JEWS IN SUITS

Dress cultures

Series Editors: Reina Lewis & Elizabeth Wilson

Advisory Board: Christopher Breward, Hazel Clark, Joanne Entwistle, Caroline Evans, Susan Kaiser, Angela McRobbie, Hiroshi Narumi, Peter McNeil, Ozlem Sandikci, Simona Segre Reinach, Arti Sandhu

Dress Cultures aims to foster innovative theoretical and methodological frameworks to understand how and why we dress, exploring the connections between clothing, commerce and creativity in global contexts.

Published:

Delft Blue to Denim Blue: Contemporary Dutch Fashion edited by Anneke Smelik

Dressing for Austerity: Aspiration, Leisure and Fashion in Post-war Britain by Geraldine Biddle-Perry

Experimental Fashion: Performance Art, Carnival and the Grotesque Body by Francesca Granata

Fashion in European Art: Dress and Identity, Politics and the Body, 1775-1925 edited by Justine De Young

Fashion in Multiple Chinas: Chinese Styles in the Transglobal Landscape edited by Wessie Ling and Simona Segre Reinach

Modest Fashion: Styling Bodies, Mediating Faith edited by Reina Lewis

Niche Fashion Magazines: Changing the Shape of Fashion by Ane Lynge-Jorlen

Styling South Asian Youth Cultures: Fashion, Media and Society edited by Lipi Begum, Rohit K. Dasgupta, and Reina Lewis

Thinking Through Fashion: A Guide to Key Theorists edited by Agnes Rocamora and Anneke Smelik

Veiling in Fashion: Space and the Hijab in Minority Communities by Anna-Mari Almila

Wearing the Cheongsam: Dress and Culture in a Chinese Diaspora by Cheryl Sim

Fashioning Indie: Popular Fashion, Music and Gender in the Twenty-First Century by Rachel Lifter

Revisiting the Gaze: The Fashioned Body and the Politics of Looking edited by Morna Laing and Jacki Willson

Reading Marie al-Khazeris Photographs: Gender, Photography, Mandate Lebanon by Yasmine Nachabe Taan

Wearing the Niqab: Muslim Women in the UK and the US by Anna Piela

Fashioning the Modern Middle East: Gender, Body, and Nation edited by Reina Lewis and Yasmine Nachabe Taan

Fashion, Performance & Performativity: The Complex Spaces of Fashion edited by Andrea Kollnitz and Marco Pecorari

Silhouettes of the Soul: Meditations on Fashion, Religion and Subjectivity edited by Otto von Busch and Jeanine Viau

Fashion in Altermodern China by Feng Jie

Fashioning the Afropolis: Histories, Materialities, and Aesthetic Practices edited by Kerstin Pinther, Kristin Kastner and Basile Ndjio

Jews in Suits by Jonathan C. Kaplan-Wajselbaum

Reina Lewis: reina.lewis@fashion.arts.ac.uk
Elizabeth Wilson: elizabethwilson.auth@gmail.com

JEWS IN SUITS

MEN'S DRESS IN VIENNA, 1890–1938

Jonathan C. Kaplan-Wajselbaum

BLOOMSBURY VISUAL ARTS
LONDON • NEW YORK • OXFORD • NEW DELHI • SYDNEY

BLOOMSBURY VISUAL ARTS
Bloomsbury Publishing Plc
50 Bedford Square, London, WC1B 3DP, UK
1385 Broadway, New York, NY 10018, USA
29 Earlsfort Terrace, Dublin 2, Ireland

BLOOMSBURY, BLOOMSBURY VISUAL ARTS and the Diana logo are trademarks of Bloomsbury
Publishing Plc

First published in Great Britain 2023
Paperback edition published by Bloomsbury Visual Arts 2024

Series design by BRILL
Cover image: SC001, Stefan Zweig Collection Addendum, Special Collections and Archives,
Daniel A. Reed Library, The State University of New York at Fredonia.

A catalogue record for this book is available from the British Library.

A catalog record for this book is available from the Library of Congress.

ISBN: HB: 978-1-3502-4420-7
PB: 978-1-3502-4421-4
ePDF: 978-1-3502-4422-1
eBook: 978-1-3502-4423-8

Typeset by Deanta Global Publishing Services, Chennai, India

To find out more about our authors and books visit www.bloomsbury.com and
sign up for our newsletters.

CONTENTS

ILLUSTRATIONS

ACKNOWLEDGMENTS

This book is the result of the research I undertook as a doctoral candidate at the University of Technology Sydney. Accordingly, it is only appropriate that first and foremost, I express my deepest gratitude to my *Doktoreltern* Distinguished Professor Peter McNeil FAHA and Professor Deborah Ascher Barnstone, whose support and wisdom have been invaluable. I would also like to express gratitude to the many academics, experts, and historians who offered research expertise and helpful feedback on drafts of my writing: Dr. Michael Abrahams-Sprod, Associate Professor Avril Alba, Professor Thea Brejzek, Dr. Christopher Breward, Professor Emeritus Sander L. Gilman, Associate Professor Michael L. Miller, Professor Andy Reilly, Dr. Elana Shapira, Professor Michael Silber, and Professor Liliane Weissberg.

Thank you to everyone who offered assistance and advice during my research trips (and online). In Austria: Dr. Marie-Theres Arnbom, Dr. Georg Gaugusch, Dr. Dieter J. Hecht, Dr. Regina Karner, Dr. Tirza Lemberger, Christa Prokisch and the archivists and librarians at the Jüdisches Museum Wien, Dr. Annika Reichwald and the staff of the Jüdisches Museum Hohenems, Magdalena Vuković at the Photoinstitut Bonartes, and many archivists and librarians at the Museum für Angewandte Kunst, Österreichische Nationalbibliothek (especially, Wilma Buchinger, Peter Prokop, and Eike Zimmer for help with images in the collection) and Maximilian Zauner at the Wienbibliothek im Rathaus. In Israel: Dr. Stefan Litt and librarians at the National Library of Israel, and Inka Arroyo, Dr. Yochai Ben-Ghedalia, and Tami Siesel at the Central Archives for the History of the Jewish People. And in the United States: Kim Taylor, at the time coordinator of special collections and archives at the Daniel A. Reed Library, State University of New York at Fredonia, her successor Mandi Shepp, who has put up with multiple emails from me requesting scans of photographs from the Zweig family collection, and archives clerk Pat Cummings-Witter.

To editors at Bloomsbury Visual Arts, Frances Arnold and Rebecca Hamilton, and coeditors of the "Dress Cultures" series, Professors Reina Lewis and Elizabeth Wilson, thank you for your support and helpful feedback in transforming my doctoral dissertation into a more concise monograph. Thanks to professional editor, Hazel Baker, who provided copyediting services during the writing of my dissertation, and to the copyeditors at Bloomsbury for fine-tuning the manuscript. Any remaining errors are my own.

To those who kindly shared family stories and photographs—even if not mentioned in the final version of this book—thank you for your generosity in taking the time to speak with me: Eva Bostock (*z"l*), Betty Buchner (*z"l*), Susie Carleton, Eva Engel OAM, Erika Fulop (*z"l*), Selma Kahane (*z"l*), Ruth Kurschner, Dr. Harry Rich, Fritzi Ritterman (*z"l*), Egon Sonnenschein, Hedy Spencer, Susan Warhaftig, William Winston, and Lisl Ziegler (*z"l*).

My fellow educators at the Sydney Jewish Museum have been a great source of support and encouragement during the final stages of writing, and I thank you for picking up the slack at work: Dr. Breann Fallon, Jeffrey Fletcher, Sandy Hollis, Jeanette Kidron, Dr. Rebecca Kummerfeld, Ilana McCorquodale, Jillian Rome, Kaitlin Sim, and Lee-Anne Whitten.

Finally, the research and writing of this book would not have been possible without the unconditional love, support, encouragement, and levelheadedness of my family: my husband, Pasko Schravemade, my parents, Ilana and Morris Kaplan, my siblings, Michael, Hadassa, and Chana Kaplan, my *kvelling* grandmothers, Miryam Wise and Lena Kaplan, and the many aunts, uncles, and cousins both here in Australia and around abroad, including Odette Kesler and David Cronin, who hosted me for over a month in Toronto between conferences and research appointments, and Paul Kesler and Alexi Wood who drove me across the Canadian-US border to a research trip at SUNY Fredonia. A special "*Dank*" must go to my cousin Isabelle Neuburg of Reinach, Switzerland, for many things, including the "care packages" of Swiss chocolate, and your kindness and patience in helping me with translating German texts when I could not always find the right English words or turns of phrase.

A NOTE ON PLACE NAMES

Naming conventions of cities, towns, and villages throughout Eastern and Central Europe is fraught with trouble. Electing to use a particular version of place names often reveals a certain political agenda. Many of the places referenced in this book were subject to name changes based on which side of the border they fell at any given period. Even within Austria-Hungary, those places that found themselves well within the borders of the Dual Monarchy were known by different names by the various ethno-linguistic groups who populated them.

Throughout this book, I refer to places within Austria-Hungary by the German-language version of their names, as these are the names by which the German-speaking Jewish population of Austria generally knew and referred to them. Thus, for example, the present-day Czech city of Brno—former capital of the Austrian crown land of Moravia—is referred to by its German name "Brünn." The first reference to a place gives the current name in the local language in parentheses: for example, "Brünn (Brno)." Those cities with names widely used in English will be substituted for the German version; thus, *Wien* and *Praha* are referred to as "Vienna" and "Prague," whereas Bratislava, which has no English equivalent, is referred as "Pressburg."

INTRODUCTION

> Itzig Faitel was a small squat man. His right shoulder was slightly higher than his left, and he had a sharp protruding chicken breast upon which he always wore a wide heavy silk tie ornamented by a dull ruby and attached to a breast plate. The lapels on both sides of this tie ran top right to bottom left so that when Faitel moved along the curbstones, it appeared as though he were rearing down the sidewalk to the other side or going in a diagonal direction. Faitel could not be convinced that the arrangement of his clothes came from the rhombic shift of his chest cage. This is why he complained terribly about Christian tailors. After all, the suits which he wore were always made from the finest worsted.
>
> Oskar Panizza, *The Operated Jew* (1893)

This book examines the role dress played in the construction and performance of masculine Jewish identification(s) and its influence on the framework of antisemitism as a marker of Jewishness in Vienna during the late nineteenth and early twentieth centuries. Dress played an important dual role in this context of coping with and responding to antisemitism and the changing patterns of Jewish identification. The "democratized" men's suit of the mid-nineteenth (and throughout the remainder of the) century promised its wearers the democratization of appearance. The suit was important because in its purported "simplicity" and "sameness" it allowed its wearers to participate in society as "equals," regardless of social, economic, religious, or ethnic background, and offered the individual the illusion of blending in, of disappearing, in a sense, into the body politic.[1] This is particularly significant when considering the history and culture of nineteenth-century and early twentieth-century European Jews, as the adoption of the suit as a symbol of respectability and ideal masculinity parallels the assimilatory and acculturation values held by many urban Jewish men.

That a person is somehow able to look Jewish is a persisting myth that has resulted in a wide variety of stereotypes from visual to verbal. Historically, European Jews were subject to physiognomic scrutiny and particular traits came to be considered "Jewish." Manifestations of Jewish bodily difference that had previously been used in Christian European literature and visual art to express the spiritual corruption of the Jews and Judaism were later "explained" in nineteenth-century scientific and medical discourse as being the results of Jewish "racial" difference. Expanding on former models of anti-Jewish bias, the nineteenth-century variety that came to be known as "antisemitism"—a term coined by the German publicist Wilhelm Marr (1819–1904) in 1879/1881[2]—was influenced by contemporaneous interest in fields such as anthropology, eugenics, and sociology.[3] Racial antisemitism was influenced by the prevalence of Social Darwinism and theories concerning the hierarchy of human races in which Jews, along with other non-European peoples, were considered racially inferior. For the intensely antisemitic Social Darwinists and German nationalists, supposed Jewish racial inferiority was dangerous not only in the biological effects it could have on the Gentile body politic through the mixing of "races" but also in the negative elements Jews were purported to bring to civilization through political, social, and economic modernization.[4] It was expressly during the broad period of emancipation and acculturation that "antisemitism" as a racial and political category emerged. As many Jews embraced various aspects of secular German culture, including modes of appearance, they became harder to recognize as Jewish. Consequently, xenophobes required new markers of visual Jewishness to single out their victims from the German body politic.

Many Jews in *fin-de-siècle* Vienna were culturally, linguistically, and sartorially indistinguishable from their Gentile counterparts. This segment of society produced many individuals who, after having overcome the social barriers placed in the path of assimilating and acculturating Jews, would involve themselves in every aspect of *fin-de-siècle* Viennese society: politics, finance, and industry, science and medicine, academia, culture, and the arts. Many of the individuals associated with Vienna's modernist milieu were of Jewish heritage—in whatever way they classified themselves as such, if at all, or were classified by others. An obvious, albeit often overlooked, element in their refashioning of self was clothing. Through adopting modern, European attire during earlier periods of Jewish modernization, Jews were able to broadcast their dedication to secular Enlightenment ideals, and their willingness to participate in Gentile society in a clear and visual manner that was at once recognizable to others. The importance of clothing in the formation of self has been addressed by numerous scholars. As an element of outermost appearance, the clothes an individual wears can inform others of many intersections of subjectivity, such as religious, cultural, socioeconomic, sexual, political, and professional. Dress, however, is not always straightforward in communicating the complexity of its wearer's subjectivity, and often requires an understanding of subtle and nuanced contexts and factors bearing on the individual.

By the *fin de siècle*, most Viennese Jews were the product of earlier acculturation (and in some cases assimilation) on the part of their parents, grandparents, and, sometimes, earlier ancestors. They themselves did not replace the traditional Ashkenazi garb, such as a kaftan and large *yarmulke* (skullcap) or kerchief, for modern suits and frocks. However, the engagement of these individuals with particular sartorial styles, whether conservative or avant-garde, made certain statements about their Jewish subjectivities (or lack thereof) to Vienna's Jewish and wider Gentile societies. Nor were the implications simple. The preference for certain styles of dress was not always understood in a positive light to indicate Jewish dedication to modern, secular society and German culture. On the contrary, and particularly in light of rising antisemitism, acculturated, fashion-following Jews ran the risk of being considered self-serving parvenus. A Jewish individual's clothing preferences, patterns, and practices could and did result in certain styles attracting a Jewish coding in the eyes of wider, non-Jewish society. This was also the case for other non-sartorial fashions and forms of leisure, such as patronizing the coffeehouse, theater, or certain art forms, thus influencing external perceptions of *Jewishness*.

Beautiful Clothing, Ugly Bodies: *Der operierte Jud'*

At the time of its publication in 1893, few of its intended readers would not have instantly recognized the central motif of Oskar Panizza's novella *Der operierte Jud'* (*The Operated Jew*): fine clothing cannot conceal the repulsive and foreign Jewish body. Panizza's novella presents the perceived corporeal traits of Jewishness in the story's title character. Even that character's name, Itzig Faitel Stern, evokes antisemitic stereotypes—with "Itzig" used as a common derogatory and stereotypical "Yiddishized" name for Jewish men in the German-language realm.[5] Itzig Faitel Stern's appearance— visual, behavioral, and linguistic—is a grotesque caricature of the Jew as he existed in the German imagination during the period in which the novella was written and published.

Der operierte Jud' was published in Leipzig, Imperial Germany, but the antisemitic tropes employed throughout would have been familiar to Viennese readers. Indeed, the Austrian capital of the *fin-de-siècle* and interwar periods has been characterized as a European capital of antisemitism, where unsavory attitudes toward Jews permeated all facets of political and cultural life. Adolf Hitler himself, the great specter of twentieth-century antisemitism, commented on Vienna's role as a "school" in his hatred of the Jews.[6] Although Austrian Jewry had been emancipated in 1867 and there was no persecution of Vienna's Jewish population on an official governmental level, antisemitism continued to function on many levels within Viennese society and was an omnipresent force in official arenas, as well as in spheres of day-to-day life.

Panizza, like other authors, drew on rhetoric that argued Jews were biologically incompatible with Germans and other Europeans, expressly at a time when Jews in Germany and Austria both enjoyed the same civil rights as their Gentile counterparts, and shared many of their secular, cultural ideals. Although focusing primarily on Itzig Faitel Stern's body, Panizza's descriptions of the title character's attire are equally important. Throughout the novella, there is reference to the notion of the Jew as a conspicuous consumer, adorning himself with beautiful and expensive clothing in an attempt to cover up his corporeal "ugliness." But moving beyond this motif of Jewish duplicity through the use of clothing, Stern's adoption of such sartorial modes is representative of the wider modernization of Jewry, in which Jews adopted modern, European clothing as a means not to mask their Jewishness but, rather, to present themselves as fully fledged members of society. Whether they desired complete assimilation and the loss of Jewishness, or simply acculturation as both modern Europeans and Jews, they saw no reason why they should dress different from those around them. Stern's emphatic explanation of his sartorial preferences sums up this perspective, "Why shoodln't I buy for me a new coat, a bootiful hat—menerá, fine wanished boots—menerá, me, too, I shood bicome a fine gentilman after this Deradáng! Deradáng!"[7]

The central theme of the novella is the alleged ugliness and ungainliness of the Jewish body and an attempt to repair its inherent damaged nature through material and behavioral self-fashioning. Panizza, as a psychiatrist and thus a member of the medical community, writes from a position of self-appointed authority, warning readers of the dangers contained in the follies of cosmetic surgery. The physicians who attend to Faitel Stern's transformation become obsessed with the task of transforming the "ugly" Jew into a beautiful paragon of Aryan masculinity; they are presented as alchemists vainly striving to turn lead to gold. But the driving force behind these attempts is the Jew himself, a man infatuated with German culture, exacerbated by his inability to truly master it. Stern's tragic end is Panizza's warning of the impossibility of Jewish assimilation.

The novella's message can be encapsulated in an analogy of fine clothing used to mask the body's true form, which, in line with contemporaneous views on gender and consumption, Panizza asserts is inelegant for men to do, but entirely acceptable for women.[8] The transformation—cosmetic, sartorial, linguistic, behavioral—of the Jew Faitel Stern into the German "Siegfried Freudenstern" is not only a metaphor for sartorial refashioning of self[9] but also a comment on the perceived femininity of the Jewish man. The insane manner in which Stern subjects himself to medical procedures to correct his posture, change his natural complexion and hair color, and his rigorous dialectal training are akin to the donning of stiff, new clothing that forces the wearer to be conscious of his bodily presence and thus curate his mannerisms in order to achieve sartorial and behavioral harmony. Although Panizza's outline of the operations undergone by the title character is less concerned with clothed identity,[10] the meticulous nature with which Faitel Stern attends to his bodily transformation is reminiscent of accounts of the dandified sartorial preparation of such figures as George "Beau" Brummell (1778–1840).[11] A caricature appearing in the Viennese satirical journal *Kikeriki* in 1897 ridiculed this purported corporeal refashioning. A Jewish character similarly named Itzig, and whose caricatured appearance naturally bears resemblance to the stereotypes of Panizza's Itzig, undergoes equally ridiculous corporeal refashioning before attending the Vienna city ball in order to appear less Jewish (Figure 0.1).[12]

The manner in which Stern/Freudenstern enthusiastically responds to such novel procedures and treatments, such as the bleaching of his skin and hair,[13] recalls the stereotype of the fashion-conscious Jew—an expression of the individual's desire to be seen as fashionable in order to erase Jewish difference or else transform Jewish difference into a fashionable vice.[14] And all of these treatments are paid for with Jewish money by Stern/Freudenstern's grandfather, Solomon Stern, who is cast as the archetype of the scheming Jew who uses his wealth to entice and, when that fails, bully others into doing his will.[15]

The climax of the novella sees a violent regression of the beautiful Aryan Siegfried Freudenstern into the hideous Jew Itzig Faitel Stern under the effects of alcohol. This regression happens first behaviorally and linguistically and is followed by a monstrous physical unraveling in which his body resumes its original repulsive contorted form.[16] The "lesson" imparted by the novella reflects the common antisemitic trope of late nineteenth- and early twentieth-century European societies as diverse as Austria,

Figure 0.1 Caricature from *Kikeriki* 37, no. 3 (January 10, 1897): 1. Courtesy of ANNO/Österreichische Nationalbibliothek, Vienna.

France, and England: that the Jew can never successfully mask his origins. He might adopt new modes of behavior, speech, or dress in an attempt to dissociate himself from typical models of Jewish identification. But, as the playwright and unofficial leader of the Viennese literary group *Jung Wien*, Hermann Bahr (1863–1934), wrote in a review of Theodor Herzl's play *Das neue Ghetto* for the newspaper *Die Zeit* (January 8, 1898), in adopting German modes of identity, the Jews were estranged from their former identities and "go about as half-humans here and there, deprived of their power, reduced to creatures with empty understanding, uncanny to others, and a torture to themselves."[17] In this manner, Itzig Faitel Stern's operation is akin to surgery that keeps a malicious disease at bay—a disease for which there is no cure: Jewishness. Although employing numerous anti-Jewish motifs, *Der operierte Jud'* does not position itself as an antisemitic work of fiction intended to malign Jews for their Jewishness, but rather a cautionary tale about the dangers of self-mutilation in the face of supposedly inherent and unchanging Jewish bodily difference.

Defining Jewishness

In order to analyze Jewish men and their patterns of dress, a close reading of how Jewishness functions is required. The term "Jewishness" is simultaneously potent but opaque. It can refer to a number of elements relating to Jewish identity. Jewishness and Jewish identity are inextricably linked with the religion of Judaism. Individuals who identify as Jewish may or may not express religiosity in any sense. Likewise, individuals born of Jewish heritage who may not consider themselves Jewish may be labeled as such by others, as has been the case throughout history. Historically, the Jew's place in European society was precarious. Prior to the emancipation of Western and Central European Jewry during the nineteenth century, their situation and the rights accorded them varied depending on where they lived. Since the Middle Ages, Jews had been considered a theological enemy in Christian Europe, and laws restricting their residential, professional, and familial patterns were widespread across the continent.

Historically, the term "Jew" has been understood to refer to the Jewish man— as opposed to the Jewish woman (or "Jewess"), who has served a different, albeit connected, role throughout Western cultural history. This view was influenced by a number of factors, including the differing meanings of male and female sexuality in Western culture in which the image of "the Jew" developed.[18] In his study, *The Jew's Body* (1991), Sander Gilman demonstrates that certain corporeal differences, both real and imagined, between the Jewish and Gentile (male) bodies stem largely from the Jewish tradition of circumcising male infants, practiced as a symbol of the biblical covenant between God and the patriarch Abraham. The circumcised phallus is "crucial to the very understanding of the Western image of the Jew at least since the advent of Christianity,"[19] and, along with other Jewish characteristics, has persisted throughout Western, Christian societies, even in their most secularized forms.[20] The very act of circumcising Jewish male infants eight days after birth meant that the practicality of Jewish/Gentile bodily difference was cemented from the beginning of a male's life. As Sigmund Freud asserts in his essay "Little Hans: Analysis of a Phobia in a Five-year-Old Child," (1909) circumcision and antisemitism are intrinsically linked. Describing what he terms the "castration complex," Freud claims the lack of foreskin creates a sense of fear in Gentile men from the earliest age that "gives them the right to despise Jews."[21] For the Christian tradition, the circumcised penis serves not only as a sign of Jewish difference but also as a bodily reminder of the Jewish rejection of Christ—"the traditional sign of the special relationship between the (male) Jew and God, becomes here a false sign,"[22] superseded by the relationship between God and the Christians, the new chosen people.

Jews, like other people, however, did not go around naked with the sign of the covenant visible to all. Beyond this ultimate sign of Jewish corporeal difference, notions of "Jewishness" referred to the various external markers of Jewish identity, both physical and behavioral characteristics often considered negative by the Gentile majority.[23] To read certain literature or patronize modernist art and architecture could be taken as an indicator of an individual's Jewishness—even if she or he was Jewish neither by religion nor by heritage. Likewise, congregating in certain localities, listening to certain types of music, to be engaged in certain professions or pastimes, or dressing oneself in a certain way might cause a person to be seen as somehow "Jewish." Given Jewry's status as a "religious" community by the Christian majority, conversion would in theory dissolve an individual's Jewishness, as she or he no longer practiced nor associated with the Jewish religion or community. Concurrent with their emancipation across Europe, the hatred and persecution of the Jews evolved from a theologically based anti-Judaism to the racially and politically motivated "antisemitism" that was strongly influenced by such contemporaneous sciences and ideologies as eugenics and Social Darwinism.[24] As a result, the ability of a Jewish individual to abandon her or his Jewishness and disappear into the Gentile body politic by adopting Christianity was jeopardized.[25] With the increasing racialization of Jews and Judaism by racial scientists during the latter half of the nineteenth century, these new Christians were often reminded by coreligionists that they had been born Jews.[26]

The emancipation of Western and Central European Jewry over the course of the nineteenth century resulted in Jews being granted the legal status of citizens in the nations in which they lived. As fellow citizens, their Judaism was reduced to a religious identity, which many chose to discard in favor of the Christianity of their dominant society. Jewish identity thus came to connote much more than the Jewish religion and its traditions. The individual could now identify as Jewish on religious, ethnic, or cultural terms—or some combination thereof. Furthermore, Jewish self-identification was now a state that Jews themselves defined, not something dictated from the outside—as had been with the case of Jewishness.[27] As a result of their legal emancipation, Jews were now permitted to reside wherever they desired, practice professions that were formerly denied to them, and participate in the civic and political life of the nations in which they lived. In short, the Jew, as an individual, was now a fully fledged member of the nation.

Theory, however, did not mesh with practice. During the course of the nineteenth century, Jewish citizens living in various European nation-states, such as France and

Germany, continued to be seen as the Other.[28] They were imposters who, despite the official view of the state that had granted them citizenship, were inherently different and did not "belong" to the nation. While a Jew might identify as German, pledge loyalty to the state and German culture, others saw him at best as an impersonator, whose inherent "racial difference" prevented him from ever truly becoming a part of the German body politic.[29] The German experience—of which we must include Viennese (and to an extent, wider Austrian) Jewry on account of its German cultural character—was not consistent prior to the creation of the German *Reich* in 1871, from which Austria was excluded, and the experiences of Jews varied in the various kingdoms, principalities, duchies, and free cities that would be unified under the Prussian crown. Post-1871 German Jewry differed greatly from Habsburg Jewry, much of which was also culturally German, who resided in differing cultural spheres and under different political circumstances that became standardized only after the 1867 Austro-Hungarian *Ausgleich* (compromise). During the final decades of the nineteenth century and the first four decades of the twentieth, the Austrian capital was one of the most important centers of Jewish life and culture in Central Europe, and its Jewish population was a multifaceted group. Despite the stereotypes that persisted, Viennese "Jewishness" took multiple forms, with dress serving as a medium through which this "Jewishness" came to be recognized.

The Male Suit

Studies of Jewish dress tend to focus on sartorial difference or the function of Jews in the global fashion system.[30] This book, however, addresses the way in which acculturating Viennese Jewish men conformed to wider sartorial conventions. The suit, in particular, played a significant role in communicating its wearer's social and economic status, as well as his political and ideological sentiments. In some ways, the tailored suit has been characterized as a uniform of sorts. Cultural theorist Eduard Fuchs argued at the beginning of the twentieth century, "A person wears a uniform voluntarily only when he is also spiritually overwhelmed by the ideas embodied in it; and every specific piece of clothing embodies in its way very specific reigning or influential ideas."[31] In this manner, Jewish sartorial modernization in Europe can be understood as linked to ideals of *Bildung* (self-cultivation) and *Sittlichkeit* (respectability) that were held in esteem by many acculturating Jews across Central Europe. The adoption of modern dress was not simply a matter of "fitting in," but rather a statement about the wearer's dedication to the ideals the style of clothing represented.

Donning the suit was a statement of the individual's desire to embody the modern "ideal man."[32] Whether politically conservative or progressive, religiously observant or secular, assimilationist or sympathetic to various forms of Jewish ethnic consciousness (including Zionism and Diaspora Nationalism), middle-class Jews by and large became accustomed to mainstream cultural aesthetic tastes in Vienna. By the latter decades of the nineteenth century, during which the *Österreich-Israelitische Union* (Austrian-Israelite Union)—the political lobbying organization founded in 1884 by parliamentarian Joseph

Samuel Bloch representing Jewish interests, including the fight against antisemitism—and the *Sozialdemokratitsche Arbeiterpartei Österreichs* (Austrian Social Democratic Workers' Party) were founded, Theodor Herzl published his treatise on the Jewish State (*Der Judenstaat*), and Karl Lueger of the antisemitic Christian Social Party was mayor of Vienna, bourgeois Viennese Jews were sartorially indistinguishable from other middle-class Viennese.

The common thread between them was the suit, what dress historian Christopher Breward describes as "a well-fitted set of garments to be worn at the same time, although not necessarily of matching cloth."[33] Often consisting of a jacket, trousers, and waistcoat worn with a collared shirt and a variety of neckwear (ties, cravats, or bow ties), Anne Hollander presents the male suit as offering men an ideal masculinity and asserts that the "uniformity" of the clothed male body since the nineteenth century is a sign of men's "desire to look similar."[34] David Kuchta argues in his study of the three-piece suit that this new form of menswear represented the competition between the aristocracy and the bourgeoisie for cultural superiority.[35] The adoption of an early form of the suit by Charles II of England (1630–85) in 1666 symbolized the transformation of male respectability characterized by the sartorial sobriety that still reigns today.[36] For Michael Zakim, the suit was a democratic enabler that came to represent a "specifically American civic uniform,"[37] which symbolized conformity, both visual, as well as intellectual and behavioral. Likewise, Breward has characterized the adoption of the lounge suit during the late nineteenth century as offering "a relaxed sense of modernity" for men of varying professional classes.[38] In this manner, Breward describes the suit "as a foundational 'idea' of modern society in the industrial West."[39] However, in addition to serving as a symbol of industrialization and modernization, Breward has characterized the suit and other elements of "respectable" male dress at the *fin de siècle* as offering male consumers a multitude of ways to fashion the self.[40] In contrast to the characterization of the male suit as a symbol of what the British sociologist John C. Flügel described as the "Great Masculine Renunciation" of sartorial splendor in favor of sobriety,[41] Breward's study reveals that men of differing socioeconomic classes actively engaged in clothing consumption and sartorial self-fashioning. Similarly, Michael Carter argues that the way the suit is worn enables the individual to express multiple meanings, from formality to informality, dandyist precision to scruffy bohemianism.[42] The Jewish man's adoption of the suit as a standard form of dress signified his entry into a sartorial fraternity of sorts that surpassed ethnic, national, and class boundaries. In doing so, he visually declared his place in a wider European society rather than as an alien Other, while at the same time developing and expressing multiple identifications.

* * *

This book proposes a new narrative of the relationship of men, clothing, and their Jewish identification. Drawing upon fashionable dress, folk costume, religious dress, avant-garde and oppositional dress, typologies which are often considered separate from one another, it proposes a new way of reading men and clothing cultures within Vienna's iconic cultural milieu. Comprised of six chapters, the first section of this book (Chapters 1 and 2) situates Jewish men within the wider frameworks of Vienna's cityscape and fashion industry, before focusing on in-depth case studies.

Chapter 1 acquaints the reader with the Jews of Vienna during the *fin-de-siècle* and interwar periods, as well as the Austrian capital within the historical context of this study: at first a wealthy power center of the vast, multiethnic and multilinguistic Austro-Hungarian Empire, and subsequently a disproportionately overpopulated capital of a small, landlocked republic. Like the Gentile population, Viennese Jews were situated across the socioeconomic, political, and cultural spectrums, as well as spatially throughout the city. I present a cross section of this diverse "community" and situate the Jewish body spatially and sartorially in the city during the period under investigation. Chapter 2 examines the ways in which Vienna's Jews were imbricated in the world of dress and fashion, and its repercussions for perceptions of Jewishness, in particular the notions of self-fashioning and "masking" through dress. Although Viennese Jews were involved in all sectors of the fashion and luxury trades, this chapter focuses on those examples pertaining to men's tailoring and accessories. I present the examples of this Jewish participation in fashion through examples of designers, retailers, and consumers. These examples are situated within the wider context of men's tailoring and its related notion of the elegant gentleman.

The remaining four chapters present specific themes within the metanarrative of Jews and dress in Vienna. Chapter 3 explores the management of appearance and dress in the context of acculturation and assimilation, focusing on the dress of Vienna's leading rabbis, and the dress and visualization of two Viennese public figures concerned with the Jews vis-à-vis the wider Austrian nationality question: Joseph Samuel Bloch and Theodor Herzl. Chapter 4 addresses the role of Viennese Jewry in the urban/rural divide. This is examined through patterns of attire of Jews in the capital and as urban visitors to the Salzkammergut region, referring to visual and literary texts. The symbolic meanings of the suit and rural folk costumes are compared and contrasted in order to analyze their respective roles in both Jewish self-fashioning and the perpetuation of external negative perceptions of Jewish men as "rootless" cosmopolitans who belonged in neither the "German" provinces nor the supposedly "Jewish" city. Chapter 5 continues along this line of inquiry and examines antisemitic caricatures that appeared in popular satirical journals. In this chapter, widespread stereotypes and their intersections with notions of the dressed body are analyzed under recurring themes that were used to gauge widespread antisemitic sentiment and perpetuate it. Chapter 6 "tests" the theories and notions raised in earlier chapters and offers new insights into the importance of dress in the construction of multifaceted masculine Jewish self-identification in Vienna through an examination of the dressing of five celebrated Viennese writers of Jewish origin: Sigmund Freud, Arthur Schnitzler, Stefan Zweig, Peter Altenberg, and Karl Kraus.

The conclusion demonstrates that despite an advanced stage of acculturation, Viennese Jews remained a highly conspicuous Other. While modern dress and other forms of visual and material culture offered Jews multifaceted ways of self-identification, the specter of antisemitism and the image of "the Jew" was strongly ingrained in wider

Viennese society. Here, the National Socialist Anschluss of Austria in March 1938 is offered as a conclusion to this complex chapter of Viennese Jewish history. The conclusion reiterates the central theme of the book: that clothing was as central to the construction of identity as it was to external perceptions of the people who wore them. Just as Panizza demonstrated through his depiction of the laughable caricature Itzig Faitel Stern unable to hide his Jewishness beneath fine clothing, dressing in modern attire offered little protection against antisemitism.

CHAPTER 1
EUROPE'S THIRD MOST JEWISH CITY

From *Kaiserstadt* to *Wasserkopf*: Vienna before and after 1918

With respect to their nationality, the Viennese are mainly Czechs—but also Jews, "Cossacks," Slovaks, Gottscheers, Carniolans [Slovenes], etc. There are also a few Germans who gather in the "German Association" from time to time and gradually reach an awareness of their national identity. Pure German [*Reindeutsch*] is only spoken by member of the Laube-Theater and the judicial defense attorneys—the latter, however, only during their pleas with the *k.k.* [Imperial-Royal] regional court.

> *Franz Friedrich Masaidek,* Wien und die Wiener aus
> der Spottvogelsperspektive *(1873)[1]*

By the end of the nineteenth century, Vienna was a *Weltstadt*, a modern metropolis and dual capital of a vast empire that drew migrants from all its provinces and beyond its borders. These migrants came from varying linguistic, ethnic, cultural, and religious backgrounds, each bringing their own culture and traditions into the mix of what Michael John and Albert Lichtblau have referred to as "*Schmelztiegel Wien*" (Viennese melting pot).[2] At the turn of the twentieth century, Vienna's diverse population reflected the wider ethnic and linguistic plurality of the Austro-Hungarian Empire, consisting of Germans, Czechs, Italians, Poles, Magyars, Slovaks, Slovenes, Ruthenians, Serbo-Croats, Bosnians, and Romanians. Judging from the diversity of its population, *fin-de-siècle* Vienna might be seen as an urban manifestation of the Habsburg myth of supranational cooperation. However, despite the mix of cultures, traditions, and languages that existed in Vienna, one leading ethno-linguistic group dominated and dictated the cultural hierarchy of the Austrian capital: Germans. In his satirical 1873 travel guide, Franz Friedrich Masaidek presented Vienna's Germans as an embattled, yet steadfast hegemonic minority surrounded by a growing foreign population, made up predominantly of Czechs and Jews.[3] Written as a form of satire, Masaidek's guide sheds light on rising anxieties during a period of industrial and urban growth, rising nationalism, and financial instability. Vienna's Germans were not besieged by an overwhelmingly foreign population that was slowly eroding the city's German character—if anything, in adapting to Vienna's German hegemony many migrants adopted the ideals of modern German national identity. However, it does reveal the perception of the complicated nature of Viennese, and by extension Austrian, identity during the latter half of the nineteenth century.

Just two years previously, Austro-Germans (or German Austrians) had witnessed the unification of neighboring Germany under the leadership of Prussia. For the most part, German-speaking Austrians belonged to the wider sphere of German history.[4] During the late nineteenth century, Austria was a political entity but had not developed into a nation-state in the same manner as France or, exerting a greater impact on the Austrian "nationality question," Germany.[5] For many German nationalists, the amalgamation of the many independent kingdoms, duchies and grand duchies, principalities, and free cities proved to be a cause for celebration. But for Austro-Germans watching from across the border, the proclamation of the German *Reich* (empire) on January 18, 1871, at the Palace of Versailles only served as a reminder of their exclusion from the emerging German nation-state in the aftermath of Austria's defeat by Prussia in the war of 1866. Nevertheless, the establishment of the German Empire in 1871 emboldened German nationalists in Austria, such as Georg Ritter von Schönerer (1842–1921), who was elected to the Austrian *Reichsrat* (Imperial Council) in the aftermath of the 1873 stock market crash and would combine pan-German nationalism with emerging racial antisemitism.[6]

While the status of Jews within Austrian society was a constant source of concern for German nationalists, the wider question of Austrian nationality was equally pressing. In addition to Jews, Austro-Germans found themselves in conflict with Austria's many non-German ethno-linguistic communities, usually over questions of linguistic and cultural autonomy.[7] The most notable conflict between "nations" of the Habsburg lands was that between Germans and Magyars. After centuries of Habsburg German rule the Magyar population of the Kingdom of Hungary, dissatisfied with its political and cultural disenfranchisement, began to voice its dissent and aspirations for independence.[8] Magyar national rebellion would come to a head during the 1848–9 revolutions that swept across the continent, taking advantage of widespread political unrest and emerging national aspirations. Although the rebellion was quashed by Austria and its Russian allies, and its leaders exiled, Magyar dissatisfaction with Austro-German political and cultural hegemony would continue to simmer over the next two decades until the 1867 Austro-Hungarian *Ausgleich* (compromise) that came in the wake of Austria's defeat by Prussia a year previously. The *Ausgleich* created the Dual Monarchy of Austria-Hungary and effectively solved the problem of German-Magyar rivalry, with each half maintaining its own parliament and laws, while being united under a single monarch, Franz Joseph I (1830–1916).

Not all nations of Austria-Hungary were as fortunate as the Magyars to achieve equal hegemony alongside the former German overlords. In the aftermath of the *Ausgleich*, the former Polish nobility of the Austrian crown land known officially as the Kingdom of Galicia and Lodomeria (henceforth referred to as Galicia) were granted a degree of cultural and political autonomy that culminated in their own Polish *Sejm* (parliament), which placed them further up the national/ethno-linguistic hierarchy than Ruthenians and Jews.[9] Austria's Czech population was not as fortunate. Czechs and the Czech language never achieved the same level of autonomy or equality as German, as had been awarded to Magyars and Poles in Hungary and Galicia, respectively. Any attempt to place Czech on an equal footing with German was met with fierce opposition from German nationalists and liberals alike—a notable case being Cisleithanian minister-president Count Kasimir Felix Badeni's (1846–1909) language ordinance of April 5, 1897, that declared German and Czech to be dual languages of the Austrian administration in the crown lands of Bohemia and Moravia.[10] Nationalistic and linguistically inspired conflicts extended beyond these cases on both sides of the Leitha river, making Vienna (dual) capital of a splintering empire held together by dynastic loyalty to the house of Habsburg.

It was in this political and nationalistic context that Vienna's position as simultaneously "German" and "Austrian" can be understood. While other European states had during the course of the long nineteenth century become home to singular, reigning "nations" that simultaneously dominated and appropriated elements from their subordinates, the lack of an underlying Austrian national culture left a void into which competing nations scrambled, all vying for supremacy. In the face of rising nationalism, a myth of supranational Habsburg unity was utilized and perpetuated in arenas as diverse as the government, military, arts, and industry. Edward Timms has asserted that Vienna's "unified city culture was essentially a myth, concocted by writers encapsulated in their coffee houses."[11] The Austrian capital's fractured cultural character reflected the wider Austrian cultural identity or nonidentity. Austria, as a political construct based around its imperial family and military (since 1867 distinct from its Hungarian half), was made up of multiple ethno-linguistic groups that could simultaneously assert a strong ethnic identity as well as their loyalty to the Austrian state and its ruling house of Habsburg. German language and culture played an important role in the development of the Austrian identity.[12] Prior to the formation of the Austrian Empire at the beginning of the nineteenth century, the Habsburgs had also provided the rulers of the (predominantly German) Holy Roman Empire until its dissolution in 1806. Although only one of the empire's many official languages,[13] German reigned supreme as the de facto language of the administration in the Austrian half of the empire.

By the end of the nineteenth century, Vienna had grown from a small, walled city into a sprawling metropolis whose burgeoning population was drawn from all corners of the Dual Monarchy. The growth of Vienna's population throughout the latter half of the nineteenth century was immense and based on two main factors: (1) immigration from other parts of Austria-Hungary and further afield, and (2) the removal of legal prohibitions on residency. In addition to increased migration from the provinces, the physical expansion of the city in 1890, which saw the inclusion of outer-lying villages as new city districts, raised Vienna's total population from 827,567 to 1,364,548.[14] Germans were the most prevalent ethno-linguistic group; however, the city was also home to many individuals of non-German origin. As the "Imperial and Royal" (*kaiserlich und königlich*) capital situated near the edge of the empire's German crown lands and fairly close to the Hungarian frontier, Vienna with its culturally hegemonic German population served as a litmus test that forced those "foreign" immigrants who wished to enter the realm of cultural and civic influence to adapt themselves and their families to the powers of *Deutschtum* (Germanness).[15] Thousands of migrants, such as those who spoke Czech, Hungarian, Polish, or Italian, replaced their traditional vernaculars and cultures with those of the dominating Germans. Many assimilated completely and effectively became Austro-Germans, the only sign of their origins being in the continued use of non-German family names—such as Masaidek himself, whose surname suggests Czech origins, despite bemoaning that Czechs and Jews were taking over his city.[16]

The city's ethnic and linguistic diversity in the face of the relative linguistically homogenous population of its surrounding German crownlands would have a negative outcome in the post-Habsburg period and would lead to increasing support for German nationalism (and later, Nazism) among the city's German population. Prior to the dissolution of the Dual Monarchy Vienna's status as (dual) capital was not only in name, but the seat of Habsburg power represented the myth of multiethnic and multilinguistic dynastic loyalty throughout the empire. So large and diverse a population was fitting for so vast an empire. However, after the Dual Monarchy's dissolution in 1918, Vienna with its population of two million (around a third of the entire Austrian population) was capital to a vastly reduced territory and was referred to as a *Wasserkopf*—a hydrocephalus or "bloated head" of a severely truncated body.[17] With the establishment of new nations out of the ruins of Austria-Hungary, thousands of non-German Viennese returned to their ancestral lands.[18] Nevertheless, the city's population remained diverse, at least in its ethnic and linguistic origins, if not in its day-to-day language and culture, with many of its inhabitants continuing to adopt German and fashioning themselves as modern "Austrians."

Vienna: A "Jewish City" or a City for Jews?

During an age of industrial progress and mass migration, Jewish immigrants made up a significant and highly visible segment of the overall migration to the *Kaiserstadt*. With the removal of its final barriers to Jewish residency and professional practice, Vienna saw a massive Jewish immigration over the remainder of the nineteenth century. From a total of 6,217 (2.2 percent of the total population) in 1857, by 1890 the Jewish population had swelled to 118,495 (8.7 percent).[19] Immigrant Jews who came to the capital from the same crown lands as other immigrants fashioned themselves in a similar manner, along sartorial, behavioral, and even cultural-religious lines.

Since the Josephinian Edicts of Toleration during the late eighteenth century (1781 and 1782), many Jews throughout the empire had adopted the German language, modern European dress, and secular education, and had undergone a change in professional patterns.[20] The migration of Jews to Vienna during the nineteenth century occurred in waves. The largest group of Jewish immigrants to arrive in Vienna after Franz Joseph I began repealing the prohibition on Jewish settlement in the city after 1848[21] were those from the Austrian crown lands of Bohemia and Moravia, where they had long abandoned many of the particular "traditional" practices and had begun the process of acculturation.[22] They were followed by Jews from Hungary (mainly present-day Burgenland and Slovakia), who although often more religiously Orthodox than their Bohemian and Moravian counterparts, had also embraced certain aspects of *Deutschtum*.[23] Finally, toward the end of the century and increasingly during the First World War, the largest migration came from Galicia.[24]

Prior to the arrival of thousands of Galician Jews fleeing the advancing Russian army during the First World War—a recent study estimates between 80,000 and 130,000[25]—Vienna's Jewish immigrants were by and large already proficient in the German language and practitioners of German culture.[26] Despite the stereotype being uneducated and culturally backward, many of the early Galician immigrants had achieved a level of acculturation prior to their arrival in Vienna, and included among this group were the parents of renowned founder of psychoanalysis Sigmund Freud (1856–1939), as well as Moritz Szeps (1835–1902) and Moriz Benedikt (1849–1920), editors of the leading Viennese dailies *Neues Wiener Tagblatt* and *Neue Freie Presse*, respectively. Indeed, until the interwar period, the official policy of the *Israelitische Kultusgemeinde* (Israelite Religious Community, henceforth referred to as IKG), the official, state-sanctioned Jewish communal body responsible for overseeing communal and religious affairs, was one of integration, with rabbis and other community leaders encouraging Jewish participation within wider German Viennese culture and society—albeit remaining true to their Jewish or *mosaisch* (Mosaic) faith.[27] Later Galician immigrants, however, were typically poor, religiously Orthodox, Yiddish-speaking *Ostjuden* (east European Jews) who dressed in styles that marked them as outsiders in the highly acculturated Viennese Jewish milieu. These newcomers were considered an embarrassment to their established coreligionists, who were afraid the arrival of "uncouth" migrants would undo the inroads they had made into Austro-German society.[28] However, not all Galician Jews segregated themselves from wider society in the "Jewish" districts; many desired and made an effort to acculturate just as migrants in the earlier decades had.

By 1923, there were 201,513 Jews in Vienna, accounting for 10.8 percent of the total population. This number, however, includes only those who identified as Jewish by religion and not those Jews who had converted to Christianity or declared themselves *konfessionslos* (unaffiliated with any religion).[29] After Warsaw and Budapest, Vienna was the "third largest Jewish city in Europe."[30] Despite the recent growth of Vienna's Jewish population, the city's newfound importance as one of Europe's Jewish capitals recalled its earlier history as an important center of European Jewry. During the Middle Ages, Vienna's small but prominent Jewish community had been one of the most important in the German-language sphere. However, in 1421, the Habsburg Archduke Albrecht V (1397–1439) enacted anti-Jewish decrees that resulted in the community's destruction through forced conversion, massacre, and expulsion in a period referred to as the *Wiener Gesera* (Viennese decree), after which Vienna would be known among European Jews as the "city of blood."[31] From that time until 1848, Jews were periodically invited to and expelled from the Austrian capital, with many other towns and cities under Habsburg dominion maintaining similar limits or bans on Jewish residency. Prior to the ascension of Franz Joseph I to the Habsburg throne in 1848, only a handful of privileged, wealthy Jewish families were given permission to settle in the city on account of the benefit they brought to the Habsburg court. The patriarchs and sons, mostly financiers, industrialists, and merchants, often served in the traditional role of *Hofjuden* (court Jews) in loaning money to and performing financial services for the Habsburgs.[32]

Over the two decades following the failed 1848–9 revolution, restrictive measures against Jews were slowly repealed until the last of them, coinciding with the *Ausgleich* in 1867, granted all of Habsburg Jewry equal rights. During this period, most Jews took up residence in Vienna's second district, the Leopoldstadt, originally a marshy area between the Danube and one of its canals, where Jews had historically settled when prohibited from living in the city itself. Throughout the remainder of the century, Jews—both immigrants and Viennese-born—settled throughout the city. However, the respective residential patterns of Jews and Gentiles in Vienna served to further segregate these groups. Viennese Jews were largely resident in the Innere Stadt, Leopoldstadt, and Alsergrund (districts I, II, and IX), thus further alienating them from the bulk of Vienna's population who lived in districts beyond the Gürtel (the Vienna Beltway). Scholarship on Jewish residency in Vienna at the *fin de siècle* focuses predominantly on these three inner-city districts—referred to by Michael John and Albert Lichtblau as the "*Dreieck*" (triangle).[33] By the turn of the twentieth century, just over half of all Viennese Jews (55.2 percent) resided in these three districts—home to only 17.8 percent of all Viennese.[34] The remaining 44.78 percent of Viennese Jews resided in other "non-Jewish" districts.

The Leopoldstadt persisted as the most "Jewish" of the city's districts. Although Jews never accounted for the majority of the district's residents (by the turn of the century only 36.4 percent),[35] they remained a highly visible element in the district's urban character, resulting in the pejorative moniker "*Mazzesinsel*" (matzo island).[36] Toward the end of his life, the merchant and community leader Sigmund Mayer (1831–1920) recalled the shtetl-like atmosphere of the Leopoldstadt before and during the Jewish Sabbath on Friday afternoons and Saturdays:

A number of the retail shops owned by Jews which, naturally, were located mostly on lively streets, were now closed on Saturdays. They formed, so to speak, black spots in the row of elegant shops and luminous display windows. In Leopoldstadt, one saw many women hiding their beautiful hair in an ancient pious manner underneath the Orthodox headdresses, covering up to the middle of the forehead. One noticed men who, thinking it sinful to smoothen the cheeks and chin with a blade, rushed into dreadful barbershops on Fridays, where their faces received the characteristic blue color due to calcium hydroxide, slightly offset with orpiment. One saw Jewish maids carrying the ancient Saturday meal, "Schaloth," its praises sung by Heine, into the *Schalothstube* and collecting it from there later.[37]

Mayer's description suggests that the average Leopoldstädter Jew was Orthodox and from more traditional communities, such as those in Galicia and Bukovina, or small provincial, Bohemian, Moravian, and Hungarian towns, as opposed to the already Germanized Jews from larger cities. Many of the Leopoldtsadt's Jewish residents, especially recent arrivals from the east, lived in relative poverty, with large families crowded into very small apartments. Kurt Tauber described his family's living conditions after relocating to

Vienna from Sopron after the First World War as "very meager," his parents and younger brother sharing the bedroom, himself and two siblings in the lounge, and the maid on a cot in the kitchen. With no bathing facilities at home, the Tauber children were taken to wash at a public bath once a week.[38] Such conditions were typical in the lives of most Viennese, whether Jew or Gentile.

Despite its "traditional" character, the Jewish population of the Leopoldstadt was not homogenous. Kurt H. Schaffir, the son of a Viennese mother and Polish father, remembered a childhood in the Leopoldstadt. A picture of middle-class respectability, Schaffir described his family home at Taborstrasse 21A, one of the district's main thoroughfares, as

indeed a beautiful apartment. Three large, high-ceilinged rooms all faced the front, each with large windows, affording a splendid view of the hustle and bustle of the Taborstraße, four floors down. The largest of the three rooms also had a bay window, so that you could look up and down the street as well.

These rooms were entered from a narrow hallway, and on the other side of the hall was a large kitchen, bathroom, a toilet and another small bedroom which faced the rear of the building. A maid's room—entered from the kitchen only— also faced the back, and there was a small balcony in the back as well. . . . The three front rooms were tastefully wallpapered—one in blue, one red and one yellow, a crystal chandelier illuminated each room—testimony to the marvel of electricity which had recently been introduced.

The blue salon was the most elegantly furnished. Its chandelier was the most ornate and the furniture was a reddish polished wood. A large, glass enclosed bookcase occupied most of one wall, opposite the sofa and coffee table. The grand piano easily fitted into one corner, leaving a large open area in the center of the room. A Persian rug covered the entire floor.[39]

To these fine, middle-class spaces, the addition of modern clothing was to be expected. Despite these evocative word pictures of rooms, similarly detailed evocations of clothing worn by their inhabitants are rare. Where clothing does appear in memoirs, it is usually written by women about women. This points to one of the challenges of writing about men's fashion. Although many accounts exist, it is probably true that it was more common in the past to describe women's clothing. There is a well-established understanding in dress history that women's dress is better documented than men's partly due to the lack of material surviving in museum collections.[40]

Jews of all classes and backgrounds resided in the supposedly "Jewish" Leopoldstadt, and there was "no conspicuous segregation between 'German' and East European Jews such as existed in other European and American cities during the same period, even though comparable social, cultural, and political tensions were similarly present."[41] Yet, many Viennese Jews—both acculturated and those who maintained their "traditional" east European practices and rituals—insisted in their memoirs that limited social interactions took place between the two groups. Auguste Glauber, for example, recalled the many refugees from Galicia who arrived in Vienna during the First World War, describing how acculturated Jewish families such as hers avoided the refugees "whenever possible."[42] Writing her memoirs decades later, Glauber remorsefully admitted to giving up a friendship with a refugee girl, "because I was told to do so."[43]

Jewish Kaleidoscope: A Cross Section of Vienna's Jewish Community

To understand the issues concerning the dress of middle-class Jewish men and their multifaceted identifications in Vienna, it is important to understand the contextual situation of Jews in Vienna, including the political, religious, and social patterns, moving beyond the binary east/west divide. How an individual in *fin-de-siècle* Vienna may have expressed his or her understanding of Jewishness differed from their coreligionists in Berlin, Warsaw, or Paris, expressly because of Austria's wider "nationalities" question. Correspondingly, Viennese Jews identified as Jewish in different manners. The variety of Jewish identification, from differing cultural backgrounds and degrees of religious observance, meant that there could be no single, all-encompassing definition of Jewish identity applicable to Jewry across time. Judaism, as a set of religious beliefs and practices, made up only one criterion of Jewish identification and Jewishness. In this regard, Viennese Jews chose to practice their Judaism on a spectrum of observance, from strict, traditional Orthodoxy, to a lightly reformed variety of Judaism, and outright secularism and negation of religiosity. In addition to Judaism as a religious identification, Jews also chose to identify as a race, an ethnicity, or a cultural community. Conversion, intermarriage, and a range of choices connected to opportunity and risk created a diverse community in which many remained "Jewish" in name only. Viennese Jews—like their coreligionists elsewhere— chose to convert to the dominant religion: Catholicism. In fact, Vienna had the highest rate of conversion from Judaism to Christian denominations of all major European cities.[44] Some converts were eventually absorbed by the dominant society. Most were not. Often, Austrian Jews converted to Christianity but remained within a "Jewish" milieu, marrying other converts, and continuing to move within Jewish circles, even attending church services with their former coreligionists.[45] Others declared themselves *konfessionslos* or remained members of the community while discarding all forms of religious practice.

Vienna's Jewish milieu was strongly shaped by individual Jews' experiences of acculturation and assimilation. The phenomena of acculturation and assimilation are distinct, despite their regular interchangeable use in literature including memoirs and biographies. Raymond H. C. Teske Jr. and Bardin H. Nelson have argued that assimilation is an intricate process that may affect both individuals and groups.[46] An individual does not assimilate simply by adopting certain modes and lifestyles of another group. True and complete assimilation requires the acceptance of the "out-group" into whose midst the individual wishes to assimilate.[47] This study draws on the definition of assimilation described by Leo Spitzer—in turn derived from a model introduced by Milton M. Gordon[48]—as "*a process of adaptation and adjustment on a continuum*" composed of three levels:

(1) *acculturation*, or cultural/behavioural assimilation, indicating the modification of cultural patterns and symbols by subordinate group members in conformity with those of the dominant group; (2) *structural assimilation*, describing the subordinate's large-scale entrance into institutions, associations, professions, fields of economic activity, clubs, and locales from which its members had previously been excluded; and (3) *fusion* or *amalgamation*, referring to the final, completing stage of the continuum, when persons from the subordinate group would merge entirely with the dominant, through intermarriage, losing their previous identity by becoming virtually indistinguishable from members of the society at large.[49]

The first stage of assimilation is most evident in examining the lifestyle patterns of Viennese Jews, including factors such as dress, language, and their overall adoption of secular German culture as their own. However, as Viennese Jewry was diverse, different segments of this population reached the stages of assimilation in varying degrees. Taking the IKG as indicative, Viennese Jewry reached the first stage, acculturation, and to a certain extent, the second stage, structural assimilation.[50] Prior to settling in Vienna, many Jewish migrants from other parts of Austria-Hungary had already become acculturated but did not necessarily assimilate into the wider Gentile society. By adopting the German language for both professional and daily use, modern sartorial fashions of the co-territorial middle-class Gentile population, and providing their children with secular German education, Habsburg Jewry signaled its desire to become contributing members of the wider society. Such acculturation had often been achieved prior to their legal emancipation, thus rendering the acculturated Jews as "sojourners in the dominant world, not full members of it."[51] Even after their complete emancipation in 1867, many Habsburg Jews remained "sojourners," not because they were estranged from Austro-German culture, but because they were largely ostracized by Gentile society and lived as a parallel society alongside it.[52]

An additional problem with assessing the success of Jewish assimilation in Vienna is that assimilation is a process that must be undertaken by the individual, whereas many of nineteenth-century Vienna's Jewish élite—including political, religious, and lay leaders—maintained an assimilatory standpoint that sought to present Viennese Jewry collectively as "Germans of the Mosaic faith."[53] Pursuing assimilation as a group hindered chances of successful, that is, complete, integration.[54] Utilizing the German sociologist Georg Simmel's notion of the Stranger, Zygmunt Bauman characterizes Jews as representing the quintessential strangers within European society who have thus been used in much scholarship as the typical case study on assimilation.[55] In Simmel's original essay, he differentiates the "stranger" from the "wanderer." While the latter "comes today and is gone tomorrow," the former "comes today and stays tomorrow. He is, so to speak, the *potential* wanderer: although he has not quite overcome the freedom of coming and going."[56] Simmel, himself a product of the Jewish assimilatory project,[57] offers the history of European Jews as a "classical example" of this phenomenon—often connected to trade and the trader's position within wider society.[58] Consequently, the Jew in Gentile European society occupied the role of the stranger, an "internal" foreigner, in that unlike the foreigner who comes and goes to and from his native land, the "foreign" Jew occupied a semi-permanent position among the body politic but not as part of it. Forming a community of faith (and, in some instances, class) the Jews sat outside the imagined confines of the "nation." In his study *Modernity and Ambivalence*, Bauman describes the impossibility of successful collective assimilation thus:

> Ethnic-religious-cultural strangers are all too often tempted to embrace the liberal version of group emancipation (erasing of a collective stigma) as a reward for individual efforts of self-improvement and self-transformation. Frequently they go out of their way to get rid of and to suppress everything which makes them distinct from the rightful members of the native community—and hope that a devoted emulation of native ways will render them indistinguishable from the hosts, and by the same token guarantee their reclassification as insiders, entitled to the treatment the friends routinely receive. The harder they try, however, the faster the finishing-line seems to be receding. When, at last, it seems to be within their grasp, a dagger of racism is flung from beneath the liberal cloak. The rules of the game are changed with little warning. Or, rather, only now the earnestly "self-refining" strangers discover that what they mistook for a game of emancipation was in fact a game of domination.[59]

While there may have been instances of assimilation into Gentile Viennese society by individual Jews during the late nineteenth and early twentieth centuries, Viennese Jewry as a whole did not assimilate into Austro-German circles. One of the primary reasons that Austrian Jewish assimilation remained incomplete was widespread antisemitism, particularly during the second half of the nineteenth century, a period of rapid Jewish modernization and eventual emancipation.[60] However, the absence of an Austrian national culture or identity beyond shared fate as Habsburg subjects also played an integral role.

The idea of "Austria" comprised all individuals regardless of ethnic origin, or *Volksstamm*, which was officially determined by everyday speech.[61] This meant that Austro-Hungarian Jews could be counted in the government census as any of the Dual Monarchy's official nationalities but not as Jewish nationals, despite their shared religion, historical experience, (in some cases) linguistic traditions, and the persisting attitude that Jews consisted of a separate race, nation, or people. Thus, a German-speaking Jew in Vienna or Bohemia was counted in the government census as a German. However, a Jew in Galicia who spoke Yiddish as her *Umgangssprache* (daily vernacular) might be counted as a Pole or German due to the fact that Yiddish was not considered among the official languages of the Dual Monarchy (nor a language at all and, instead, a jargon or "bad German") and due to her working knowledge of the Polish language as a result of her location and daily interactions with Gentile Poles.[62] While "Jew" was not counted among the official nations of the empire, it existed as a religious category under the terms *"israelitisch"* (Israelite) or *"mosaisch"* (Mosaic).[63] Marsha L. Rozenblit asserts: "Possessing no territory, no common spoken language, no normal economic distribution, and no political aspirations, to the nineteenth century observer the Jews did not display the usual attributes of a nation."[64] Thus, the Austrian *Vielvölkerstaat* (multiethnic state) with its ethnically and linguistically mixed population and lack of uniting national identity further complicated the possibilities for Jewish assimilation.

Despite denying its Jewish subjects the ability to identify as Jewish "nationals," the state's acceptance of them as loyal Austrians only reinforced Jewish loyalty to the Habsburg Empire—"the *Gesamtstaat*, and not an Austrian national or ethnic culture, which did not exist."[65] Joseph Samuel Bloch, the Galician-born rabbi and deputy for the district of Kolomea-Buczacz-Sniatyn in the Austrian *Reichsrat* (parliament), believed Austrian Jewry to be not simply "the most loyal devotees of the monarchy, [but] they are the only unconditional Austrians in this federation."[66] Patriotic Jews were not the only Austrians to share this attitude. A funeral scene in Franz Theodor Csokor's 1936 play *3. November 1918*, in which soldiers bury their colonel, perpetuates this supposed Jewish ultra-Austrianness and therefore "foreignness" in his inability to identify with the concept of nation. While other soldiers shovel soil into the grave of their colonel calling out their respective homelands among the Austro-Hungarian crown lands, the Jewish staff doctor Grün offers "Earth from Austria."[67] Perhaps an exaggeration, but Austria's multiethnic character afforded its Jews the ability to identify in varying ways. Rozenblit refers to a "tripartite identity" in which Jews were able to identify politically as Austrian, culturally as German, and ethnically (and/or religiously) as Jewish.[68] Likewise, Lisa Silverman notes that after the dissolution of the empire, Jews in the First Austrian Republic adapted this tripartite identity to identify as politically Austrian, ethnically Jewish, and culturally Viennese.[69] In this manner, many Viennese Jews became highly acculturated, adopting the language and cultural mores of middle-class Germans, but choosing to assert their Jewish identity—whether faith-based, cultural, or ethnic.

The notion of widespread Jewish assimilation in Vienna is further complicated by the fact that within the crown lands that would become the First Republic of Austria after the dissolution of the Habsburg Empire, Austrian Jewry was situated predominantly in Vienna.[70] The Austrian capital itself maintained a precarious position in the Dual Monarchy's German provinces. The multiethnic character of "Austrian culture" was, for the writer Robert Musil (1880–1942), a "perspective flaw belonging to the Viennese point of view."[71] Multiethnic, cosmopolitan Vienna—and during the interwar period, "Red Vienna," seen as a hotbed of left-wing radicalism[72]—was reviled by those in the provinces as a particularly Jewish city, despite Jews only ever reaching 10.8 percent of the city's total population (in 1923).[73]

The higher-than-average rate of conversion out of Judaism in the Catholic-oriented Vienna of the late Habsburg period does not indicate a triumph of Catholicism over Judaism in terms of the religious convictions of the converts. Like their counterparts in other parts of Europe, Viennese Jews converted for a variety of reasons, including social, economic, and civic factors, as well as those who did indeed convert out of truly religious conviction.[74] Thus, the dominant role of Catholicism in Vienna was not one of a solely religious nature but one that was all-encompassing. Converting to Catholicism—and to a lesser degree Protestantism[75]—was often seen as a means of facilitating "total assimilation into Western culture" in Vienna and other European cities.[76] Yet, a majority of those Jews who did convert continued to be seen as "Jewish" by both Jews and Gentiles. Marriages between Jewish converts to Christian denominations or those who had declared themselves *konfessionslos*, and those who remained Jewish were common, thus augmenting the rate of recorded intermarriage among Jews and "non-Jews."[77]

But what did it mean to be Jewish in Vienna or how might Jewishness be defined in this time and place? It was the two ends of the spectrum of diverse Viennese Jewry—the acculturated élite and the so-called "Polish Jews" or *Ostjuden*, that correspond to Hannah Arendt's binary opposites of Jewish assimilation, the parvenu and the pariah—that often set the tone for external manifestations of Jewishness: the former with its obsessive desire to assimilate and the latter with its inability and often unwillingness to do so.[78] As with the studies that focus predominantly on Viennese Jewry in districts I, II, and IX, numerous memoirs and biographies of Viennese Jews during the final decades of the nineteenth century and early decades of the twentieth century have painted a portrait of a community that was largely "assimilated," fabulously wealthy, and deeply involved in the development of the city's modernist culture.[79] Most of Vienna's Jewish population, however, were middle- to working class. The illustrious *Ringstraßenfamilien* (Ringstrasse families)—Auspitz, Ephrussi, Epstein, Gutmann, Königswarter, Lieben, Schey, Rothschild—belonged to a small socioeconomic tier that was, in addition to maintaining ostentatious lifestyles, socially incestuous. Marriages were made between the sons and daughters of wealthy families in an attempt to marry one's children into the right families. By limiting the spousal pool available to their children, the Jewish élite were able to keep wealth within a select group and forge professional ties with other wealthy families, not dissimilar to those unions made by the European aristocracy.[80]

Although memoirs, such as Edmund De Waal's *Hare with Amber Eyes* (2011) and Tim Bonyhady's *Good Living Street* (2014), present a limited snapshot of Viennese Jewry as a whole, they offer a glimpse into the complexities of Vienna's Jewish financial élite, its precarious position within Viennese society, and its relationship to the art world. The idea was that the correct manner of dress, behavior, education, and fashioning one's environment in a certain aesthetic style could transform a newly wealthy parvenu from the provinces into a highly esteemed and respected member of Vienna's upper class. This attitude was influenced by notions of *Bildung* (self-cultivation) and *Sittlichkeit* (morality or, in this context, respectability), which were central to the phenomenon of Jewish assimilation and acculturation in German-speaking Europe—a descendant of the *Haskalah*, the project of Jewish self-fashioning, often referred to as an Enlightenment, that began in the eighteenth century. Although translated as "education," *Bildung* refers to the concept of self-cultivation from a cultural perspective. To be "*gebildet*" was not only to be well educated in the formal sense but for the individual to have undergone a conscious self-fashioning along the lines of contemporary cosmopolitan educational and cultural values. In this manner *Bildung* and *Sittlichkeit* went hand in hand.[81] Élite *Ringstraßenfamilien* were a minority, albeit a highly conspicuous and powerful one, among Viennese Jewry. While its members enjoyed collecting valuable works of art and racehorses, or being seen at the theater or the famous *Konditoreien* Demel and Sacher, poorer Jews in the Leopoldstadt or working-class districts struggled to feed their families. The many unknown Jews, unable to afford the lifestyles of their immensely wealthy coreligionists, or the clothes and trinkets to visually assimilate into polite society, often remained easily identifiable as Jews, having retained the traditional sartorial, behavioral, linguistic, or cultural markers of (eastern) Jewishness.

Often these élite families were nominally Jewish. They were, like other Jews in Vienna—those who had not resigned from Judaism by either converting to Christianity or declaring themselves *konfessionslos*—members of the IKG and other community bodies and organizations. They participated at various levels from tax-paying members to being actively involved in community affairs. Many families in this socioeconomic tier were completely secular and did not participate in the religious or cultural aspects of Jewish life; that is, they did not attend synagogue regularly or celebrate the Jewish holidays, and some even converted to Christianity. They were the polar opposites of recently arrived immigrants, both culturally and economically. In the social hierarchy of Vienna's Jewish population, the *Ringstraßenfamilien* sat firmly at the top, while poor, traditionally Orthodox immigrants found themselves at the bottom.[82]

The palaces and villas of this Jewish élite, often home to more than one branch of the family, each occupying a different floor of the building, were decorated in the most resplendent styles with highly sought-after works of art lining the walls and custom-made furniture and fittings. Moriz and Hermine Gallia, perhaps slightly lower down the social ladder from the *Ringstraßenfamilien*, owned and lived in a grand apartment house at Wohllebengasse 4, a mere few minutes' walk from the palace of Baron Albert von Rothschild, which was located at the present-day Prinz-Eugen Strasse 20–22 in Wieden (district IV).[83] The building was designed by the architect Franz von Krauß, and many of the interiors by the celebrated Secessionist designer Josef Hoffmann.[84] A house on the Wohllebengasse, a short lane several streets back from the bustle of the *Innere Stadt*, conveyed a very different sense of material and aesthetic identification to those residing in *Ringstraßenpalais*. The Gallia family's existence was by no means modest. Like the *Ringstraßenfamilien*, they lived in the lap of luxury, albeit of differing tastes. While those with homes on the Ring tended to style themselves and their environments in mock-aristocratic, historicist opulence,[85] the Gallias and others, including art patrons Fritz and Lili Waerndorfer, and the author Richard Beer-Hofmann, championed emerging forms of artistic modernism.[86] However, an apartment house on the Wohllebengasse, albeit a luxurious one, was somehow less conspicuous than the brilliance of the Ringstrasse—or "Zionstraße von Neu-Jerusalem" (Zion Street of New Jerusalem) as the satirist Masaidek acerbically referred to it.[87]

Vienna's large *Bildungsbürgertum* (educated middle class)—among which the Gallia family can be counted, albeit at the wealthier end of the spectrum—was situated lower down the socioeconomic ladder between the *Ringstraßenfamilien* and Jewish working class and gave birth to many renowned literary and cultural figures. Arthur Schnitzler, Richard Beer-Hofmann, Karl Kraus, Theodor Herzl, and Stefan Zweig can be counted among its more famous sons. These men were the sons of professionals such as doctors and lawyers, engineers, industrialists, and businessmen, and many of their peers went on to follow in the footsteps of their fathers. Some, such as Schnitzler, Beer-Hofmann, and Zweig were the Viennese-born sons of immigrant parents from other parts of the Dual Monarchy, while others, such as Kraus and Herzl, were immigrants themselves, arriving in the capital as children or as young men. The Jewish *Bildungsbürgertum* lived typically in the Jewish districts (I, II, and IX) but also elsewhere.[88] Often they were upwardly mobile and looked toward the Jewish financial nobility for their cues on the social graces. Stefan Zweig spent his childhood and youth in the Ring's vicinity, first in a family apartment on the Schottenring, later as a student in rooms in Buchgasse—a fitting name for one who would go on to become one of the most renowned and widely translated authors during his time[89]—and Tulpengasse. His parents, Moriz and Ida Zweig, like other Jews of their socioeconomic class, placed a great deal of importance on education, and had Stefan educated at the renowned *Gymnasium* on Wasagasse in Alsergrund.[90]

The *Bildungsbürgertum* was usually secular. Like the Jewish *Ringstraßenfamilien*, its members' connection to Judaism was mostly in name. In his biography of Stefan Zweig, Oliver Matuschek describes how the Zweig family celebrated neither Hanukkah nor Christmas, despite the latter's widespread celebration among secular Jewish families.[91] They were Jews and did not hide the fact, but nor did they broadcast it. This was not uncommon among other Jews of this class, both those famous and unknown. When Rosalie Landstone, the mother of Arthur Schnitzler's English translator Hetty Landstone (née Landstein), visited the author at his Viennese home in 1929, she reported in a postcard to her daughter in London that there was "nothing to make 'Shabos' [*sic*] with."[92] Other families of the same class took a more traditional approach to Judaism and Jewish identification. There are numerous references to Jewish identity and culture, and the Jewish milieu of his upbringing in Friedrich Torberg's famous collection of anecdotes of pre-1938 Vienna, *Die Tante Jolesch*.[93] Harry Rich (né Reich), born in 1926 to a typical middle-class immigrant family from Bohemia, recalls a "traditional" Jewish upbringing in Alsergrund, regularly celebrating the Jewish holidays and occasional visits to the local synagogue on Müllnergasse.[94] Similarly, Elisabeth "Lisl" Ziegler (née Schacherl), born in 1917, also grew up in Alsergrund. Although her family was not particularly religious, her atheist father would dutifully take Lisl and her sister Fritzi to synagogue on the Jewish holidays, when they would deliver flowers to their more observant mother.[95] In contrast, Ludwig/Lajos Schischa, an Orthodox immigrant from Mattersdorf (Mattersburg) in the formerly Hungarian Burgenland, was more concerned with Torah-study and attending synagogue than anything else—according to family lore (Figure 1.1).[96]

Fidelity to Jewish traditions was an issue that varied among Viennese Jewry. Among families of earlier arrivals in the city from Bohemia, Moravia, and Hungary (during the post-1848 era), religious practice varied between traditional Orthodoxy, Liberalism (with services in the original Hebrew and Aramaic, and sermons in German),[97] and secularism.[98] To many, Judaism was both an ethnic and confessional identity that worked in tandem with their German cultural identity. Like their Christian German counterparts who adhered to either the Catholic or Protestant faith, their religious persuasion and

Figure 1.1 Family of Ludwig (Lajos) and Ida Schischa, Vienna, *c.* 1920s. From L-R: Max, Leopold ("Poldi"), Edith, Ida, Ludwig, Eugen ("Jenő"), and Helene/Ilona. Courtesy of Susan Warhaftig, Sydney.

membership of the IKG was simply a formality of civic society, albeit one that played a large role in Austrian bureaucracy. As in neighboring Germany, of all the Jewish organizations active in Vienna during the late nineteenth and early twentieth centuries, only the IKG was state-sanctioned and recognized as being responsible for all civic and religious matters of the community.[99] This mirrored the state's acknowledgment of the Jews as a purely faith-based community—Austrian citizens of the Mosaic faith, similar to the assimilatory aspirations in neighboring Germany.[100] Such importance placed on religion in the sociopolitical identity politics of the Austro-Hungarian Empire made the accepted Jewishness of religiously unaffiliated Jews all the more difficult to reconcile and complicated the notion of who was Jewish.

Yet, neither members of the Jewish élite, the *Bildungsbürgertum, konfessionslos,* nor converts to Christian denominations successfully assimilated into the dominant Gentile society. On the contrary, they were easily identifiable as Jews and, like their poorer coreligionists, they were assaulted in various cultural spheres from both ends of the political spectrum. From the Right they were cast as dangerous revolutionaries and/or enemies of the German *Volk,* and from the Left as blood-sucking parasitic capitalists.[101] These polarizing images of Jews and Jewishness certainly affected the daily experience of the many Jews who did not conform to these external perceptions.

Viennese Jewry was not the homogenous group so often depicted in the contemporary antisemitic press and literature. Vienna's Jewish "community" was a vibrant population that was made up of diverse social, cultural, religious, economic, and political communities. Herein lay the vulnerability. Rather than help in its favor to reject xenophobic representations of Jews, its heterogenous character only further complicated notions of Jewish identification and Jewishness, allowing this oft-maligned and socially isolated segment of Viennese society to be attacked from all sides of the cultural and political arenas.

CHAPTER 2
FASHIONING THE SELF, DRESSING SOCIETY
DRESS AND IDENTITY IN EUROPE'S THIRD JEWISH CAPITAL

Participating in Fashion: Viennese Jews and Dress

Clothing and other aspects of visual self-fashioning played a central role in the acculturation and urbanization of Vienna's Jewish population. It was both by adopting widespread modes of dress and by their contribution in creating and transmitting fashions to the wider society—as designers, manufacturers, retailers, fashion journalists, and consumers—that Viennese Jews publicly expressed their status as modern, urban cosmopolitans and equal participants in Viennese culture. This sartorial self-reinvention among immigrant Jews gave rise to a recurring trope in late nineteenth- and early twentieth-century Europe: the accusation that Jews were somehow attempting to conceal their Jewishness. Using examples from literary fiction, contemporaneous fashion and lifestyle magazines, photographs, and other visual examples, this chapter explores the role of Viennese Jews in that city's fashion and dress industries, as well as the role of dress in the acculturation process.

For assimilating and acculturating Viennese Jews, their complete emancipation in 1867 signaled the permission to enter wider Gentile society. However, the dismantling of administrative discrimination had not extended to the social sphere, and many within the Dual Monarchy continued to harbor prejudices against Jews. The logical solution for some Jews was the complete rejection of their past.[1] This generally meant a change of name, religion, residence, and—if not already undertaken—the adoption of both modern styles of dress and the language and culture of the majority. The abandonment of all traces of Jewishness would, in theory, facilitate complete assimilation. However, more often this was not the case. Many of those Jews who left Judaism by changing their religion—as many affluent and middle-class Jews did—or by declaring themselves *konfessionslos*, remained "Jewish" through their involvement in circles consisting largely of other converted or irreligious Jews.[2] Whether an individual was able to assimilate successfully, or merely acculturate to the dominant German culture was often determined by factors beyond his or her control. An individual may have desired to disappear into the dominant cultural and ethnic group, but desires and intentions did not guarantee complete assimilation. As Peter Gay explains, among the various forms of German antisemitism that emerged parallel to the emancipation and acculturation of Jews during the latter decades of the nineteenth century, a common form was one that targeted Jews expressly for their eagerness to become German and their increased rate of acculturation.[3]

The assimilatory process of most Viennese Jews did not extend past the first stage (acculturation). Gay argues that assimilation "took several generations, several intermarriages, possibly a change of name and of residence, before the past of the new Christian faded into invisibility."[4] Thus, their incomplete assimilatory process left them as acculturated Jews, regardless of whether they chose to practice Judaism or not. Highlighting the multidirectional isolation faced by acculturating Jews, Jacob Golomb refers to such individuals as *Grenzjuden* (marginal or borderline Jews), individuals who "were alienated from their religion, and tradition, but had not been fully absorbed into secular Austrian society."[5] Similarly, Sander L. Gilman describes the acculturation of German Jewry more widely as a borrowed value system that led to both a loss of identity and the external accusation of Jewish deviousness through concealment.[6] Viennese Jews desiring full assimilation as well as those content to remain Jewish participants in German culture faced accusations of masking their Jewishness.[7] Franz Friedrich Masaidek warned his readers that the "*anständigen*" (respectable—which is to say, acculturated) Jews were far more dangerous than their traditional coreligionists, as they deceived Christians about their true intentions.[8]

The accusation against Jews of masking their religious or ethnic identity was often related to clothing choice, with the belief that true Jewish garb was that of the *shtetl* and not modern European fashions. What made this sartorial artifice "dangerous" in the eyes of its detractors was its historical connotation with sin, seduction, and the pervasion of nature.[9] Writing in his self-published journal, *Die Fackel*, in 1906, the Viennese satirist Karl Kraus argued that clothing was unable to mask the body or true aspects of human nature, but rather "articulate[s] the unconscious essence of man with the greatest clarity. It tells us directly and bluntly about the innermost part of man from which all desires, thoughts, and experiences arise."[10] This trope commonly appeared in antisemitic literature in which Jewish figures were caricatured dressed in opulent styles and in the latest fashion, while still retaining the behavioral patterns and visual markers of the *Ostjuden*. The Viennese satirical magazine *Kikeriki* (1861–1933) regularly contained xenophobic content ridiculing Austria-Hungary's various ethnic groups; however, those targeting Jews and Czechs tended to be more aggressive than others. This typically included grotesque caricatures of Jews that followed traditional physical and behavioral stereotypes. One telling example features an elegantly dressed sow in a frock and wide plumed hat on her way to attend the theater (Figure 2.1). The caption reads: "Pfui, man kann in gar kein Theater gehen, alles viel zu *schweinisch!*" (One simply cannot go to the theater; everything there is just too piggish!).[11] Although not explicitly commenting on the sow's Jewishness, the German word "*schweinisch*" (piggish) is used here as a euphemism for "*jüdisch*" (Jewish). The use of a pig to represent a Jewish figure is no accident. Within the German-language realm the relationship between the figure of "the Jew" and the pig was a common trope in anti-Jewish imagery from at least the thirteenth century, with the so-called *Judensau* employed as a common motif within woodcuts and church carvings.[12] The cartoonist's focus on the theater is also significant. Along with

Figure 2.1 Caricature from *Kikeriki* 35, no. 99 (December 12, 1895): 1. Courtesy of ANNO/Österreichische Nationalbibliothek, Vienna.

the coffeehouse, the theater developed a reputation for being a preferred site of Jewish recreation and socialization, in contrast to Gentiles visiting the *Heuriger* (wine gardens on the city's outskirts).[13] The message conveyed in the caricature is quite clear: despite adopting fineries, the Jew cannot mask his or her true nature. In linking Jewishness, the theater, and fashionable dress, the notion of artifice and its association with dishonesty and immorality is brought to the fore.[14] A Jewish-coded figure dismisses the theater, and yet dressed in styles of hyperbolic proportions she too appears in a costume, and thus is a product of this realm of falsity.

As a result of linking an underlying Jewishness with an external layer of fashionable clothing, it was inevitable that the much more ancient figure of the parvenu would come to the fore. Fashionable clothing came to be seen as inherently "Jewish," in contrast to the simple clothes of the working-class Christian, or the *Tracht* (traditional costume) of rural peasants. Therefore, the adoption of fashionable styles of dress came to affirm rather than negate Jewishness. This widespread notion was internalized and purveyed by Jews themselves. The characters in Arthur Schnitzler's 1924 novella *Fräulein Else* are undoubtedly members of the Viennese Jewish bourgeoisie struggling with the supposedly conflicting notions of *Sittlichkeit* and Jewishness.[15] Although the characters' Jewishness is never outwardly stated, it is expressed through the title character's internal monologue. When Else is implored by her mother in a letter to seek the financial aid of one her fellow guests at the South Tyrolean resort of San Martino di Castrozza, a certain

Herr von Dorsday d'Eperies, she describes her family's would-be benefactor as "still quite nice-looking with his pointed beard, going grey. But I don't like him. He's a social climber. What good does your first-class tailor do you, Herr von Dorsday? Dorsday! I'm sure your name used to be something else,"[16] a clear reference to the tendency of some Jews to change their names in an attempt to appear less Jewish.[17] Else continues:

No, Herr von Dorsday, I'm not taken in by your smartness, and your monocle and your title. You might just as well deal in old clothes as in old pictures. . . . But, Else, Else, what are you thinking of? Oh, I can permit myself a remark like that. Nobody notices it in me. I'm positively blonde, or reddish blonde, and Rudi looks like a regular aristocrat. Certainly one can notice it at once in Mother, at any rate in her speech, but not at all in Father. For that matter, let people notice it. I don't deny it, and I'm sure Rudi doesn't.[18]

In this unabashed confession of her own Jewishness, there is a sense of self-deprecation and simultaneously a sense of guilt about the internalized social antisemitism and its influence on Else's own sense of Jewish identification. The passage is revealing, as it comments on "normalized" Jewish views on Jewishness and the complicity of Jews in the perpetuation of this negative image. Here, through his fictional character Else, Schnitzler gives a voice to the complexities of Jewish identification in contemporary Vienna. Else's internal monologue presents the conflicting views of identifying as a Jew: shame, scorn, pride, and indifference. This is underpinned by Else's reference to Jewishness in all but name. The readers know exactly what she is referring to—the "Jewish look" or a particularly "Jewish" manner of speaking (*Mauscheln*) influenced by Yiddish—despite not daring to utter it. And Schnitzler takes this notion of masking one's true identity further through the use of dress. Dorsday is described by Else as a sort of a fop: a follower of fleeting fashions rather than adhering to the conventions of respectable dress— dressing in an inappropriate manner—"His tie is too loud for an elderly man. Does his mistress choose them for him?"[19]—alluding to the stereotype that Jewish men—and women—have no sense of style, and that Dorsday must turn to others for advice, even if that advice is incorrect. Furthermore, Dorsday is portrayed as a stereotypical Jewish coward, a huckster, and a murderer,[20] with its connotations of the biblical figure Judas Iscariot, in contrast to the innocent Else, who is a victim of the crimes of others—a sacrifice for her father's sins. However, Dorsday is not the only character inscribed with stereotypically Jewish characteristics. In addition to Else's reference to her mother's obvious Jewishness, her brother Rudi and cousin Paul are presented as Jewish playboys, her father the crooked Jewish speculator, and her Aunt Emma as a hysterical snob who, following Else's psychotic breakdown, comments to her son, "You don't really suppose, Paul, that I'll travel to Vienna in the same carriage with her like this. One might have unpleasant experiences!"[21]

The perceived link between upwardly mobile Jews and clothing as a form of self-fashioning that Schnitzler highlights through his fictional characters was often used in satirical cartoons depicting the failed attempt of an individual to hide his or her

Jewishness.[22] Postcards from Vienna and other parts of the empire—indeed throughout Europe and further afield—commonly depicted scenes populated by individuals with stereotypical, grotesque Jewish features—large hooked noses, misshapen bodies, dark, curly hair, thick lips, and protruding ears—dressed in fine clothing, characters made all the more grotesque through the juxtaposition of corporeal ugliness and material beauty. A postcard in the archives of Vienna's Jewish Museum, date-stamped 1912, depicts a throng of middle-aged and elderly men with stereotypical Jewish features loitering in front of the Viennese Stock Exchange. The grotesque, misshapen features of the men are complemented by their finely tailored suits and coats in the latest fashions. The men appear to be haggling over stocks and sharing the latest gossip in fraternal camaraderie.[23] Another example, date-stamped July 1903, depicts a diverse crowd strolling in the Prater: fashionably dressed Jews, a flamboyantly attired fop, and ramrod-straight, impeccably groomed officers of the Austro-Hungarian army. The Jews affect aristocratic airs and stroll in a manner conveying confidence and comfort with their place in this society.[24] However, such caricatures present a one-sided negative view of Jewish assimilation. They convey the notion that Jews wished to assimilate into mainstream society at all costs and do not consider the possibility that Jews may have used acculturation and the adoption of modern dress to develop modern, specifically Jewish identities.[25]

Jews participated in the world of fashion and created identities independent of external, often negative, characterization, through their engagement within the fashion industry. In the purveyance of sartorial fashions, Jewish entrepreneurs, retailers, and designers were able to take control of their visual appearances and present new styles to the wider society. One sector of the clothing industry in which they excelled, particularly in German-speaking Europe, was the development of the department store. Following in the wake of earlier enterprises including dry goods stores, drapers, clothing warehouses, and novelty stores, department stores developed simultaneously in London and Paris, during the second half of the nineteenth century and spread throughout Europe, to the Ottoman Empire, across the Atlantic to the Americas, and European colonies in Africa, Asia, and the Pacific. Initially designed to provide a luxury retail experience, with entrepreneurs eager to generate profit, the department store evolved over time into establishments catering to different socioeconomic classes.[26]

Although Jews were not responsible for the creation of early department stores in Britain and France, over the course of the nineteenth century, many Jewish entrepreneurs in the German-speaking world, took advantage of the newly acquired rights that came with their emancipation and the changing retail patterns in the larger cities.[27] In many ways, the prevalence of Jews in the development of department stores can be viewed as an extension of traditional Jewish involvement in the "rag trade"—a result of Jews being denied entry to craft guilds and other professions during earlier periods. In his study of Jewish-owned German department stores, Paul Lerner highlights the connection between department stores and traditional Jewish professional patterns, particularly the Jew as a peddler. Like the Jewish peddlers, he claims, who were dependent on their ability to conduct trade across national, ethnic, and linguistic boundaries,

The department store in a sense institutionalized the circulation of the itinerant peddler, bringing diverse goods and populations together under one roof, but in a setting where the consumers, modern mobile spectators, circulated around stationary displays of commodities that had come to rest after their long journeys.[28]

The rise of the department store was also built, in part, upon the earlier development of the ready-made clothing industry, which provided an important segment of the apparel sold in early incarnations of such establishments.[29] The rise of the ready-made clothing industry created a rift between its customer base and those who continued to frequent tailors and dressmakers for bespoke garments. These ready-made clothes were often of poor quality because their production was "organised by 'clothiers'—that is, merchants— many of whom had themselves never made a suit and whose artistry was manifest instead in the profitable coordination of cloth, labor, and credit."[30] This model of business was a contrast to the artistry of tailors who had not only honed their skills over a longer period but also engaged directly with the customer's body.[31] The contrast was also manifest in language. Writing of the ready-made clothing industry in North America, Michael Zakim notes: "By the 1840s New York City business directories published two separate listings for men's clothing stores: clothiers' 'warehouses' and tailors' 'establishments'," not only separating the physical spaces in which the trade took place but also dividing the customer base by the common, working-class and traditional, elitist notions denoted by these spatial descriptions.[32] However, as Christopher Breward has demonstrated in his study of male sartorial patterns in nineteenth-century London, the class boundaries between customers of ready-made clothing and those who frequented bespoke tailors were not fixed. Many men, including those who moved in the upper echelons of society, purchased certain garments from bespoke tailors while sourcing others from other retailers.[33] Still, the prestige of bespoke tailoring often won out over other forms of clothing consumption. At times, participation within this industry precluded involvement in its consumer base. The Viennese businessman Wilhelm Mährischl owned a business that exported ready-made men's garments and accessories to other parts of Europe, including Scandinavia and Switzerland. His daughter Fritzi Ritterman (1913–2019) recalled that despite her father's involvement in the industry—or perhaps as a result of it—the Mährischl family did not purchase clothes from department stores or other retailers, but rather frequented the services of dressmakers and tailors.[34]

The development of the *Konfektion* (ready-made clothing) and department store industries in Germany and Austria-Hungary was largely due to the efforts of Jewish entrepreneurs.[35] While Paris and London were dominating forces in the world of fashion during the nineteenth and early twentieth centuries, esteemed for *haute couture* and tailoring, respectively, Berlin and Vienna received acclaim for *Konfektion*.[36] A close exchange of creation and ideas developed between these cities, and what was known as "Parisian" style in the *Konfektion* industry was often the product of German and Austrian firms. For example, the trade journal *Chic Parisien: journal special pour modèles des Paris et Vienne*, which was distributed throughout Europe, and as far as Australia and New Zealand, was printed in Vienna between 1898 and 1940 by the publishing house

A. Bachwitz.[37] This publishing house, with its offices at Löwengasse 47 in Vienna's third district, published other fashion-related material, including the early twentieth-century trade journal and catalogue for tailors, *Herren-Mode-Welt*. Founded by a German-Jewish immigrant Arnold Bauchwitz (1854–1930), who later changed his name to Bachwitz, the eponymous firm was one of Austria's leading publishers of fashion-related material during the early twentieth century. In her 1935 study of German fashion magazines, Lore Krempel asserted that Bachwitz alone published forty different titles in various European languages, including German, French, English, Portuguese, Spanish, Czech, Italian, Serbian, Hungarian, and Dutch.[38]

Many leading department stores in the German and Austro-Hungarian empires— and later in the Weimar Republic and Austria-Hungary's successor states—were owned and/or founded by individuals of Jewish origin; of note were Adolf Jandorf's Kaufhaus des Westens (KaDeWe) and Hermann Tietz's Warenhaus Tietz in Berlin, and August Herzmansky and Alfred Abraham Gerngroß's eponymous department stores in Vienna.[39] Uri M. Kupferschmidt asserts that the prevalence of Jewish-owned department stores was as much a result of "mobility and migration" as "entrepreneurial imagination and flexibility."[40] The Jewish-owned department stores and other fashion businesses in Vienna were not exceptional but, rather, typical of the transnational nature of both the fashion system and world Jewry.

In Vienna during the second half of the nineteenth and early decades of the twentieth centuries, Jews' representation in the textile and luxury industries was disproportionate to their share of the wider population. In his 1936 volume on the so-called "Jewish Question," Georg Glockemeier boldly claimed that Jewish-owned businesses dominated Vienna's main shopping streets:

> Anyone who has walked down the street with open eyes during the last years, has had the opportunity to convince themselves about this intrusion. One could see how the Jews have taken over one shop after the other in the good commercial streets. In Vienna's main shopping street—the Mariahilferstrasse, all the way to the Gürtel—the Jews owned about 30 percent of the stores before the war, today approximately 60 percent. On the basis of storefronts alone, today about 80 to 90 percent of the Mariahilferstrasse is Jewish.[41]

Published during a period of increasing concern over the "Jewish Question" and Austria's own concern for its national image, Glockemeier's volume was undoubtedly clouded by contemporary anxieties. Although based on anecdotal evidence, this account is preceded by statistics outlining the proportions of Jews in various Viennese industries. These statistics included, for example, those relating to textiles and apparel: 45 percent of men's hatmakers, 40 percent of jewelers, 67.6 percent of furriers, 25 percent of leather merchants, 34 percent of milliners, 60 to 80 percent of shoe manufacturers and merchants, 9.5 percent of bag makers, 73.75 percent of the textile trade, and 93 percent of the linen trade.[42] It is the case that Jews dominated fashion retail; therefore much of Vienna's population wore clothes designed, manufactured, or retailed by Jews.

However, the impact of Jews on Vienna's clothing trade was reciprocal. The evolving textile and dress industries of the nineteenth century helped many Jewish families on the road to financial respectability and offered them an entry ticket into the so-called "second society." The writer Stefan Zweig characterized this as only the means to achieving the true Jewish desire, namely the acquisition of knowledge:

> Getting rich, to a Jew, is only an interim stage, a means to his real end, by no means his aim in itself. The true desire of a Jew, his inbuilt ideal, is to rise to a higher social plane by becoming an intellectual. Even among Orthodox Eastern Jews, in whom the failings as well as the virtues of the Jewish people as a whole are more strongly marked, this supreme desire to be an intellectual finds graphic expression going beyond merely material considerations—the devout biblical scholar has far higher status within the community than a rich man. Even the most prosperous Jew would rather marry his daughter to an indigent intellectual than a merchant.[43]

Zweig's ideas about Jews and scholarship are undoubtedly exaggerated, revealing more about his own attitudes on the topic than any certainties. However, his words carry a modicum of truth. The efforts of fathers involved in manufacture resulted in comfortable financial situations that afforded sons, such as Zweig himself, the opportunity to occupy themselves with more intellectual and creative pursuits.[44] This attitude is helpful in understanding the prevalent role wealthy Jewish families played in supporting emerging modernist art and design.

In 1903, the Secessionist designers Koloman Moser (1868–1918) and Josef Hoffmann (1870–1956)—neither of whom were Jewish—together with the textile manufacturer and arts patron Fritz Waerndorfer (1868–1939), founded the design collective known as the Wiener Werkstätte. Waerndorfer was born to a Jewish family, but converted to Protestantism with his wife Lili (née Hellmann, 1874–1952) in 1902 and anglicized the spelling of his original surname "Wärndorfer."[45] Raised in an upper-middle-class family, he was exposed to the art world and its utilization by acculturating Jews as a way of affirming their dual Jewish and Viennese identifications during Vienna's so-called *Gründerzeit*, the period of economic prosperity between the revolution of 1848/9 and the 1873 stock market crash.[46] In this manner Waerndorfer and his family were not unique in their patronage of modernist art and design, with other wealthy Jews among the Wiener Werkstätte's patrons, such as the industrialist Moriz Gallia (1858–1918) who served on its board.[47] Evolving out of the Vienna Secession—the *fin-de-siècle* art movement concerned with creating new artistic forms for a new century and a new supranational Austrian aesthetic in rejection of historicist traditions (of which Moser and Hoffmann were among the founding members)—the Wiener Werkstätte produced and marketed a wide range of carefully designed products, including furniture, ceramics, silverware, decorative art, graphics, stationery, textile, and sartorial accessories, that were very popular among Vienna's very Jewish *Bildungsbürgertum*. The Jewish customer base grew so important that by the end of the first decade of the twentieth century, the Werkstätte offered a series of greeting cards marking *Rosh Hashanah* (Jewish New

Year) and depicting patterns from its range of popular textile designs. The Werkstätte opened stores outside Vienna in locales frequented by this segment of society, such as the popular Bohemian spa towns Karlsbad and Marienbad, as well as Zürich and New York.[48]

Jewish individuals were involved with the Werkstätte beyond the roles of financial backers and customers—there were also many Jewish designers.[49] The Wiener Werkstätte was dissolved in 1932, but many of the Jewish-owned department stores and fashion houses continued to operate until their forced closure or "Aryanization" after the Anschluss in March 1938. The Aryanization of the Jewish firms not only destroyed this Jewish industry but also led to the loss of the city's title as a European (and worldwide) fashion capital, a loss from which Vienna has never recovered.[50]

Textile and *Konfektion* manufacture and department store ownership were not the only segments of the dress industry in which Viennese Jews engaged. Several Jewish families or individuals established luxury fashion salons and tailoring ateliers catering to a wealthier customer base. Of note was the tailor and outfitters Wilhelm Jungmann & Neffe. A native of Sankt Georgen (Svätý Jur), Wilhelm Jungmann (1838–1914) opened his first Viennese store in 1866 at Rudolfplatz 1, before relocating to a new address at Salvatorgasse 3, both in Vienna's Innere Stadt. After a number of failed partnerships, Jungmann was joined in the business by his nephew and brother-in-law Wilhelm Dukes (1849–1938), a trained dressmaker and native of Komorn (Komárom/Komárno), and the pair registered the name Wilhelm Jungmann & Neffe in 1873.[51] In 1881, the firm received the honor of bearing the title of *kaiserlicher und königilicher Hoflieferant* (Imperial and Royal Court Purveyor), that same year moving to new premises at Albrechtsplatz 3 (today Albertinaplatz)—prime real estate behind the Viennese Hofoper where the business continues to operate to this day.[52] In addition to bearing the prestigious title of *k. und k. Hoflieferant*, Wilhelm Jungmann & Neffe boasted an élite clientele in both Vienna and abroad, including members of the Habsburg and Italian monarchies, Princess Pauline von Metternich, and the Duchess of Württemberg.[53] The business enjoyed esteem throughout the remainder of the nineteenth century and into the twentieth century, and demonstrated an ability to adapt to the times during the post-Habsburg era. Originally catering to a female clientele and offering fabrics of French origin, by the 1920s, Dukes pivoted the firm's focus toward a male clientele and English fabrics.[54] A customer registry from the 1920s and 1930s lists the addresses of customers in various districts populated by Vienna's middle- and upper-middle classes, as well as addresses outside the Austrian capital. Among the customer details are many names common among Viennese and other central European Jews, such as Abeles, Austerlitz, Breuer, Deutsch, Eckstein, and Friedländer.[55]

Wilhelm Jungmann & Neffe was not the only prominent Jewish-owned clothing atelier in Vienna during the late nineteenth and early twentieth centuries. Among the many renowned Viennese clothing establishments catering to either male or female clientele, or at times both, Goldman & Salatsch, Kniže & Comp., Maison Blanc, E. Braun & Co., Heilmann Kohn & Söhne, Heinrich Grünbaum, Heinrich Grünzweig,

G. & E. Spitzer, and Ludwig Zwieback & Bruder can be counted.[56] Like Jungmann and Dukes, the founders of these firms were commonly immigrants to the Imperial and Royal *Kaiserstadt* from Bohemia, Moravia, and Hungary.[57] These men and women were of the generation that saw official barriers preventing Jewish involvement within professional fields begin to crumble. However, resistance to Jewish involvement in wider society remained socially entrenched and was often expressed in rhetoric regarding the destruction of traditional—that is, "German"—retail cultures by the emergence of large Jewish-owned department stores and smaller retailers offering wares of supposedly "foreign" origin.[58]

Male Sartorial Politics in Vienna: Tailoring and the Allure of the English Gentleman

While the high visibility of Jews within Vienna's dress and luxury industry certainly contributed to notions of modern fashion's "foreignness"—at least in the minds of antisemites—the moniker had earlier origins and can be traced to the Congress of Vienna (1814–15). In the period leading up to the Congress, Viennese fashion, including its men's fashions, developed largely in the shadow of other societies, dominated in particular by English and other west European styles.[59] Reingard Witzmann argues that rather than being leaders of fashion, pre-Congress Viennese originality lay in its adaptation of foreign attire.[60] Drawing fashionable aristocrats and their modes of dress from all over Europe, the Congress has been described as "the catalyst in the development of a distinctive Viennese style."[61] The visiting statesmen and aristocrats—as well as their wives and households—required the services of skilled tailors and dressmakers to cater for their ceremonial and civilian sartorial needs. This brought the clothing styles of differing European aristocracy to Vienna, in particular the English, who "had long been isolated by the continental blockade and therefore had developed fashions and behaviors that seemed strange to the rest of Europeans."[62] In addition to its importance in shaping the political boundaries of Europe in the wake of Napoleon's defeat, the Congress of Vienna served as a showcase for European sartorial styles—perhaps a precursor to the modern fashion show, with memoirs by participants commenting on the dressed appearances of other attendees.[63] The Congress set Vienna on the road to becoming one of Europe's fashion capitals. The following year, 1816, saw the publication of Vienna's first fashion magazine, *Wiener Modenzeitung*, aimed at the cultural élites of Viennese society.[64] As the century progressed, Vienna continued to develop its fashion industry.

Despite a penchant for nostalgic fashions inspired by alpine folk dress (to be discussed in Chapter 4), the predominantly "national" influences on Viennese fashion during the remainder of the nineteenth century were France and England. Perceived as pinnacles of Western culture, France and England were held in high esteem by Vienna's acculturated Jewish bourgeoisie and upper classes, not in spite of but as a result of their dedication to *Bildung* and *Deutschtum*.[65] Gerda Buxbaum asserts that Paris "dictated" Vienna's cultural milieu at the *fin de siècle*, not only in the context of dress fashions but in all aspects of Viennese culture.[66] The families of the writers Stefan Zweig and Peter Altenberg, for example, immersed themselves in the language and culture of France. French was regularly spoken in the Zweig household, which served the young Stefan well later in life when working on German translations of poetry by French and Belgian writers, and fostered a deep love for the language and culture in which he felt equally at home as in his native German. In his biography of Zweig, Oliver Matuschek postulates that the central character Edgar in Zweig's 1911 story *Brennendes Geheimnis* (Burning Secret), whose bourgeois mother regularly addresses her son in French, is the author's fictional double.[67] Likewise, Altenberg, a decade older than Zweig, was exposed to French language and culture at a young age by his Francophile father, whom the author recalled was happiest when relaxing in a dark red fauteuil reading Victor Hugo and French periodicals.[68]

Sartorially, France and England had a great impact on both female and male fashions in Vienna. Fashion salons catering to middle- and upper-class women continued to look toward France for inspiration and direction, and periodicals were published under French titles such as *Chic Parisien* and *le Grand Tailleur*. Men's tailors and outfitters looked toward the English for cues to sartorial respectability. However, gendered clothing fashions were not rigidly divided between French and English style; for example, Jewish businessman Heinrich Grünbaum's eponymous store on the Graben specialized in both French and English women's clothing.[69] Buxbaum comments on the strong influence English culture exerted over Viennese women's sports and leisure attire, inspired by Empress Elisabeth's (1837–98) penchant for sport and modest, functional attire.[70]

The dominance and prestige of English male fashions are clearly evident in the regular use of English sartorial terms in tailoring journals and men's lifestyle magazines during the first three decades of the twentieth century, as well as the names of men's fashion houses. Heinrich Neumann's fashion salon on the Kärntnerstrasse, which catered to Vienna's élite,[71] traded under the name Old Bond Street, while the (unrelated) Neumann family's department store used the name Metropolitan Clothing Palace; these serve as just two examples of English-language names used as an expression of quality.[72]

That English tailoring reigned supreme in the world of men's sartorial fashions in continental Europe during the latter half of the nineteenth century and into the twentieth century is so broadly accepted within the field of dress history that it is often taken for granted when considering men's dress beyond Britain. One reason for this may very well be that such sartorial fashions were so ubiquitous that, despite their supposed London origins, men's tailoring developed a more "global" image of (at least aspiring toward) middle-class respectability and sobriety—with slight regional variations, of course— unlike the omnipresence of Paris within the world of women's fashions.[73] Indeed, the regular use of English-language terms within the tailoring profession, across linguistic boundaries, as well as the regular use of English names for businesses bear witness to the widespread Anglophilia that engulfed many continental European societies.[74] The penchant for English tailoring among middle-class European men, be they in Vienna, Madrid, Warsaw, or Copenhagen, can be seen as part of a wider Anglophilia that exceeded sartorial fashions: England and English culture as a bastion of modernity, sobriety, and respectability. David Kuchta demonstrates that the tailored suit served as an aesthetic manifestation of the "politeness" associated with the English gentleman.[75] The notion of politeness (or gentility, perhaps) has resonance when considering the Anglophilia of Viennese Jewish bourgeoisie with its emphasis on the ideals of *Bildung* and *Sittlichkeit*.[76] Thus, although references to English dress and correct behavior within a Viennese context are less explicit, the implied meaning of dressing in "English" tailoring went beyond appearing as a fashionable member of society.

At the end of the nineteenth century, the architect Adolf Loos (1870–1933) extolled the virtues of English tailoring in the Viennese liberal press. Such forms of "modern dress" were for Loos more than sartorial fashion, but rather one cog in a wider system of modern culture and civilization.[77] Men's tailoring, in this manner, would be used as a tool to refashion a nation within the context of modernity: a uniform of sorts for the modern man—both materially and aesthetically, but also symbolically.[78] In contrast, the constant flux of women's dress fashions and widespread reports of the "latest from Paris" in the press created an image less of uniform stability but rather one of ever-changing novelty.

This attitude to fashion was both influenced by and perpetuated ideas about the masculine–feminine binary and the social and biological roles of the sexes in society,[79] which was reflected in the manner in which sartorial fashions were transmitted to male and female consumers, respectively. In the second half of the nineteenth century, fashion magazines or journals in many major European cities took on a specifically feminine connotation, were directed at a female readership, and predominantly focused on women's and children's clothing, with occasional reference to menswear. Literature on men's dress, however, was presented in a different context. In Vienna prior to the revolutions of the middle of the nineteenth century, men's fashions, like that of women's, were regularly depicted in fashion and advice literature in the form of detailed colorful plates, such as those that appeared in the *Wiener Zeitschrift für Kunst, Literatur, Theater und Mode* (1816–1949). During the second half of the century, however, men's dress fashions were often published in trade journals for industry practitioners, with monotone and color fashion plates published alongside detailed tailoring instructions and information on new styles: cut, fabric, details.[80] It was not until the period of the First World War and its aftermath that Austrian fashion and lifestyle magazines, in the manner that had been available to women for several decades, were marketed at a wider male readership.[81]

Beyond England's reputation as the capital of men's sartorial elegance, the spread of modern tailoring across Europe (and further afield) was made possible by the advent of the ready-made.[82] This novel development in both men's and women's dress not only created new price ranges that offered previously costly styles at a lower price to a wider cross section of urban and rural societies but also contributed to the standardization of men's dress across the continent.[83] By the end of the nineteenth century, newspapers throughout Europe contained advertisements for men's tailoring emporiums targeting all levels of society, from the boutique ateliers to large discount bazaars and warehouses. But regardless of their different target consumers, many shared the similarity in promising fine "English" clothing.[84]

In addition to the countless advertisements promising male consumers fine English clothes, by the beginning of the twentieth century it was not uncommon for Austro-Hungarian newspapers to publish short articles on the state of men's dress in England and to a lesser extent in France (these were often reprinted from other publications).[85] In Austria-Hungary, for example, reports in newspapers and tailoring journals offered advice to male readers on how to dress in ideal English tailoring. These articles contained detailed descriptions of the latest styles of garments (jackets, waistcoats, trousers, outerwear, headwear, and other accessories), advice for what a well-dressed gentleman should wear in particular social settings, and the dress of certain public figures.[86] Britain's Edward VII—still Prince of Wales at the time some of the articles were published—was a particular favorite. Not only was Edward held up as a paragon of elegance, but his clothing choices were also described as a way of encouraging male readers to take an interest in their dress.

An article appearing in a June 1898 issue of the *Neues Wiener Tagblatt* described Edward's purported preference for waistcoats.[87] The author's seemingly innocuous description of the Prince of Wales's attire is presented as a way to convince male readers to take an interest in, or at least be aware of, popular fashions. Perhaps the logic of publishing information about men's dress in dailies was a way of exposing men to ideas about fashion in smaller increments, a way to create familiarity with and acceptance of "fashion" among male populations in the face of widespread attitudes about the frivolity of fashion in the face of male sobriety.[88] The article's anonymous author claimed that the "tyranny" of men's fashion was by no means as extreme as that of women, but it certainly existed. Excluding the "eccentricities" and "absurdities" of the *Gigerl* (fop), men's fashion is known for its uniformity that well-dressed men around the world adhere to.[89] The origin of such elegant uniformity, according to the author, was of course London. The Prince of Wales was praised as a leader of men's fashion, and the author took the opportunity to describe his newest waistcoat choice—"'the B. B. Waistcoat'— nach 'Beau Brummel'[*sic*]"—in great detail. The author claimed that Edward's adoption of this single-breasted style was a result of the double-breasted variety becoming too tight for his "starke Figur"—a polite reference to Edward's substantial girth. In addition to the Prince of Wales, Lord Chesterfield—whom the author counted among the best-dressed young men in London—was described appearing in the new fashion three days after its debut.[90]

The notion that England was the cornerstone of male elegance continued into the new century, with the publication of magazines dedicated to men's dress and lifestyles that continued to hold up the English gentleman as a yardstick of masculine respectability. The *fin-de-siècle* tailoring journal published under the English title *Fashions for Gentlemen*, published by Rudolf von Waldheim and Josef Eberele,[91] offered readers a series of monotone and color plates (printed in Austria by L. Patois of Paris) of the latest male fashions, with drafting and cutting instructions as well as information on the new styles printed in both English and German—similar to those published in the London-based journals (Figures 2.2 and 2.3). The journal's English title is a clear indication of the perceived superiority of English male fashions, but the listing of

Figure 2.2 Tailoring fashion plate by the John Williamson Company Limited, London, 1913. Copyright: Metropolitan Museum of Art (New York).

Figure 2.3 Tailoring fashion plate by the John Williamson Company Limited, London, 1914. Copyright: Metropolitan Museum of Art (New York).

offices in Paris, London, New York, Vienna, Berlin, Milano, Copenhagen, Brussels, and St. Petersburg implied that the fashions featured within were truly international. The styles depicted in the 1912 issues included, for example, "modern" sack suits with both single- and double-breasted jackets and tapered trousers with turned up cuffs, in light-colored, pinstripe fabric; knee-length frock coats; a morning coat with contrasting, pinstriped trousers; a short sport coat (*Sportüberzieher*), and a raglan coat. The detailed garment information provided alongside the fashion plates and drafting instructions not only enlightened the readers about appropriate fabric types but also compared the new styles with the old in great detail. For example, the April 1912 issue stated the main differences between the latest morning coat fashion and that of the previous season were the fuller and wider design of collar and lapels, the higher position of the front button closure, the narrower sleeves, and the overall longer jacket (Figure 2.4).[92]

Waldheim and Eberle also published a similar journal during the same period under the title *Wiener Herrenmode*, with text in both English and German. Like *Fashions for Gentlemen*, *Wiener Herrenmode* provided fashion plates (both color and monotone) along with tailoring instructions and information about the new styles. The fashion plates in this publication featured both young and mature-looking gentlemen in various sack suits (single- and double-breasted), frock coats, morning coats, overcoats in various styles and cuts (again, single- and double-breasted, with exposed and hidden buttons, fitted and loose, and some with contrasting collars and lapels), evening wear, including both full evening dress (white tie and tails) and dinner jackets (black tie, satin lapels), and sport and leisure attire (including breeches and Norfolk jackets for hunting and riding). The models carried canes, wore a range of footwear (shoes with spats, patent leather slippers, riding boots, hobnailed hiking boots) and headgear (top hat, bowler, panama, homburg, or cap), depending on the social occasion they were dressing for. The fabrics varied as well: plain, striped or tweed (particularly for leisure attire) in black, brown, various shades of gray, blue, and green. Overall, the styles depicted in *Wiener Herrenmode* were similar to those that appeared in *Fashions for Gentlemen*. What differed in the *Wiener Herrenmode* fashion plates was that many of the plates depicted models in recognizably Viennese surroundings: on the Ringstrasse, before the Austrian parliament building, outside the *Wiener Hofoper*, and in the Prater (Figures 2.5 and 2.6). Presenting generic styles as Viennese to an international audience, the publishers sought to stake a claim for Vienna in the world of male fashion.[93]

The publication of specific periodicals dedicated to men's dress indicates changing attitudes toward fashion as an acceptable preoccupation for men. During the early twentieth century, such publications encouraged their readers to take an interest in their dressed appearances. In its first issue, the short-lived Viennese journal *Die Herrenwelt* (1916–17) assured its male readers that the time had come to pay more attention to their dress, and that concerning oneself with fashion and one's sartorial appearance was no longer "unmanly," the concern of the "mentally deficient," or those "who had not much else going on upstairs."[94] The time for man to air his intellectual superiority through disregarding his dress had come to an end.[95] According to the editor, dressing tastefully was as important as cleanliness.[96] In this manner, the magazine focused not only on

Figure 2.4 Fashion plate from the Viennese tailoring journal *Fashions for Gentlemen* (April 1912). Courtesy of Österreichische Nationalbibliothek, Vienna, Austria.

Figure 2.5 Fashion plate from the Viennese tailoring journal *Wiener Herrenmode* (December 1911). Courtesy of Österreichische Nationalbibliothek, Vienna, Austria.

Figure 2.6 Fashion plate from the Viennese tailoring journal *Wiener Herrenmode* (January 1912). Courtesy of Österreichische Nationalbibliothek, Vienna, Austria.

"tasteful" attire but on all manner of "tasteful" masculine lifestyles. The clothing styles featured the ubiquitous lounge suit and morning and frock coats, all in dark, subdued colors. The illustrations were printed in black and white; however, the advice for color combinations included (overwhelmingly) black, white, various shades of gray, blue, brown, and green. In the journal's first issue, dated January 1916, for instance, a table titled "Wie man sich richtig kleidet" (How to dress correctly) listed various occasions and the correct combination of garments to be worn at each, including the appropriate colors. For example, to an afternoon visit or a 5 o'clock tea (*5 Uhr-Tee*), gentlemen were advised to wear a black jacket with a waistcoat in the same fabric with white insert or unicolor "fashion vest" (*Modeweste*), black trousers with gray stripes, "Zylinder oder Melon" (top- or bowler hat), a dark overcoat, white shirt with faint white or black horizontal striped breast and white linen cuffs, a not-too-high turndown stand collar, a black-gray patterned ascot, middle-gray or dark brown buckskin gloves, lace-up patent leather shoes with buckskin or cloth inserts, or spats in the same color as the gloves. Finally came the jewelry: gold or platinum cufflinks, with colored precious stones to match the tiepin, and a thin gold watch-chain. Very clear instructions, indeed.

Die Herrenwelt presented its readers with the correct, gentlemanly modes of dress and behavior, thereby offering them an insight into the lifestyle of the nobility and the financial élite. And yet, members of these social tiers would have had no need for such a journal as they already knew how to behave and dress. Rather, the journal's readership was drawn from those who wanted to fashion themselves in the same manner.[97] Gesa C. Teichert maintains that although an important source of information for sartorial self-fashioning, fashion journals and guides could teach its readers only so much. It was important for men to learn how to dress properly through upbringing and bourgeois socialization.[98] Publications like *Die Herrenwelt* would have been particularly important supplements for both assimilatory- and acculturation-minded Jews. For those already assimilated and acculturated, the magazine would confirm what they knew about the correct fashion (both clothing and other aspects of lifestyle) of the Viennese upper classes. For those who had set out on the difficult journey of acculturation (e.g., *Galitsianer* Jews who had arrived from Austria's eastern crown land during the years the magazine was published, as well as other Jewish immigrants from the Dual Monarchy's other provinces), the publication could serve as a manual for how to dress and conduct oneself in both the public and the private spheres.

Published in the midst of the First World War, *Die Herrenwelt* displayed an amount of patriotism that appealed to anti-English sentiment, asserting that the English tailoring industry had been devastated due to the internment of the superior Viennese immigrant tailors, thus robbing the English of their best practitioners.[99] Unsurprisingly, the English influence on the Viennese bourgeoisie, indeed on dress and its terminology, continued to run deep, and despite the Anglophobic language, the magazine continued to feature the same "English" styles and reference English male fashions and fabrics, but with subtle allusions to the superiority of Austrian and German products.[100]

Similarly, certain editions devoted more attention to "Austrian" (or rather "German") sartorial modes. The fourth issue of the journal, published in July 1916, focused specifically on the gentleman's correct appearance while on the *Jagd* (hunt), including the various social situations a man might find himself in while on a hunting trip. It is apparent throughout memoirs, biographies, and in photographs that while many Viennese Jews saw themselves as urban cosmopolitans (and not *völkisch* peasants of Austria's alpine

Figure 2.7 Selma and Max Imbermann (on the right) with friends, Austria, 1927. Courtesy of Ruth Kurschner, NJ.

provinces), they were not averse to engaging in the supposedly "German" leisure activities such as the *Jagd* or *Wanderung* (hike), and altered their dressed appearances accordingly (Figure 2.7).[101] For Viennese Jews, asserting a modern and "Viennese" identity meant engaging in such typically "Austrian" (or German) leisure activities that presented the individual at once as both an urban cosmopolitan and a member of the wider Austrian "nation." Ulrich Furst, for example, described in an unpublished memoir regular trips to the Wiener Wald, skiing, and hiking expeditions while growing up in Vienna. During the 1920s his parents joined a Jewish alpine club after they, along with other Jews, were expelled from the *Deutsche und österreichische Alpenverein*.[102]

Such styles of dress were commonly adopted by many members of Vienna's bourgeoisie, as well as by Jews and Gentiles in other parts of the Dual Monarchy and its successor states, and correspond to those featured in a variety of Viennese men's fashion and lifestyle magazines from the same period, such as *Der gut angezogene Herr, Der Herr von heute, Der Herr und seine Welt*, and *Die Bühne*.[103] By the 1920s, perhaps indicating a break with popular styles of the prewar era, the attire featured in Viennese men's fashion magazines had evolved from the stark blacks, grays, and browns of the prewar era into a variety of colors and fabrics for the "well-dressed gentleman," with multiple options for a variety of social situations. An editorial in the 1936 autumn/winter issue of *Der gut angezogene Herr* preached individuality through dress but implored the reader to trust the advice of his tailor or outfitter, and the magazine continued to supply charts and tables indicating the correct combination of garments, fabrics, and colors to be worn in different situations, albeit less rigid than those printed in *Die Herrenwelt*.[104] Similarly, indicating the emerging influences of Hollywood, America was regularly referenced alongside England as a leader in men's style, and American icons, such as the actor Adolphe Menjou, were regularly featured as icons of male style.[105] Vienna was not unique in this regard; other major cities of Austria-Hungary's successor states saw an increase of journals and magazines dedicated to men's fashion and lifestyle, similarly taking British and American men as yardsticks for sartorial and behavioral elegance and refinement.[106]

Linked to the ideals of *Bildung* and *Sittlichkeit*, these publications regularly preached simultaneous refinement of dress and behavior, as well as the harmony of a man's dress with both his environment and peers. In a 1936 editorial on the correct dress choices for weddings, the editor of *Der gut angezogene Herr* asserted, above all, the importance of environmental harmony before following trends. The editor used the example of a guest appearing in evening dress at a ceremony where the bridal couple dressed in simple *Trachten* (folk costumes)[107] as being "arrogant and almost ridiculous."[108] In the same manner, urban dressing revealed a delicate balance between environmental harmony and individuality. In his memoir, the aforementioned Ulrich Furst (né Fürst) recalled his father's mockery when he deviated from conventional bourgeois modes of dress in favor of exploring his own individual tastes:

> There was a time when I needed a new suit. Mother went with me to buy one and, for the first time, I could pick it myself. I selected a medium-dark reddish brown suit, as I was tired of the dark grey suit Father and all the other men of the older generation wore and wanted something a little more youthful. When I brought it home, Father made one of his famous dry comments: "You look like a pig breeder from the Puszta." But I liked my new suit despite this nasty remark, and wore it quite often.[109]

Accessories also played an important role in a man's overall appearance. Magazines implored men to pay as much attention to their accessories (such as scarves and ties) as they did to their evening wear and furs.[110] It was important to maintain an elegant outward appearance, and this could be achieved by following strict codes of dress rather than falling prey to popular fashions. In 1931, the journalist Edgar Liss warned readers of *Der Herr von heute* of the dangers of excess and extreme in sartorial patterns. Elegance was achieved through attention to detail, while inelegance could be easily seen in those who displayed exaggerated styles, such as overly wide shoulder pads and trouser legs, garish ties, and pointed shoes. In sum, Liss warned, "the line [between elegance and inelegance] is difficult to describe, but all to easily crossed."[111]

Advice on Clothes: Jewish Designers and Retailers

Prior to the publication of magazines catering to men's dress and lifestyles in the interwar period, journalistic pieces on men's dress and style were often anonymously penned or else under pseudonyms—perhaps relevant considering the preexisting attitudes toward "fashion" and men who took an interest in it. One of the key figures to write publicly on the matter was the aforementioned Adolf Loos. Although better known for his architectural designs and creations, Loos was a frequent commentator on the state of Austrian society and all areas of its design industry, including clothing. For Loos, writing about clothing and other aspects of the design world went beyond an interest in aesthetics. He strongly believed that design was an indicator of a society's place in the modern world and a tool by which to measure the extent of its modernization. Austria, according to Loos, despite its wealth, was a backward society desperately in need of a design reform that would lead it into the twentieth century and modernity.[112] In both his architectural projects and the essays he published in the Viennese press, Loos sought to educate the Austrian public and encourage it to reform its retrograde manners, including abandoning the popular taste for *Jugendstil* and Art Nouveau. Dress was particularly important in this respect. Loos saw dress as built structures, architecture for the human body. How could society truly become modern in his new and rationally designed buildings if the people inhabiting them continued to dress in outdated, irrational clothing? To be modern was to exist in a modern environment, wear modern clothes, and use modern appliances. To Loos, historicizing styles included *Jugendstil*, which had similarities to Rococo, *Japonisme*, and eighteenth-century taste.[113]

Loos, like so many of his colleagues in the various fields of the *Wiener Moderne* (Viennese Modernism), was an immigrant to the Habsburg *Kaiserstadt*. A native of the Moravian capital, Brünn (Brno), Adolf Franz Karl Viktor Maria Loos[114] was raised solely by his mother Maria from the age of nine, after the death of his stonemason father. Maria Loos likely considered *Bildung* to be of great importance, for her young son was educated locally in Brünn, followed by a short period at a Benedictine *Gymnasium* in Melk, Lower Austria, where he failed his exams. Loos's education was turbulent and saw him shunted from one institution to another: Reichenberg (Liberec), Brünn, Dresden, Vienna, and Dresden again. Finally, after spending three years in the United States (1893–96), Loos returned to Austria-Hungary and settled in Vienna.[115]

Although Loos was not Jewish, many of the individuals in his professional and social circles were—as were two of his three wives.[116] As Janet Stewart explains in her study of this architect and his cultural criticism, Loos wrote very little regarding Jews, partly because he found himself very much amidst a liberal bourgeois milieu that was largely made up of acculturated Jews.[117] In this sense, the "Jewish difference" of the individuals Loos associated with was irrelevant. These were individuals whom he believed had already set out to adopt modern culture and were centrally placed to modernize Austrian society.[118] Although notions of inherent Jewish difference were as widespread in Vienna as in the rest of the German-speaking world, they were not universally held. Loos was one such individual who dismissed concerns of racial difference and actively sought to develop a modern Viennese identity that would include Gentiles and Jews alike.[119] Indeed, Loos's writings on the topics of male dress and style are of central importance to the study of Jewish men and their dress in *fin-de-siècle* and interwar Vienna.

Loos played an important part in the response to the Jewish crisis of identity in Vienna during this time. Enjoying warm relationships with members of Vienna's Jewish

Bildungsbürgertum, he worked actively with patrons and financiers, both Jewish and Gentile, to refashion modern male identities. Many of his clients were members of the men's apparel trade. These included the Jewish-owned tailoring firm Goldman & Salatsch, whose new tailoring workshop and shop interior in 1896 were among Loos's first professional commissions. Among his closest associates can be counted Karl Kraus and Peter Altenberg, who were in a way rebels among acculturated, middle-class Viennese Jewry. Both were known critics of the very class from which they had sprung.[120] Like these two Jewish friends and colleagues, Loos criticized what he considered the hypocrisy and excess of the acculturated Jewish upper-middle class, some of whom served as patrons to Secessionist artists and designers, including his archrival, Josef Hoffmann. To Loos, Secessionist style, with its applied ornamentation and organic forms, was an indication of the failed assimilation of Viennese Jews on account of their disproportionate representation among the movement's patrons.[121] Like Hoffmann, Loos also catered to many Jewish clients, but his stark geometric designs, devoid of applied ornamentation and neo-Rococo references, were the antithesis of the ostentatious designs of the Secession. In an undated essay titled "Die Emanzipation des Judenthums" (The Emancipation of Jewry), Loos compared the Jewish patronage of Secessionist artists and designers to a return to traditional Jewish garb:

> Jews who have long since put aside their caftans are happy to be able to slide back into one again. For these Secession interiors are only caftans in disguise, just like the names of Gold and Silberstein, like the names of Moritz and Siegfried. One could recognize them by it. True, there are Aryan Moritzes and Siegfrieds, just as there are Aryan owners of Hoffmann interiors. They are exceptions. One recognizes them by it. Let me not be misunderstood. I have nothing against a strong, vigorous emphasis on the Jewish. I do not take issue with the man in the caftan. I respect the man who calls himself Moses or Samuel. But I deplore the man who wishes to overcome his caftan and his name of Samuel and relapses into Olbrich and Siegfried. That would bring us back to the same patch. In the new ghetto. And these unfortunates believe that they are emancipating themselves from Jewishness with Olbrich or Siegfried. Just eating ham isn't enough.[122]

In this short, undated piece, Loos encapsulates the issue of assimilation and acculturation in Vienna: the strong desire of many to discard their Jewishness, but their failure to do so as a result of deeply rooted antisemitism in the society and a lack of understanding of its hidden codes.[123] Loos's tone is symptomatic of the general attitude toward Jews and Jewishness in many parts of Europe at the *fin de siècle*, when acculturating and assimilating Jews were commonly seen as disingenuous and therefore a greater threat to the Gentile body politic than their coreligionists who were visibly and unashamedly Jewish.

As Elana Shapira has demonstrated, many Jewish patrons of the arts were not fixated on obfuscating signs of Jewishness, but rather focused on creating new forms of secular Jewish identification independent of the Gentile élite.[124] In doing so, they commissioned artists and architects to design living quarters and workplaces that broke away stylistically from the former modes of the bourgeois milieu with its penchant for historicism and heavy Biedermeier-style furniture that conveyed a sense of stability and sobriety.[125] By being among the first to adopt novel architectural and decorative styles (in the same way they had previously adopted changing patterns of dress over the course of the nineteenth century), wealthy Jewish patrons boldly asserted their identities as modern "Europeans" entering a new century.

As the antithesis to Hoffmann and the Secession, Loos offered his own design principles for Jewish acculturation. In the context of Viennese modernism, acculturating Jews who were eager to fashion a place for themselves in Viennese society, while at the same time choosing not to conform to middle-class conventions, were happy to join Loos in a partnership of refashioning the modern Viennese self. This partnership was not simply that of artist (Loos) and patron (Jews), but a reciprocal one in which both parties collaborated to fashion new models of masculinity for the new century. Shapira offers the professional relationship between Loos and Michael Goldman, owner of the tailor's workshop and boutique Goldman & Salatsch, as an example of this partnership: "Goldman supplied Loos with a suit appropriate for presenting his cultural agenda in public, and Loos tailored his authorship to 'suit' the need of Goldman, an assimilated Jewish businessman, to succeed at the center of a European city among the leading representatives of major society."[126]

Later, Loos would collaborate with Fritz Wolff, proprietor of the men's outfitters Kniže (1910)[127] located on the Graben and designer Ernst Deutsch-Dryden. Born in Vienna to Hungarian Jewish parents,[128] Ernst Deutsch, who anglicized his name to Deutsch-Dryden, was better known for his work as a graphic artist in Vienna and Berlin before the First World War, and for his work as women's wear designer in Vienna and, later, New York and costume designer in Hollywood after his relocation to the United States in 1933.[129] Widely recognized as a talented and influential designer, and an equally elegant dresser, Dryden's collaboration with Loos and Wolff "produced an unbeatable mix of talent,"[130] making Kniže, alongside Goldman & Salatsch, the most renowned menswear establishment in interwar Vienna—a reputation that persists until today. The "English style" Loos praised in his essays and had incorporated into his designs for Goldman's business were similarly present in his architectural designs for the Kniže boutique, an approach shared by Deutsch-Dryden in developing the company's clothing and overall branding.[131]

Despite his regular collaboration with Jews, they rarely appear in Loos's writing. He does not specifically distinguish them from other "Austrians." Stewart asserts that Loos points to Jews as an example of the sartorial modernization of Austria's citizens. In arguing for the adoption of the modern suit in preference to *Volkstrachten* (folk costumes), Loos says "that he has never heard a Jew argue that the Jews in Galicia should continue to wear the caftan."[132] Thus, acculturating Jews are presented as a contrast to Germans in the fashioning of modern Austrian identity. As a mixture of languages, ethnicities, and cultures, Loos's Austria "has more in common with English culture than with the customs of the Upper Austrian peasant who, although geographically closer, is temporarily dissociated from modern Austria,"[133] and is appropriately positioned to adopt the culture of the Anglophone world. This includes, primarily, the adoption of modern clothing and conveniences over folk lifestyles and aesthetics.

At the *fin de siècle*, Loos wrote a series of short essays dealing with the very topic, which were published in Viennese newspapers and journals, notably the liberal, Jewish-owned *Neue Freie Presse* that included many Jews among its editorial staff and subscribers.[134] Several of these pieces dealt with various topics related to men's dressing and all came down to the single argument: a man should be well dressed.

> To be dressed correctly! I feel as if I have revealed in these words the secret that has surrounded the fashion of our clothes up until now. We have tried to get at fashion with words like "beautiful," "stylish," "elegant," "smart," and "strong." But this is not the point. Rather, it is a question of being dressed *in such a way that one stands out the least.* A red dress coat stands out in a ballroom. It follows that a red dress coat is unmodern in a ballroom. A top hat stands out at the ice-skating rink. Consequently it is unmodern to wear a top hat while on the ice. In good society, to be conspicuous is bad manners.[135]

It is apparent that Loos's notion of correct dressing follows dandyist methods of simple, albeit meticulous, modes of dress.[136] The dandy as a historical figure who has passed into semi-mythical status became the yardstick by which sartorially elegant men were measured. Originating as an archetype from the "arch-dandy" George "Beau" Brummell, the dandy as a sociocultural type refers to the man for whom dressed appearance, or appearance in general, is of paramount importance.[137] Like Loos, it is not enough for the dandy to appear beautiful; rather, he must be well dressed, meaning maintaining an appearance of effortless elegance. A man who obviously strives to appear elegant fails.[138] To Loos, a man's appearance should be carefully contrived but never conspicuous.

Loos's rejection of applied ornamentation did not equate with "minimalism." On the contrary, the architect maintained a distinction between decoration and ornamentation. Panayotis Tournikiotis asserts, "For Loos *decoration*—the purposeful use of simple forms and the honest use of materials—was indispensable in his otherwise spare constructions."[139] His lack of applied ornamentation came from a rejection of what Gottfried Semper celebrated as his *Bekleidungstheorie* (theory of cladding) in his two-volume work *Der Stil der technischen und tektonischen Künsten oder Praktische Ästhetik* (*Style in the Technical and Tectonic Arts, or Practical Aesthetics*) (1860–63). To Loos, cladding represented unnecessary surface dressing.[140] This is evident in photographs of Loos's own sitting room (a reconstruction of which exists at the Wien Museum in Vienna). While free of ornamental architectural motifs and surface dressings that were present in both historicist architecture of the previous generation, as well as the designs of Loos's revivals at the Viennese Secession, the room is not free of objects or decorative elements. Rather, the objects that make up this milieu—books, a clock—*objets d'art,*

Figure 2.8 Caricature from *Kikeriki* 30, no. 22 (March 16, 1890): 3. Courtesy of ANNO/Österreichische Nationalbibliothek, Vienna.

and Persian rugs—indicate his preference for a level of comfort and function of the accumulation of material culture.[141]

Superfluous ornamentation was personified in the figure of the *Gigerl*, whom Loos railed against in his writings. The term "*Gigerl*" has often been mistranslated as "dandy" when, in fact, the two terms denote very different figures. While a dandy can be understood as a social critic who sets the tone of stylish consumption external to contemporary accepted fashions, the *Gigerl*—more suitably translated as "fop" or peacock—is a man frivolously concerned with his outward appearance and a keen follower of fashion (Figure 2.8).[142] As Loos notes, "the [*Gigerl*] always wears only that which *the society around him considers* modern"[143]—rather than becoming one who dictates fashion himself. To Loos, the archetypes of the dandy and *Gigerl* were manifested in the national characters of England and Germany, respectively. Being well dressed— that is to say, a "dandy"—meant dressing in the reserved and practical manner of the English, rather than that of the Germans, who "express their individuality through odd styles and unusual wardrobe creations and through rather adventurous neckties."[144] As a nation of *Gigerln*, the Germans were accused by Loos of concerning themselves with being beautiful rather than being correctly dressed, in contrast to the English, whom Loos characterizes as the arbiters of sartorial taste. The latter clearly understood that correct dressing meant dressing appropriately for any given social situation and not, like the *Gigerl*, "standing out."

The first step to modernizing Austria, then, would be to encourage its multiethnic populace to turn away from Germany as the yardstick for civilization and follow the ways of England and, in a large part, the United States. To Loos, these nations had achieved a level of modernity that Austria could aspire toward.[145] While Austria's supranational identity was threatened by the narratives of competing nations, Loos saw British and American supranationalism as "an idealisation of Western culture and therefore modern culture."[146] Clothing was therefore an important factor in this equation, for it not only served as an exclusionary criterion for specific cultural identities but also surpassed them. As an individual who paid close attention to the centrality of dress in the fashioning of modern male identity, Loos recognized the important role dress played in the so-called American dream:

> An American philosopher says somewhere, "A young man is rich if he has a good head on his shoulders and a good suit in the closet." That is sound philosophy. It demonstrates an understanding of people. What good are brains if they do not express themselves in good clothes? For both the English and the Americans demand of an individual that he be well dressed.[147]

More than a passive reflection of identity, clothing was a sign of conscious self-fashioning. Michael Zakim argues that the suit "aspired to wed dynamism to self-control, two latently conflicting principles whose unity was fundamental for industrial success."[148] For "modern" or "modernizing" men, the suit was equally important in that these two "latently conflicting principles" could be expressed through sartorial identity, thereby providing an image of stability for society. Thus, "[i]n his idealised England and America, in comparison, the eradication of traditional dress codes means that everyone has the right to be well-dressed."[149]

It was in this paradigm of modern "English" dress and interiors that Loos found an answer to the question of both Austrian identity and Jewish acculturation. For a people who were considered "citizens of the world since presumably they did not have their own country,"[150] collaborating with Jewish retailers (such as Goldman and Wolff) and designers (such as Deutsch-Dryden), Loos fashioned his clients' homes and businesses in "English" styles with its traditions of sartorial prestige and precision. By dressing his Jewish and Gentile clients as English gentlemen, both in their clothing styles and in the interiors they inhabited, Loos made a clear statement that acculturating Jews were not *Gigerln* pitifully chasing after emerging and fleeting fashions, but rather "guaranteed that his clients would be identified with the cultural persona of the English gentleman and therefore appeared as respected and distinguished members of Western society."[151]

CHAPTER 3
REFASHIONING THE SELF
ACCULTURATION, ASSIMILATION, AND CLOTHING

The notion of self-fashioning refers to the manner in which an individual recreates—or refashions—his or her identity and for a variety of reasons. In his study of early modern English writers, Stephen Greenblatt asserts that the fashioning of self involved the creation of an identity that an individual desired to broadcast to society, "a distinctive personality, a characteristic address to the world, a consistent mode of perceiving and behaving."[1] Greenblatt's notion of self-fashioning focuses on literary tastes and behavior rather than sartorial modes. Nevertheless, clothing and material culture play an important role in the shaping of identity. As John Styles argues, clothes play a central role in the fashioning of the individual, as they are ever present and highly visible, and very deliberately reveal or conceal certain aspects of the body.[2] Self-fashioning, like assimilation and acculturation, is an essentially personal process that must be undertaken by the individual, but can be undertaken simultaneously by groups of individuals with the same goal.

Within the context of acculturation and assimilation during the *fin-de-siècle* and interwar periods, Viennese Jews actively engaged in sartorial and behavioral self-fashioning as a way of asserting membership of modern German culture and society, or else to allow the individual to develop new modes of identification as an alternative to accepted conventions. In this manner, modernizing and upwardly mobile Viennese Jews challenged preexisting notions of Jewishness and Jewish identification, from both within their communities and outside them. Parallel to linguistic self-fashioning in the wake of the Josephinian Edicts of Toleration in 1781 and 1782 were its visual and behavioral counterparts. Steven Beller asserts that Viennese Jews and other Austrian Jews took their cultural cues from the Protestant North, rather than the "reactionary" Catholic South.[3] While most Jewish converts to Christianity opted for Catholicism over Protestantism, the orientation toward the culture of Prussia over that of Austria created a further divide between Austria's "German" Jews and its Catholic Austro-German population.[4] The issue of how religion was intertwined with language and ethnicity in the question of nationality was a complicated one. Although the state considered the question of an individual's national identity to be one determined by language alone, religious denomination played an unofficial, albeit important, role on an everyday scale.

A person could speak German, practice Catholicism, and still on account of her or his "racial origins" be regarded by the wider community as a Jew. The question as to what Jews were—a religious community? a race? a nation?—is beyond the scope of this book. However, the inconsistency of categorizing Jews confounded Jews and Gentiles alike and was exacerbated by the wider nationalities question of the Dual Monarchy.

Most Austrian Jews—excluding the many Yiddish-speaking, religiously Orthodox, and Hasidic Jews in Galicia and Bukovina—had long adopted High German as their *Umgangssprache* (everyday vernacular).[5] In light of this linguistic adaptation and the link between officially recognized nations and languages, German-speaking Jews should have been recognized as German nationals. Indeed, they were, officially. In practical terms, however, this was not always the case, and Jews continued to be viewed by many as a separate national, ethnic, or racial group. This was particularly evident with the rise of nationalist movements in Central and Eastern Europe during the latter half of the nineteenth century. Acculturated, German-speaking Viennese Jews found themselves in a precarious limbo between a hostile in-group (Germans) with whom they had been instructed—and in many cases, wanted—to identify and an unrecognized *Volksstamm* (nationality or ethnicity) with whom they were prohibited from identifying.[6]

While Jews were not the only non-German ethnocultural group living in Vienna, one of the key differences between them and, say, the 102,974 self-identifying Czechs who called the city home in 1900[7] was that the latter maintained linguistic, cultural, and historical ties to a territory within the borders of the Dual Monarchy. Jews, who were considered by others and considered themselves as "foreign" and having roots in the Levant, had no national claims or historic ties to particular regions of the empire, and—increasingly after their emancipation—could be found living in most if not all Habsburg crown lands. Ever since their arrival in Europe during antiquity and for a variety of reasons, including religious, cultural, and external factors, Jews were unable to establish fixed and centralized "national" roots in the lands in which they lived—which were, after all, scattered across the length and breadth of the continent—but continued to maintain cultural and religious connections to each other and the idea of a historical and spiritual homeland in Palestine. Additionally, at different periods throughout their history in Europe and in certain locales, Jews were granted a degree of autonomy that effectively marked them as a separate nation, which many continued to see themselves belonging to.[8] Consequently, Jews defy the modern European category of nation as it developed over the eighteenth and nineteenth centuries.

The result of their historic experience and connection to their coreligionists across national, linguistic, and dynastic borders had made Jews into a transnational people. In her study of South Asian women and standards of beauty in North America, Vanita Reddy describes the methodology of her study as one that "typically takes as its object the act of migration and crossing borders as distinctly gendered processes."[9] Certainly this is also true of Jewish acculturation, a phenomenon played out across an equally transnational plane. Referring to memoirs and biographies, contemporary newspapers and magazines, among other texts, Marion A. Kaplan has examined the dual role of the Jewish mother in imparting her children both a strong sense of Jewish identification and an appreciation of German culture and dedication to *Bildung*.[10] Women, Kaplan demonstrates, were often more traditional in their observance of Judaism than their husbands, a deciding factor being the influence of the domestic sphere on women's lives in Germany during the nineteenth century. In this sense, Jewish women played a greater role in maintaining Jewish transnational identity than their male counterparts.

Although Kaplan's study focuses on Jews in Imperial Germany, the same can be said of Viennese Jews who, like their German counterparts, had begun the process of acculturation prior to their respective emancipations in 1867 and 1871. Indeed, the stronger sense of Jewish identification in Austria was largely the result of the *Vielvölkerstaat*.[11] Like their Germanized Czech and other non-German counterparts in Vienna, acculturated Jews existed (unofficially) as a distinct *Volksstamm* and tended to remain connected to one another, moving in the same social circles, marrying other Jews, even after converting to Christian denominations, or having themselves declared *konfessionslos*. An example can be found in Fritz Stern (1904–92), co-owner of Alumetag aluminium manufacture. Orphaned at a young age, Stern was raised in the household of his maternal grandfather, the rabbi Aron Friedmann (1833–1911), and aunts, where he was exposed to Orthodox Judaism. Upon reaching the age of bar mitzvah, Stern dutifully laid *tefillin*, at the behest of one of his more observant aunts, until the age of sixteen when he gave up religion and became interested in Social Democracy, probably under the influence of his aunt Friederike Freidmann (1882–1968), a well-known pedagogue and associate of the psychotherapist Alfred Adler (1870–1937). In 1923, Stern took the definitive step to distance himself from Judaism and declared himself *konfessionslos*.[12] Nonetheless, four years later, Stern married Margarethe Czopp, the daughter of Jewish immigrants from Galicia and Hungary.[13] Despite Stern's disdain for Judaism, his marriage to Czopp is recorded in the Index of the Jewish records of Vienna and Lower Austria.[14]

As a transnational people, and because of family and professional connections, Viennese Jews commonly maintained connections not only with their coreligionists in Vienna but also with communities abroad. The Ephrussi banking family, originating in the Russian city of Berdichev (Berdychiv, Ukraine)—a city of great importance in the history of both Hasidism and the Haskalah[15]—maintained familial and professional connections beyond Austria's borders in France and Russia, remaining citizens of the latter until the First World War.[16] Likewise, the wealthy families of Viennese intellectuals and cultural figures, such as Berta Zuckerkandl-Szeps and Stefan Zweig, had connections in countries such as France and Italy[17]—to say nothing of the many Jews with connections in Galicia or across the border in the Russian Empire. In his study of Vienna's 929 richest individuals prior to the First World War, Roman Sandgruber argues that the Jewish financial élite made up almost two-thirds of Vienna's millionaires.[18] Sandgruber observes how some of the millionaires concerned themselves with the development of Viennese culture, such as the literary salon of Adolf and Mathilde (née Schey von Koromla) Lieben or Viktor Ephrussi's interest in art and science.[19]

The modernization and acculturation of European Jewry during the eighteenth and nineteenth centuries had a strong hand in weakening the longtime bonds between Jews living in different countries. Raphael Mahler (1899–1977), the Galician-born Israeli historian, for example, deemed "that by jettisoning Yiddish they [Moses Mendelssohn and the Berlin *Maskilim* who encouraged the adoption of German language and culture] were destroying one of the chief foundations of Jewish culture."[20] By removing the connecting language between Jews and encouraging their entry into mainstream, Gentile society, a sense of cultural distinction was, indeed, eroded. What resulted in the most extreme cases, however, was a group who although culturally indistinguishable from the Gentile majority, were still separated by social, religious, ethnic, and class barriers.

Rabbis and Their Clothes: An Example in Modernization

During the nineteenth century, within the context of the modernization of European Jews and Judaism, there was a backlash against a transnational Jewish identification. Many rabbis—both Reform and Orthodox—sought to highlight the Jews' loyalty to the states in which they lived. More than being loyal to them, the Jews were fully fledged members of those nations: they were Germans (or French, Hungarians, Poles, etc.) who practiced the Mosaic faith. The refashioning of rabbis from devout, Talmudists concerned only with the scriptures and spiritual well-being of their flock to spokesmen for their communities, literate in both Jewish and secular German scholarship, was central to recasting Jews as modern Europeans.[21]

The dress of religious leaders is not likely to be encountered in fashion histories, belonging as it does to the history of dress or costume. Yet, religious leaders of varying denominations were prominent in European societies and were heavily represented in the visual arts. Religiously speaking, connections to communities beyond the borders of the Dual Monarchy strongly influenced the notion of transnationality in a manner that was not uncommon in other religious denominations. The interaction and contact between Viennese rabbis and lay leaders to others outside of Vienna and Austria helped strengthen a transnational Jewish identity. European Jewry with its long history of migration had an equally long history of transnational rabbinical exchange. Rabbis, who were long exchanged between communities across political and cultural borders, served as more than mere spiritual leaders but often as mediators between their communities and Gentile authorities.[22]

The Jewish religion along with the (classical) Hebrew and Yiddish languages had been uniting factors between communities separated across wider political and cultural-linguistic spheres. In Vienna alone the most prominent rabbinical figures of the nineteenth century—Isak Noa Mannheimer, Lazar Horowitz, Adolf Jellinek, Moritz Güdemann, and Joseph Samuel Bloch—were migrants to the *Kaiserstadt*, and only two—Jellinek and Bloch—were natives of the empire.[23] But far from simply fostering and maintaining transnational connections with other Jewish communities, Viennese rabbis played an important role in the modernization and Europeanization (or Germanization) of Austrian Jewry.

Viennese Jewry could not have achieved the high levels of cultural and structural assimilation without the help of various community institutions and organizations. In a city in which the separation between the Catholic Church and state was practically nonexistent, Protestantism and Judaism, as minority religions, were mandated and governed by state-sanctioned institutions administering to the spiritual and civic needs (such as births, deaths, and marriages) of their adherents.[24] As such, rabbis, like Catholic priests and Evangelical ministers, were faith leaders not simply concerned with the spiritual well-being of their flock but also served in a role akin to civil servants. Prior to the emancipation of Habsburg Jews in 1867, Viennese rabbis, like their counterparts in other European cities, played an important role in the modernization and acculturation of their communities. However, the beginning of modernization within Vienna's small Jewish community during the early decades of the nineteenth century was championed by the congregants themselves in an attempt to mimic the reforms of congregations in Hamburg and Berlin.[25] In his function as head of the community, the merchant Michael Lazar Biedermann was responsible for bringing the Copenhagen-born son of Hungarian immigrants Isak Noa Mannheimer (1793–1865) to serve as a rabbi in Vienna's newly built synagogue on the Seitenstettengasse, which he consecrated in 1826.[26] As Jews were not permitted to reside in Vienna at the time—excluding the small, wealthy community of "tolerated" Jews—and thus the position of rabbi was not recognized by the state, Mannheimer's official position was that of a "religious teacher."[27]

Mannheimer's efforts at revolutionizing Judaism through reformed synagogue services, Jewish practice, and religious writings played a central role in transforming Viennese Jewry from a foreign "nation within the nation" to modern Europeans who would eventually be emancipated by the state to enjoy the same rights as their Gentile counterparts. This is not to suggest that religious reform alone was responsible for the emancipation of Jews in Austria-Hungary; however, the community's efforts at refashioning its external appearance undoubtedly played a part in attempting to make Judaism and Jewry appear respectable in a modern European sense. Radical reforms were simultaneously occurring in other Jewish communities in Europe and beyond, such as replacing Hebrew with the local vernacular for prayers, the removal of references for the return to Zion, and proposals to commemorate the Sabbath on Sunday, rather than Saturday, in accordance with Christian denominations.[28] Indeed, under Mannheimer's leadership the Viennese congregation was influenced by some of the reforms taking place in other German congregations. Marsha L. Rozenblit explains that although influenced by the reforms occurring in other communities, Viennese Jews rejected the more radical reforms of some German congregations and instead preferred the aesthetic reform of the synagogue service.[29] The reform of Judaism in Vienna was not exclusive to those who were considered "reformists." A number of "traditional" or "Orthodox" rabbis worked with the reformers in discarding some of the more obsolete practices of Ashkenazic Judaism. For instance, the Bavarian-born Lazar Horowitz (1803–68), head of Vienna's Orthodox community during the *Vormärz* period, in collaboration with Mannheimer abolished the practice of *metzitzah b'peh* during the circumcision ceremony.[30]

Along with the ritual reforms were the reforms in the structure of the synagogue service. Unlike in Germany and Hungary, in which a schism developed between the respective Reform/Neolog and Orthodox communities,[31] the Reform-oriented and Orthodox factions of the Viennese community came to a compromise that resulted in a particular *Wiener Ritus* (Viennese Rite). The main prayers of the synagogue service would continue to be recited in Hebrew by the *khazzan* (cantor) with others recited quietly by the congregants, while the sermon would be delivered in German. Men and women would sit separately, with the latter seated in balconies above the main gallery or else in a separate side gallery (as was common even in more radically reformed German congregations).[32] The community also proposed the introduction of an organ into the synagogal proceedings; however, as a result of opposition from more traditional factions of the community, it was not used during the Sabbath and festival services (unlike in Hungarian Neolog synagogues).[33] In this manner, and with the employment of an all-male choir supporting the cantor, the Viennese synagogue service was redesigned to resemble Christian equivalents.[34] Overall, from its beginnings in the early nineteenth century, the *Wiener Ritus* was foremost concerned with the aesthetic reform of Judaism and Jewry, with the dual aim of making Judaism appealing to a younger generation of Jews and simultaneously signaling Viennese Jewry's dedication to the Fatherland.[35]

The modernization and aesthetic reform of Viennese Judaism included the transformation of the figure of the rabbi into one that reflected the Christian vocational role. The Habsburg administration, in a wider push to turn Jews into loyal and productive Austrians following Joseph II's Edicts of Toleration in the late eighteenth century (despite not awarding them equal rights), introduced changes to the role of rabbis in society.[36] Rabbis were expected to be proficient in German and broaden their educational training beyond Judaism. Additionally, there were expectations from their own congregations. Rozenblit explains, "Viennese Jews expected their religious leaders to be trained and to function like a Protestant minister. Instead of traditional Talmudical learning, his education had to provide him with a solid grounding in philosophy, theology, and Bible."[37] Nonetheless, it appears that traditional Jewish education remained central to an aspiring rabbi's training, as is evident of Vienna's leading rabbis during the latter half of the nineteenth century, namely, Mannheimer, Adolf Jellinek, and Moritz Güdemann, who had all received, in addition to a secular, German education, a strong grounding in traditional Talmudic learning at both traditional *yeshivoth* and modern rabbinical seminaries.[38]

In accordance with the aesthetic reform of Judaism that was central to the *Wiener Ritus*, Viennese rabbis, like their counterparts in other European countries, adapted the style of their synagogal vestments to resemble those of Evangelical pastors and Greek Orthodox priests. This was neither novel nor surprising, for clothing had played an important role in the modernization of European Jews since the Enlightenment.[39] That rabbis—as pastoral and spiritual leaders—should adopt new styles of dress in preference to more traditional or "oriental" modes that had been prevalent in earlier times and remained in use in Eastern Europe was a natural step on the path to Jewish acculturation. Prior to the advent of Reform (or Liberal) Judaism, the image of the rabbi dressed in a kaftan and fur cap or large *yarmulke* was as common throughout Ashkenazi Europe as the beard and earlocks. Such styles, which continued to be worn in the East after the widescale modernization of many Western and Central European Jewries during the eighteenth and nineteenth centuries, are purported to have come from the attire common among the Polish *szlachta* (nobility) of the sixteenth and seventeenth centuries—themselves purportedly influenced by Ottoman styles.[40] Prior to their modernization, rabbis and other Jewish men in the German lands (including Bohemia and Moravia) were as likely to be seen attired in the same manner as their counterparts in Poland and Russia. This was largely influenced by the transnational nature of Ashkenazic communities during the period, in particular, that many "German" rabbis and *roshei yeshiva* (deans of traditional rabbinical seminaries) were of Polish origin.[41]

The modernization of rabbinic dress had its origins in Italian and Dutch communities of the late Renaissance period where, as Asher Salah argues, cantors and prayer leaders dressed in a manner meant to mark their ceremonial role—that is, by wearing a special mantle that was "either a particularly sumptuous *tallith* of silk or a garment similar to the *cappa*, the mantle worn by university doctors."[42] The later sartorial modernization of nineteenth-century rabbis was not exclusive to those communities following a path of reform.[43] A lithograph dated 1847 by E. Schier of the German Orthodox rabbi and opponent of Reform Judaism, Samson Raphael Hirsch (1808–88), depicts a young bearded man in a dark, cassock-like robe, with white collar and clerical bands and a high, rounded hat (Figure 3.1).[44] So attired, Hirsch appears in similar sartorial mode to Samuel Holdheim (1806–60) and Abraham Geiger (1810–74), his contemporaries and proponents of the Reform movement he so strongly opposed (Figures 3.2 and 3.3). This approach to rabbinical garb was not exclusive to Germany and the German rabbinate. Variations were common in other

Figure 3.1 Lithograph of Rabbi Samson Raphael Hirsch, *c.* 1847. Courtesy of Alamy.

Figure 3.2 Portrait of German rabbi, Dr. Samuel Holdheim (1806–60), undated. Courtesy of Abraham Schwadron Portrait Collection, National Library of Israel, Jerusalem.

Figure 3.3 Portrait of German rabbi, Dr. Abraham Geiger (1810–74), undated. Courtesy of Alamy.

Figure 3.4 Zadoc Kahn, chief rabbi of France photographed by Nadar, Paris (1875–95). Courtesy of Alamy.

"modern" European congregations, both Reform and Orthodox, in both Western and Eastern Europe. In France, for example, illustrated and photographic evidence depicts Chief Rabbi Zadoc Kahn (1839–1905) dressed in similar black cassocks with lace bands (Figure 3.4). The choice of headwear differs in the low, black, wide and curled brimmed hats that resemble the *Capello romano* worn by Catholic clerics.[45] In contrast, the attire of the British chief rabbi, the Hanover-born Nathan Marcus Adler (1803–90) and his son and successor Hermann Adler (1839–1911) appears closer to their German counterparts (Figures 3.5 and 3.6).

Thus, rabbinical sartorial reform in Vienna was in line with the wider sartorial modernization of European rabbis. A large *tallith* (ritual prayer shawl) was exchanged for a narrow, scarf-like variety that could be draped over the shoulders rather than enveloping its wearer's entire body. Rabbis adopted the wearing of a *Talar* (cassock or gown) similar to Christian preachers, in contrast to the traditional kaftans worn by their predecessors and Hasidic counterparts, a high white collar and clerical bands, and tall brimless hats reminiscent of the *kalimavkion* worn by Greek Orthodox clerics or the *biretta* of Catholic priests (Figure 3.7).[46] They continue to be worn today by cantors and rabbis in certain European congregations as well as by some associated with Anglo-Orthodoxy in the British Commonwealth of Nations. These new garments did not necessarily possess religious or spiritual significance (albeit their adoption by faith leaders undoubtedly imbued them with such), but rather were part of a wider attempt to

Figure 3.5 Nathan Marcus Adler, chief rabbi of the British Empire photographed by Herbert Rose Barraus, 1889. Courtesy of Alamy.

Figure 3.6 Hermann Adler, chief rabbi of the British Empire photographed by W. & D. Downey, 1892. Courtesy of Alamy.

Figure 3.7 Portrait of Rabbi Dr. Adolf Jellinek, *c*. 1891. Courtesy of Alamy.

Figure 3.8 Lithograph of Isak Noa Mannheimer by Eduard Kaiser, 1858. Courtesy of Wien Museum, Vienna.

bring decorum into the synagogue,[47] and the adoption of these garments was part of the acculturation of Jewry and the performance of Judaic rituals. Furthermore, the adoption of sober black garments, with their connotations of Protestant values of asceticism and industriousness, by European rabbis also situated wearers in the long tradition of black clothing as a marker of prestige, religious piety, scholarship, and discipline in European Christendom.[48]

Photographs, painted portraits, and engravings depicted Viennese "preachers" ("*Prediger*" in German) in much the same manner outlined previously. It is telling that in the absence of the *tallith* there is nothing in the sartorial appearance of these religious leaders to suggest that they are Jewish (Figure 3.8). That the rabbinical cassock differed from those worn by Catholic priests and Protestant ministers in Vienna is evident in the tailoring textbook of the Vienna Tailor Academy during the early twentieth century, which included separate drafting instructions for the garments worn by the three religious leaders and specified, in particular, different sleeve styles for each.[49] However, more immediately obvious is the style of headwear donned by rabbis in contrast to their Christian counterparts; in a church, male heads go uncovered as a sign of respect, while the opposite is true of the synagogue. In contrast to the portraits of Christian preachers of the period, those of Viennese rabbis dressed in this garb maintain this fundamental difference. The robes and bands may signify mainstream Austrian Jewry's dedication to *Deutschtum* and *Bildung*, but the continued presence of the *tallith* and rabbinical/cantorial hat (whether resembling the Greek Orthodox *kalimavkion* or the Catholic *biretta*)[50] declares a dedication to a Jewish identification; assimilation—even among the supposedly Jewish élite—can and will go only so far.

In contrast to such images that serve as a public proclamation of Jewish identity, albeit of a modern, European variety, are those photographs of Viennese "preachers" in "private." Studio photographs of Viennese rabbis dressed in civilian clothing, that is, bareheaded and in modern suits, present an interesting contrast. For example, an undated photograph of Vienna's chief rabbi (appointed 1892) Dr. Moritz Güdemann (1835–1918), an opponent of the Reform movement who had been educated at the Jewish Theological Seminary in Breslau,[51] can be contrasted with "official" portraits in which he appears in the sartorial identity of rabbi. An undated photograph of Güdemann in rabbinical hat and robe complete with white clerical bands (Figure 3.9) contrasts with another photographic portrait of the rabbi. In the "unofficial" portrait, Güdemann reclines in a winged chair covered by a fur throw. His head is bare and his dress is civilian: double-breasted frockcoat, waistcoat, and trousers. Between the index and middle fingers he holds a cigar (Figure 3.10). Unlike the other portraits, which include sartorial clues to his rabbinical identity, Güdemann's attire appears no different than that of other Jewish and Gentile members of the bourgeoisie. In a peculiar twist, these images reverse the maxim of the Haskalah to "be a man in the street and a Jew at home"—his public sartorial identity is very clearly and unambiguously "the Jew in the street" in the face of the more general "private" persona of the "man at home."

Figure 3.9 Moritz Güdemann, undated photograph. Courtesy of Abraham Schwadron Portrait Collection, The National Library of Israel, Jerusalem.

Figure 3.10 Moritz Güdemann photographed by N. Chefez, Vienna, undated. Moritz Guedemann Collection AR 7067, LBI Photograph Collection, Call no. F 001 AR 7067. Courtesy of Leo Baeck Institue, New York.

Between East and West: The Myth of *Ostjuden* And German Jews in Vienna

The role of rabbis in the modernization and visual refashioning of Viennese Jewry has added significance in the context of the internal "national" quandary within the community. Vienna's Jewish population, consisting of individuals from all cultural and linguistic spheres of the Austro-Hungarian Empire and further afield, was a microcosm of Habsburg Jewry. However, it was not a unified one, with many divisions separating Jews of differing socioeconomic status, political ideologies, or geographic origins. The typical cultural model of Viennese Jewry that appears in memoirs and biographies is the division of the community into two main groups—and in some cases two parallel communities. The first consisted of "German" (or Germanized) Jews who were culturally assimilated, that is, they adopted the German language if they had not already done so previously, as well as modern, secular lifestyles and dress, they were educated in a secular manner, and mixed, to an extent, with Gentiles of the same socioeconomic tiers. In contrast were the "Polish Jews" or *Ostjuden* (as they were referred to increasingly after 1914),[52] the bearded, earlocked, kaftan-wearing Jews from Galicia, Bukovina, and beyond, who were often uneducated in the secular sense, spoke Yiddish as their vernacular and German with a strong accent, were religiously Orthodox, and isolated from Gentile society.[53]

Memoirs and recollections of Viennese Jews of their lives before the Shoah also highlight a separation between "eastern" and "western" Jews in the Austrian capital. In some cases, acculturated western Jews completely rejected their eastern coreligionists. Otto Grossman recalled, "To us the sight of an orthodox Eastern Jew with beard and temple-ringlets in his kaftan was ridiculous, as was his language. Or was it a language? To us it was a corrupt and comically-sounding German."[54] However, many Viennese Jews retained a sense of (sometimes reluctant) responsibility and fraternity to their culturally unassimilated eastern coreligionists, donating their time and money to charitable causes and joining organizations, such as the Österreichisch-Israelitische Allianz (Austrian-Israelite Alliance) to safeguard Jewish interests and improve the plight of the easterners. Hans Stein, for example, whose family lived in a Döbling apartment (district XIX) in the vicinity of the upper-middle-class *Cottageviertel* recalled:

> Every so often men in tattered suits came to pay a visit. We called them Schnorrers, Jews who said they needed money to buy food. Those Jewish men had their well-appointed route in the city. They knew exactly where to go. If they did not come at the usual time, we became worried and talked about them. We did not know their names, so we gave them fictitious names. These customers were mostly Polish Jews, the underdogs of the Jewish hierarchy of Vienna. We were the Western Jews; "they" came from the East, speaking with a distinct accent. The outsiders. We did give them money when they needed it.[55]

Stein's candid recollection of his acculturated family's reaction to their less fortunate coreligionists highlights the derision the *Westjuden* felt for the *Ostjuden*, but also reveals how pity and warmth can co-reside. This binary model of east/west Jewry, however, is a simplification of the diversity of Viennese Jewry during the late nineteenth and early twentieth centuries, and the reality was far more complex.

Over the course of the nineteenth century, with the steadily increasing number of Jewish migrants from Galicia, Bukovina, and across the Russian border, those same regions were seen as the last frontier before the barbarity of the Orient, if not barbarism itself. This is highlighted in the novels and stories of Galician-born Karl Emil Franzos (1848–1904), of which Robert S. Wistrich writes:

> Those tales entitled *Aus Halb-Asien* (Out of Half-Asia), published in two volumes in 1876, ostensibly described the border regions of the Austro-Hungarian Empire (Galicia, Bukovina, Romania, western Russia). In fact, they were "not merely a geographical designation but a condition of the mind," a metaphor for Europe as a realm of light and love, in opposition to its polar opposite, Asia, a jungle of darkness, barbarism, and violent hatreds. The *Ostjuden* were "half-Asian" precisely because they lived within these social and cultural boundaries. They were an unfortunate *product* of this unredeemed world of religious fanaticism, national oppression, superstition, and backwardness. It was in this special sense that Franzos coined his famous formula "Every country gets the Jews it deserves."[56]

This sarcastic observation cannot be truer in the sense that every country gets the people it deserves. The social, economic, and political conditions of those lands shaped the behavior of the Jews no more nor less than they did the behavior of its Gentile inhabitants. But Franzos and other "Germans" were mistaken if they thought that barbarism and violent hatreds were exclusively endemic to Asia or the easternmost parts of Europe. The same petty hatreds existed even within the supposedly enlightened imperial capital.[57] This "half-Asian" characterization that was so freely applied to the *Ostjuden* lulled the *Westjuden* into a false sense of security. They believed they were "European," when they, too, like their more "primitive" coreligionists, were seen by other Europeans equally as half-Asians who had learnt the ways of the cultured nations of the West—an ape in a dinner jacket, as in Franz Kafka's 1917 short story, *Ein Bericht für eine Akademie* (*A Report to an Academy*).[58] Even Jews of Galician origin bought into the East/West binary. For some the figure of the *Ostjude* encapsulated all that was negative in Jewishness. Viennese-born Kurt H. Schaffir, whose father was a native of Bialystok and whose maternal family originated in Galicia recalled of his childhood:

> We were strongly cautioned to avoid any appearance of Jewish mannerisms in public. Some of our neighbours [*sic*.] or parents of classmates spoke Yiddish at home, and we picked it up a bit ourselves. But it was considered a corruption of the German language, used only by uneducated Jews who had not mastered proper German, and we never spoke it in school or in public.[59]

The binary model of Viennese Jewry, Germanized Jews, and *Ostjuden* is far too limited to explain the complexities and issues pertaining to notions of Jewishness in Vienna.

"Eastern" was a subjective designation: German Jews considered Austrians "eastern," and Jews in the west of Germany—historic Ashkenaz—considered Berliners, many of whom had arrived from Posen (Poznań) after its incorporation into Prussia at the end of the eighteenth century, as eastern.[60] Nor are the terms "Germanized" or "German Jews" suitable. Viennese Jewry was, by and large, linguistically German regardless of geographical origin, socioeconomic class, or degree of religiosity. Even those segments of the Jewish population that commonly used Yiddish or other languages among themselves were proficient in German. In reality, Viennese Jewry during the late nineteenth and early twentieth centuries can be divided into multiple overlapping subcategories, such as the assimilated, acculturated, Jews of varying degrees of Orthodoxy, Hasidic, secular but culturally Jewish, and multiple varieties of "national" Jews (such as Zionists and Diaspora Nationalists).[61]

Individuals in these sociopolitical/cultural-ideological subgroups could be found in all socioeconomic classes. They lived in different types of homes furnished in varying aesthetic styles, educated their children in different manners, spoke different languages, engaged in different leisure activities, were members of various cultural and political organizations, worked in a variety of professions and occupations, and, of course, dressed differently. This was often determined by an individual's socioeconomic status and cultural milieu. For example, while an immigrant from Galicia may not have been able to afford to purchase his clothing at the men's tailoring atelier Goldman & Salatsch and had to resort to buying them from a cheaper, ready-made clothing warehouse, such as those advertised in the city's Jewish newspapers,[62] photographic evidence reveals that poorer members of the community readily adapted to conventional sartorial fashions. Many Viennese Jews, regardless of socioeconomic status or geographical origin, possessed many mutual values, particularly with regard to family and education.[63] The lower-middle-class or working-class immigrant Jews from Galicia, for example, were closer to their Germanized middle- and upper-middle-class counterparts than Gentile members of the same socioeconomic classes in the value they placed on education.[64] Joseph L. Tenenbaum, a *Galitsianer* from Sasów (Sasiv) and later well-known American urologist and Zionist leader, came to Vienna as a young man to study medicine. In his Yiddish-language semi-memoir, *Galitsiye: mayn alte heym* (1952), Tenenbaum devoted an entire chapter to Vienna, a city he placed on par with Lemberg:

> Vienna—I don't know which city is more beloved to me: Lemberg or Vienna. To me, it is a bit like asking a child, "whom do you love more: father or mother?" My answer is the same childish: "both!" Both cities are dear to my heart. Even though throughout my life I have visited many countries and lived in many cities, the two cities—Lemberg and Vienna— remain engraved in my brain and rooted in my soul that no new home whatsoever can suppress. I look at Paris, the wonderful and beautiful Paris, with its boulevards and café tables, and I see Vienna with its arcades. [. . .] But Vienna—who and what can compare with the city of my student years, when I studied medicine at the world-class university—Vienna, the city of Strauss's waltzes, Schubert's melodies, and Gustav Mahler's symphonies. The city

of Adolf Sonnenthal, Josef Kainz, and the prima donna Selma Kurz. Vienna of art, love, and song. Vienna of Arthur Schnitzler's *Reigen*.[65]

Tenenbaum's description of Vienna—the typical images of tourist guidebooks—is romantic and more than a little contrived. However, his attitude was not uncommon among wider Habsburg Jewry, especially *Galitsianers* who identified wholeheartedly with Vienna and the Habsburg myth of multiethnic fraternity. Beyond serving as a city of refuge for those fleeing the advancing Russian army during the First World War, for Galician Jews, Vienna's allure as a sprawling metropolis with financial and cultural opportunities was attractive—the same as for those in other parts of the Dual Monarchy. In addition, the appeal of liberal German language and culture, introduced and perpetuated simultaneously by the Josephinian reforms of the end of the eighteenth century and Galician *Maskilim*, meant that by the beginning of the twentieth century, Galician immigrants were no strangers to *Deutschtum*, even if not dedicated practitioners of it themselves.[66]

Eva Bostock (née Lemler) was born in the working-class district of Ottakring (district XVI) in 1919 to Orthodox parents from Galicia. The family, like many of their neighbors—Jews and Gentiles alike—was very poor and lived in a small flat with a shared toilet and sink on the outside landing. Eva's father, Berl Lemler (also known by his German name "Bernhard"), a native of Kraków, worked occasionally as a cantor and performing odd jobs at the local Ottakringer synagogue. Her mother Lina (also known as "Liba," née Beutel) came to Vienna with her Hasidic father and siblings from the Galician shtetl Złoty Potok (Zolotyi Potik), and upon arrival in the Austrian capital began teaching herself to read and write in German. Given the relatively small Jewish population of Ottakring, most of Eva's interaction with other Jews took place at home or at the synagogue, while most of her school peers were Christian.[67]

Despite their traditional origins, the Lemler family was part of a growing number of *Galitsianer* Jews who had moved away from a strictly traditional lifestyle. Although they attended synagogue regularly, kept a kosher home, and observed the Sabbath, Berl and Lina Lemler embraced the sartorial modes of modern Europeans. In photographs included in Eva's unpublished memoir, Berl and Lina wear modern attire: Berl in a suit, white-collar shirt and tie, with trimmed moustache, and Lina in a dark floral blouse (or possibly dress) with a fashionable waved hairstyle.[68] Their children, too, appear, in clothing typical of the period. In particular, one a photograph from 1935 depicts their son Adolf with friends that appears to have been taken in a rural setting with mountains in the background. "Dolfi" wears a *Trachtenjanker*—the typical fulled wool jacket worn as traditional Austro-Bavarian attire, and popular among urban visitors to the country.[69] Only Lina's father, Zvi Hersch Beutel, retained the appearance of the "typical" *Ostjude*. Eva recalls her grandfather as an elderly Hasid who sat at home and studied the Talmud all day.[70] Visually, Zvi Hersch Beutel lived up to his granddaughter's recollections decades later. In an undated photograph, he sits in shirtsleeves and wearing what appear to be pyjama trousers, clasping a cane and deeply engrossed in a book. His long white beard and large satin *yarmulke* clearly mark him as an Orthodox Jew.[71] Although only a generation removed from the urbane style of his daughter and son-in-law, the cultural divide appears far greater.

The Lemler family was by no means an anomaly. Many publications, including memoirs and biographies, particularly those published in English, have focused largely on Jews residing in the *Dreieck* (districts, I, II, and IX), regardless of social class. Evelyn Adunka and Gabriele Anderl have documented the vibrant Jewish life in Ottakring and Hernals, exploring the heterogenous character of this small community.[72] Not only were the clothing choices of Berl and Lina Lemler part of a wider provincial-to-urban adaptation that also characterized migrants from Bohemia, Moravia, and Hungary, but the generational divide between older and younger immigrants from Galicia was very common during the period. While some Galician immigrants retained their traditional lifestyles and patterns of appearance, many adopted the modern styles of dress worn by their Viennese-born coreligionists. In his memoir, George Clare described how his mother's Galician family had adopted the aesthetic codes and tastes of the Viennese bourgeoisie. Recalling a Passover *Seder* (a ritual feast or ceremony) at his maternal grandparents' apartment on the Türkenschanzplatz (district XVIII), he writes:

> We were fourteen sitting around the extended dining-room table with its gold-damask tablecloth, sparkling glasses, gold-rimmed plates and shining silver. The ladies wore long dresses and were adorned with their best jewellery, the men had dinner jackets, and on their heads bowler hats instead of the traditional yarmulkas, the skullcaps of the Orthodox Jews. At Stock Exchange Councillor Schapira's Seder evening city hats were *de rigeur*.[73]

Many Jews from Galicia and other parts of Eastern Europe had been influenced by modernism and societal change, therefore abandoning "traditional" garb long before migrating to "Western" cities like Vienna. Photographs of Galician immigrants both before and after the First World War reveals the tendency of youth, in particular, to embrace modern sartorial styles, perhaps indicative of a general youthful disposition toward "fashion." Nuchim Kürschner, a native of Monasterzyska (Monastyryska), relocated to Vienna to study chemistry in the early 1920s where he was known by the German name "Norbert." In Vienna, Kürschner immersed himself in the wider cultural milieu—attending the opera, concerts, theater—as well as the Jewish sports association Hakoah. Most of his peers including his later business associate, Salomon Walter, were recent arrivals from Galician towns and villages. Surviving photographs of Kürschner, Walter, and members of their circle depict dapper young men, dressed in tailored suits, in the same manner as their Viennese-born counterparts (Figure 3.11).[74]

Patterns and preferences of dress did not vary much between Viennese Jews of differing geographical origins, and only slightly between socioeconomic classes determined more by an individual's ability to purchase the latest fashions. In his account of his Jewish Viennese ancestors, Edmund De Waal describes his great-grandmother Emmy Ephrussi's (née Schey von Koromla) expensive taste in clothing and penchant for dressing up for the camera in historicist costume[75] alongside her husband Viktor's more studious and

Figure 3.11 Nuchim/Norbert Kürschner and Salomon Walter (first and second on left) with friends, Vienna, *c.* 1932. Courtesy of Ruth Kurschner, NJ.

less flamboyant appearance, following the stereotypical modes of gendered sartorial consumption.[76] Similar gendered patterns of attire are visible in the representations of the Gallia family. Gustav Klimt's famous portrait of Hermine Gallia (1904) presents the subject dressed in an exquisite avant-garde gown similar to those worn in a number of Klimt's other portraits of the wives of wealthy, often Jewish, art patrons.[77] Hermine's attire in the painted portrait reflects the same Secessionist aesthetic identity the family sought to embody in their apartment on the Wohllebengasse with interiors by the celebrated Secessionist designer Josef Hoffmann.[78] And yet, this mode of dress does not correspond with Hermine's typical dress habits as they appear in photographs included in the family history written by her great-grandson Tim Bonyhady. Although in the photographs included in Bonyhady's book Hermine is by no means "plainly dressed," her attire is conservative, following accepted bourgeois fashions, rather than the Secessionist styles of Klimt's portraits. Few images of her husband Moriz appear throughout the book, and in those that do, including a 1901 portrait by Ferdinand Andri, he appears in the stereotypical role of conservative Jewish plutocrat in dark suit and tie, white collar, clasping a cigar between his fingers.[79] This same model of conservative and sober male sartorial respectability alongside a more elaborate and flamboyant femininity was common across Vienna's upper and middle classes. For Jews, in particular, adhering to these gendered sartorial codes possessed the dual meanings of social respectability and conforming to Gentile society.

The aesthetic transformation of Jewry extended beyond choice of attire. As Viennese rabbis had sought to instill in their congregants, education—in both the formal sense and *Bildung*—was essential to participating in modern Austrian society.[80] It was commonly held that rigorous primary and secondary schooling would prepare a student for university. In his memoir, Stefan Zweig commented on the symbolic meaning for Jewish families of having at least one son graduate with a doctorate,[81] especially when fathers had been unable to study themselves as a result of restrictions placed on Jewish enrollment at Austrian universities. While his older brother Alfred was sent to work in their father Moriz's textile business, Stefan, already having shown an aptitude for writing as a *Gymnasiast*, was sent to university. To Zweig, this was pure vanity, and in a letter to the German-Swiss novelist Hermann Hesse, dated March 2, 1903, he lamented the pressures placed upon his shoulders as a result of his parents' "vanity."[82] The importance placed on education crossed class and geocultural boundaries among Vienna's Jewish population. Despite their family's financial situation, the education of children was very important to Berl and Lina Lemler, the former of whom had been educated at the music academy in Kraków. Their daughter Eva was sent to study at a *Humanistisches Gymnasium* with hopes that she would go on to study medicine at university and graduate as a doctor.[83] Great importance was also placed on "classical" culture, which included violin lessons and participation in the school's orchestra, as well as trips to the opera house and theater.[84] Particularly during the interwar period, due to the increasing popularity of Jewish forms of cultural expression among Viennese Jews,[85] especially the youth, the multilayered Jewish identification that had developed toward the turn of the century whereby one could be both culturally Viennese and Jewish continued to evolve, denying the binary characterizations Jewish/German and East/West.

Asserting National Consciousness: Joseph Samuel Bloch and Theodor Herzl

With the rise of antisemitism as a political force in Austro-German society, it became apparent to many Jews that the imagined East/West binary was irrelevant. It was increasingly difficult for Jews to assert a German national identity and be accepted as such. In his study of Polish Chicagoans, Dominic A. Pacyga asserts that "ethnicity is often a choice,"[86] and indeed there is some truth to these words when one considers the aforementioned moniker "Germans of the Mosaic faith" or Rozenblit's tripartite model of Jewish identification. However, in the pseudo-scientific rhetoric of the latter part of the nineteenth century, the Jew and the German (or Aryan) were mutually exclusive concepts. The Jew could not be a true member of the German nation as his (perceived) inherent racial difference was incompatible with the "true" European races.[87] Nonetheless, as Steven Beller has demonstrated, Jews were simultaneously faced with expectations to assimilate into the wider society.[88] The Jewish response to this contradiction varied, turning to different models of Jewish self-identification. Some rabbis, too, played a part in this shift, with many in the German-speaking lands who had previously stressed the exclusively religious nature of Judaism—characterizing their flock as Germans of the Mosaic faith or "Israelites" with its spiritual connotations, rather than "Jews"— now spoke of Jewish peoplehood, albeit a people who remained loyal to the nations in which they lived. Moritz Güdemann, for example, was an opponent of nascent Zionism and claimed in 1895 (one year prior to the publication of Theodor Herzl's pamphlet proposing the establishment of a Jewish State), "I have always believed that we are not a nation, or rather more than a nation: I believe we had the historic mission to propagate universalism among the nations and that we were therefore more than a territorial nation."[89] In addition to rabbis, other community leaders—both official and self-appointed—took part in the debate regarding Jewish nationhood. Two prominent examples of a turn to Jewish nationalism among "leaders" can be found in the figures of Joseph Samuel Bloch (1850–1923), the rabbi turned Reichsrat deputy for the Galician district of Kolomea (Kolomyia), and journalist turned self-appointed messiah, Theodor Herzl (1860–1904).

Bloch and Herzl were not quite contemporaries being born a decade apart. Their family backgrounds and upbringings placed them at opposite ends of the supposed East/West binary. One of them received a traditional, Orthodox education on the Dual Monarchy's margins, while the other was born into a secular, acculturated household in one of its largest cities. While Bloch was impressed by Herzl's presence and passion, he was less inclined to support the latter's Zionist cause, albeit not responding with ridicule or a moratorium of silence on the matter.[90] However, they shared a number of similarities: both came of age in a period of mounting political antisemitism that influenced their self-identification as Jews, both were immigrants to the *Kaiserstadt*, and, furthermore, both were fierce proponents of the notion of Jewish nationhood, albeit from differing perspectives. In their function as public figures, Bloch and Herzl were harangued in the press and simultaneously had an impact on the image of Austrian Jewry.

Joseph Samuel Bloch and the Ideal of Supranational Austria

Like many leading figures of the Jewish community at the time, Bloch was a migrant to the Austrian capital. He had been born and raised in Dukla, Galicia, by poor, Orthodox parents, and received both a traditional Jewish and secular education at a traditional *kheyder* (primary school), *Gymnasia*, and universities in Lemberg, Eisenstadt, Magdeburg, Liegnitz (Legnica), Munich, and Zürich, receiving his doctorate at the last. Before being engaged as the rabbi of Floridsdorf, at the time a municipality on the outskirts of Vienna (later to become Vienna's twenty-first district in 1904), Bloch held rabbinical posts in Rendsburg, Kobylin, and Brüx (Most).[91] However, Bloch was known less for his rabbinical service than for his fight against antisemitism and for the rights of Jews in the Austrian political arena, for which he drew the ire of antisemites. It was his public debate against the theologian August Rohling regarding the latter's involvement in the trial of the Tiszaeszlár blood libel in 1883 that propelled Bloch into the public arena.[92] Among his accomplishments were the establishment of the *Oesterreichische*

Wochenschrift in 1884 (in circulation until 1920)[93] and the *Österreichisch-Israelitische Union* (OIU) (Austrian-Israelite Union) in 1886, with the resolve "to elevate and foster Jewish consciousness [*Stammesbewusstsein*], to create a front against the rapidly spreading 'semitic anti-Semitism' and as much as possible, to suppress all tendencies which seek to sharpen religious and radical antagonisms."[94]

Although sympathetic to some elements of Zionism, the variety of Jewish nationalism Bloch preached as part of his political platform differed from it and other varieties of nationalism in Europe in its lack of territorial claims. In contrast, Bloch fashioned himself as an Austrian patriot and proud Jew, asserting the right of Jews as equal members of the national mosaic that made up the Austrian state. Rather than identifying as Germans, Bloch believed Austrian Jews should adopt a tripartite variety of self-identification "embracing Jewish ethnicity and an Austrian political or civic consciousness while leaving the question of cultural affinity to each individual."[95] In an age in which Austrian national identity was nonexistent, and most "Austrians" identified nationally with their *Volksstamm*, Jews wishing to express an Austrian national identity, particularly those in Galicia and Bukovina, found themselves in a difficult predicament. For German-speaking Jews, especially in Vienna, Bohemia, and Moravia, identifying as German nationals was easy enough—despite antisemitic discourse that argued they could not—due to the Habsburg administration's view of nationality being linked to language. Yiddish-speaking Jews in the eastern crown lands, however, were unable to identify as "Jewish" nationals, as Yiddish and Hebrew (the latter, although not commonly spoken, was used for ritual purposes and community records) were not recognized as languages of the Austro-Hungarian Empire.[96] Rather, they were permitted to identify themselves in the censuses and official documents as members of any of the other recognized nations. Many declared themselves to be German or Polish—the former was closest to Yiddish, and many Galician Jews were proficient in the latter—despite the widespread social, economic, and cultural divide between Jews, Germans, and Poles in Galicia.[97] And yet, many Galician Jews considered themselves "Austrians" and found themselves enamored with Franz Joseph I.[98] It was in this Jewish subculture that Bloch was born and raised.

For his part, Bloch recognized the loyalty of the Jews to the empire as a result of Franz Joseph's benevolent toleration of his Jewish subjects. The Jews, he claimed, were the true Austrians, the "Grundstock" (foundation) of the potential Austrian nation,[99] in contrast to the empire's other nations that had fallen victim to rising nationalisms from both within and outside the Dual Monarchy. As Bloch's son-in-law Max Grunwald noted, "The Austrian German regarded himself as a German, the Austrian Pole as a Pole, and so on. Only the Galician Jews regarded themselves as Austrians."[100] For Bloch, the identification with Austria and supranational identity were important in light of the Jew's place in Gentile society. It is telling that the title chosen for his periodical identified with Austria, "in contrast to the *Deutsche Wochenschrift* edited by [Heinrich] Friedjung."[101] Bloch firmly believed that a supranational Austria in which the Jews could gain an equal footing alongside their fellow Austrians of different ethnic backgrounds would provide the most secure environment in which Austrian Jewry could continue to contribute to and participate in the wider society.[102]

Bloch's dedication to Austria's supranational identity and Jewish political consciousness aroused the indignation of many in the Austrian political and civic arenas.[103] However, as a public Jewish personality, regardless of his political alignment, he would have been bait enough for antisemites. The proud Jew fighting back against discrimination was a growing tendency among various brands of Jewish political consciousness across Europe.[104] Bloch was savaged in the Viennese press and literary community. For example, Franz Friedrich Masaidek's collection of *Lose Gedanken* (*Loose Thoughts*) refers in large part to Vienna's Jewish population, and Bloch is one of the handful of well-known individuals mentioned by name. In one instance, Masaidek notes, "Ein Rabbi Bloch fördert den Antisemitismus mehr als zehn Schönerer," in reference to the antisemitic pan-German politician and agitator Georg von Schönerer (1842–1921).[105]

For antisemites Bloch was a manifestation of the arch-Jew in Gentile society, pushily forcing his agenda on poor, decent folk. In his function as a symbol of Jewry, the reality of Bloch's appearance mattered little to his detractors. "Rabbi Bloch" was no *Galitsianer* with long beard, *peyes* (earlocks), and *shtrayml*. There is a dearth of surviving images of Bloch; however, in those that do survive he appears as a typical, aging, urban middle-class gentleman with neatly trimmed beard and hair, wearing pince-nez and dressed in a tailored suit—not dissimilar to those "private" photographs of his colleague Moritz Güdemann (Figure 3.12). In contrast, caricatures that appeared in the Viennese satirical magazine *Kikeriki* present Bloch as a stereotypical rabbi wearing a tall cantor's hat and long black kaftan, with an unkempt beard and long hair, complete of course with protruding lips and a large nose.[106] In fact, the only resemblance between the real Bloch and his caricatured personage is that both wore spectacles (Figure 3.13). While serving as the rabbi of the Floridsdorf congregation, Bloch likely donned the uniform associated with his profession. However, in his political career as a parliamentary delegate representing the district of Buczacz-Kolomea-Sniatyn and member of the Polish club, he would certainly have dressed according to modern European standards. Like Masaidek, the publishers of the magazine found in Bloch a convenient manifestation of Jewish politics in its entirety, regularly appearing in visual caricatured form or mentioned by name in written segments. The divorce between the reality of Bloch's sartorial (and physical) appearance and his portrayal in the antisemitic press is no accident. Grunwald notes, "'Doctor Bloch,' as the Jews called him, or 'Rabbi Bloch,' as his enemies called him, became the obvious representative of the Jewish race."[107] As a representative of the "Jewish race"—who happened to be a congregational rabbi, no less—Bloch would play an appropriate role for the enemies of his people: the meddling Jew, a proponent of a supranational Austria jeopardizing the efforts of the nationalists in Germanizing the Austrian half of the Dual Monarchy.

In spite of his rabbinical uniform in the synagogue, his sartorial identity in other arenas was typical of the Viennese middle class and thus a demonstration of his self-perception to wider society. However, his typical bourgeois dress patterns outside of rabbinical "office hours" made little difference to his overall image. After being "betrayed" by his colleagues in Polish club and losing his seat in the Austrian parliament in 1895,[108] Bloch continued his fight against antisemitism. His journal remained in circulation until 1920, in which he penned and edited numerous articles concerning the situation of Jews throughout Austria-Hungary and further afield.

Figure 3.12 Joseph Samuel Bloch, Vienna, photographed by S. Weitzmann, Vienna, undated. Courtesy of Alamy.

Figure 3.13 Caricature of politician and newspaper publisher Ernst Vergani and *Reichsrat* deputy Joseph Samuel Bloch from *Kikeriki* 30, no. 1 (January 2, 1890): 1. Courtesy of ANNO/Österreichische Nationalbibliothek, Vienna.

Theodor Herzl: A Bourgeois Nationalist

Theodor Herzl's attitude toward Jews and the idea of a Jewish nation were complex and often contradictory. Unlike Bloch, Herzl was not an elected politician nor an official community leader, but rather a self-appointed messiah. While surviving photographs of Bloch are scarce, a wealth exist that depict Herzl at different stages of his life, both formal studio portraits and more relaxed family snaps. In examining these images, it is apparent that Herzl used sartorial styles to express his political and cultural sentiments—this was by no means unique to Herzl, as we shall see in Chapter 6; however, the choices he made regarding his clothing as part of a wider self-fashioning are significant, especially when considering the lasting impact his legacy has left on world Jewry. Although leader of a Jewish nationalist movement, Herzl's political endeavors to establish a Jewish national home and new modes of Jewish identification should not preclude him from being considered a cosmopolitan. His political visions were, after all, the product of his cosmopolitan, bourgeois background—his German, middle-class upbringing in Budapest, transnational family connections, and legal and journalistic postings in Vienna, Salzburg, and Paris.

Like many of his contemporaries, Herzl did not undergo a metamorphosis from the kaftan-wearing *Ostjude* to the *Frack*-wearing *Westjude*. Born in 1860 to Jakob and Jeanette Herzl, members of Budapest's Jewish bourgeoisie who had already embraced the ideals of *Bildung* and *Sittlichkeit* before the birth of their son, it was in this city that the young Theodor (also known in Hungarian as Tivadar) would live until the family relocated to Vienna in his eighteenth year after the death of his older sister Pauline. Herzl's early life, until his embrace of Zionism, has been characterized as one of discernable assimilation and estrangement from his Jewish roots. This, however, was not the case, with the Herzl family living in the heart of Budapest's "Jewish" quarter, next door to the city's main synagogue on the Tabakgasse (Dohány utca) where his father attended services, and the strong familial Jewish influences during his upbringing, all of which is apparent in his own biographical writings and diaries.[109]

Georges Yitshak Weisz and Robert S. Wistrich have argued in their respective studies that the Herzl family was steeped in Jewish tradition and maintained connections with a number of rabbinical figures, despite their acculturation, providing the young Theodor's childhood with a very "Jewish" coloring.[110] Indeed, it was only after joining *Albia*, a German nationalist *Burschenschaft* (student fraternity) while studying law at the University of Vienna that he turned away from his Jewish origins in favor of the German nationalism popular during the final decades of the nineteenth century. He resigned from *Albia* in 1883 as a protest against the fraternity's toxic culture of antisemitism manifested in a speech marking the recent death of Richard Wagner delivered by fellow *Burschenschaftler* Hermann Bahr (1863–1934), the later leader of literary circle *Jung Wien*, indicating Herzl's strong sense of Jewish identification despite his dedication to German culture.[111] After graduating from university, Herzl worked briefly as a legal clerk in Vienna and Salzburg before devoting himself to writing and journalism. He wrote a number of plays, stories, feuilletons, and other articles, some of which were published in the *Berliner Tageblatt*, before he was finally offered a position as the Paris correspondent for the *Neue Freie Presse*, while travelling through the south of France with his wife Julie (née Naschauer) in 1891.[112] It was in Paris that Herzl witnessed the notorious Dreyfus Affair, which has been credited with leading him to Zionism as the answer to the "Jewish Question."[113]

However, prior to his embrace of Zionism, Herzl had other plans for the "grand" refashioning of the Jewish people. One early proposal focused on the mass conversion of Europe's Jews, with the Viennese leading by example. Vienna's Jews, Herzl surmised, would be paraded through the streets of the Austrian capital, converging on St. Stephen's Cathedral where they would undergo a mass baptism, recalling imagery of a biblical nature.[114] So theatrical a scenario is symptomatic of what Michael Burri describes as Herzl's self-styled nobility as a consequence of his bourgeois upbringing,[115] explained by Steven Beller as typical of Herzl's fascination with the pomp and ceremony of the aristocracy. "Herzl was so plainly a dandy, an aesthete and a snob, fascinated by aristocrats and ideas of chivalry," remarks Beller.[116] His grand plans were also likely influenced by the 1879 pageant along the unfinished Ringstrasse in celebration of the Imperial couple's (Franz Joseph and Elisabeth) silver wedding anniversary.[117]

Herzl's Zionist ideals were different from the national revivals of Central Europe that were inward-looking and self-idolizing, that actively rejected external influences as detrimental to the survival of a pure national culture, or at best recharacterized borrowed elements as indigenous. On the contrary, Herzl's Zionism celebrated little "Jewish" national culture at all, but rather borrowed enthusiastically from the "indigenous" cultures among whom European Jews lived, specifically Germans. In the preface to an English edition of Herzl's 1902 utopian novel *Altneuland* (*Old-New Land*), Jacques Kornberg asserts that Herzl rejected the inward-looking bigotry of *Ostjuden* who closed themselves off from the enlightened cultures of others.[118] Indeed, as a member of Vienna's Jewish bourgeoisie with its dedication to *Bildung*, *Sittlichkeit*, and *Deutschtum*, Herzl wished to fashion his Jewish State by borrowing many elements from German culture. His views are evident in *Altneuland* as well as his 1896 pamphlet on the Jewish State (*Der Judenstaat*). Disappointed by the growing antisemitism, Herzl redirected his love of the German culture into a new form of *Deutschtum*. Essentially, the creation of a Jewish State in Palestine, Argentina, Uganda, or elsewhere would constitute the creation of a culturally German colony of Jews, in which *ungebildete Ostjuden* would be transformed through the adoption of modern European culture as their own. In so doing, they would also serve as proxy colonizers for "real" Europeans, bringing enlightened German culture to the uncivilized native inhabitants of the land.[119]

Aesthetics and style played an important role in Herzl's political fancies, including the integral role clothing played in the refashioning of self. Although references to sartorial styles and their effect on an individual's bearing are scarce in Herzl's writings, those instances in which explicit mention of clothing is made are telling because of the manner in which they fit into his wider discussions of self-ennoblement. In his pamphlet on the establishment of a Jewish national state, for example, Herzl proposed that prior to their departure from European ports, the poor, un-acculturated emigrants—the Zionist pioneers who would serve as the state's first citizens—would be provided with new clothing, not "as alms, which might hurt their pride, but in exchange for old garments," imbuing the emigrants with "the symbolic meaning 'You are now entering a new life.'"[120]

The year following the publication of his 1896 treatise, Herzl insisted that delegates to the First Zionist Congress in Basel dress in white tie, claiming that "festive clothing makes most people stiff. From this stiffness a respectful tone emerged."[121] Both his sartorial choices and the manner in which Herzl has been visually depicted confirm his attitudes toward clothing and behavior. Admirers remarked on Herzl's noble and "oriental" appearance, especially in relation to his full, "Assyrian" beard. Turning away from his youthful antisemitism as a *Burschenschaftler*, in 1929 Hermann Bahr would romanticize his first encounter with young Herzl, describing an "assyrischen schönen Jüngling," (Assyrian, beautiful youth), reflecting widespread attitudes (among Jews and Gentiles) toward Jews as an oriental people.[122] Yet, whether much of Herzl's image was self-constructed needs to be tested against the role of visual conventions in shaping depictions, either via portrait photographers or by means of other visual artists.

Arthur Kamczycki explores the development of Herzl's noble image through artistic representation. The Galician-born German Zionist graphic artist Ephraim Moses Lilien (1874–1925) frequently depicted Herzl in biblically themed illustrations. The images ignored Herzl's role as cosmopolitan journalist and political lobbyist, instead showing him in the guise of biblical figures of power and esteem, such as Moses, Joshua, the High Priest Aaron, angels from various biblical episodes, and powerfully built slaves and farmers in a combination of contemporary Bedouin and ancient Assyrian attire.[123] In presenting Herzl as the personification of these Israelite heroes, Lilien's image not only expresses the hope of a future Jewish return to the land of their ancestors but also presents the Zionist foundations laid by Herzl in biblical proportions (Figure 3.14).[124] Lilien's choice to dress these Herzlian figures in styles resembling contemporary Bedouin attire rather than historical clothing is not an accident.[125] By presenting the Zionist leader in stylized contemporary Levantine garb, the division between Herzl's highly tailored appearance and the Zionist notion of Jewish return to the land of their ancestors

Figure 3.14 Ephraim Moses Lilien, *Moses*, 1908. Courtesy of Alamy.

is diminished. Here Herzl's Jewish—that is to say, "foreign" or "oriental"—identity is brought to the forefront to argue the case for Jewish Statehood in Palestine.

There is a peculiar contrast in Lilien's naked, scantily clad, and oriental-garbed depictions of the Zionist leader—a strong, sculpted body drawing allusions to Greek mythology and contemporaneous naturalist cultures celebrating male virility and strength[126]—and Herzl's polished sartorial identity. By representing heroes of Jewish history through Herzl's personage, Lilien created a direct link between contemporaneous discourse on Jewish national (spiritual and physical) revival with its demands of redemption through physical labor, and the urban gentility of Herzl's milieu, a milieu completely unsuited to the physicality his discourse called for. Herzl himself was typical of Vienna's Jewish *Kaffeehausliteraten* (coffeehouse literati), a demographic he would criticize in *Altneuland*. The Zionist journalist, Erich Burin, ridiculed this segment of German (including Austrian) Jewry, chastising the lethargy of so-called "*Kaffeehausjuden*" (coffeehouse Jews) steeped in "Gojim naches" as the antithesis to the healthy individual who thrives with physical exercise amidst nature.[127]

Lilien was not the only Jewish artist who cast biblical allusions onto representations of the Viennese Zionist leader. Richard I. Cohen notes that the 1908 portrait of Herzl by Polish-Jewish artist Leopold Pilichowski (1869–1933) was inspired by earlier representations of Moses (Figure 3.15).[128] Cohen describes the manner in which Herzl is dressed: in ceremonial black, his hat and cane in his left hand, "overlooking the Promised Land, to which his right hand points limply."[129] The overall mood is somber and even a little foreboding. The dark landscape behind Herzl is certainly no land flowing with milk and honey, as described in the Torah, but, rather, gloomy and swamp-like, as many early Zionist pioneers found it after arriving in the latter decades of the nineteenth century. Perhaps the large body of water Herzl stands above is the Sea of Galilee, and the gloomy landscape a reference to *fin-de-siècle* Zionist efforts to rid the areas of Jewish settlement of malaria by draining the swamps.[130] In this manner, the detail of Herzl's figure in contrast to the more abstract representation of the landscape, such as his regal stance, the serious expression on his face, and his tailored European attire, suggests a wish to recreate the land in the Zionist image.

Unlike Lilien's illustrations depicting Herzl in art nouveau styles swathed in Levantine robes or Assyrian regalia (when dressed), in harmony with an orientalist depiction of Palestine, Pilichowski's subject is dressed in a manner more accurately representative of Herzl's clothing habits. Here the Zionist founding father, proudly surveying the land, appears in the guise of eighteenth- and nineteenth-century European "explorers," divorced sartorially, culturally, and ideologically from the object of their colonizing efforts. However, Pilichowski's sartorial representation of Herzl is not far from the truth. Although dressed in regal black—tonally reminiscent of the seventeenth-century Spanish fashions present in Dutch portraits of male respectability and power—the formality of European dress as divorced from the reality of Levantine cultures can be observed in those photographs taken during Herzl's 1898 tour of Ottoman Palestine. In one photograph taken prior to an audience with the German Kaiser Wilhelm II (Figure 3.16), Herzl poses solemnly with other similarly dressed members of the

Figure 3.15 Leopold Pilichowski, *Portrait of Theodor Herzl*, 1908. Courtesy of Alamy.

Figure 3.16 Theodor Herzl (middle) with members of the Zionist delegation (L-R: Joseph Seidner, Moses T. Schnirer, Max Bodenheimer, David Wolffsohn) in Jerusalem before an audience with Kaiser Wilhelm II (1898). Courtesy of Alamy.

Figure 3.17 Portrait of Theodor Herzl, published by Verlag Max Jaffé, Vienna, *c.* 1902. Pf 6123 E1. Courtesy of Wiener Bildarchiv/Österreichische Nationalbibliothek, Vienna.

Zionist delegation before the walls of Jerusalem and the Tower of David. Standing in eveningwear beneath a clear sky and amidst the harsh Levantine landscape of dry shrubs and rubble, it is apparent that Pilichowski's portrait is no exaggeration. Adopting *Frack* and *Zylinder* as the uniform for his role as a Zionist "statesman," Herzl's common clothing does not differ in tone. The sobriety of attire—what John Carl Flügel referred to as the "Great Masculine Renunciation"[131]—was by no means exclusive to Herzl. His colleagues are dressed in the same manner, the formality of their dress an influence of the ideals of *Bildung* and *Sittlichkeit* and their corresponding translation into sartorial self-fashioning. This sober masculine style was not one of simplicity. Rather, there is a sense of dandyish precision in Herzl's dress patterns; his attire is carefully selected for the situation at hand, in this case to declare his role as a self-styled statesman and the perceived "nobility" and importance of his task.

Although he regularly appeared attired in monochrome, there was both diversity and intent in his sartorial styling. One particular photographic portrait of Herzl is worth mentioning. Taken at the turn of the century, the photograph is important not only because of the man it depicts but also because of the solemnity and dignity it conveys (Figure 3.17). The image was considered so iconic that it was later cropped and used as a de facto official portrait of Herzl and hung in the so-called Independence Hall in Tel Aviv (at the time a room in the Tel Aviv Museum of Art) where David Ben Gurion declared Israeli Independence on May 14, 1948 (Figure 3.18). The uncropped, original image presents Herzl standing in three-quarter profile, his hands gripping the back of a

Figure 3.18 David Ben Gurion declaring independence of the State of Israel beneath a portrait of Theodor Herzl, Tel Aviv, May 14, 1948. Courtesy of Alamy.

chair while he stares contemplatively ahead. Although his clothing here is similar to that worn in other portraits, it is representative of the public dressed identity he wished to convey: a black frock coat with half-satin lapels, lapelled waistcoat, high white collar, and black bow tie. This outfit is not an evening *Frack* for a formal setting but rather the more casual version used for business, presenting Herzl as a man of action. Herzl decisively chose the dandified black of self-styled nobility.[132] With his elegantly stark attire and stern countenance, Herzl conveys the noble dignity he wished to instill in the refashioned Jewish nation and the seriousness of this mission. Gripping the back of the chair, he stares thoughtfully ahead, perhaps ruminating on the future of his "nation." In addition to his dress, other aspects of his styled appearance, such as his neatly brushed hair and long graying beard, express a sense of seniority, wisdom, and respectability. Kamczycki attests to the important role that Herzl's beard played in his self-ennoblement.[133] In the final decade of the nineteenth century, while living in Paris at a time when the culture of ancient Mesopotamia was fashionable, Herzl grew a full "Mesopotamian" beard. In this way, Herzl attempted to adapt to local, Parisian fashions. Upon returning to Vienna where his "oriental" beard visibly marked him as non-German, that is to say, as Jewish, his newly acquired hirsute appearance made a clear and unabashed statement about his Jewish self-identification.[134] Herzl's revised "Jewish" appearance at this time corresponded to his changing views on the Jewish Question and stood in contrast to both his former German-styled grooming and his unsavory opinions about his coreligionists.[135]

*   *   *

The sartorial identity of Viennese rabbis and other public Jewish figures during the late nineteenth and early twentieth centuries came about alongside a series of deliberate strategies of Jewish modernization. In adhering to the professional modes of their colleagues in other European societies, Viennese rabbis both knowingly and involuntarily signified their dedication to the ideals of European intercultural exchange that were an important part of the tenets of *Bildung* held dear by their bourgeois congregants. By donning a specific rabbinical uniform, with slight variations, that was also worn by their colleagues in London, Amsterdam, Rome, Paris, or Hamburg that clearly marked their Jewish identification, Viennese rabbis were in effect perpetuating the antisemitic stereotype of the rootless Jewish cosmopolitan. Their garb may have resembled those of their Christian counterparts of varying denominations, but its distinctiveness as the uniform of Jewish faith leaders highlighted their separateness from local leaders of other faiths, instead drawing them closer to their Jewish colleagues and congregations beyond Austria's borders. Thus, it can be argued that the idea of demonstrating and being part of a deliberate strategy of Jewish modernization—by the Orthodox, Galicians, and prominent acculturated "German" Jews— often had negative repercussions for the image of the Jew within antisemitic discourse as will be explored in the following chapters. In the attempt to modernize their attire and grooming, Viennese Jews often found themselves in a sartorial paradigm that would be perceived as somehow "Jewish," regardless of its more universal elements.

As the example of Joseph Samuel Bloch has shown, and in spite of his rabbinical uniform in the synagogue, his sartorial identity in other arenas was typical of urban, middle-class Viennese and thus a demonstration of his self-perception and that of the society. However, his typical bourgeois dress made little difference to his overall image. Although his professional role as rabbi of the Floridsdorf congregation and its corresponding uniform formed only one part of his multifaceted public identity, it was for his public status as a Jew of note that Bloch came to be recognized. Bloch's "Jewish" public roles as rabbi and campaigner against antisemitism linked him to the broad network of Jewry beyond the borders of Austria-Hungary, rather than to the Austrian political arena within which he struggled for equality for all peoples of the Dual Monarchy. This serves as a contrast to Herzl and his visibly Jewish (albeit non-traditional) appearance, perhaps a visual manifestation of his exclusively "Jewish" nationalist agenda. In this regard, their respective backgrounds are not insignificant in their approaches to Jewishness within the context of nationhood: Bloch, the self-taught and refashioned Eastern Jew and proud Austrian, and Herzl, the German-oriented, bourgeois Western Jew turned Jewish nationalist.

CHAPTER 4
STRANGERS IN THE CITY
"ROOTLESS" JEWS AND URBANITY IN VIENNA

In 1890, a poem titled "Die armen Antisemiten" ("The Poor Antisemites") appeared in the satirical Viennese magazine *Kikeriki*, lamenting the "Judaization" of society:

Alles verjudet, alles verjudet,
Ihr habet wahrlich Recht,
Die Astronomie schon ist verjudet,
Sie wird zum Judenknecht.
Nun will als Normalzeit man erwählen
Wie ist Euch das unbequem,
Und an Protesten wird's Euch nicht fehlen:
Den Meridian von—"Jerusalem"![1]

The author's use of the term *"Normalzeit"* was a likely reference to standardized time that came with the expansion of long-distance train services.[2] It is no coincidence that the beginnings of mass migration to Vienna from its far-flung provinces coincided with the advent of rail travel in Austria (later, Austria-Hungary). While the early decades of the nineteenth century saw the development of local horse-drawn railways, it was not until the 1830s that Austria opened its first long-distance railway (Vienna to Kraków) operating with steam-powered locomotives. The remainder of the century saw the construction of additional railways linking the capital to its provincial centers. While early railways were financed by industrialists, notably Salomon Mayer von Rothschild, founder of the Austrian branch of the prominent Jewish banking family, the state began nationalizing railways toward the middle of the century and continued to invest in further constructions during the century's remainder.[3] The greater mobility rail travel afforded Austria-Hungary's population was a central factor in the state's modernization and the transformation of Vienna from the relatively small seat of Habsburg power to the centralized metropolis it was by the eve of the First World War. The anxiety surrounding the "Judaization" of Vienna was linked not only to the increased migration of Jews to the capital but also to the involvement of Jews in the railway's development and its transnational reach. As Kurt Grunwald asserts:

> utilizing their almost proverbial international connections with relatives and business associates in other countries, they [the Jewish entrepreneurs] made an important contribution to the evolution of an international capital market

and substantially assisted the infra-structural development of the economically backward parts of the continent.[4]

Jews, of course, were not the only migrants who were attracted by the social, economic, and cultural opportunities life in the capital offered. However, their increasing presence in the city was duly noted and their visibility in daily life was in part responsible for emerging negative images of Vienna, as highlighted in scurrilous caricatures, sketches, and poems published in the satirical press. While Vienna had always attracted migrants from across Europe, earlier bans on Jewish residency in the city as well as many of Austria's other German provinces rendered their presence negligible. With the emancipation of Habsburg Jewry in 1867, Jews were permitted to settle anywhere in the empire. While small communities formed among other Austro-German locales, Vienna remained the dominant center of Jewish life and culture in Austria's German provinces. Vienna, with its large (and growing) Jewish population, came to be seen by inhabitants of the relatively *Judenfrei* German provinces as teeming with Jews. Already in the 1870s, Franz Friedrich Masaidek referred to Vienna as "*Neu-Jerusalem*" (New Jerusalem) and sarcastically noted the presence of "*deutsche Eindringlinge*" (German intruders).[5] In truth, although Vienna's Jewish population had grown from less than one thousand at the beginning of the nineteenth century to 146,926 at the beginning of the twentieth, the city's overall population had grown as well. Consequently, over the course of the nineteenth century, Jews never accounted for more than 10.1 percent of the total population.[6] Even during the early 1920s, when the number of Viennese Jews was at its highest point (201,513), Jews accounted for only 10.8 percent of the city's population.[7]

This chapter analyzes the notion of Jewry and cosmopolitanism and its alienating effect on the image of "the Jew" in Gentile society. The urban/rural binary was especially pronounced during the interwar period when Austria's Jewish population was largely confined to Vienna (in contrast to Bohemia, Moravia, and Galicia during the Habsburg era) and in light of the fact that Jews now functioned as the ethnic minority par excellence amidst an overly Austro-German population. This is examined through patterns of attire of Viennese Jewish visitors to the Austrian provinces using examples of photography, written descriptions, and literary fiction, including Hugo Bettauer's 1922 satirical novel *Die Stadt ohne Juden* (*The City without Jews*). Meanings of clothing and "fashion" within an urban/rural binary were significant here. The symbolic meanings of the suit and rural folk costumes are compared and contrasted in order to analyze their respective roles in both Jewish self-fashioning and in the perpetuation of external, negative perceptions of Jewish men as "rootless" cosmopolitans who belonged in neither the "German" provinces nor the supposedly "Jewish" city of Vienna.

Vienna: A Cosmopolitan *Weltstadt*

From 1850 to the end of the century, the Austrian capital and its population swelled from a small, walled city to a bustling metropolis. The first step on the path to Vienna's expansion saw the incorporation of the *Vorstädte* (suburbs) between the walled city and the Linienwall, the eighteenth-century city fortifications between the suburbs and outlying villages. This was followed by Franz Joseph I's decision to raze the city walls and commission the building of the Ringstrasse in 1857, thereby connecting the old city to the newly incorporated districts (II–IX). Although fashioned as a grand boulevard encircling the historical city center, the Ringstrasse did little to bridge the gap between old and new. For most, with its administrative buildings and palaces (*Ringstraßenpalais*) of the nobility and newly wealthy financial élite, the Ringstrasse simply served as a substitute for the old walls.[8] In his scathing attack on the *Kaiserstadt's* new grand boulevard with its government buildings and palaces constructed in a mixture of conflicting historicizing styles (which included Greek revival, neo-baroque, neo-renaissance and neo-gothic), Adolf Loos decried the Ringstrasse, declaring it had transformed Vienna into a "*Potemkin'sche Stadt*" (Potemkin City)—a laughing stock of the modern world.[9]

Despite Loos's misgivings, the city continued to act as a magnet that drew both migrants and tourists alike. The grand, sweeping Ringstrasse, a thoroughfare through which visitors and locals alike could marvel at the imposing surrounding buildings and upon which the city held numerous parades and pageants, served as a stage where the individual could parade themselves before and within a new urban society.[10] Throughout the remainder of the nineteenth century, the villages beyond the city limits were incorporated as new districts and the Linienwall, separating them from the rest of the city, was demolished and replaced with the Gürtel, the Vienna Beltway, another ring-like road. With this newly expanded city area and population drawn to it, architects set about designing new projects, both public buildings and private residences, to transform the dual capital of the Austro-Hungarian Empire into a world-class metropolis.

By the end of the century, Vienna, which had already become a center for economic, scientific, cultural, and artistic development, was fast becoming a *Weltstadt* (metropolis). During the *Gründerzeit*, businessmen and their families flocked to the Austrian capital, taking advantage of its geographic centrality to conduct their affairs and manage concerns throughout the empire. With their newfound wealth, they commissioned celebrated architects from across Europe—of note, the Viennese Heinrich von Ferstel (1828–83), the Bavarian-born Ludwig Förster (1797–1863), and the Danish Theophil von Hansen (1813–91)—to design luxury city palaces and apartment houses.[11] Eager to prove themselves worthy and equal members of the élite, these newly-rich families, many of whom were Jewish, also used their wealth to purchase and commission artworks from Vienna's leading artists, both established and avant-garde, such as Hans Makart (1840–84) and Gustav Klimt (1862–1918).[12]

The assertion of identification was not simply a matter of proving the worth of the nouveau-riche in the face of "old money." For Jewish magnates in particular, the resurgence of antisemitism that came with the rise in nationalist sentiment in the wake of the 1873 stock market crash meant that the refashioning of identity could also involve the development of new identities—neither Jewish nor German—in the absence of an overarching Austrian one, save for loyalty to the Kaiser. The nonexistence of an overarching Austrian national identity was manifested in the tendency of Habsburg subjects to identify with the varying ethno-linguistic groups that made up the multiethnic Dual Monarchy.[13] For the most part, Viennese Jews were fiercely loyal to German culture, Franz Joseph, and the Austrian state. Refashioning themselves as modern Austrians served Viennese Jews of varying cultural and socioeconomic backgrounds well, helping them deal with exclusions from increasingly hostile and nationalistically defined group identification, and in many ways gave them an answer to the absence of an Austrian national identity.[14]

In *fin-de-siècle* and interwar Vienna, as in much of Central and Eastern Europe, terms such as "cosmopolitan" and "international" were often used as euphemisms for "Jewish."[15] This was influenced by a number of factors, not least the "transnational" character of European Jews. Although they were loyal Austrians and dedicated participants in German culture, Viennese Jews maintained familial, professional, religious, and even cultural ties to Jews in other cities and towns of the empire and beyond its borders. While Jews were by no means the empire's only ethnic group to maintain extra-national ethnic or cultural networks, a prime difference between them and other ethnicities was their lack of territorial claims within the borders. They were, in the minds of many, a rootless, non-European people.[16]

Citing the eighteenth-century French philosopher Denis Diderot, Margaret C. Jacob characterizes the figure of the cosmopolitan as "a stranger nowhere in the world."[17] However, given the negative connotations of cosmopolitanism in the context of antisemitism, it is more fitting to consider the opposite: a stranger everywhere in the world, as a reflection of Zygmunt Bauman's notion of the stranger as the embodiment of ambivalence:

> There is hardly an anomaly more anomalous than the stranger. He stands *between* friend and enemy, order and chaos, the inside and the outside. He stands *for* the treacherousness of friends, for the cunning of disguise of the enemies, for fallibility of order, vulnerability of the inside.[18]

However, Viennese Jews did not characterize themselves as strangers in their city. Despite the ties they shared with Jews beyond the empire's borders, their complete emancipation in 1867 made them fiercely loyal to the empire and its monarch.[19] Likewise, the process of acculturation that had begun with the Josephinian Edicts of Toleration at the end of the eighteenth century created a strong sense of familiarity and belonging in German culture. Cosmopolitanism among Jews—in the manner of being "worldly," that is culturally informed—can be understood as the result of the Haskalah and the dedication to the ideals of *Bildung* it inspired.

Michael L. Miller and Scott Ury raise the question of dual Jewish (the specific national) and cosmopolitan (the international) identities in light of a perceived assimilationist drive in cosmopolitanism.[20] Being cosmopolitan did not mean an individual abandoned his or her "roots" or culture in favor of others. Historically, urban European Jews were seen as cosmopolitan not in spite of their Jewishness, but because of it. Jews were perceived as cosmopolitan due to their supposed rootlessness, their urban residential patterns (insinuating a lack of connection with the "land"), and their tendency to make themselves at home in different societies, as well as maintaining professional practices and relationships with other Jews across national and political borders.[21] Stefan Zweig, for example, was considered a cosmopolitan due to his dedication to "internationalism,"[22] and although not religiously observant, took a keen interest in his Jewishness and issues relating to it.[23]

But what was the relationship of accusations of "cosmopolitanism" and "rootlessness" to dress, particularly the dress of urban Jews? If the cosmopolitan stranger makes a point of engaging with cultures different from his or her own—that is to say, takes an "international" outlook—then it follows that cosmopolitan dress patterns and styles will incorporate elements of other cultures.[24] The sartorial habits of acculturated, middle-class Viennese Jews as members of the wider middle class resembled styles favored by their contemporaries in other major urban centers. The relative uniformity of male dress fashions in modern cities across Europe attests to what Eduard Fuchs referred to as the political power of the bourgeoisie.[25] The standardization of bourgeois dress was international and a result of industrialization, which erased national difference and created a sartorial "bourgeois social order."[26] Fuchs argued in 1902 that the dominance of London in the world of male fashion was a result of England's dominant role in the development of bourgeois thought and culture, as well as London having "become the true enduring metropolis of the bourgeois world."[27] This puts things into perspective regarding the role of Jews in the bourgeoisie. In late nineteenth and early twentieth-century England, Jews were a small minority (and a minority in the English bourgeoisie), most having arrived as poor migrants fleeing persecution and economic hardship in the Pale of Settlement.[28] How then, if England is historically linked with the development of the bourgeoisie, did the Jew become representative of that class in the German-speaking world? The answer lies in the Jew's visibility as a member of the middle class, and that class's visibility in public life.

The public/private binary and its impact on bourgeois culture has been an important structuring device in much cultural investigation, but its simplicity makes it problematic and open to critique.[29] The personas that developed in the public and private arenas did not exist in a binary model, but rather as a fluid continuum that adapted to the setting in which the individual found themselves. In *fin-de-siècle* Vienna, the self-fashioning of bourgeois personas was strongly influenced by the body inhabiting public arenas including the street, workplaces, retail establishments, and coffeehouse. The public sphere afforded the individual an opportunity to construct and perform an ideal self, as Tag Gronberg emphasizes:

> *Selbstdarstellung*, the public and theatricalized representation of the self, has often been cited as a distinctive feature of nineteenth- and turn-of-the-century Vienna as an urban stage, as a city structured for, and by, the display of the self. The daily afternoon stroll (*Korso*) along the Ringstrasse epitomized this culture of appearance.[30]

The intimacy of the home played a similar role in the fashioning of private personas.[31] Although scholars have addressed the notion of contesting public and private personas that developed through cultural forms such as architecture, decorative arts, and literature,[32] clothing and the spaces in which they are worn have also played an important role in defining these identities. Architects such as Josef Hoffmann and his rival Adolf Loos were acutely aware of this. Their designs for houses and apartment renovations made use of different textures that fostered a sense of theatricality—in the case of Hoffmann interiors—and *Gemütlichkeit* (coziness or congeniality)—in the case of Loos—providing patrons with a kind of stage upon which they might perform a carefully constructed persona within the family sphere or else to their guests.

While the space through which the body moved or came into contact with was an important vehicle for the refashioning of self, clothing, which came into direct contact with the body, was doubly important for the manner in which an individual both perceived him- or herself and was perceived by others. Wrapped in clothing, the body is not separate from its sartorial trappings, but is inherently defined by them—what Anne Hollander characterizes as the complete body.[33] Different clothing styles came to denote different meanings and were thus adopted for the different situations in which the individual found themselves. Diderot, for example, addressed this notion of privacy and comfortable clothing in a lament for his discarded dressing gown.[34] More than simply a eulogy for a garment that made him feel secure and fostered creative productivity, Diderot's discarded dressing gown encapsulates the notion that different garments carry different contextual meanings. His two dressing gowns, as garments worn in the intimacy of the home, denote not only the private sphere but also his craft as a writer carried out in this space, as opposed to the publicity of the street. Although Diderot wrote his essay in the eighteenth century, the idea of intimate clothing that he addressed developed further throughout the following century.

Outside the private sphere, public institutions like the coffeehouse served multiple purposes including the development of bourgeois culture, fostering cosmopolitanism, and modernizing Jewry. A counterpart to the intimacy of the home or salon, the coffeehouse had long been a site of socialization, information sharing, cultural development, and masculine bonding. Loos recognized the coffeehouse's importance in his modernizing efforts and sought to harness the institution's existing role in male self-fashioning in his coffeehouse designs.[35] For acculturating Jews, this very "Viennese" institution was equally important to their own self-fashioning. As a liminal environment between the private sphere of the home and the public arena of the street, the *Wiener Kaffeehaus* served as a refuge from both the intolerance of wider society and the traditional Jewish milieu many of them had abandoned.[36]

In contrast to the home where an individual was able to invite guests into his or her intimate sphere, the coffeehouse was a public space individuals were able to visit without receiving an invitation. Although a public arena that was (technically) open to men of different class backgrounds, the *Wiener Kaffeehaus* as an intimate realm of human socialization sat on the border between public and private spheres. The coffeehouse was a primarily interior space removed from the highly public arena of the street (although some coffeehouses did offer seating on the pavement in front of the establishment, known locally as a *Schanigarten*). Within, patrons were afforded the possibilities to interact with each other or else remain solitary spectators. The intimacy of the coffeehouse was significant in fostering a sense of fraternity among male patrons and was vital to the fashioning of new gendered and classed personas.[37] The sense of *Gemütlichkeit*, combined with the twin ideals of *Bildung* and *Sittlichkeit*, was fostered through the relationship between dress and spatial design, the architecture/fashion nexus that has been addressed by scholars such as Elana Shapira and Mark Wigley.[38] As already pointed out in Chapter 2, to Loos, the fashioning of modern male identities, indeed any modern identity, encapsulated all facets of the designed, including, most importantly, clothing and space. In his advice to "modern men," he encouraged a harmony of aesthetics based on pure and simple design.

In 1899, Loos was commissioned to design the interior and façade of the modernist Café Museum,[39] which architectural historian Panayotis Tournikiotis asserts was designed to reproduce "classical" Viennese coffeehouses of the 1830s.[40] Café Museum served as a meeting point for a number of Viennese and foreign writers, including those who were engaged in the development of Jewish national literary culture through their writings in Hebrew and Yiddish.[41] This multilingual literary activity, of course, fits into the cosmopolitan narrative of the coffeehouse as a junction between cultures, languages, and ethnicities reflected in the "founding myth" of the *Wiener Kaffeehaus*.[42] Like his design for the Goldman & Salatsch boutique and workshop three years earlier, the design of Café Museum marked an important point in Loos's career. It served as an architectural reflection of Loos's sartorial image; in the words of Elana Shapira, it "served as a distinguished business card that reflected Loos's correct self-presentation."[43] Utilizing design motifs and typologies of architecture associated with a gentlemen's club, and "fashionable" prints by the American artist Charles Dana Gibson in the café's eponymous back room (designed as a ladies' parlor),[44] Loos made a clear statement on the perceived masculinity of the coffeehouse. But it was not through Loos's architectural design alone that the importance of masculine self-fashioning was addressed. Although not always explicitly referenced in his designs, sartorial self-fashioning played a central role in Loos's performance of identity. This meant that dress was deeply embedded in all aspects of his endeavor to design the modern man, even when not obvious.

Several years later (in 1907–8) Loos designed his American Bar (also known as the "Kärntner Bar") in a side passage off the Kärntnerstrasse in Vienna's first district. More than his previous coffeehouse design, Loos's American Bar actively engaged with questions of male identity and cosmopolitanism in *fin-de-siècle* Vienna due to the design of the space, specifically his use of colors, lighting, choice of textiles and other materials, and the manner in which they dealt with issues of gender and public space.[45] While coffeehouses did not make a habit of prohibiting entry to female patrons, Loos's American Bar actively enforced a policy of male-only patronage.[46] In contrast to the homosocial feminine environment of the *Kaffeehaus*, Loos's new bar offered

an alternative space to the coffeehouse—a male sanctum influenced by the model of American bars and British gentlemen's clubs, in which Loos uses a masculine architectural language to both articulate a stance in opposition to the ornamental decorative "feminine" style of the Secessionists, and to provide a setting in which the social structure of coffeehouse culture is redefined to exclude women.[47]

Writing for the *Wiener Allgemeine Zeitung* (February 22, 1909), Peter Altenberg defended the prohibition against female patrons, based on what he considered unsuitable furnishings for the female body, its dressed appearance, and performance of femininity.[48] By designing a public house that followed what he believed to be modern American standards of design, Loos wished to create a space akin to the liminal site of the coffeehouse, in which men could fashion a new form of masculinity on a blank plane unencumbered by the "fairer sex," by the femininity of Secession style, or by traditional Viennese modes of masculinity. Rather, in line with his overall views about male style and behavior, Loos took the example of the Anglophone world in rejecting the localized *Schlamperei* (slovenliness) of Vienna's cultural milieu and orienting the city with the international.[49]

The ambiguity of the coffeehouse that Loos sought to address in his own designs played a crucial role in developing the image of Viennese bourgeois culture beyond both the private sphere of the home and the public sphere of the street during the second half of the nineteenth century. As a space neither entirely public nor private, the coffeehouse was an appropriate setting for the development of "alternative" cultures that did not fit into the accepted canon of dominant or national cultures. Numerous texts have highlighted the importance of the coffeehouse both in the metamorphosis of Central European Jews into modern Europeans and in the simultaneous development and assertion of Jewish identification in the Austrian capital.[50] But the strong Jewish presence in the coffeehouse was not welcomed in all quarters. In May 1900, a piece appeared in the feuilleton section of the *Wiener Zeitung* under the title "Wiener Kaffeehäuser" penned by the paper's chief editor Friedrich Uhl. In the piece, Uhl romanticized the *Kaffeehäuser* of past times—of *Alt-Wien*, a time associated with Biedermeier *Gemütlichkeit*—highlighting the period between 1830 and 1870.[51] There is subtle subtext concerning the change in nature of the *Kaffeehaus* after 1870. This period in which Austrian Liberalism reigned supreme saw a greater civic integration of Jews into Viennese society and the exponential growth of the Cisleithanian capital's Jewish population.[52] With their integration into Viennese society, Jews became a more visible element in the public sphere, including coffeehouses.

The idea that the coffeehouse was a fertile ground for the cultivation of artistic and intellectual discourse was not a development of the *fin de siècle*. The coffeehouse evolved as one of the significant sites in the development of the public sphere throughout the seventeenth and eighteenth centuries,[53] and continued into the nineteenth century as a site of male socialization and information sharing. The coffeehouse's role in the social milieu of Vienna's Jews is noteworthy. With the abandonment by many Viennese Jews of their traditional religious practices, Steven Beller observes that the coffeehouse became a secular replacement for the synagogue and *Beth Midrash* (house of study), traditional sites of masculine Jewish socialization and learning, creating consequences for the image of Viennese coffeehouses in general.[54] Indeed, the prevalence of Jewish coffeehouse patrons can be understood as a result of the coffeehouse's public status where no one was barred entry, in contrast to other social arenas, such as the Habsburg court, aristocratic salons, or nationalistic *Burschenschaften* (student fraternities).[55] Mary Gluck argues that the coffeehouse, existing between the private and public realms, "created a new public space receptive to protean, destabilizing energies of modern life."[56] In this alternative public arena, the notion of Jewish difference, indeed, the perceived oriental nature of Jews in European society, was able to exist in harmony with the myths surrounding the genesis of Viennese coffeehouses. Coffeehouse orientalism provided a fertile environment in which the Jew could exist as an "insider" and not an alien Other.[57] The coffeehouse was a venue that did not bar patrons from entry based on ethnic or religious background; hence many urban Jewish men flocked there, both to socialize and conduct business.[58] As a result, as highlighted by Uhl's short essay, the *fin-de-siècle* coffeehouse developed a particular "Jewish" coding. In contrast, the *Heuriger*—the "provincial" wine garden on the city's outskirts—was seen as "ultra-Aryan" and a refuge from the "Jewish" urban environment.[59]

Visualizations of *fin-de-siècle* Viennese coffeehouses offer a compelling view into the nature of male socialization in Vienna with regard to the insider/outsider status of coffeehouse patrons. Carl von Zamboni's photograph of Vienna's Café Griensteidl, taken prior to 1897, that first appeared in the Viennese illustrated newspaper *Die vornehme Welt*, depicts male patrons in the coffeehouse's salon (Figure 4.1). Despite its designation as a coffeehouse, there appears to be little actual drinking of coffee taking place. In fact,

Figure 4.1 Photograph of Café Griensteidl by Carl von Zamboni for the illustrated newspaper *Die vornehme Welt*, before 1897. Wien Museum Inv.-Nr. 98654/2, CC0. Courtesy of Wien Museum, Vienna.

among the pile of newspapers strewn haphazardly across the center table, only glasses of water—complimentary with a customer's order of coffee—appear. It has been argued that the actual consumption of coffee was secondary to the main function of the coffeehouse: a site for recreation, social interaction, and dissemination of ideas.[60] In this manner, Uhl described the coffeehouse's superiority to other similar venues (such as taverns and beer and wine gardens) in its ability to facilitate the socialization of its patrons—no doubt free of the effects of alcohol:

> Man geht zum Bier, man geht zum Wein, man geht zum Nachtmahl, und das Kaffeehaus besucht man weniger und vor Allem des Plauderns willen. Die Wiener liebten und lieben die Gesellschaft, sind am liebsten heiter mit den Heiteren. Das Kaffeetrinken in Kaffeehause [sic] war ihnen eigentlich Nebensache.[61]

> (One goes out for a beer, a wine, or for dinner, but less so to the coffeehouse [for refreshment], where one goes primarily for a chat. The Viennese have always loved—and still do—being in the company of others, are always cheerful, but best among the cheerful. Thus, actually drinking coffee at the coffeehouse has always been of less importance to them.)

The men in Zamboni's photograph might serve as a visualization of what Uhl describes. These men, middle-aged and elderly, sit at their tables, caught in mid-conversation, reading an issue from the complimentary array of international and local periodicals, a few peering at the camera's lens in a bemused manner. They are dressed in ubiquitous dark lounge suits and leather shoes. Although the lounge suit—generally black or of other muted colors—of the late nineteenth and early twentieth centuries became a uniform of sober, modern masculine respectability across professional and class boundaries,[62] the occupants of this photograph are by no means identically dressed. Darker jackets are paired with trousers in lighter fabrics, while some of the men wear suits of what appear to be matching fabrics. Lapel height and style vary among the coffeehouse patrons as do jacket lengths. Variety can also be seen in the cut of each man's collar, or whether he wears a necktie, cravat, or bow tie around his neck. Heads are bare, as is appropriate for an indoor setting, with hats and coats hung by the back wall. A sole behatted figure wearing the *Zylinder*, popular among men in Europe and its colonies during the period, hovers in the doorway—either arriving or leaving. All men have grown some form of facial hair; most sport a moustache, but a few have short, neatly trimmed beards. The *Sitzkassiererin* (female cashier) provides a contrast to this hirsute masculinity, standing among four men in the doorway, to this male-dominated environment.

As sites of Jewish socialization, there was a connection between the Synagogue and the *Kaffeehaus*, drawn through the similarity of dress styles worn in both. The sartorial styles adopted by the men in Zamboni's photograph resemble those portrayed by the Jewish artist Emil Ranzenhofer (1864–1930) in a series of watercolors depicting Viennese synagogues—not the small, Orthodox prayer rooms frequented by Vienna's Galician immigrants, but the large, palatial synagogues or "temples" that catered to the Jewish upper and middle classes.[63] The construction of such exquisite palatial synagogues—in Vienna and other European cities—during the nineteenth century can be understood as a symbol of the confidence in and expectations of their position in wider European society that Jews maintained. Architectural historian Rudolf Klein asserts that "there has seldom been such a strong and constant link between architecture and ethnic, religious and cultural identity as there was in the synagogues that the emancipated Jews erected."[64]

Like Zamboni's coffeehouse photograph, Ranzenhofer's synagogue interiors present an absence of women. The figures who dominate are men, dressed in frock coats and a variety of hats—top hats, bowlers, homburgs—for a Jewish man must keep his head covered in the "house of God," unlike in the coffeehouse, with prayer shawls thrown over their shoulders as they pray in their pews as part of the *minyan* (prayer quorum). In this series of paintings, the women's gallery in the balconies above the men's sanctuary remains ominously vacant, perhaps a reference to the supposedly masculine nature of the synagogue (Figure 4.2). At the very least, these male-dominated images might be understood to comment on the active participation of men in Orthodox synagogal proceedings, in the face of the passive female role.[65] Women appear in one scene depicting a marriage ceremony in the Moorish-revival *Synagoge in der Tempelgasse* (also known as the *Leopoldstädter Tempel*). In this scene they are in the background and out of focus, albeit in brightly colored frocks, in sharp contrast to the dull grays and browns of the men (Figure 4.3).

The types of clothing depicted in Ranzenhofer's synagogue interiors are the typical bourgeois styles of male sobriety and respectability, and do not in any way appear particular to a religious setting. Eric Silverman observes that Jews have long reserved their best clothing for the synagogue, especially on high holidays.[66] While such a practice of dressing may have been more apparent in the context of the shtetl,[67] in cosmopolitan Vienna where standard fashions prevailed among the Jewish middle class, as among others, the distinction between clothing worn for sacred and profane purposes was less apparent. Certainly, clothes worn in the synagogue intimated a sense of decorum; however, so too was it in other public arenas such as the theater, opera, or semi-formal events. The dress patterns of Ranzenhofer's male figures resemble those worn by the subjects of Zamboni's photograph. The photograph is an indication of the power of the suit in affording men of different faiths and ethnic backgrounds the opportunity to participate in modern society. Although the identities of the men in the photograph remain unknown, it is possible that some of them are Jewish: after all, this particular coffeehouse was a favorite meeting place of the renowned *Jung Wien* literary group, many members of which were Jewish.[68] Additionally, given the prevalence of antisemitic bodily stereotypes at the time this photograph was taken, it is possible that some of the men in this image may have been perceived as Jewish due to their physical characteristics.

The *Wiener Kaffeehaus* played host to Jews of varied identifications. Acculturated Viennese Jews who had estranged themselves from their religious inheritance found a home in this quintessentially Viennese and simultaneously cosmopolitan institution. The coffeehouse also played host to those Jews who remained loyal to Jewish identity and the religious traditions of Judaism, with many kosher establishments operating throughout

Figure 4.2 Emil Ranzenhofer, *Synagoge in der Schopenhauerstraße*, watercolor, 1902. Pk 3020, 15. Courtesy of Wiener Bildarchiv/Österreichische Nationalbibliothek, Vienna.

Figure 4.3 Emil Ranzenhofer, *Synagoge in der Tempelgasse*, watercolor, 1902. Pk 3020, 13. Courtesy of Wiener Bildarchiv/Österreichische Nationalbibliothek, Vienna.

the city, particularly in the second district.[69] The consequence was the "Judaization" of the coffeehouse, which according to Steven Beller, like Jews themselves so central to the development of a modern Viennese culture, remained on the periphery as an outsider.[70] The clothes these Jewish men wore in the *Kaffeehaus* were likewise important in the assertion of their identification. As a "private" or intimate public space, the coffeehouse demanded public respectability and decorum of its patrons. The clothes a man wore to the coffeehouse corresponded to those he would wear in other "public" arenas. As a hybrid space that existed between the privacy of the home (or the exclusive Jewishness of the Synagogue) and the publicity of the street and other public arenas, the coffeehouse served its Jewish patrons as a transitional arena between their specific (Jewish) and general (Viennese) identities.

The Jew in the City and the Goy in the Country: Vienna as a Dangerous Jewish Metropolis

It would be all too easy to attribute the prejudice toward Vienna as a "Jewish" city to mere xenophobia, but the Austro-German variety of antisemitism was influenced by numerous factors including racial, religious, and socioeconomic bias.[71] The Christian Social politician, Karl Lueger (1844–1910), who served as mayor of Vienna from 1897 until his death, made use of this variegated antisemitism in his political platform, alternating between different segments of the Jewish population as the target of his attacks based on the sentiments of his audience. He was "Der schöne Karl" presenting himself as a *völkisch* friend of the people and a champion of the lower-middle and working classes.[72] As an immensely popular, albeit divisive, figure—Franz Joseph prevented his instatement as mayor of Vienna three times due to his perceived rabble-rousing until bowing to public pressure in 1897—Lueger's legacy lasted into the interwar period. In a satirical short story, "Der heilige Lueger" (The Holy Lueger), the title reflecting the mayor's cult-like status, the psychoanalyst Fritz Wittels (1880–1950), the son of Jewish immigrants from Galicia, portrayed Lueger as a saint-like "father" of the downtrodden who saves the virtue of a provincial spinster from ruin. Originally published in 1909, a year before Lueger's death, in Wittels' anthology *Alte Liebeshändel*, the story was reprinted in a March 1925 issue of the society magazine *Die Bühne*, with accompanying illustrations.

The tale concerns a spinster named Athanasia from the Lower Austrian town of Maria-Enzersdorf who travels to the capital in order to visit her idol, described as "the most beautiful man in Vienna, affectionately called 'the handsome Karl' by the ladies. They were all in love with him, and because he could not marry them all, he did not marry at all."[73] However, the naïve and kind Athanasia finds herself out of her depth in this dangerous metropolis, and falls prey to a plump little man with dark eyes and a beard, and who speaks in "light, singing tones."[74] Not only do this man's physical characteristics bring to mind Jewish bodily stereotypes, but his singsong voice can also be understood as a reference to the stereotypical manner in which Jews were thought to speak, sometimes referred to pejoratively as *Mauscheln* (from the western Ashkenazic

Figure 4.4 Illustration by Sipos for Fritz Wittels, "Der heilige Lueger," *Die Bühne* 2, no. 17 (March 5, 1925): 31. Courtesy of ANNO/Österreichische Nationalbibliothek, Vienna.

pronunciation of the name "Moses").[75] The accompanying illustration reinforces the idea of a sinister Jewish villain (Figure 4.4).

To avoid ambiguity as to the man's "racial" identity, Wittels has Athanasia encounter the man in the vicinity of the Taborstrasse, a very Jewish-coded location as the main artery of the heavily Jewish-populated Leopoldstadt. After Athanasia spends the night with him, "der schwarze Lueger" announces his intention to go to the *Rathaus* and adds, "Oh dear, by ten o'clock I will have already devoured three Jews!" playing up to Lueger's antisemitic reputation.[76] When Athanasia later meets the real Lueger and confesses her predicament, his valet Pumera exclaims incredulously, "Really! Can't you hicks tell the difference between a Jew and our esteemed mayor?"[77] However, Lueger takes pity on the spinster and is portrayed as the chivalrous opposite to the scheming Jew. The moral of the story is not that Jews are sinister and depraved beings ready to sully the virtues of innocent Gentiles at every opportunity, but rather a satire on the manner in which Lueger was held up to be a saint-like hero of the "real" (German) Austrians.

Lueger has remained a controversial figure in the historiography of Vienna, held up both as a vehement antisemite and as a champion of the people who used antisemitism only as a means to rally the masses, toning down his rhetoric once appointed to the office of mayor. In his memoir, the community leader Sigmund Mayer criticized Lueger for his hypocritical antisemitic rhetoric while maintaining cordial relations with members of the Jewish community.[78] Similarly, Joseph Samuel Bloch, with his extensive experience combatting antisemitism in public forums, noted that while he was steadfast in his parliamentary opposition to Lueger, he was the least burdensome—"von allen Geistern die verneinen, war Lueger mir am wenigsten zur Last."[79] While Lueger's antisemitism, however benign and opportunistic, remains deplorable, it is telling that an individual such as Bloch should hold such an opinion of him.

The Jew as a symbol of urban decadence, as satirized in Wittels' story, became a standard idea anchored in the antisemitic discourse of the latter half of the nineteenth century. This was, in part, connected to contemporary medical discourse. By the turn of the twentieth century, it was an accepted "fact" in European medical circles that Jews were physically inferior to Gentiles and especially prone to neurasthenia.[80] Jewish physicians, too, notably Cesare Lombroso and Martin Engländer, accepted this notion, but rather than attributing it to inherent racial characteristics, they argued that Jewish neurasthenia was a result of environmental circumstances. The modern city, as a chasm of depravity causing a debilitating sensory overload in its inhabitants, was seen as the main cause of mental and physical illness in the modern world.[81] The Jew, as Sander Gilman notes, came to be seen as "both city dweller par excellence as well as the most evident victim of the city."[82] And Vienna, as home to Europe's third largest Jewish population, was a prime target for that characterization.[83]

As a contrast, Cisleithania's German provinces came to be seen as the antithesis of the modern, "Jewish" city.[84] The very small Jewish populations throughout the predominantly German crown lands had additional implications for Vienna's image after the dissolution of Austria-Hungary in 1918, when Austrian Jewry, like the wider Austrian population, was limited to a greatly reduced territory. The city's enormous post-Habsburg Jewish population now separated by newly defined borders from its smaller Austrian satellites scattered throughout the former crown lands of Bohemia, Moravia, Galicia, and Bukovina, played a role in cementing the notion of the capital as a Jewish metropolis.[85] The collapse of the empire and the exiling of the Imperial and Royal family in 1918 gave way to the Social Democrats, who took over the city's mayoralty from two decades of Christian Social rule in 1919. As Lisa Silverman asserts, the combination of Social Democratic governance, an enlarged Jewish population, and the overall disproportionately multiethnic population in the face of the republic's more ethnically homogenous Austro-German population, made the capital "[loom] large as a dangerous 'Jewish' metropolis—superficial, ugly, crass, corrupt, depraved, socialist, capitalist, materialist, decadent, modern, and immoral."[86] Similarly, the still precarious Austrian "national" identity had been transformed from one of multiethnic/multilinguistic dynastic loyalty to one of German national homogeneity.[87] No longer one "minority" among many, Jews now served as the ideal Other alongside the new republic's predominantly German population. This is not to claim that Vienna was suddenly seen as "Jewish" in the interwar period. Indeed, this perception had emerged during the second half of the nineteenth century and Vienna was often derided as "*Neu-Jerusalem*" in antisemitic literature, particularly certain neighborhoods, such as the so-called "*Zionstraße*" and "*Mazzesinsel.*" Rather, the factors outlined earlier worked in tandem to cement this image during a period of gross uncertainty regarding the Austrian state's future and national identity.

Among those to call attention to the enlarged and now more concentrated Austrian Jewish population and its consequences for Austrian public life was Georg Glockemeier who, in his 1936 book *Zur Wiener Judenfrage*, presented a long list of statistics and analyses of Jewish involvement in various sectors of Viennese society, from commerce and industry to the liberal professions.[88] In the book's foreword, Glockemeier observed the contemporary political and civic discourse on the so-called Jewish Question, citing well-known figures who had taken part in the debate, claiming the book's aim was to determine "a fair and timely solution to the Jewish Question."[89] One figure he cited was the Christian Social politician Leopold Kunschak—who would serve as leader of the post-Second World War Österreichische Volkspartei (Austrian People's Party)—who claimed that either the Jewish Question would be solved sensibly with regulations introduced against Jewish economic activity, or mob mentality would prevail among the Gentile population.[90] In 1919, Kunschak had proposed a *numerus clausus* for Jews in academia and public service and, in 1920, that Jewish refugees from Eastern Europe be forcibly expelled from the state or interned in a concentration camp.[91] In presenting the data, Glockemeier claimed to be an unbiased observer of the situation, but presented Jews as a race of driven business people who had "conquered" Vienna through mercantile activity disproportionate to their numbers.[92] The use of such terminology, conveying a clear inference of Jewish insidiousness, was no accident, intended as it was to insinuate the idea of a foreign minority, or strangers, dominating the "real" members of the nation. Glockemeier even went so far as to suggest that the Jews' ability to excel at commerce was due to racial peculiarities—"Und das haben die Juden ihrer Eigenart zu danken."[93]

Glockemeier's report reads as a form of fearmongering predicting a "dystopian" future in which Jews dominate at the expense of Gentiles, if the government does not intervene. There is a sense of familiarity to the 1922 novel *Die Stadt ohne Juden* (*The City Without Jews*) by Hugo Bettauer, and its film adaptation by H. K. Breslauer of the previous decade, in which Jews are expelled from Austria in response to their overwhelming dominance in all fields and industries. To scholars of Viennese Jewish history and culture of the First Republic, Bettauer's novel, with its sympathetic view of the Jewish experience and ridicule of common antisemitic anxieties is intricately connected to his murder.[94] In 1925, a year after the premiere of Breslauer's film, Bettauer, a journalist and publisher of numerous novels and the short-lived journal *Er und Sie* (*He and She*) that promoted sexual enlightenment, was murdered in his office by a dental technician with right-wing extremist views named Otto Rothstock. Bettauer, born to Jewish parents in Baden bei Wien, albeit a convert to Lutheranism, was seen by Rothstock and other adversaries in the role of Jewish deviant responsible for the pollution of "pure" German culture.

Like Glockemeier's claims of objectivity, the novel's antagonist, the fictional Christian Social chancellor Dr. Karl Schwertfeger—loosely modelled on Lueger—couches his proposal to expel Austria's Jews in "objective" terms: the Jews, he claims, are just naturally more adept at modern life and industrial practices than their Aryan counterparts and possess a natural ability to excel in and adapt to any given situation. Consequently, it is unfair that they are able to dominate Viennese society:[95]

Sehen wir dieses kleine Österreich von heute an. Wer hat die Presse und damit die öffentliche Meinung in der Hand? Der Jude! Wer hat seit dem unheilvollen Jahre 1914 Milliarden auf Milliarden gehäuft? Der Jude! Wer kontrolliert den ungeheuren Banknotenumlauf, sitzt an den leitenden Stellen in den Großbanken, wer steht an der Spitze fast sämtlicher Industrien? Der Jude! Wer besitzt unsere Theater? Der Jude! Wer fährt im Automobil, wer prasst in den Nachtlokalen, wer füllt die Kaffeehäuser, wer die vornehmen Restaurants, wer behängt sich und seine Frau mit Juwelen und Perlen? Der Jude![96]

(Let's have a look at little Austria of today. In whose hands is the press and consequently public opinion? The Jew! Who, since that ominous year of 1914, has amassed billions upon billions? The Jew! Who controls the tremendous circulation of cash, occupies the leading positions in the banks, and stands at the pinnacle of all industries? The Jew! Who owns our theaters? The Jew! Who drives around in automobiles, splurges in nightclubs, fills the coffeehouses and best restaurants, and decks himself and his wife with jewels and pearls? The Jew!)

From a post-Shoah perspective, *Die Stadt ohne Juden* appears an almost prophetic warning of what was to come some two decades later. Bettauer's tale offered a speculative scenario of societal decline after the expulsion of Vienna's Jews, originally enforced as a means of improving the destitution of the city's population. Not only practicing Jews but also converts to Christianity and their children, as well as the children of mixed marriages, are ordered to leave the city and Austria as a whole (of course, in the novel it goes without saying that the only place in Austria in which Jews live is the capital). However, unlike the reality of the Jewish experience in Vienna after the Anschluss of March 1938, the novel ends on a happy note. With the city's continued economic decline, the government decides to reverse the expulsion and Jews are invited back into the city with open arms—a climactic ending sees the mayor standing before the city's population to officially welcome the first returnee with the warm greeting, "mein lieber Jude!"[97]

One of the novel's central themes is that Jews are a significant factor in what makes Vienna a cosmopolitan city. The expulsion of the Jews results in the capital's transformation, a large part through clothing and material culture. Gone are the Jewish politicians, bankers, *Konfektion*-moguls, and coffeehouse literati, and in their place a former cosmopolitan metropolis is transformed into a giant provincial town populated by *Tracht*-wearing provincials. Formerly well-dressed people trade in their stylish suits and frocks for *völkisch* attire. Department stores attempt to advertise rustic fabrics—Loden, fustian, cotton, and flannel—as the top Parisian fashions,[98] and as far as the eye could see, men dressed "old and young in loden jackets, knee breeches, and green alpine hats on their heads. And the women! Most of them dressed in Dirndl costumes, which, while certainly very fetching in the open country, here looked like caricatures, like bad jokes."[99] In fact, one of the few elegantly dressed inhabitants of this dystopian city is the Jew Leo Strakosch, masquerading as a Gentile Frenchman Henri Dufresne, whose dark blue suit, patent leather shoes, and expensive silk tie attracted attention in a crowded *Wienerwald* inn[100]—a highly Aryan-coded environment in contrast to the Jewish *Kaffeehaus*. Strakosch's fashionable alter ego, although one that evokes a sense of refined manners and urbane cosmopolitanism, both marks him as an essential Other among a homogenous *völkisch* population, and likewise brings to mind tropes of Jewish deviousness. Like his contemporaries, Bettauer, perhaps unwittingly, perpetuates the notion of Vienna as a city in the control of the Jews. Scott Spector notes that in attempting to highlight the contribution of Jews to Viennese society, Bettauer falls prey to the same antisemitic tropes of Jewish domination.[101]

This satirical text does not simply offer a speculative scenario concocted from the mind of a novelist. As a Jewish-born convert to Lutheranism, Bettauer was certainly aware of the toxic levels of antisemitism in his hometown. Nor was this work of fiction novel in its depiction of a city that was overrun with Jews. *Die Stadt ohne Juden*, although a satire of the destructive nature of xenophobia, was very much a piece of its time. The publication of the novel and its film adaptation during the 1920s is pertinent to the Austrian capital's large Jewish population in the face of the provinces' comparatively insignificant numbers.[102] Additionally, the high representation of many Jews in all arenas of Viennese civic and political life, despite being a minority, provided Bettauer's audience with a peculiar speculative scenario in the event of an actual expulsion.

Trachtenmoden and the Suit[103]

The "Jewishness" of Vienna in the face of the "non-Jewish" provinces was not an idea that concerned Austria's Gentile population alone. Many Austrian Jews during the latter Habsburg and interwar periods also perceived the provinces to be somehow "non-Jewish" and they dealt with this in different ways. To some Jews, the absence of large established Jewish communities in Austria's provinces—particularly in the Salzkammergut region— was attractive and a determining factor in choice of holiday destination, whereas for others, the natural beauty of the location, removed from the stress of urban life, exerted a stronger influence.[104]

It would be inaccurate to suggest that certain towns were desirable holiday destinations for Jews alone. *Sommerfrischen* in the Salzkammergut became popular during the nineteenth century for both Gentile and Jewish upper- and middle-class Viennese. Certain towns were esteemed for their distinguished summer visitors, such as Bad Ischl, which had served as a holiday destination to the Habsburgs since the middle of the nineteenth century.[105] The esteem brought to the town by the presence of the Imperial and Royal family was an attraction for bourgeois Viennese—especially Jews, many of whom considered themselves among Franz Joseph I's most devoted subjects. Describing the overwhelming popularity of "Ischl" among Jewish *Sommerfrischler*, Friedrich Torberg quoted the Jewish comedian Armin Berg who mused sarcastically, "There are 500 million Chinese in the world, and only 15 million Jews . . . why then does one not see *one single* Chinese in Ischl?"[106] Ischl was not the only preferred holiday destination of Viennese Jews, and while some individuals, such as Peter Altenberg, preferred towns in which they could avoid other Jewish tourists,[107] it was common for Viennese Jews to take their holidays in the same locales.[108] The *Cur-* and *Fremdenlisten* published in many *Sommerfrischen* during the early decades of the twentieth century regularly listed common Jewish-sounding names of visitors from across Austria-Hungary and abroad including their temporary addresses at local hotels, pensions, or private villas. For example, among the names listed in the *Ischler Cur-Liste* of June 16, 1900, were the typically Jewish names Bardas, Bernstein, Freund, Friedmann, Goldberger de Buda (a renowned Hungarian industrialist family), Hirschfeld, Hirsch, Kohn, Konberger, Krausz, Löwy, Politzer, Popper, Spitzer, Stein, Stern, Weintraub, and Weiss.[109]

While holidaying in these locales, many Jews adopted the sartorial modes associated with the provinces and rural populations, commonly referred to as *Trachten* or, in an attempt to emphasize the ethnic and thus exclusionary nature of the garments, *Volkstrachten*. Over the course of the nineteenth century, *Trachten* were increasingly utilized as a form of national self-display within the wider context of emerging ideas revolving around European "nations" and nation-states. While originating as ceremonial or "formal" attire among rural populations, *Trachten* came to symbolize more than the rural communities in which they originated but were presented as a sartorial manifestation of cultural and ethnic distinction. In the foreword to his 1858 *Die deutsche Trachten- und Modenwelt*, the Austrian art historian and later director of the k. k. *Österreichischen Museum für Kunst und Industrie* (Imperial and Royal Austrian Museum for Art and Industry), Jakob von Falke asserted that more than a reflection of national character, German *Trachten* constituted an essential "Baustein" (building block) to the understanding of German cultural history.[110] As social and cultural critics argued in the decades leading up to the First World War and into the interwar period, *Volkstrachten* were imbued with significance as sartorial symbols of cultural, ethnic, and national homogeneity and hegemony. However, within the German cultural and linguistic sphere (including Austria), no single form of *Volkstracht* existed, nor did they remain static but rather, like other forms of dress, were influenced by external factors.[111] *Tracht,* as a form of fashionable dress—that developed into the type of clothing sometimes referred to in fashion magazines and pattern books as *Trachtenmoden*—was influenced, like other forms of fashionable dress in earlier centuries, by members of the Imperial and Royal family adopting it outside its original contexts.[112]

Particularly during the last two decades of the nineteenth century and into the twentieth, *Trachten* remained in the public eye. In addition to their presence as embodied garments, *Trachten* were addressed in editorials and feuilletons published in some of Vienna's largest daily newspapers, including *Die Presse, Wiener Zeitung,* and *Neuigkeits Welt-Blatt.* In the wider context of rising nationalism across Europe, *Trachten* were used not only by the Austro-Hungarian state in an attempt to make the multiethnic Dual Monarchy seem relevant but also by proponents of nationalism. The very notion of national costume, like national identity itself, was an invented one.[113] Sartorial styles defined as national dress or costume were used to define the boundaries of a nation's body politic.[114] Standardized national dress did not exist for Austria's Germans or other nations of the Dual Monarchy, but rather, different rural communities maintained their own practices of dressing for ceremonial contexts such as attending religious ceremonies, weddings, and other milestone events, as well as rural fairs and festivals.[115]

Trachten were embraced by proponents to evoke a sense of German distinctiveness and exceptionality, especially in the context of pan-German nationalism. In this context, *Trachten* were presented as honest, *einheimisch* (indigenous), a sense of tradition in a turbulent, modernizing world, in contrast to fashion, a foreign entity that destroyed traditional civilization and turned the population into slaves of novelty.[116] Writers and social commentators idealized rural populations in "traditional" *Trachten* as bastions of tradition unencumbered by the modern world and its fleeting fashions.[117] The sense of foreign intrusion that "fashion" evoked with its French (and to a lesser extent English) connotations, had an added layer of significance in the context of antisemitism and the prevalence of Jews in the fashion, textile, and luxury industries. This detail was not lost on antisemitic commentators who took the opportunity to rail against Jews for polluting the German body politic through imported foreign fashions and destroying traditional business practices.[118]

Of course, in Vienna's urban environment *Trachten* were not typical attire and were instead reserved for ceremonial contexts, a form of "resort wear" when visiting the country, or as a costume at themed balls. And most people, Jewish and Gentile, wore clothing that corresponded to conventional urban dress. For men this meant tailored garments of some kind: jacket, shirt, and trousers, and typically a waistcoat as has been described in previous chapters. However, in the face of the tailored suit's symbolic role as a sartorial democratizer,[119] masculine forms of *Volkstrachten*—in their most generic incarnation a pair of *Lederhosen* and *Trachtenjanker*—might be understood as having the opposite effect: a sartorial symbol of exclusion, or at least cultural/national particularity. Lillian Bader (née Stern) remembered her childhood excitement over holidays in the Salzkammergut, in a large part linked to the clothing of the local population she was able to describe in detail many decades later:

> They were dressed in their Sunday best: they wore green vests, short leather pants and green half stockings which left their knees bare. Their boots were hobnailed. A brush of chamois hair was stuck in the wide green ribbon which adorned their hats.
>
> Our peasant land-lady [*sic.*] received us with a curtsey. She, too wore her Sunday outfit, the most prominent feature of which was a kerchief of black taffeta which covered her head. In the back it was tied in a big wing-like bow, which stood out stiffly to the left and right of her face and fell down to her waist.[120]

For Bader, the experience was added to by the thrill of being able to dress like the locals in a *Dirndl*. Dressing is rarely a passive act and choosing what garments to wear in any given situation can be a statement of both conformity and rebellion. Just as Vienna's nascent fashion press implored its readers to adhere to sartorial templates appropriate to one's context, wearing *Trachten* while hiking or relaxing at a *Sommerfrische* was a matter of following accepted social norms and not necessarily a declaration of German national ideology.

Numerous visual and written evidence of Viennese Jews' embrace of *Trachten* while on holiday abound in museum and library archives, as well as private family collections around the world. These range from the famous to the unknown. Many photographs from the collection of the Freud Museum in London depict relatives of Sigmund Freud dressed in *Trachtenmoden*—more often women and children than men. In one well-known photograph, Freud's sons Oliver, Jean-Martin, and Ernst, posed in identical *Trachtenjanker*, *Lederhosen*, alpine hats (commonly referred to as "Tyrolean" or "Styrian" whether they came from those regions or not), *Wadenstutzen* (knitted knee socks), boots, white shirts, and neckties, standing before a typically "rural" backdrop with corresponding props (Figure 4.5). It is entirely possible that the portrait was taken in Vienna as a form of pantomime as was not uncommon among urban residents. However, a family memoir written by Freud's eldest son Jean-Martin offers anecdotes relating to the family's dress habits, including when on holiday in rural locales, typically in Bavaria. The younger Freud recalled the difference in details of the *Lederhosen* worn

Figure 4.5 Ernst, Jean Martin, and Oliver Freud dressed in *Trachtenmoden*, *c.* 1900. IN264. Courtesy of Freud Museum London.

by him and his brothers, following Styrian traditions, to that of local Bavarian boys and men.[121]

Freud's comments on his family's practice of dressing and wider social norms are poignant in light of his familiarity with his Jewish origins. Despite being raised by a father who openly scoffed at religion, Jean-Martin Freud's memoir reveals a childhood exposure to religious practices and the wider Jewish community on the part of his relatives, especially his Orthodox maternal grandmother, Emmeline Bernays.[122] Throughout his memoir Freud makes regular reference to his Jewish extended family, their lifestyles, and awareness of the prevalent antisemitism in Vienna, as well as his simultaneous ease in Austro-German society. Such a memoir, should, however, be read within the context in which it was produced. Published a decade after the Shoah, Freud's memoir, like others written by Viennese Jewish survivors and refugees, perpetuates a narrative of almost complete integration—both cultural and social—that was destroyed with the Anschluss.[123] Like memoirs that lament the lost world of Viennese Jewry before the Anschluss, photographic evidence has been used for similar purposes. Photographs depicting individuals dressed in "authentic" *Trachten* or *Trachtenmoden* are many, but alone they serve as little more than evidence of widespread sartorial fashion. It is with additional information about the individuals depicted and their wider context—through the mediums of diaries, letters, memoirs, or oral history—that such images are imbued with meanings as reliable sources.[124] When understanding the varied political, cultural, and religious sentiments and ideologies of Jews who wore *Trachten*, the result is more nuanced.

The way a photograph of Viennese couple Grete and Fritz Stern intersects with their daughter's memory of Austrian patriotism is a case in point. "They were true, true Austrians, and I shall show you pictures of what it meant," was how their daughter Eva described Grete and Fritz.[125] The pictures in question are typical of those in many other family albums and archival collections, depicting smiling children, women, and men holidaying in rural settings in generic forms of *Dirndl*, *Lederhosen*, and hobnailed boots, their heads often covered with scarves or alpine hats. Referring to the photographs in the same context, they serve in the function to support a claim of "Austrian" national identity—in all the complexity it entails.[126] This is not to dismiss claims that the Sterns were "real" Austrians, especially when considering Marsha L. Rozenblit and Lisa Silverman's models of tripartite German-Austrian/Viennese-Jewish identification.[127] While multidimensional identification among non-Jewish Austrians was certainly a reality, its implications for Viennese Jews were divisive and exclusionary. With the increasing levels of antisemitism during the interwar period, and its unifying function among various non-Jewish segments of the population,[128] it was harnessed within antisemitic discourse to highlight an inherent Jewish "difference"—whether religious or ethnic—that prevented Jews from being true Austrians.

It is in this context that Eva's comments about her parents' Austrian-ness are significant, albeit typical of the post-Shoah narrative of pre-Anschluss Viennese Jewry. While both Grete and Fritz Stern came from traditional immigrant families, they, like many Viennese Jews, turned away from religion in favor of a secular lifestyle. Their daughter Eva recalled her childhood home in Vienna as secular, and her parents' negative attitude toward religion.[129] Both placed more importance on their political ideology, that is, their support for the Austrian Social Democratic Party. In one poignant photograph Grete and Fritz are dressed in styles that publicize their dedication to their Austrian loyalties: Grete in a

Figure 4.6 Grete and Fritz Stern dressed in *Trachtenmoden*, Austria, 1937. Courtesy of Eva Engel, Sydney.

modern version of a *Dirndl* with an apron and headscarf, and Fritz in a *Trachtenjanker*, *Lederhosen*, long white socks, and a *Tirolerhut* (Figure 4.6). Despite their rural attire the couple wear elements of apparel that indicate their urban Viennese identity rather than a rural idyll. Grete wears what appears to be fashionable, possibly high-heeled shoes. Her *Dirndl* is blue with black and white stripes in a floral pattern, typical of the *völkisch*, albeit fashionable, attire depicted within the pages of contemporary Viennese pattern books (Figure 4.7). Fritz's attire is closer to that of authentic *Trachten*, but small details stand out as urban: he wears a smart collared shirt with a faint stripe, and a loud, polka-dotted tie. This dress is thus a form of *Trachtenmoden* rather than authentic *Trachten* and would have "outed" Grete and Fritz as urban visitors to the country—with its antisemitic connotations.

As a Viennese businessman, Fritz Stern most likely wore a suit as his regular attire, reserving *Trachten* with their nationalistic connotations for special occasions, as was typical of urban, middle-class Viennese and indicated by surviving photographs (Figure 4.8). It would be tempting to connect the suit's democratizing power with Stern's political ideologies; however, wearing such attire was common among men across the political, religious, ethnic, and class spectrum. Certainly, small details of styling and appearance existed between men across these categories; for example, the quality of cut and fit had an impact on the overall look of a man's dressed figure. *Trachten*, however, can be understood as the opposite to the suit's equalizing function: while any man could don a suit without fear of critique, the political and national symbolism associated with *Trachten* meant that those who donned the latter put themselves at risk of criticism if they did not fit neatly into the perceived national category. This came to a head in June 1938, three months after the Anschluss, when the police chief of Reichsgau Salzburg announced a *Trachtenverbot*—to be later instituted in other parts of the Reich—that deemed "non-Aryans" (a euphemism for Jews, of course, or those considered Jewish under the Nuremberg Laws of 1935) were forbidden from dressing in German *Trachten*—in both authentic and popularized form. The *Trachtenverbot* highlighted specific forbidden garments including, but not limited to, *Lederhosen*, *Joppen/Janker*, *Wadenstutzen*, alpine-style hats, and *Dirndl*. Anyone in breach of the rules was subject to a fine of 133 Reichsmarks or two weeks' imprisonment.[130] Although by 1938 the majority of Austrian Jews lived in Vienna and did not regularly wear *Trachten* outside specific contexts, such styles of dress played an important role in their understanding and performance of modern Austrian and Jewish subjectivities. However, the *Trachtenverbot* reveals the extent to which Jews were wearing "traditional" German attire and the ambiguity of the urban/rural divide that played on the anxieties of antisemites and German nationalists. For Grete and Fritz Stern, the ban came as a great blow to their loyalty to the idea of the Austrian nation.[131] As a sartorial symbol of national identity, the political aspect of *Trachten* was not new. However, by making it illegal for certain people to wear such garments, Hanns Haas has commented, "*Tracht* was no longer a beautiful form of casual attire, but rather a '*Sache des Volkstums*',"[132] and the implications for who did and did not belong were now clearly and legally defined.

*   *   *

Figure 4.7 Fashion plate from pattern-book *Wiener Modenzeitung*, no. 105 (June 1937): 17, depicting *Trachtenmoden* for women. Courtesy of ANNO/Österreichische Nationalbibliothek, Vienna.

Figure 4.8 Unidentified Jewish family, Austria, undated. AU/Ph 356. Image courtesy of the Central Archives for the History of the Jewish People, Jerusalem.

Despite earlier critique and ridicule, and the sartorial-based persecution of the Nazi era, *Trachten* remained a powerful symbol of self-fashioning for many Austrian Jews. For some who would flee to the safety of other countries after the 1938 Anschluss, *Trachtenmoden*, along with other aspects of their Austrian culture, would travel with them. Shortly after the Anschluss, the Sterns fled Austria, being given permission to enter Switzerland on account of Fritz's business connections to an enameling plant near Zürich that he used for his aluminum ware company. From Switzerland Fritz secured a job in Sydney, Australia, where the family sojourned for eleven months before relocating to Auckland, New Zealand, in late 1939. Among the possessions they were able to take out of the so-called "Ostmark" were *Trachtenmoden*, including Grete's blue *Dirndl* that is now housed in the archives of the Sydney Jewish Museum.[133] Such garments, however, inherited new meanings in their exile and were used predominantly as a form of fancy dress (Figure 4.9), as opposed to functional clothing or symbols of national identity—raising additional questions in the context of what historian Konrad Kwiet has referred to as the "re-acculturation" of German and Austrian refugees.[134]

As discussed in Chapter 2, the dress patterns of Viennese Jews had a direct influence on antisemitism, including accusations that Jews were trying to mask their true origins. Adopting the dress of the dominant group, whether in Vienna or the Salzkammergut, went beyond trying to erase or mask an individual's origins.[135] This practice of dressing can be understood as a continuation of the modernization process Jews underwent in the eighteenth and nineteenth centuries. The donning of *Volkstracht*—like that of a tailored suit in preference to a kaftan, or High German in favor of Judeo-German or

Figure 4.9 Eva Engel (née Stern) with a fellow refugee child wearing *Trachtenmoden* in Auckland, 1940. Courtesy of Eva Engel, Sydney.

Yiddish—announced an individual's self-positioning within the wider society as both Jew and Austrian.[136] To these Jews, the adoption of popular forms of dress and culture did not signify their rejection of their Jewish identities, but rather that they, too, like other ethnic groups in Austria-Hungary and later the First Republic, were modern Europeans and not a relic from the past. Like the suit with its multitude of symbolic registers that promised its wearers the possibility of respectability, equality, and invisibility, *Volkstracht* was a highly coded form of dress that offered its wearers a particular visual identity but often resulted in one with very different repercussions.

CHAPTER 5
DER KLEINE COHN
DRESS AND THE FUNCTION OF MOCKING THROUGH
CARICATURE

Caricatures: Critical Perspectives

In his 1921 study of Jewish caricatures, Eduard Fuchs asserts that caricatures are an important tool to gauge public sentiment, and thus draw from existing prejudices.[1] Fuchs attests to the power of caricature as a "source of truth" (*Wahrheitsquelle*) in historical inquiry: not as a true representation of the subjects depicted, but rather as a means to measure and test the mood of society.[2] Similarly, Thomas Milton Kemnitz argues that the importance of such images to historians lies in what they reveal about their creators' attitudes and emotions toward individuals and events.[3] Such images play an additional role in attempts to shape public opinion and attitudes, and have at various times been utilized for propaganda.[4] In this manner, caricatures are important tools for reading widespread perceptions of Jewishness in *fin-de-siècle* Vienna, particularly those in connection with clothing. This is because these visual art forms showed the stereotypical and satirical figuring of the Jew in ways that are not necessarily understood from reading written texts.

Although the terms "cartoon," "caricature," and "political/satirical print" have been used as synonyms, John Richard Moores argues that the interchangeable use of such terms obscures their specific meanings.[5] Caricature, for example, refers specifically to the distortion of the physiognomic features and characteristics of certain individuals (or groups).[6] Satire, however, lampoons not only physical and behavioral attributes, but has often taken widespread opinions and beliefs as subjects. Mark Bills asserts:

The difference between the two traditions typifies the unique position of later satirical imagery and its ability to utilise diverse influence. Caricature, or the systematic distortion or exaggeration of personal appearance, was also associated with high art, with an academic tradition that drew on anatomy, rules and theory. Physiognomy provided the theory, whilst rules and instructions emerged for drawing, identifying it as a distinct discipline. It is an art of wit and politeness. In contrast, satire was associated with low culture. Its images were often symbolic and draw on popular folk imagery such as the symbolism of popular emblem books. Text was an important element in expounding its point beyond ambiguity. It often lacked humour and can be characterized by its bigotry and service of propaganda at a time of religious or political divide in London.[7]

Despite the differences in these terms, caricature was regularly employed in social satire and was central to the creation of stereotypes.[8] Lawrence H. Streicher, for example, argues that caricature "underlies [cartoons, comic strips, and animated films] and is present in each."[9] The images examined in this chapter are all examples of caricature; they represent certain Jewish stereotypes prevalent in Viennese and wider European culture of the time, but not all are examples of satire.

Scholars have argued that satirical caricatures that have appeared in print media have their origins in the satirical prints that gained popularity in eighteenth-century London, from there spreading to continental Europe, and as far as the American colonies.[10] An urban phenomenon, these images were produced by printers and made available to the public for purchase or by public display. Sartorial fashions were common targets of caricatures in journals and satirical prints which were circulated among all socioeconomic tiers. Writing about caricatures of popular fashions in the Georgian era, Diana Donald argues that the importance of such images is found "not only in giving a valid impression of styles of dress in the Georgian period, but also at a deeper level, in conveying social attitudes of the time."[11] Ann Taylor Allen asserts that caricatures and the satirical journals they were published in "can help the historian understand one of the most important and least tangible facets of social change—the concomitant development of the perceptions, attitudes, and values of the people affected."[12] However, there is a danger of treating caricatures as a reflection of society's mores and visual practice, particularly in relation to fashion, which often existed as visual representations prior to becoming widely adopted sartorial modes.[13] As Donald stresses:

> Attitudes to fashion were confused and ambivalent. The comedy of the caricatures connected an underlying anxiety, or, rather, anxiety gave them an edge and a kind of sanction. They were meant, ostensibly at least, to curb the follies of the frivolous, and illustrate the sort of behaviour that right-minded people should avoid; for morality and taste were closely associated in public mind. In this sense, caricatures were as important as fashion plates in forming the consciousness of consumers, even if the messages they sent were considerably more ambiguous.[14]

In Vienna, almost a century after the period Donald refers to, caricatures of Jewish individuals had a similar function. Over the course of the nineteenth century, Viennese Jews went from being social and political pariahs requiring permission to reside in the Austrian capital to full citizens with equal rights. Many of the Jewish caricatures served a double purpose: they maligned those depicted and simultaneously offered a wider readership a satirical avenue to deal with the changing society around them. Although comical images of Jews appeared in multiple forms such as printed on postcards, as book illustrations, and consumer goods such as figurines, walking canes, and salt-and-pepper cellars, this chapter will deal primarily with those caricatures appearing in satirical Viennese magazines. With their heavy visual content and overall dedication to satire, popular periodicals are appropriate and compelling vehicles through which the perception of Jews in wider society can be understood. Although Jews were not the singular focus of the journals (which focused predominantly on contemporary political events in Austria and throughout Europe), they remained a regular source of ridicule and were caricatures in both visual and written form.

The journals employed caricatures as a typical device with which to consider the "Jewish Question." Caricatured Jewish archetypes were a mainstay of European satirical press. The malicious images that appeared in the pages of journals and magazines had their origins in medieval representations of Jews.[15] Although Jew-hatred of the medieval period was predominantly expressed from a religious Christian perspective, the characteristics and features attributed to Jews were reused in the racially and politically based "antisemitism" that developed during the nineteenth century. Like many of the woodcuts, engravings, paintings, and sculptures of the Middle Ages—for example, the notorious *Judensau* that appeared on many churches and other buildings in the German-speaking lands[16]—the *fin-de-siècle* caricature employed deformed physical features and corrupt attributes to symbolize the internal character of its subject.[17]

A popular example from the *fin de siècle* can be found in *Der kleine Cohn*, a small, deformed Jew, whom William Collins Donahue refers to as "a kind of anti-Semitic mascot of Wilhelmine culture."[18] Although a satirical figure of Imperial Germany, *Der kleine Cohn* found his way into Viennese culture, appearing in the satirical press and in songs, and also depicted on postcards.[19] Writing of cartoons in the American press during the late nineteenth and early twentieth centuries, Matthew Baigell argues that Jews were singled out above all minority groups for ridicule: "they were money-hungry shylocks and thieving Fagins, social climbers, arsonists ready to claim insurance for property loss, and disagreeable, scheming parvenus who could take advantage of any situation in which they found themselves."[20] The same archetypes appeared in the Viennese satirical press.

Jews in Viennese Caricature and Satire:
Personalities and Stereotypical Types

The political, economic, and civic changes in Viennese society during the second half of the nineteenth and early part of the twentieth centuries had a profound impact on the Jewish experience in Vienna and the symbolic role(s) Jews played in the wider society. The economic prosperity of the *Gründerzeit* in the post-1848 period created a false sense of security for Viennese Jews, many of whom—not least the Jewish élite who built splendid palaces and apartment houses on the newly constructed Ringstrasse—took advantage of the new professional and social channels now open to them. The May 1873 stock market crash served as a salutary reminder to many Viennese Jews who believed that their newly granted equality had put an end to the anti-Jewish bigotry.[21] In many quarters of Viennese society, Jewish stockbrokers—and Jews in general—were blamed for the crash, igniting long-held notions of Jewish monetary practices in combination with a new class-based antisemitism. During this period, the notion of antisemitism developed into a variety of anti-Jewish prejudice that was based on race and class rather than religious biases and was exacerbated by the racial pseudo-science of the nineteenth century.[22] This new form of Jew-hatred was further cultivated by rising nationalist movements throughout the empire, including the pan-German variety and various forms of Slavic nationalism ranging from the Young Czechs to Pan-Slavism.[23] A supposed biological Jewish difference was exploited by antisemitic German nationalists, first, to bolster the cause for German cultural, political, and racial superiority and, second, to struggle against what they perceived was a reactionary Austrian political entity that combined diverse ethnic and cultural elements.[24]

Jewish difference was highlighted visually in the form of humorous images that appeared in numerous Viennese daily and weekly periodicals. Ann Taylor Allen asserts that the huge increase of *Witzblätter* (satirical journals) in nineteenth-century Europe was a product of the general development of print media during the period and the increasing literacy levels of the public.[25] The Jewish caricatures appearing in the pages of the *Witzblätter* regularly used the most extreme behavioral and bodily stereotypes, taking the figure of the immigrant "Polish Jew" or *Ostjude* as the main frame of reference. It was not only the overtly antisemitic nationalist periodicals that pursued such a line of Jewish representation; negative stereotypes of Jews also appeared in more Liberal-leaning journals, including *Figaro* (1857–1919) and its supplement *Wiener Luft*, and especially during the interwar period, *Die Muskete* (1905–41), which Julia Secklehner describes as offering "weak" antisemitism.[26] The appearance of seemingly antisemitic caricatures in Liberal papers is unsurprising. Many middle-class Viennese Jews adhered to Liberalism during the latter half of the nineteenth century and in their desire to assimilate into the wider Viennese bourgeoisie, or to assert their place in society as modern Jews and Europeans (or Germans), they eschewed the culturally unassimilated *Ostjude* and his "backward" way of life.[27]

To be sure, Jews were not the only group to be pilloried in the pages of Viennese print media during the late nineteenth and early twentieth centuries. Magazines like *Kikeriki* (1863–1933) attacked other ethnic, national, and religious groups as well, such as Catholics, the Ottoman Empire, Russians, Bulgarians, Serbs, Czechs, English, and even Germans. Likewise, the satirical journal *Der Floh* (1869–1919) ran a regular piece titled "In der Volksküche" (In the Soup Kitchen), which caricatured the various ethnic groups that made up the Austro-Hungarian Empire. By depicting in written form a conversation between a group of men, each representing a different national or ethnic group, the journal drew attention to the stereotypical characteristics and features of each *Volksstamm*. No one was left unmocked.[28] However, despite the regular appearance of caricatures ridiculing Austria's other ethnic groups, those depicting Jews were often more aggressive.

The guise under which Jews appeared in the caricatures published in the Viennese satirical journals varied in form and contained multiple meanings. Just as Jeffery W. Beglaw has demonstrated in his study of anti-Czech caricatures in *Kikeriki*, Jewish cartoons often appeared as recurring archetypes or themes.[29] These changed over time and were influenced by political and civic events, both locally and abroad, that influenced general attitudes toward, and public opinion of, Jews and Jewishness. While the physiognomic depiction of Jews in the images remained much the same during the late nineteenth and early twentieth centuries, the social and sartorial role of Jewish characters varied. Common Jewish types that appeared in caricatures in *Witzblätter* included the assimilation-minded Jewish parvenu, the wily and money-grubbing Jewish stockbroker or businessman, the Jewish *Gigerl* or fashion victim, and the ubiquitous, work-shy, and parasitical *Ostjude* whose characteristics seemed to be the basis for every other Jewish character. These caricatures corresponded to common Jewish archetypes in wider society during the period at both ends of the political spectrum. Nevertheless, these differing archetypes were two sides of the same coin: the Jewish man (and woman), whether impoverished *Schnorrer* or wealthy parvenu, almost always possessed the stereotypical physiognomic features of dark curly hair, beady scheming eyes, large fleshy lips, and protruding, hooked noses. What differentiated these caricatured "types" was their clothing. Each figure was differently attired; however, the styles ranged from threadbare rags, such as the kaftan of the *Schnorrer* and rabbi, or the European-style but scruffy garments of used-clothes dealers and peddlers, and the fashionable styles of modern European men worn by the professionals and industrialists.[30]

The prevalent physiognomic similarity between caricatured Jewish archetypes—what David Low referred to as "tabs of identity"[31]—at times made the visual distinction between them difficult to ascertain. Thus, written text, in the form of captions below or speech balloons in the images, served an important role in transmitting a Jewish character's socioeconomic, cultural, or professional identifier to the audience.[32] For example, many images depicted Jewish caricatures in the typical dress patterns of Eastern European Jews; however, the captions below the images present these figures speaking High German or even the Viennese dialect. These Jewish caricatures can be compared with those whose captions are written in a way that mimics perceived Jewish patterns of speech (Yiddish or *Mauscheln*). At other times, Jewish figures, although visibly characterized by the material trappings of middle-class respectability (such as fine clothing and occupying expensively decorated interiors), are presented speaking in a corrupted form of German, implying that beneath such trimmings, upper- and middle-class Jews were no different from their poor, culturally unassimilated coreligionists.

The Ugly/Beautiful Binary

One of the most virulently antisemitic examples of Viennese satirical journalism at the *fin de siècle* and up to its closure by the Dollfuß regime in 1933 for its allegiance with the then-banned Nazi Party[33] was the journal *Kikeriki*. Originally published by the journalist and dramatist O. F. Berg (1833–86)[34] as a liberal and anti-clerical satirical journal, *Kikeriki* repositioned itself during the 1890s as increasingly hostile to Jews, in particular in the lead-up to and after the populist antisemitic Christian

Social Party leader Dr. Karl Lueger's election and induction as mayor.[35] During this time, the publication fashioned itself as an organ of Lueger's Christian Social Party, and depictions of Jews, who had previously appeared in a more light-hearted manner alongside comical representations of other groups, became more defamatory.[36] As one of "the most widely read . . . and most popular journal[s] in Austria-Hungary,"[37] *Kikeriki* surely had a large impact on general attitudes toward Jews and Jewishness at a time when political parties were exploiting widespread xenophobia and nationalistic sentiment. While other satirical publications contained blatantly antisemitic cartoons, the extent of their Jew-baiting did not match that of *Kikeriki*, which by the end of the nineteenth century seemed to have adopted the primary intention of ridiculing and demonizing Jews.

A recurring theme in *Kikeriki* was the notion of the Jewish parvenu using his wealth to buy his way into high society. "Ugly" Jewish figures were caricatured as forcing themselves into a Gentile milieu though bribery or using their wealth to unsuccessfully transform themselves into respectable members of Viennese society. In such images, this idea was regularly presented through the adoption of fashionable clothing. However, not all images of Jews were exclusively a comment on perceived Jewish mannerisms. An image appearing in the journal in February 1890 used this trope to highlight a contemporary geopolitical issue, the imprisonment of the claimant to the French throne, Philippe, Duke of Orléans (1869–1926), that same month for entering Paris in violation of the 1886 law of exile. Suggesting that had Philippe been a wealthy Jew or masqueraded as one, he would have been welcomed with open arms, the cartoon depicts Marianne, the personification of France, warmly receiving the duke, who struggles under several sacks filled with millions of francs (Figure 5.1).[38] Covering the latter's face is a mask of grotesque proportions complete with stereotypical Jewish hooked nose, protruding lips pulled into a grimace, thick, dark, arched brows, and heavily lidded eyes. These exaggerated features are contrasted with the duke's fine clothes: a top hat, short morning coat, high collar, and form-fitting trousers ending in dainty heeled shoes. The implication is not so much concerned about the duke's predicament, but rather that the ugly and foreign Jew can (and does) buy his way into respectable society but will forever be contrasted unfavorably with the beauty of his material surroundings and possessions, and those among whom he lives. Without the caption, this image is easily misread as a comment on Jewish parvenus in France, rather than a comment on a foreign political issue. Caricatures and satirical images operate on many levels simultaneously, and this example is no exception; the image refers to the political predicament, supposed French hypocrisy, and the stereotypical visual and behavioral characteristics of Jews. Although the caricature does not take the Jew as its main subject, by placing the figure of the Jew in the image's foreground, the cartoonist perpetuates widespread attitudes about Jewishness. This visual foregrounding would have had direct implications for the audience's reading of the image with regard to an understanding of Jewishness, particularly for those who were illiterate or who may not have bothered to read the caption.

Although a variety of visual Jewish archetypes existed in the Viennese *Witzblätter*, the "ugly" Jewish body juxtaposed with material beauty was a common trope used

Figure 5.1 Caricature from *Kikeriki* 30, no. 14 (February 16, 1890): 4. Courtesy of ANNO/Österreichische Nationalbibliothek, Vienna.

to convey the perceived threat Jewishness posed to Gentile, Austro-German society. Following these concerns, the ugly/beautiful binary was employed by antisemites to separate acculturated middle-class Jews, often visually indistinguishable from their Gentile counterparts, from the body politic. The ugly/beautiful binary thus utilized "tabs of identity" to contrast corporeally "ugly" Jews with material beauty.

Alongside the "ugly" Jew, the "beautiful" Jew was similarly used in satirical caricatures. The caricature of the "beautiful" Jew, or rather the Jew in beautiful clothing, reveals the problematic nature of acculturation in an age of rising nationalism and racial-scientific discourse. In adopting the language, culture, and visual markers (including sartorial) of a Gentile majority over the course of the eighteenth and nineteenth centuries, many *Westjuden* were virtually indistinguishable from their Gentile counterparts by the *fin de siècle*. A caricature in *Wiener Luft* from January 4, 1890, depicts a stereotypical Jewish couple in their home. Both man and woman have the same features (excluding the male pattern of baldness): corpulent, hooked noses, protruding lips, and dark curly hair. Although not grotesquely exaggerated as in *Kikeriki*, these "Jewish features" are contrasted with the couple's opulent surroundings and attire (Figure 5.2).[39] By juxtaposing stereotypical bodily and behavioral markers of Jewishness with material elegance, caricatures of lavishly dressed Jews not only played a part in revealing the "true" nature of acculturated Jews but also had repercussions for the image of sartorial elegance and fashion. An image published in the January 21, 1900, issue of *Kikeriki* reveals this

Figure 5.2 Caricature from *Wiener Luft: Beiblatt zum "Figaro,"* no. 1 (January 4, 1890): 1. Courtesy of ANNO/Österreichische Nationalbibliothek, Vienna.

Figure 5.3 Caricature from *Kikeriki* 40, no. 6 (January 21, 1900): 2. Courtesy of ANNO/Österreichische Nationalbibliothek, Vienna.

perceived association (Figure 5.3). With the title "Die Hofball-Toiletten aus 'Maison Spitzer," the image depicts fashion personified as an ugly, overweight Jewish woman sitting atop a throne marked "Spitzer"—a renowned Jewish-owned clothing atelier—surrounded by female members of the aristocracy all surging forward, their purses and banknotes held out.[40] In this instance there is a direct link between Jewish "ugliness" and the vulgarity of fashion with its foreign and frivolous connotations.

Figure 5.4 Caricature from *Der Floh* 29, no. 23 (June 6, 1897): 5. Courtesy of ANNO/Österreichische Nationalbibliothek, Vienna.

Another related trope of the ugly/beautiful model is that which juxtaposes Jewish "ugliness" with Gentile "beauty." This binary representation was widespread in European societies and was manifest in both visual and literary forms. The diary of author and socialite Alma Schindler (1879–1964) is full of nasty remarks about the physicality and behavior of Jews—despite spending much of her time in their company and later marrying two Jewish men (Gustav Mahler and Franz Werfel). In an entry from 1901, she fantasizes about marrying the Jewish composer Alexander von Zemlinsky (1871–1942), pointedly remarking, "how ridiculous would it look . . . he so ugly, so small—me so beautiful, so tall."[41] The contrast of the Jew's "ugliness" with the non-Jew's physical "beauty" was also expressed in the depiction of inner character: the Jew's corporeal "ugliness" and incorrect attire was a physical manifestation of immoral character, while the Gentile's "beauty" and sartorial respectability was a sign of his or her purity and goodness of character. An image appearing in *Der Floh* (1897) highlights this notion. Two "ugly" Jewish men regard a reputable-looking couple strolling in their Sunday best, the ill-fitting and scruffy clothes of the Jews providing a contrast to the sartorial respectability of the young couple (Figure 5.4).[42] The caption beneath the image does not specify whether the young couple are Jewish or not. Given that one of the two Jews comments that he arranged their marriage, it is not unlikely that this handsome couple is supposed to be Jewish as well. However,

Figure 5.5 Caricature from *Kikeriki* 30, no. 2 (January 5, 1890): 1. Courtesy of ANNO/Österreichische Nationalbibliothek, Vienna.

what is important here is that they are drawn without Jewish bodily stereotypes and therefore serve as a contrast to the two "ugly" Jews.

An exaggerated Jewish physiognomy could also be used to highlight negative aspects of non-Jewish behavior. For example, *Kikeriki*'s regular depictions of Vienna's mayor from 1889 to 1894, Johann Nepomuk Prix (1836–94), include stereotypical Jewish features (large nose, protruding lips, high-domed forehead) to highlight negative aspects of his character. A caricature from the front page of the January 5, 1890, issue accused Prix of being money-grubbing and mismanaging the city's funds (Figure 5.5).[43] This and other depictions of Prix in the journal bear little resemblance to the mayor as he appeared in various portraits of the period. Another way in which Jewish "ugliness" was used to comment on the behavior of Gentiles was to highlight the stupidity of antisemitism. For example, a caricature from the journal's April 27, 1890, issue portrays a family of "ugly," large-nosed Jews admiring beautiful flowers in the *Rothschildgarten* while an indignant antisemite with a small button-nose fumes that the Jews with their large noses are stealing the flowers' beautiful scent (Figure 5.6).[44] Nonetheless, this caricature can likewise function on another level. Through the character of the antisemite the cartoonist levels an accusation of Jewish avarice, claiming that even their physicality consumes more than they are entitled to, to the detriment of others.

Figure 5.6 Caricature from *Kikeriki* 30, no. 34 (April 27, 1890): 3. Courtesy of ANNO/Österreichische Nationalbibliothek, Vienna.

The Ubiquitous *Ostjude*

The figure of the *Ostjude* exemplified the cultural perception that Jews were unattractive and remained a constant threat in antisemitic discourse and its visual manifestations. In a similar manner to the ugly/beautiful binary used to separate acculturated Jews from the Gentile body politic, the figure of the *Ostjude* was employed as the ultimate personification of Jewish difference in Viennese society. This ultimate Jewish difference was manifested in the eastern archetype through various elements of his character: bodily, racially, linguistically, religiously, culturally, and—importantly—sartorially. For both the antisemite and the *Westjude*, the *Ostjude*'s "traditional" garb or tattered clothes served as a sartorial marker of his inner qualities: depraved, dirty, and foreign. Clothing was thus used to highlight two models of supposed Jewish difference: (1) the deception of Jews whose fine clothing did not correspond to the bodies they covered, and (2) old clothing as an indicator of outsider status.

A prominent example of clothing used as an antisemitic motif can be found in a caricature titled "Ein Surrogat" from *Wiener Luft* (February 1, 1890) (Figure 5.7), in which a pair of *Ostjuden*—father and son—dressed in tattered rags converse amidst filthy surroundings. Both wear long kaftans with ragged hems and sleeves, large boots, and the stereotypical high-crowned felt hats that, although bearing little resemblance to the actual headwear styles of Hasidic men, were omnipresent in antisemitic caricatures. Both have long, wispy sidelocks (*peyes*) and the father has a ragged beard in contrast

Figure 5.7 Caricature from *Wiener Luft*, no. 5 (February 1, 1890): 1. Courtesy of ANNO/Österreichische Nationalbibliothek, Vienna.

to his son's sparse growth—reference to the biblical commandment for Jewish men not to shave their facial hair (Leviticus 19:27). Their living quarters are filthy. The bed is unmade, articles of clothing, shoes, and dirty dishes lie about the floor and across a threadbare armchair, ragged coats hang on the wall, and there is a dirty, decrepit stove at the back of the room. The son scratches himself, a visual indication of not only his uncleanliness but also his discomfort at being unclean. The caption, written in mock-Yiddish with elongated vowels, reveals a family disagreement: the son wishes to visit the public baths, while his father expresses exasperation and accuses him of being a spendthrift ("*As De bist a Verschwender! Sennen mer nix erst vorgestern bei dem groißen Regen geworden naß bis auf der Haut?*").[45]

The multilevel meaning conveyed is that not only are *Ostjuden* dirty and foreign (inferred by their incorrect German) but also miserly. This caricature also contains a message of intergenerational conflict, with the added inference that the son will become his father, as he is starting to resemble him. Along with physiognomic and linguistic characteristics, old and tattered clothes are clearly understood as transparent symbols of Jewishness and correspond contextually to social and medical discourse on Jews and venereal disease.[46] In this manner, the Jewish father and son depicted in a filthy room, in dirty, threadbare clothing, and discussing personal hygiene appeals to the reader's prior knowledge of social discourse on Jews and venereal disease. Such images also make use of the historical representations of Jewish dealers of used clothing. Depictions of Jews in this sartorial guise are, in a sense, comforting to the antisemite: they present the Jew in his supposedly natural form who is therefore rendered less threatening.

The conflation of all Jews with *Ostjuden* was a common theme in such caricatures. The archetype of the Jewish parvenu had his origins in the newly arrived *Ostjude*: an exchange of the kaftan, *shtrayml*, and sidelocks for *Frack*, *Zylinder*, and Franz Joseph-style whiskers was a recurring theme. During a period of increased Jewish acculturation in Vienna, which saw Jews across various socioeconomic tiers becoming linguistically, culturally, and sartorially indistinguishable from their Gentile counterparts, the physiognomic resemblance between *Ostjude* and *Westjude* in satirical cartoons was no accident. Such images were not merely a comment on the shared origins of both "types," but a clear statement about the nonexistence of the *Westjude* in the eyes of antisemites. The social discourse among acculturated upper- and middle-class Jews positioned them as distinct from their eastern coreligionists. In Jewish circles, the figure of the *Ostjude* was a construction of acculturated Jews to deflect antisemitism away from themselves and onto unacculturated coreligionists.[47] However, to the antisemite there was no difference; and this was reflected in caricatures that maliciously characterized the difference between the *Ost-* and *Westjuden* as a purely sartorial and material one.[48] If clothing and other material trappings were the only things that separated the acculturated *Westjude* from his eastern coreligionists, then once they were removed what was left was Jewish foreignness.

In addition to appearing as the quintessential visual manifestation of the Jew, the *Ostjude*'s language was employed as a tab of identity.[49] Jews were commonly caricatured speaking *Mauscheldeutsch*, a Yiddishized, grammatically incorrect German, complete with stereotypical exclamations such as "*mboh*," "*chammer*," and "*e soj*." It matters little whether Jews were dressed in the attire of the Hasidim or in modern fashionable garments, as the

Figure 5.8 Caricature from *Wiener Luft*, no. 1 (January 4, 1890): 2. Courtesy of ANNO/Österreichische Nationalbibliothek, Vienna.

stereotyped form of speech was common throughout caricatures in the various satirical journals. A caricature in *Wiener Luft* (January 4, 1890) (Figure 5.8) satirizes the widespread dedication to *Bildung* and European culture among Viennese middle-class Jews. Two men are depicted in mid-conversation. Outwardly, there is little to define them as Jewish: they are drawn with stereotypical hooked noses, but their sophisticated facial hair (one with whiskers and moustache and the other with a neat full beard) and their well-fitting modern clothing carry no indication of Jewishness that was otherwise suggested through sartorial ignorance. On the contrary, there is a sense of hyper-stylishness, particularly with regard to the man on the left. Although appearing in the guise of a wealthy plutocrat, dressed in double-breasted overcoat with a fur collar and *Zylinder*, details of his appearance such as his blasé stance, monocle, and hat sitting at a slight angle give him the appearance of a fashion-conscious *Gigerl*. His acquaintance, dressed in a coat with an upturned collar, a wide-brimmed hat, sporting long hair, and a portfolio under his arm, does not appear as a respected and sober member of the middle class but, rather, some sort of bohemian intellectual reminiscent of the poet Peter Altenberg. In addition to the details of their attire and their typically Jewish-sounding names—Morgenstern and Sonnenschein—their Yiddishized speech in the caption highlights these men as Jewish:

Morgenstern: Sonnenschein! biste gewest bei der Aufführung der *neunten Sympfenie* von *Beethoiven* [*sic*]?

Sonnenschein: Mboh! wie hast *neunte* Sympfenie? Jach geh' nür zü erschte
   Sympfenien!
(Morgenstern: Sonnenschein! Were you at Beethoven's *Ninth Symphony*?
Sonnenschein: Mboh! What do you mean *Ninth Symphonie*? I only go to *first*
   symphonies!)

By contrasting the Jews' respectable dressed appearance with their incorrect German and
cultural naivety, the caricature both comments on the supposed incompatibility of Jews
with the ideals of *Bildung* that so many of them held dear, and it connects the bourgeois
Jews of Vienna's inner districts to religiously traditional, culturally unassimilated Jews of
the Leopoldstadt and Brigittenau (districts II and XX).[50]

The Jew as Upwardly Mobile Parvenu

Binary modes of Jewish difference have played a large role in the imagining of the Jew in
antisemitic discourse. Another common binary model of Jewish representation divided
Jews between pariahs and parvenus, as highlighted by Hannah Arendt.[51] With the increasing
cultural, economic, academic, social, and political success of Jews during the latter half of
the nineteenth century, satirical magazines in Central Europe would increasingly portray
Jews as nouveau-riche parvenus, in contrast to an older model of the Jew as a dispossessed
pariah.[52] It meant little that Jews were not the only members of a growing liberal-minded
bourgeoisie. Allen notes, "despite his attempts at assimilation, the Jew was never portrayed
simply as another ambitious bourgeois, but always as a crude and recognizable racial type."[53]

The parvenu/pariah binary was regularly employed in caricatures and satirical cartoons
in depicting Jews as crass social climbers or (equally crass) destitute human vermin.
Such caricatures were especially effective in that that they used all manner of antisemitic
stereotypes to ridicule the assimilatory process at all stages, from acculturation to complete
integration with the wider Gentile population. A common visual trope was the disheveled
eastern peddler's transformation into the corpulent, wealthy plutocrat dressed in fine
clothing and living in opulently decorated rooms.[54] In the images that utilized this trope,
clothing played an all-important role. When the shabbily-dressed *Schnorrer* exchanges his
shtetl garb for well-tailored European clothing, his change of attire does not simply reflect
the amassing of wealth. A change of dress patterns is never simply just a change of clothing;
it is also an expression of the individual's self-image. Joanne Entwistle asserts, "The body
as a vehicle of the self has to be 'managed' in daily interaction and failure to manage one's
body appropriately can result in embarrassment, ridicule and/or stigma."[55] By changing
out of his fraying kaftan, worn boots, and typical "Jewish" hat into the ubiquitous lounge
suit and a pair of polished boots and spats, the Jew candidly expresses his desired entrance
into modern European culture and his reinvention as a cultivated European. The presence
of this notion in such images is all the more important due to the contemporary antisemitic
discourse that denied the Jew the possibility of reinventing himself as anything other than
a Jew. The result was the transformation of the pariah into the parvenu.

The figure of the Jewish parvenu was attacked by antisemites and (some) Jews alike for the crass manner with which he sought to insert himself into the upper echelons of society.[56] Theodor Herzl's utopian Zionist novel *Altneuland* (1902) is in many ways a critique of what he considered the parvenu behavior of Viennese Jewish élites.[57] Rejected by the woman he loves in favor of the physically inferior Leopold Weinberger, a personification of contemporary antisemitic stereotypes, the young lawyer Friedrich Löwenberg finds himself disgusted with Vienna's Jewish bourgeoisie of which he is himself a part (as indeed Herzl was). Löwenberg decides to abandon civilization and become the companion of the elderly eccentric American millionaire Kingscourt (a misanthropic, originally Prussian, aristocrat named Königshof). The novel, full of praise for the Zionist project, and the noble pioneers of "The New Society" in Ottoman Palestine, is peppered with contempt for assimilatory-minded Jews who scoff at the idea of Jewish national autonomy. Herzl's "New Jews," decent, hard-working, and outwardly proud of their Jewish identities, are sharply contrasted with the decadence and self-destructive parvenu behavior of the Viennese hypocrites Grün, Blau, Walter Schlessinger, and the Weinberger-Löffler family, who are quick to ridicule efforts of Jewish self-determination at the beginning of the novel. The contrasting characters represent what Arendt refers to as the pariah and the parvenu,[58] and it is in the New Jew's proud nature that she/he can overcome pariah status.

The binary nature of these groups is manifested in their corporeal and sartorial evolution; at the beginning of the novel the immigrant Eastern European Littwak family is presented as impoverished and physically frail pariahs dressed in rags. After their relocation to Palestine, they are transformed into erudite nobles in the land of their ancestors (using a clear Zionist trope of biblical origins), seamlessly elegant and harmonious in the fine clothing of the modern European and the Oriental surroundings. In contrast, the parvenus of Vienna, living in the lap of luxury, are transformed into the same comical figures depicted in contemporary satirical caricatures, personified by Ernestine Löffler's metamorphosis from the beautiful and fashionable society debutante into the corpulent and garishly opulent middle-aged matron who comically tries to hold onto her youth. Setting the Zionist message of the text aside, Herzl's novel is a classic example of Jewish self-critique and is strongly linked to the so-called Jewish Question in *fin-de-siècle* Vienna, albeit in a non-satirical manner.[59] Such Jewish self-critique, which has been described as a form of self-hatred, is unsurprising. The antisemitic stereotypes in Herzl's novel were widespread in Viennese society and resemble those in magazines like *Kikeriki*. As such, these widespread tropes were internalized even by Jews themselves.[60]

The scorned bourgeois Jews of Herzl's *Altneuland* are lampooned for their clannishness in the face of their desire to assimilate. The figure of the upwardly mobile parvenu was also mocked for his desire to abandon his Jewishness. One way in which this was attempted was conversion and intermarriage. At the *fin de siècle*, Vienna had the highest rate of Jewish apostasy of any European city.[61] Viennese Jews left Judaism by either converting to Christianity or declaring themselves *konfessionslos*. They did this for a variety of reasons, including genuine religious conviction, a desire to marry non-Jews, to facilitate social and professional advancement, and other personal reasons.[62] In this manner, intermarriage was common in Vienna and—along with conversion—was used

Die confessionelle Schule.

Was jetzt getrennt der Hohn, der Spott . . .

Vereinigt einst der Liebesgott.

Figure 5.9 Caricature from *Der Floh* 30, no. 40 (October 2, 1898): 4. Courtesy of ANNO/Österreichische Nationalbibliothek, Vienna.

by antisemites (as well as some Jews) as evidence of a Jewish tendency toward social climbing.[63] Intermarriage between Jews and Gentiles was a common target of ridicule in satirical caricatures (Figure 5.9).[64] It was not only the perceived aesthetic divide between the "ugly" Jew and "beautiful" Gentile that such images highlighted; they also gave a voice to the double accusation that Jews took Gentile partners purely for self-advancement and thus befouled the Gentile body politic.[65]

Satirical cartoons addressing the issue of intermarriage also attacked the Gentile party involved. Caricatures published before and after the First World War pilloried young Gentile women for liaisons with older, wealthy Jewish men who shower them with expensive gifts.[66] In images addressing the issue of mixed relationships, both parties are lampooned for their opportunism: the young and beautiful *demimonde* eager to befoul herself in return for material comfort, and the lecherous old Jew for preying on young beauties in order to enhance his image in a milieu impressed by appearances. This raises an interesting question regarding the nature of the parvenu and assimilation. Such cartoons clearly select as their targets so-called Jewish parvenus hoping to raise their social status and insert themselves into high society. However, exactly which segments of high society the parvenu aspires to is less obvious.

The general accusation—one based on the experiences of a limited number of tolerated wealthy Jews, often in other European capitals[67]—targeted Jewish "infiltration" into aristocratic and upper-class circles. In *fin-de-siècle* and interwar Vienna, however, Jewish socialization with members of the upper echelons of Gentile society was an exception to the overwhelming social experiences of Viennese Jews, whose nobility were a more "closed" group, marrying their children to each other, and were often excluded from the Gentile aristocracy.[68] Fears of Jewish infiltration were not unfounded, albeit unlikely. While there were instances of ennobled families "assimilating" into the (non-Jewish) aristocracy—such as the family of the famed writer Hugo von Hofmannsthal—the likelihood of Jews from lower socioeconomic tiers becoming assimilated into élite Gentile circles was less likely.[69]

Three Jews on a Park Bench: Jews as Inward-Looking Conspirators

The closed nature of Jewish communities, especially in instances of heightened antisemitism on the part of the dominant Gentile population, was a common theme in Central Europe. The classic image of Jews conspiring together against their Gentile "hosts" was widespread in the German-speaking world. Antisemitic postcards from various German and Austrian towns during the late nineteenth and early twentieth centuries used this archetype for both malicious and sentimental purposes.[70] The trio of Jews gossiping on a park bench was only one manifestation of this image; at times the number in the group was smaller or larger, and the setting also changed. This archetype, albeit satirizing Jewish clannishness, was not simply one of ridicule but one that had far more serious connotations. Although caricatures of Jewish friends or business associates might highlight stereotypical professional habits or cultural peculiarities, these seemingly harmless images carried implications of a Jewish deviousness that was dangerous to Gentile society.

This stereotypical role applied, like others, to both easily identifiable *Ostjuden* and their westernized counterparts. The earlier example from *Wiener Luft* (Figure 4.8) of the two seemingly-westernized Jews discussing their artistic tastes is more than a mockery of artistic snobbery and philistinism; it also carries the accusation of Jewish domination over Vienna's artistic scene.[71] Similarly, a caricature from the same magazine not only pointedly mocks Jewish business practices but also makes a statement about the proportion of the retail trade dominated by Jews (Figure 5.10).[72] The caption reveals that the two Jews, one dressed in the respectable lounge suit, cravat, and pince-nez of the bourgeoisie, the other in a somewhat shabbier coat and hat, discuss the former's method of squeezing his competitors out of business through his advertising. There is no shortage of caricatures concerning the shady business or social practices of Viennese Jews in which they are depicted as conspirators. For example, some months later, *Wiener Luft* published an image in which two adult Jews enthuse over a child's "education" in his father's business practices—in particular the child's ability to forge his signature (Figure 5.11).[73] Such caricatures highlight the widespread contemporary stereotypes and fears about Jewish dishonesty and dominance in certain professions and industries.[74] This was pointed out in the early twentieth century by Werner Sombart, who emphasized the link between Judaism and capitalism in his 1911 volume *Die Juden und das Wirtschaftsleben*.[75] Such concerns were rife in European societies, particularly when Jews were a highly conspicuous segment of urban settings. In Vienna, where in 1890 they constituted 8.7

Figure 5.10 Caricature from *Wiener Luft*, no. 3 (January 18, 1890): 4. Courtesy of ANNO/Österreichische Nationalbibliothek, Vienna.

Figure 5.11 Caricature from *Wiener Luft*, no. 14 (April 5, 1890): 4. Courtesy of ANNO/Österreichische Nationalbibliothek, Vienna.

percent of the total population, most Jews were very poor, with only a third of the total Jewish population being able to afford to pay the IKG taxes.[76] But none of this prevented antisemites like Karl Lueger from stirring up fears about Jewish economic dominance over the lower-middle and working classes.

However, beyond the economic threat that Jews were thought to pose to the fabric of society, equally worrying was the threat many believed they posed by way of their supposed racial and cultural peculiarities. Interestingly, while this racial "threat" was highlighted in caricatures that commented on intermarriage or Jewish-Gentile socialization, it was more commonly highlighted in those images in which Gentiles were replaced by large numbers of Jews or groups of Jews attempting to enter Gentile-designated environments. Dressed in a variety of attire—kaftans and fur hats, evening wear, business suits, or the fashionable styles of holiday resorts, including *Volkstrachten*—Jews were depicted in almost every social situation, and often to the exclusion of Gentile figures. The fear embedded in such images was not the racial contamination that Jewish-Gentile socialization would result in, but rather the threat of Jews outbreeding Germans and becoming the dominant "race" in Vienna and its provinces. A 1906 *Kikeriki* cartoon depicts a crowd of Jews in Bad Ischl who wear fashionable attire that marks them as foreign urban visitors to this provincial town (Figure 5.12).[77] Not only are the Gentiles absent, but its crux, highlighted by the caption, suggests a Jewish ridicule of *Goyim*. Although the Gentile is invisible in the

Figure 5.12 Caricature from *Kikeriki* 46, no. 53 (July 5, 1906): 3. Courtesy of ANNO/Österreichische Nationalbibliothek, Vienna.

cartoon, his presence is felt through the little boy's exclamation: "Bape, Bape, auf der Esplanade ist ein Mann, der einen Christen nachmachen kann!"[78] In a cruel twist of fate, the Gentile ridicule of the Jew is turned on its head with the Jews in this image laughing over the peculiarities of the *"Christen"* (Christians).[79] Not only have Jews "replaced" a Gentile populace, but they have also become emboldened enough to ridicule them in a prominent public setting.[80]

Fears of "Jewification": An Increasing Jewish Population

Another typical trope related to the *Ostjude* that appeared in antisemitic caricatures was the notion of "Jewification," whereby it was feared that Jews were taking over Vienna. Although Germans had cultural and linguistic hegemony over other "nations" in the Cisleithanian half of the Dual Monarchy,[81] Austria's status as a *Vielvölkerstaat*, whereby no single nation was officially dominant over the others, created difficulties for interethnic relations and for the overall notion of Austrian identity. Jeffery W. Beglaw demonstrates that Cisleithanian minister-president Count Kasimir Felix Badeni's (1846–1909) *Sprachenverordnung* (language ordinance) of 1897 that declared the equality of both the Czech and German languages in the crown lands of Bohemia and Moravia emboldened Czech national confidence while simultaneously placing Germans on the warpath, not only in the crown lands but in the Austrian capital, too. Beglaw's study shows that among the various "themes" addressed in anti-Czech political and social cartoons, a common trope appearing in *Kikeriki* was the notion of Czech migrants swamping the Empire's "German" capital.[82] Although Austro-German anxieties about non-Germans taking over the capital were not new, the anti-Czech sentiments at the *fin de siècle* are an appropriate example of the wider national conflicts during the period.

Likewise, Germans feared growing Jewish influence in a city that had formerly been closed to Jewish migration. The *fin-de-siècle* cartoons depicting a Jewish "takeover" of

Figure 5.13 Caricature from *Kikeriki* 46, no. 14 (February 18, 1906): 2. Courtesy of ANNO/Österreichische Nationalbibliothek, Vienna.

the city were not new. Earlier satirical outputs, such as Franz Friedrich Masaidek's *Wien und die Wiener aus der Spottvogelperspektive* (1873), satirized in visual and written form the widespread fears about the growing Jewish and Czech communities and the effects they would have on the political, economic, and social life of the capital. Already in the 1870s, Masaidek had characterized these concerns in images of city parks overcrowded with Jews.[83]

The cartoons addressing these concerns that appeared in the *Witzblätter*, like the aforementioned "Ischl" cartoon, often followed a certain formula: they took place in traditional "German" environments, implying a sense of foreign intrusion; the individuals depicted might be dressed in outlandish styles, pointing to a supposed Jewish inelegance and hankering after fashion; and few or no Germans were present, suggesting a complete Jewish usurpation of power. A *Kikeriki* cartoon from February 1906 suggests the next parliamentary addendum (Figure 5.13).[84] Among the fictional future ministers of the Austrian parliament are no Gentiles, just "ugly" Jewish men in ill-fitting ceremonial garb. Particularly (intended) humorous depictions are the bandy-legged Minister of War, complete in ceremonial officer's uniform, and the Minister of Religion, who wears a cassock and sports a tonsure, but has the appearance of a Hasidic rabbi with his stereotypical Jewish facial features and long, scraggly beard.[85] In addition, the protocol under his arm includes the subtitle "Talmud." The Minister for Trade, in contrast to his colleagues who are at least dressed in ceremonial garb, even if comically ill-fitting, has been drawn simply as the stereotypical Galician peddler carrying his pack over his shoulder and dressed in typical kaftan and hat. While the other figures engage with each other, the new Minister for Trade breaks the fourth wall, grinning at the readers, possibly expressing amusement at the "Jewification" of Austrian politics.

In a similar vein, a satirical image from *Wiener Luft* comments on the Jewish overpopulation of the city (Figure 5.14)[86]—an anxiety that persisted to plague antisemites over the ensuing decades. Two clearly non-Jewish gentlemen stand in a public space filled with people. The visitor to Vienna, dressed in a checked overcoat with fur-lined collar and cuffs, and a top hat, asks a local, who is far more modestly

Figure 5.14 Caricature from *Wiener Luft*, no. 9 (March 1, 1890): 2. Courtesy of ANNO/Österreichische Nationalbibliothek, Vienna.

dressed in overcoat and bowler, where he might find the Judengasse, to which the latter replies exasperatedly, "Perhaps you could tell me where it isn't?"[87] Although neither of these men possess tabs of identity that would indicate they are Jewish, this sense of answering a question with a question has a strong "Jewish" connotation. Sander Gilman refers to this kind of representation of a particular Jewish roundabout way of speaking as "the hidden language of the Jew," which, like Yiddish and *Mauscheln*, indicates Jewish deviousness and depravity in antisemitic discourse.[88] Upon closer inspection, all the figures populating the background scene are Jews. Even the individuals inspecting the crowd from their balconies and the decorative caryatids adorning the building have stereotypical Jewish features. The shop windows, too, display Jewish individuals inside, and their signs announce the typically Jewish names of the owners, such as *Veitl*, *Veigelsto*[ck], and *Mandelste*[in/ern]. In this scene, a "genuine" Viennese sarcastically informs a visitor that the city is so overrun with Jews, a specific *Judengasse* is redundant, the implication being that the whole city has been reconfigured.

During periods of political and social unrest, such cartoons appeared in the pages of the journals—*Kikeriki* in particular—with greater frequency. In the wake of the First World War and the uncertainty the collapse of the Dual Monarchy held for millions of its former subjects, images depicted Jews having benefitted from the war and dominating the emerging republic,[89] "hordes" of Jewish immigrants arriving from the east (Figure 5.15),[90] and the threat Béla Kun's communist regime in the neighboring Hungarian Soviet Republic held for "German Austria."[91] While Kun and his associates did not take over Austria—ironically, they fled to Vienna upon the Soviet collapse later that year—and Jews did not usurp Austro-Germany, cartoons prophesizing or warning readers about the dangers of Jewish domination remained common. Such images persisted into the 1920s and 1930s. A *Kikeriki* cartoon from 1925 prophesizes *Stadtparkreformen* (city park reforms) and depicts the *Stadtpark* full of promenading Jews dressed in the latest

Figure 5.15 Caricature from *Kikeriki* 59, no. 26 (June 29, 1919): 7. Courtesy of ANNO/Österreichische Nationalbibliothek, Vienna.

Figure 5.16 Caricature from *Kikeriki* 65, no. 23 (June 7, 1925): 7. Courtesy of ANNO/Österreichische Nationalbibliothek, Vienna.

fashions (Figure 5.16).[92] The reforms include a direct telephone link to the Viennese Stock Exchange with live updates shown via charts and dials in an advertising column. In this reform, non-Jews are relegated to a minority where one sees "only Kohns and Shlomos—even the trees are circumcised!"[93] Below the cartoon, a caption informs in very small and easily overlooked text: "Die Wiener Stadtpark gehört den Juden. Reichsdeutsche Arier sind von seinem [*sic.*] Besuche ausgeschlossen" (The Vienna city park belongs to the Jews. Reich-German Aryans are forbidden from visiting). The specific reference to *Reichsdeutsche* is not an accident; in this manner *Kikeriki*—by this time sympathetic to emerging National Socialist ideals—warns that Jews have attained dominance over Viennese Germans, and no local Gentile would even consider visiting so strongly "Judaized" an environment.

Revenge and Ridicule: Reaction to Jewish "Intrusion"

By the time *der schöne Karl* was appointed mayor of Vienna in 1897, the antisemitic caricatures appearing in the *Witzblätter* had taken a more aggressive stance. In particular those published in *Kikeriki*, which presented itself as an organ of Lueger's Christian Social Party, anti-Jewish cartoons, and satirical verse and prose became more prevalent.[94] Jeffery W. Beglaw argues that it is impossible to prove whether *Kikeriki* was "proactive or reactive" in the nationality conflicts of the *fin de siècle*, and, instead, poses a series of questions regarding why there was an increase in xenophobic sentiment.[95] Although Beglaw's study concerns anti-Czech sentiment among Vienna's dominant German population, the same can be argued with regard to the Jews. It is irrelevant whether *Kikeriki* was responsible for influencing antisemitic sentiment in Vienna or was influenced by it; what is clear is that the journal harnessed existing antisemitism and certainly took advantage of the new administration's antisemitic rhetoric to both entertain its readers and malign the city's Jewish population. In addition to visually bemoaning the Jewish presence in Vienna, *Kikeriki* cartoons posed "solutions" for the Jewish Question to its readers. Caricatures that ridiculed Jews, making them appear comical bumbling pests, and those that hinted at taking revenge or actively "de-Judaizing" the city were prevalent.[96]

A common trope in such images was the "revenge" Lueger would now mete out upon his enemies. The front page of an issue of *Der Floh* just weeks before his induction as mayor employed this very theme (Figure 5.17).[97] Wearing a black toga and reclining

Wenn Dr. Lueger Bürgermeister wird.

Ave Caesar! Morituri te salutant.

Figure 5.17 Caricature from *Der Floh* 29, no. 12 (March 21, 1897): 1. Courtesy of ANNO/Österreichische Nationalbibliothek, Vienna.

on a throne guarded by roaring lions, Lueger as a Roman emperor, surveys his bowing subjects: political opponents swathed in togas, and two bare-chested, loincloth-clad Jews whose wrists are bound together. The caption in Latin reads: "Ave Caesar! Morituri te salutant." (Hail Caesar! They who are about to die salute you.) The caption gives no doubt that the figures before Lueger have been condemned to death (at least in a political sense), but the incoming mayor's noble stance conveys a sense of justice: punishment shall be meted out swiftly and painlessly. The divide between Lueger's political opponents, who include the former Liberal mayor Raimund Grübl (1847–98), and the Jewish prisoners is important. Not only are the two groups spatially divided but their sartorial difference places the former at a higher rank than the lowly Jews. Additionally, Lueger looks at his political opponents, avoiding the gaze of the condemned Jews, suggesting a sense of respect for the former but none for the latter.

A cartoon of a similar mood appeared in *Kikeriki* three years later; this depicted the Salzgries[98] in mourning: black banners hanging from every building and crowds of raggedly dressed Jewish peddlers sobbing inconsolably into each other's shoulders (Figure 5.18).[99] *Kikeriki*—the journal's eponymous anthropomorphized rooster mascot—asks a passerby if the display is the result of the death of a member of the Paris branch of the Rothschild family. "But no," the passerby replies, "it's because Lueger is so healthy!" Lueger's populist antisemitic rhetoric created the impression that self-assured Viennese Jews were now finally getting their due—and indeed, some of the more vulnerable members of the community (particularly the poor immigrants in the Leopoldstadt) did suffer increased abuse at the hands of emboldened antisemites.[100] However, as many liberal-minded, middle-class Jews were quick to point out, there was no reinstitution of anti-Jewish laws at the hands of the mayor who even maintained cordial relations with individual Jews and the board of the IKG.[101] The communal leader and textile magnate Sigmund Mayer (1831–1920), for example, claimed that Lueger did not dislike Viennese Jews, whose business prowess he admired, but rather disliked foreign Jews.[102] Nevertheless, Lueger's rhetoric undoubtedly emboldened antisemites in their mistreatment of Jews and made it difficult for individual Jews—including those baptized—to feel included in the ranks of the Christian Social Party and wider Austro-German society. As Arthur Schnitzler stressed:

It was not possible, especially for a Jew in the public eye, to ignore the fact that he was a Jew, since the others didn't ignore it, not the Christians and even less the Jews. One had the choice of being considered insensitive, importunate, or fresh or sensitive, shy, or suffering from a persecution complex. And even when one kept one's inner and outer composure so that one didn't show one tendency or the other, it was just as impossible to remain fully unaffected as someone could remain indifferent who let his skin be anaesthetized but had to look on with alert and open eyes as unclean knives scratched at it, cut into it until it bled.[103]

Contemporary cartoons highlight this sense of alienation. Two very similar images from *Kikeriki* reflect the sense of hostility and the sharpened division between Vienna's Gentile

Figure 5.18 Caricature from *Kikeriki* 40, no. 15 (February 22, 1900): 4. Courtesy of ANNO/Österreichische Nationalbibliothek, Vienna.

Figure 5.19 Caricature from *Kikeriki* 40, no. 14 (February 18, 1900): 2. Courtesy of ANNO/Österreichische Nationalbibliothek, Vienna.

and Jewish populations. The first, appearing in February 1900—under the title "Der Ball der Stadt Wien"—presents two silhouetted ball scenes side by side: the first consists of three Jewish couples with unruly hair, hooked noses, and protruding lips, and the second of three decidedly non-Jewish couples with proportioned features and neat hair, waltzing with more decorum (Figure 5.19).[104] Unlike the Jews, their silhouettes are tidy with discreet attire and a lack of ostentatious jewelry. The implied message of the cartoon is that in the past (prior to Lueger's ascension to the mayoral throne), the city balls were rife with Jews, but now they have recovered their decorum and good taste since the Jews have been removed. The second image published exactly six years later, also depicts a silhouetted ball scene, this time with Lueger's recognizable profile in the window dancing with a female personification of Vienna, and two lavishly dressed Jewish *Börsianer* excluded and watching the scene from outside (Figure 5.20). As the Jews regard the scene with regret, one bemoans Lueger's success and popularity in Vienna, "Waih! Der Luegerleben tanzt sech aber noch ganz rüstig mit der Vindobona!" (Oy vey! *Luegerleben* is still dancing so vigorously with *Vindobona*!).[105] The message inferred here: all is well in Vienna and the troublesome Jews have been put in their place. These two cartoons were part of a wider accusation of Jewish ostentation and "Gentile" retaliation by limiting the power their financial wealth supposedly gave them. Another cartoon from the turn of the twentieth century depicts a group of lavishly dressed Jews unsuccessfully attempting to buy their way into a court ball (Figure 5.21). The group leader, a *Frack-* and *Zylinder-* wearing parvenu, holds up a hundred-crown note as a bribe, only to be refused entry by the sentry standing guard at the palace's entrance. A sign posted on the palace wall reads: "Entry only for officers, high dignitaries, diplomats, etc."[106] The implied message is that although wealthy, the nouveau-riche parvenu does not belong among authentic, worthy members of society and that Jews should be prevented from buying their way into these circles at all costs.

* * *

Figure 5.20 Caricature from *Kikeriki* 46, no. 14 (February 18, 1906): 7. Courtesy of ANNO/Österreichische Nationalbibliothek, Vienna.

Figure 5.21 Caricature from *Kikeriki* 40, no. 6 (January 21, 1900): 3. Courtesy of ANNO/Österreichische Nationalbibliothek, Vienna.

The cartoons appearing in the Viennese *Witzblätter* during the late nineteenth and early twentieth centuries can be read as a manifestation of widespread perceptions of Jews in Viennese society. These images are important because they reveal how caricatures in cartoons and satirical images were used to depict Jews and other minorities as "Others," and in doing so employ a range of xenophobic tropes that play on the paranoia and fear of readers. Additionally, these images are critical for how they explore the ways in which clothing contributed to the conceptualization of Jewish Viennese stereotypes. As this chapter has argued, clothing played a central role in the fictive imaging of the Jew. The glaring contradictions of Jewish dress in these images, from the miserly Jew in expensive clothing, through disheveled *Ostjuden* to fashion-following Jews in ill-fitting ostentatious attire of the *Gigerl*, often bedecked with jewelry and other trinkets, reflect the contradictory nature of contemporaneous antisemitic discourse. Jews were simultaneously accused by antisemites of being dangerous schemers plotting to destabilize the foundations of society, and money-grubbing plutocrats propping up a degenerate and exploitative system. The widespread presence of these caricatured types in the Viennese press served only to bolster notions of Jewish inferiority and immorality. While the Jewish caricatures often bore very little resemblance to the collective image they sought to portray—so too with those lampooning Czechs or Magyars—they were effective in the continued circulation of antisemitic tropes. I write "collective" rather than "individual" because the antisemitic caricatures that appeared in the Viennese satirical press rarely attacked Jews as individuals but rather as a group. Even those antisemitic caricatures that did single out specific Jewish politicians or writers targeted them as representatives of Jewry as a whole rather than as individuals.

Whether a reflection of existing antisemitic sentiments or hopeful projections of changing attitudes toward Jews, the caricatures published in the pages of journals like *Kikeriki, Der Floh*, and *Wiener Luft* are evidence of ways in which Jews were made to feel and be perceived as Others in a larger, ethnically, and culturally heterogenous society. The "tabs of identity" employed to indicate a caricature's Jewishness, whether physiognomic, linguistic, behavioral, or sartorial—or a combination of these—rarely corresponded to the reality of actual Viennese Jewry, many of whom had acculturated themselves to German culture and the ideals of *Bildung, Sittlichkeit*, and *Deutschtum*. To antisemites who sought to harangue Jews, this lack of resemblance was of little importance. On the contrary, the more Jews adopted the cultural ideals and trappings of the dominant culture around them and abandoned the external signs of their Jewishness, the more virulent the antisemitic rhetoric became. The growing visual similarity between acculturated middle-class Jews and their Gentile counterparts meant that antisemites required a way to differentiate themselves from the subjects of their vitriol. More than serving as a device with which to attack Jews, these caricatures were vital in order to allay antisemitic anxieties in a changing society.

CHAPTER 6
THE MAN IN THE SUIT
JEWISH WRITERS AND THEIR CLOTHING[1]

Jews in Suits: An Introduction

This penultimate chapter examines the dress patterns and practices of five well-known Jewish writers in the Austrian capital who were active at the *fin de siècle* and the early decades of the twentieth century. These writers—Sigmund Freud (1856–1939), Arthur Schnitzler (1862–1931), Stefan Zweig (1881–1942), Peter Altenberg (1859–1919), and Karl Kraus (1874–1936)—maintained differing approaches to their Jewishness in relationship to their role as "Jewish" cultural icons at the time. How does one define "Jewish writer" in the context of *fin-de-siècle* and interwar Vienna? Is a Jewish writer someone who writes primarily on Jewish themes or in "Jewish" languages? A writer who lives according to the tenets of the Jewish religion? Perhaps one who takes an active role in Jewish public affairs? Or an individual of Jewish origins, perceived as "Jewish" no matter how far removed that ancestry was (such as the renowned Hugo von Hofmannsthal)? Determining who is a Jewish writer is much like asking the question "who is a Jew?" Certainly, other writers qualify, such as Richard Beer-Hofmann whose work explicitly addressed Jewish themes and was sometimes associated with cultural Zionism, or the many native-Viennese and immigrant writers who were actively involved in the development of Hebrew and Yiddish literary culture in the Austrian capital. However, these five authors' primary importance as literary figures was found in their wider importance to Austrian literature and their lasting status as icons of Viennese modernism. While three of the five—Schnitzler, Zweig, and Altenberg—were renowned for their fiction, plays, and biographies (in the case of Zweig), Freud and Kraus occupied the roles of "prophets": the former of the human mind and its subconscious, and the latter, a "prophet of doom,"[2] who took it upon himself to warn his contemporaries of their impending moral destruction.

Georg Simmel, whose concept of the stranger might be employed here in understanding these Jewish protagonists' simultaneous insider/outsider position within Viennese society and cultural milieu,[3] characterized fashion as a form of imitation. Fashion, he argues, can only exist along the lines of inclusion and exclusion.[4] The wearing of the suit as a standard and conventional form of Western male dress is relevant here. All five wore a suit in some form or another, whether following strict codes of male sartorial respectability as Freud did or subverting these codes and adopting more eccentric styles like Altenberg. In the same manner that wearing a suit can signal the wearer's desire to conform, the way it is worn and the details of its styling allowed its wearer to reject some of the more uniform notions the suit symbolized and express individuality.[5] It was both in the styling of the suit and in the accessories worn with it that men chose to conform to or reject societal norms.

This was certainly true for many Jewish men in Vienna during the late nineteenth and early twentieth centuries. The five writers whose dress patterns are addressed in this chapter are examples of different approaches to wearing the suit. Whether they were immigrants (Freud, Kraus) or the Viennese sons of immigrants (Altenberg, Schnitzler, Zweig), these men were raised in the broad spectrum of Vienna's Jewish middle class with its dedication to the notion of *Bildung*, *Sittlichkeit*, and *Deutschtum*. What makes them curious case studies in examining the intersection of the dressed male body and Jewishness is their alienation from the intimate world of Jewish culture that dictated the lives of their forebears—sometimes self-imposed, at others the result of upbringings. Not only did they approach their own Jewish identification from different perspectives, but the way in which they dealt with Jewishness and the so-called Jewish Question differed as well. Altenberg and Kraus, like others of their generation, took the definitive step of publicly distancing themselves from the Jewish middle class; the former in particular renounced not only his hereditary cultural-religious identification but also the sartorial and aesthetic norms of this milieu. Freud, Schnitzler, and Zweig, on the other hand, navigated their Jewish identifications and the notion of Jewishness from different perspectives: sometimes proud, sometimes ambivalent, sometimes secondary to other classifications (i.e., German, Austrian, European). They did not renounce Judaism, nor did they reject the Jewish community as Altenberg and Kraus had; however, the ways in which they approached their individual Jewish identification were not identical. Freud and Schnitzler actively and candidly addressed the Jewish Question throughout their writing, unapologetically portraying the Jewish bourgeoisie as they felt it was best represented. Zweig, however, despite his youthful flirtation with cultural Zionism, tended to avoid frank discussion of the topic in his published writings as a mature author, relegating it instead to his private correspondence with intimate associates. Like Altenberg and Kraus, Freud, Schnitzler, and Zweig's different approaches to their Jewish identification also found manifestation in their individual dress patterns, practices, and preferences.

Sigmund Freud: Godless Jew

The "father of psychoanalysis" Sigmund Freud maintained a conscious practice of dress that placed him squarely in Vienna's educated middle class. Freud's background was typical of Viennese Jewish bourgeoisie during the second half of the nineteenth century. Born Sigismund Schlomo Freud in the Moravian town of Freiberg (Příbor) to Jakob Kolloman (or Kalman) Freud and his third wife Amalia Nathansohn—migrants from the Galician towns of Tysmenitz (Tysmenytsia) and Brody[6]—the young Sigmund spent his early years in Moravia before the family relocated to Vienna by way of Leipzig. The wealth of literature on Freud's life and work highlights his relationship to his Jewishness and Jewish identification.[7] However, absent from texts that focus on Freud's Jewish identity is a discussion of the effects his background had on his dress habits. Several factors had a strong influence on his sense of Jewish identification, and thus his self-presentation, including his family's Galician origins, the lack of religious observance in the parental home, and his coming of age in the period directly after the 1867 *Ausgleich* and emancipation of Austro-Hungarian Jewry. Jakob Freud relocated his family to Vienna in 1860 after the prohibition of Jewish residency in the Austrian capital had been rescinded, but prior to Jews being granted equal status to Gentiles. The young Sigmund grew up in the Jewish environment of the Leopoldstadt which, though not the satellite *shtetl* it would become several decades later, was home to a large Jewish population.

Freud is of course best known for his pioneering works on psychoanalysis, a man concerned foremost with plumbing the depths of human psyche. However, he also placed great importance on material objects, attested to by his love of collecting ancient artifacts. His Viennese and London offices were decorated with his large collection of artifacts and fetishes from diverse cultures, his most prized possession being a Persian rug, of which Liliane Weissberg notes:

> Too precious to put on the floor, perhaps, or to hang on the wall, the rug found its place in a quite specific location, and as an object in a peculiarly liminal site. He placed it on a couch, or divan, on which his patients would rest during treatment time. Thus, it became not only one of Freud's most prized possessions, but quite literally the foundational object of psychoanalytic treatment itself.[8]

Although much has been written about Freud's collecting habits, little attention has been given in the scholarship to Freud's choices of attire. Like those of other middle-class Viennese Jewish men, Freud's dress patterns have been overlooked as visual markers in discussions of Jewish identity, assimilation, and acculturation because of their supposed sameness to styles favored by middle-class Gentile men. In his memoir Jean-Martin (also known as simply Martin) Freud presents his famous father as an elegant man concerned with his appearance. He describes his father as a typical member of the bourgeoisie, greatly concerned with common notions of sartorial decency corresponding to an individual's station in life:

> He was not the slightest bit vain in the common meaning of the word. He merely submitted without objection to the deeply entrenched medical tradition that a doctor should be well turned out: and so there was never a hair out of place on his head nor on his chin. His clothing rigidly conventional, was cut from the best materials and tailored to perfection.[9]

In this manner, Freud the son highlights in his father's clothing choices what British psychologist John Carl Flügel described as an "adherence to the social code."[10] As Elana

Shapira explains, Freud recognized the importance of clothing in the acculturation experience of Viennese Jews. Referring to a dream of Freud in which he was caught by a Gentile housemaid in a state of undress, Shapira asserts the connection between a sense of anxiety derived from undress or disorderly dress and that concerning appearances among acculturating Jews in a hostile environment.[11]

It is true that in surviving photographs Freud appears at first glance to be attired in a standard, uniform manner. However, he is not always dressed in the same garments and the diversity of his dress choices can be seen in the small details. For example, in many photographs depicting Freud in middle and old age, he appears in dark, three-piece lounge suits, white collared shirts, and crosstie. A cursory glance might suggest that the doctor's sartorial tastes and styles hardly changed over the course of his adult life, save for the obvious change of lapel, collar, and jacket styles of the wider world of men's fashion. A 1926 photograph of Freud sitting bent over a book at a table presents his appearance as typical of an elderly member of Vienna's *Bildungsbürgertum* of the period (Figure 6.1). He wears a dark, worsted three-piece suit, a shirt with a faint stripe and a necktie in a light patterned fabric, and a watch chain hanging from his waistcoat. There is nothing particularly remarkable about Freud's clothing choices here—he looks like many other older, middle-class men of the era.[12] His clothing, similar here to that worn in other images, adopts the role of an upper-middle-class intellectual's uniform.[13]

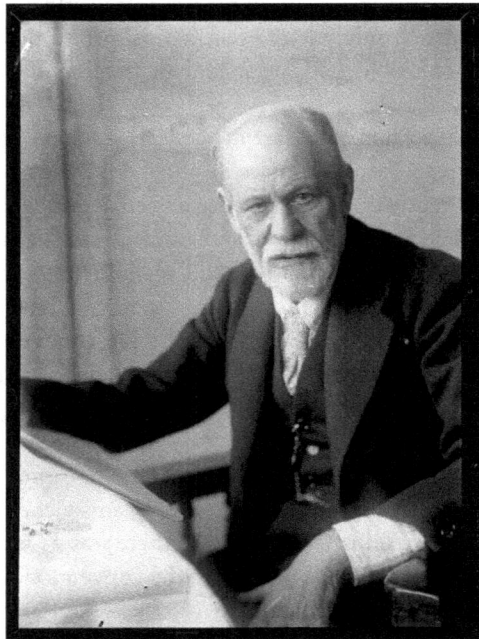

Figure 6.1 Photographic portrait of Sigmund Freud by Ferdinand Schmutzer, Vienna, 1926. LSCH 0059-C. Courtesy of Wiener Bildarchiv/Österreichische Nationalbibliothek, Vienna.

Part of a series of photographs by the renowned photographer Ferdinand Schmutzer (1870–1928) for the occasion of Freud's seventieth birthday, in which the latter poses at the table with his newspaper, documents, or cigar, the aforementioned portrait has been carefully designed to evoke the seriousness and importance of Freud's status. It is in the styling of this image as well as his own bearing and sartorial styling that Freud's status as an esteemed medical practitioner and thinker is distinguished from other men of his class. Looking up from his newspaper, with his spectacles left on the table before him, he stares back at the camera's lens in a somewhat bemused if not defensive manner, his mouth slightly open as if to offer an expert opinion to a patient— or else a man momentarily interrupted in his intellectual pursuits. His gaze searching, as if probing the subconscious of the viewer, is not unusual when considered in the context of contemporary conventions of portraiture; however, it appears significant when considered in light of the icon Freud has become. But it is no accident that Freud adopts this bearing. Appearing as he does in this image, surrounded by props that evoke middle-class values, Freud assumes the guise of both wise old man and esteemed father of psychoanalysis.

During the same year that Schmutzer took his portrait, Freud was interviewed by the German-American writer George Sylvester Viereck (1884–1962) who would publish an article about their meeting. This was the first time that Freud received an immense amount of public recognition in the wider media.[14] In his article, Viereck quoted Freud describing his relationship to the so-called Jewish Question, "My language . . . is German. My culture, my attainments are German. I considered myself a German intellectually, until I noticed the growth in anti-Semitic prejudice in Germany and in German Austria. Since that time, I consider myself no longer a German. I prefer to call myself a Jew."[15] Perhaps the sense of defensiveness in portraits can be understood as linked to Freud's relationship to antisemitism. Some years earlier, Freud was captured by the lens of Max Halberstadt (1882–1940), a Hamburg Jew, resulting in a portrait that is now perhaps one of Freud's most well-known (Figure 6.2). In the portrait Freud's dress appears almost identical to that worn in some of the Schmuzter portraits. So, too, does he bear the same defensive expression with probing gaze and furrowed brow. The air of confrontation is further enhanced by his defensive pose: his left hand on his hip, thus pushing aside his jacket and revealing more of his (rather unremarkable) waistcoat, and the phallic accessory in the form of a clipped cigar (reminiscent of the circumcised Jewish penis addressed in much of Freud's writing), lodged between the fingers of his right and pointing threateningly.[16] During his career Freud was often regarded as a renegade of sorts within the medical field, facing ridicule due to championing a novel science that challenged the academy—a science often ridiculed as "Jewish" due to the fact that many of his close colleagues and patients were Jews. Freud was well aware of the antisemitic nature of his criticism, claiming in a letter to his colleague Karl Abraham (1877–1925), a Bremen-born Berliner Jew, that the rejection he faced was certainly a result of widespread antisemitism.[17]

Within Schmutzer's series of photographs, Freud's attire varies, albeit subtly: a change of suit, shirt, and neckwear styles. A further comparison of a wide collection

Figure 6.2 Photographic portrait of Sigmund Freud by Max Halberstadt, Hamburg, February 12, 1932. IN17. Courtesy of Freud Museum London.

of photographs—both formal portraits and more casual images—confirm that Sigmund Freud responded to the change and appeal of sartorial styles. For example, a photograph (*c.* 1906) (Figure 6.3) of Freud in middle age by Ludwig Grillich presents him in formal setting, sitting proudly in a Biedermeier-style armchair. The sense of formality is not conveyed through his rather casual pose and styling of his clothes—his left leg crossed over the right at the knee, and his jacket lying open—but rather in his straight-backed posture in which he gazes solemnly into the camera's lens. Posed in a semi-relaxed manner that follows the conventions of painted portraits, he is a proud member of Vienna's *Bildungsbürgertum*, exuding cultural, intellectual, and financial stability in his posture. Although his double-breasted jacket with satin or silk lapels and trousers are in dark colors, they appear to be of different fabrics—common for the times.[18] As in other photographs, he wears a short, dark crosstie under his white collar, which itself is a crisp, lower collar in contrast to the popular high starched variety. His waistcoat, however, is patterned: a dark base fabric with lighter checkered diamonds, bars, and crosses. This slight burst of pattern amidst an overwhelmingly even range of fabrication is typical of such garments. Gesa C. Teichert characterizes the male waistcoat as sitting on the border between garment and accessory, especially in its incarnation as a bright or textured piece of attire amidst an overall sober male suit, particularly during the first half of the nineteenth century.[19] Although after 1860 the resplendent waistcoat was replaced with one that more closely corresponded to the

Figure 6.3 Photographic portrait of Sigmund Freud by Ludwig Grillich, *c.* 1906. Courtesy of the Sigmund Freud Privatstiftung, Vienna.

overall look of the suit, patterned waistcoat styles were a common male fashion of the time across age barriers.[20]

In comparing Freud's waistcoat with one worn by Alfred Zweig, older brother of renowned Viennese author Stefan Zweig, in an undated portrait, differences can be observed. The image, most likely taken during the previous, if not the same, decade, shows the elder son of a successful textile manufacturer in clothing similar to those worn by Freud (Figure 6.4). Although the fabric patterns of Freud's and Zweig's waistcoats differ, since the latter is in gridded dots, the cut of the waistcoats, including lapel and roll height, and of the jackets appear similar. The similarity of styles adopted by these men of different generations raises the issue of intergenerational following of fashion. Stefan Zweig in his oft-quoted memoir recalled the tendency of young men to style themselves in a fashion that made them appear older than their years for the purposes of social and professional advancement:

> Newspapers advertised methods of encouraging your beard to grow, young doctors of twenty-four or twenty-five who had only just qualified as physicians sported heavy beards and wore gold-rimmed spectacles even if they had perfect eyesight, just to impress their patients by looking experienced. They wore long black frock coats and cultivated a measured tread and, if possible, a slight embonpoint in

Figure 6.4 Photograph of Alfred Zweig by Atelier H. Ephron, Vienna, *c.* 1880s. Courtesy of Alfred Zweig Collection, Daniel A. Reed Library Archives & Special Collections, State University of New York at Fredonia, NY.

order to achieve that desirably staid appearance, and if they were ambitious they took a good deal of trouble to dissociate themselves from the suspect immaturity of youth, at least in their outward appearance.[21]

Here, Zweig seems to suggest that his brother Alfred's choice of attire followed that of their father's generation. Likewise, Teichert asserts that although younger men were granted greater flexibility in adopting bolder fashions, older men were expected to dress in a sober manner that expressed respectability.[22] However, whether Alfred Zweig was dressed in styles favored by an older generation, or Freud in those of the younger, the photographs indicate that Freud was aware of and receptive to popular male dress fashions. This also appears to confirm the notion that both Freud's clothing and the portrait styling (the Biedermeier-style chair to be specific) were carefully selected in order to create a visual identity that demanded respect and the right to be taken seriously by his peers and clients. Freud's son Martin expressed the same notion in describing his father as "well-turned out" and insisting on traveling to clients in a *Fiaker* (two-horse carriage) rather than an *Einspänner* (one-horse carriage) or public transport—as was more fitting of the family's financial situation and social status—in order to generate an image of bourgeois respectability.[23]

In another photograph dated 1912 (Figure 6.5), Freud is sitting bent slightly forward in a chair with the stub of an ever-present cigar or cigarette dangling between his fingers.

Figure 6.5 Sigmund Freud at home photographed by his son Martin, Vienna, 1912. IN9. Courtesy of the Freud Museum London.

Surrounded by some of his collected artifacts, such as pottery and tile fragments, a framed image, and what appears to be a reproduction of Michelangelo's *Dying Slave*, Freud, the aging Jew in elegant clothing, is juxtaposed with the sublime beauty of the naked youth. It is in the décor of this room that Freud's *Bildung* can be observed. The finely carved, albeit sturdy, wooden furniture, valuable antiques, the framed image on the wall behind him, and the parquet floor underneath are the trappings of his monetary success and upper-middle-class status. Freud, although not formally positioned, leans forward, one arm resting on the arm of his seat and the other held in front of his body; he is casual yet aware of the photographer's presence and alert to any potential harm to his person. This serves as a juxtaposition to the youth who leans back in a highly erotic manner, his body offered to the viewer's gaze and desires. In contrast, the layering of Freud's clothing, albeit following the fashions of the times, serves as an additional shield for his body. He is elegantly attired, but his clothing is casual, suited to the intimacy of domestic spaces. Atop his waistcoat and striped trousers Freud wears a velvet smoking jacket that is possibly black or another dark color, with bound edges. The combination of velvet jacket and cigarette with its connotations of intimacy and the private sphere[24] link Freud to the provocative youth and Freud's writings on the human subconscious and its desires. Like the pleasure he took in collecting artifacts of past cultures with which to furnish his rooms, Freud's subtle, albeit distinct, sartorial tastes were carefully chosen to generate his identity as a modern, cosmopolitan European.

Of the wealth of surviving photographs of Freud, a large proportion consists of images of Freud as an elderly man. Many of them are studio portraits, as are the majority of the images just discussed. However, there are a number of less formal images in which Freud, at various stages of his life, poses casually, alone, with members of his family, or with colleagues. Such images are important pieces of evidence into the life of Freud the man, the private citizen, rather than the famous psychoanalyst. Of particular interest are those images in which Freud poses with relatives, such as a family portrait from the 1870s, including his parents, siblings, and cousins, various images of Freud with his children at different stages of their lives, and those in which he appears in the guise of a kindly old man sitting with his grandchildren. The importance of these images is not simply that they offer an insight into Freud's private persona but that they also shed light on the various dress habits of his middle-class Jewish milieu.

There is a well-known photograph of Freud and his youngest daughter Anna (1895–1982), an accomplished psychoanalyst in her own right, from 1913 (Figure 6.6). Holidaying in the Dolomites (at the time still part of Austria), Freud and Anna are walking arm in arm across what appears to be a field on the edge of a forest or patch of trees. Their dress stands out in contrast to that worn in most other photographs. Whereas Freud generally appears dressed in an urban, middle-class manner (e.g., the tailored lounge suit discussed earlier), both his and Anna's dress in this photograph indicate another type of middle-class attire: that worn while holidaying in rural *Sommerfrischen*.[25] Like many other urban visitors to the country, Anna wears a *Dirndl* with puffed sleeves and an apron, apparently a generic form rather than authentic local *Tracht*. In contrast, Freud's attire is far less *völkisch*. He wears what appears to be a felt hat (perhaps a dark green—the image is black

Figure 6.6 Sigmund Freud with his daughter Anna in the Dolomites, 1913. IN48. Courtesy of the Freud Museum London.

and white) with a tuft of *Gamsbart* (chamois hair) poking out of the band—a typically *völkisch* form of *Sommerfrische* fashion. However, his overall attire, with its belted Norfolk jacket, knickerbockers worn with long socks and boots, and a white collared shirt, appears more influenced by English country fashions. Carrying a walking stick and clutching his pipe, Freud appears the country squire in tweeds, rather than a *Lederhosen-* and *Janker-* attired local. He and Anna pause mid-stroll, glancing at the camera in a placid if somewhat curious manner, as if momentarily interrupted from an intimate discussion.

The "natural" appearance of their "rural" dress and their contented nature in this rural environment suggests a sense of comfort in the dominant German culture of Cisleithania, not a self-conscious assimilatory drive. The attire depicted in the photograph matches that purportedly worn on a hiking expedition in South Tyrol (incidentally the same region where the 1913 photograph with Anna was taken) described by his son Martin:

> Father wore a conventional country suit with a soft shirt collar attached and a tie. My mother, who ordered all my father's clothes tried to reach absolute perfection, always taking the greatest care in ordinary well-cut clothes made from British cloth. Thus he appeared as respectable as he did in Vienna in his dark suits and black ties. . . . As a contrast to my parent's respectable appearance, I wore well-used leather shorts and the usual Tyrolean outfit. Although I was only sixteen, I was taller than my father and very thin at the time.[26]

Such styles of rural dress were common and conventional. In addition to donning *Trachtenmoden* while relaxing on *Sommerfrischen* or during hiking expeditions, some middle-class Viennese Jewish men also chose to attire themselves in a "conventional country suit" that aligned them sartorially and thus symbolically with the culture of the English gentleman, rather than the German—as Adolf Loos preached in contemporary newspapers.[27] Through such choices of attire, Freud embraced a wider "European" identity rather than limiting himself to the local cultural identification.

Arthur Schnitzler: Literary Bon Vivant

The celebrated dramatist and novelist Arthur Schnitzler fashioned his role as a critic of the Viennese educated middle class for whom he wrote. A product himself of this segment of society, Schnitzler used its dress modes to simultaneously express his participation in this class and his self-appointed role as its observer and critic. This dual internal-external position manifested itself in Schnitzler's youthful rebelliousness. In 1894, the Jewish Viennese salonnière Berta Zuckerkandl-Szeps (1864–1945) wrote to her sister Sophie Clemenceau in Paris describing an evening at the home of the renowned laryngologist Johann Schnitzler (1835–93).[28] During the dinner the seat next to Zuckerkandl-Szeps at the table remained vacant until its occupant arrived after the *Vorspeise* (entrée/appetizer): "a strikingly handsome, blond man, very elegant. A lock of hair fell across his forehead. I did not see his eyes as he had lowered his eyelids. A cool bow and then he sits down next to me. He is the son of the house, Arthur Schnitzler."[29] Berta was thoroughly unimpressed with the young Schnitzler's blasé conduct and complained to her husband, the anatomist Emil Zuckerkandl (1849–1910) on their way home.[30]

The image of the beautiful blond youth contradicts the prevalent stereotype of the "ugly" and "dark" Jew. Zuckerkandl-Szeps's description of the younger Schnitzler as an aloof and handsome man who stood out from the crowd at an evening among Vienna's Jewish upper-bourgeoisie is one that may have been plucked from one of Schnitzler's own short stories, plays, or novellas. Zuckerkandl-Szeps herself might have been a character from the pages of Schnitzler's fiction. A cultural critic and writer, the daughter of a Galician-born newspaper magnate and sister of chief editor of the *Wiener Allgemeine Zeitung*,[31] Zuckerkandl-Szeps played hostess (in the spirit of earlier German-Jewish women Fanny von Arnstein, Rahel Levin, and Henrietta Herz) to a salon that first met in her Döbling (district XIX) home and later in the Palais Lieben-Auspitz on the Ringstrasse, which drew artists, writers, and other cultural luminaries from Vienna and across Europe.[32] The individuals depicted in Schnitzler's literary canon strongly resemble this upper-middle-class segment of society of which he and Zuckerkandl-Szeps were both a part. Regarding Schnitzler's writing, Martin Swales complains "that the actual social range of his portrait gallery is limited. He tends to confine himself to a prosperous, upper-class milieu, concerning himself particularly with artistic and intellectual circles where so many of the chief participants were Jews."[33] This is not surprising; after all, these were the circles in which Schnitzler himself moved. In addressing questions of social discourse, Schnitzler employed the milieu he best understood as an example of a wider, universal human condition.

Schnitzler was born in the Leopoldstadt (district II) to Hungarian immigrant parents; his father Johann came to Vienna from Groß-Kanizsa (Nagykanizsa) and his mother Louise from Güns (Kőszeg).[34] By Schnitzler's own account his parents came from different socioeconomic backgrounds. He describes his paternal grandfather, Josef Schnitzler, as an alcoholic carpenter whose behavior resulted in the family falling into debt. In contrast, his maternal grandfather Philipp Markbreiter, the grandson of a court jeweler, was an accomplished physician who enjoyed playing the piano and had been raised in an environment dedicated to the ideals of *Bildung* and *Sittlichkeit*, only to fall prey to a gambling addiction. Through her mother Amalia, Louise Schnitzler (née Markbreiter) was related to the illustrious Jewish Schey family, a scion of which commissioned the building of a large palace on the Ringstrasse during the 1860s.[35]

Johann and Louise Schnitzler had settled in the Leopoldstadt prior to the birth of their eldest son Arthur. The Schnitzlers' world, although decidedly Jewish, was one of the upper- and upper-middle classes with familial and professional connections to wealthy Jewish professionals and members of the city's artistic milieu. Upon graduating from the *Gymnasium*, Schnitzler, a dutiful son of the Jewish upper-bourgeoisie, followed in his father's footsteps and enrolled at the University of Vienna in 1879 to study medicine. From there he received a Doctor of Medicine and went to work at his father's medical clinic. As Ritchie Robertson asserts, "Schnitzler found medicine uncongenial," only exacerbated by a tense relationship with his father.[36] It was the death of his father, and suffering from "auditory hallucinations" and tinnitus during the early 1890s, that helped Schnitzler find a way out of the world of medicine and the opportunity to embrace his literary passions.[37] During this same period, Schnitzler became involved with the writers who would become the *fin-de-siècle* literary group *Jung Wien* (Young Vienna),[38] meeting regularly at Café Griensteidl in Vienna's inner city.[39]

Schnitzler's foppish sartorial patterns and tastes can be understood as a reaction to the social discourse of Jewishness in late nineteenth-century Vienna, such as the increasing antisemitism that Karl Lueger utilized in his populist Christian Social political platform. However, unlike those Jews who chose to reject and hide their Jewishness in the wake of growing antisemitism, Schnitzler remained a member of the IKG, marrying under the auspices of the city's rabbinate,[40] and recording the birth of his children in the community records.[41] As a well-known author who made no attempt to hide his Jewish identity, and openly addressed the so-called Jewish Question throughout his writing, Schnitzler's carefree, foppish appearance was both a sign of his social artistic milieu and a refutation of perceived visual markers of Jewishness. Playing with the idea of the dark, "oriental" Jew vis-à-vis the blond German, it is possible that Schnitzler took advantage of his blond handsome appearance that Zuckerkandl-Szeps described to refute notions of Jewish bodily difference. Moreover, he dressed in a manner that rejected the notions of male sartorial conventionality that permeated Jewish bourgeois circles to broadcast their dedication to *Bildung* and *Sittlichkeit*. Schnitzler saw himself as simultaneously Jewish and German; to him there was no contradiction. In an undated letter found some time after his death, Schnitzler wrote of his national status:

> Neither Jewish-Zionist resentment nor the stupidity and impudence of German nationalist[s] will make me doubt in the least that I am a German writer . . . I should find it proper that authors whose language is Hebrew should call themselves Hebrew writers or Jewish writers. Neither could I object if poets of Jewish background who have hitherto written in another language became outraged at the stupidity of anti-Semitism, which would deny them membership in a nation on whose territory they were born, in whose speech they were reared and which they even helped to shape; and if, as a result, these poets abjured the beloved language hitherto employed by them and turn to Hebrew as the medium for their creative works. Such poets would thereby have obtained the right to designate themselves as Jewish poets. But as long as they continue to write in German, they must call themselves German poets . . . They are German poets as surely as Heine, Boerne, Gundolf, and a hundred others of Jewish origin are German; as surely as Brandes is a Danish writer and Proust a French writer. Just ask any genuine living German poet, ask Heinrich Mann, Thomas Mann, Gerhart Hauptmann, Hesse, Unruh, whom they feel to be more German: Wolzogen, Dinter, and that crowd, or Wassermann, Werfel, Beer-Hofmann, and a dozen others of Jewish orogin [sic.] that I could name.[42]

Like many Viennese Jews of his era when an individual's nationality was (officially) determined through language, Schnitzler approached his identity in the tripartite manner described by Rozenblit: ethnically (and religiously) Jewish, culturally German, and politically Austrian.[43]

What influence did Schnitzler's self-identification as both Jew and German have on his self-fashioning and how did this manifest itself in his choice of attire? In youthful photographs, Schnitzler appears in the same guise as the young bachelor Zuckerkandl-Szeps described in the letter to her sister: bright-eyed, his messy hair parted at the side and brushed up in a debonair manner. Portraits depicting Schnitzler as a youth in the late 1870s clearly display his foppish attire. In one portrait in particular (c. 1878) by the atelier of the well-known Josef Székely (1838–1901), Schnitzler as a *Maturant* (secondary-school graduate) wears a velvet jacket and waistcoat with bound edges and a large spotted bow below his turndown shirt collar (Figure 6.7). His fair locks are brushed back and high, and with his sparse growth of moustache, the roughly sixteen-year-old Schnitzler looks the part of dreamy aesthete. However, as a youth, Schnitzler lived in the confines of the parental home and the rules of the *Gymnasium*. Opportunities for a young man to express himself through sartorial modes were, at this point of his life, somewhat curtailed.[44]

In images of Schnitzler ranging from young adulthood to his advanced years, there is a persistent sense of the boyish foppishness highlighted in Zuckerkandl-Szeps's letter. His hair is tousled, his fringe long and brushed up and to the side. As he moves through different stages of his life, his scanty moustache grows into a full, pointed goatee and

Figure 6.7 Arthur Schnitzler photographed by Josef Székely, Vienna, *c.* 1878. AS 4 B. Courtesy of Wiener Bildarchiv/Österreichische Nationalbibliothek, Vienna.

wide moustache that lend him the appearance of hirsute virility.[45] In two photographs taken decades apart, Schnitzler's style of hair and facial hair changed little.

In the first, a studio portrait taken in 1885 at the time when Schnitzler was still a medical student, Schnitzler sits "casually" while his friend and fellow student Friedrich "Fritz" Kapper (1861–1939) leans next to him (Figure 6.8). Although the photographer's sitters pose themselves in a manner that expresses studied nonchalance, these two young Jewish men hold themselves in a highly considered manner to express their identities as young, modern men-about-town. Schnitzler crosses his legs at the knee while simultaneously balancing an open book on top and he holds a pen between the fingers of his left hand. Bent at the elbow, his left arm is held aloft, perhaps simulating the casualness of one resting his arm on the top of his upholstered chair. However, his arm does not rest comfortably. Rather, it is fixed in the air in a manner reminiscent of a marionette or carved figurine. While Kapper rests his hand directly on Schnitzler's shoulder, his pose is no less rigid. With his left leg crossed over the right, and his right hand placed on his hip, Kapper bends forward slightly and leans against his friend, careful not to place too much weight on him. The stiffness of their "nonchalant" posing is the result of contemporary conventions of photography and the exposure time that required sitters to hold their poses for a longer period of time, which Graham Clarke describes as reflecting "the method and not the medium."[46]

The use of an open book as prop is notable, not only as a conventional tool in nineteenth-century studio portraits[47] but also as a symbol of Schnitzler's dedication to literature, even though he was still at this stage of his life destined to follow his father into

Figure 6.8 Arthur Schnitzler (sitting) with Fritz Kapper, Vienna, *c*. 1885. AS 162 C. Courtesy of Wiener Bildarchiv/Österreichische Nationalbibliothek, Vienna.

a medical career. It is not only the open book and pen that express Schnitzler's rebellion against the bourgeois conventions of his Jewish milieu; his hairstyle and dress are equally important. Like Kapper, he wears his beard neatly pointed and a sharp moustache. Unlike his friend, however, Schnitzler's hair is not neatly trimmed and brushed, but worn longer and swept up across his forehead in an untidy fashion. Likewise, the dress choices of these two friends differ. Kapper wears a typical lounge suit with a high closure, a wing collar, and a discreet black bow tie. Schnitzler's dress, however, is more elaborate and matches his more "debonair" pose: the roll of his jacket lapel is much lower which, like that of his waistcoat, has bound edges. Like his friend, he wears a white wing collar, but with a large, patterned necktie beneath, and what appears to be a pearl tiepin in its knot. The portrait's sepia tone obscures the colors of the men's attire, but the tone of the image and the manner in which the light falls across the fabric of the suits suggest they are not black, but perhaps a lighter shade of brown, gray, blue, or even green.

In the second image (Figure 6.9), taken almost four decades later by the celebrated portrait photographer Franz Xaver Setzer (1886–1939), Schnitzler's attire (from what is visible in a portrait of only the writer's face and upper torso) is more severe and akin to the sober conservatism of Kapper's sartorial appearance than his own foppishness in the 1885 portrait, and more suited to a mature gentleman as per middle-class conventions.[48] He appears to be dressed in a dark—possibly black—single-breasted dinner jacket with a high break point and matching waistcoat beneath. In contrast to the patterned ties of his youth, he wears a simple, black bow tie beneath what appears to be a wing collar

Figure 6.9 Arthur Schnitzler photographed by Franz Xaver Setzer, Vienna, *c.* 1922. Courtesy of Alamy.

partially obscured by his pointed beard. Gazing seriously at Setzer's apparatus, Schnitzler is no longer a young and carefree medical student, but rather a mature and respected writer, chronicler of Vienna's *Bildungsbürgertum*. Nonetheless, there is still a sense of playfulness in the appearance of the sixty-year-old Schnitzler. Here, too, his hairstyle is similar (although one that slopes downward across his forehead rather than brushed up) and he wears the same beard and moustache, albeit fuller than in his youthful days.

The style Schnitzler wore his hair and trimmed his facial hair were only two ways in which he developed a particular image of youthful rebelliousness.[49] His choice of sartorial styles also exposes the development of a mode of identification that was at once distinct from the middle-class milieu and borrowing elements from it. In a family snapshot from 1905, he stands on the balcony of his apartment at Spöttelgasse 7 with his wife Olga (née Guszmann) and son Heinrich (Figure 6.10). Here his attire is largely concealed by his arms crossed over his chest and a large, light-colored overcoat draped over his shoulders. Leaning nonchalantly against the balcony's sturdy balustrade, he stares defiantly into the camera's lens—a contrast to a more placid Olga. He does appear to be wearing a dark suit—the manner in which the light falls across the contours of the fabric suggests his jacket may be velvet. His haughty, solemn stance, and the manner in which the drape of his coat evokes a cape or cloak, recalls portraits of the aristocracy. Leaning against the balustrade and holding a cigar between his fingers, he seems to be caught in a typical moment of private life, rather than a staged situation. This defiant manner in the face

Figure 6.10 Arthur Schnitzler with his wife Olga and son Heinrich on the balcony of their apartment at Spöttelgasse 7, Vienna, c. 1905. AS 104 B. Courtesy of Wiener Bildarchiv/Österreichische Nationalbibliothek, Vienna.

of supposed bourgeois respectability is reminiscent of Schnitzler's character Heinrich Bermann in the novel he published three years later, *Der Weg ins Freie* (*The Road into the Open*). Bermann, a middle-class Jew and son of a lawyer and politician, is a sharp critic of the mannerisms and obsessions of Vienna's Jewish *Bildungsbürgertum*.[50] To Bermann, like to Schnitzler, nothing in the world is sacred and beyond reproach. Yet, his criticism comes from the perspective of an insider, and not someone who had rejected his people, like Peter Altenberg, Karl Kraus, or Otto Weininger did. Bermann/Schnitzler is at once both an unashamed member of the Jewish bourgeoisie and its uncompromising critic.

In some images, Schnitzler's clothing preferences are somewhat subdued and embrace the favored dark tones of middle-class masculine respectability. But his dark suits are not dull. Embracing the sober tones of Victorian masculinity, the writer, like other men of his period, embellished his dressed appearance with accessories such as watch chains, neckwear, jewelry, or striking cufflinks (Figure 6.11). Nor were the clothes themselves plain. In a 1908 portrait from the atelier of the celebrated Viennese photographer Madame d'Ora—a Viennese Jewess, Dora Kallmus (1881–1963)—Schnitzler poses, knees crossed and left hand buried in his trouser pocket, the right hand resting on his thigh, in a sharp, three-piece suit of dark, woolen material (Figure 6.12). The edges of his waistcoat, jacket lapels, and turned-up sleeve cuffs are carefully bound (perhaps in satin, although it is impossible to tell from the photograph), as are the side seams of his trousers. He stares

Figure 6.11 Arthur Schnitzler photographed by Atelier D'Ora-Benda, Vienna, 1915. AS 62 G. Courtesy of Wiener Bildarchiv/Österreichische Nationalbibliothek, Vienna.

Figure 6.12 Arthur Schnitzler photographed by Madame d'Ora, Vienna, *c.* 1908. 203453-D. Courtesy of Wiener Bildarchiv/Österreichische Nationalbibliothek, Vienna.

Figure 6.13 Arthur Schnitzler with his wife Olga and children Lili and Heinrich photographed by Madame d'Ora, Vienna, 1910. 203485-D. Courtesy of Wiener Bildarchiv/Österreichische Nationalbibliothek, Vienna.

outward, his expression serious, perhaps judging the viewer. In the same year that this portrait was taken, Schnitzler published his novel *Der Weg ins Freie*, his most explicit critique of his bourgeois Jewish milieu. His choice of attire conformed to middle-class conventions, but his piercing gaze expresses a sense of discontent. Images like this are important because they not only reveal the clothing preferences of individuals but also offer an insight into the manner men straddled the conflicting influences of societal discourse on male sobriety and a desire to appear sartorially splendid.[51] In Schnitzler's case, this visual negotiation of masculine expectations also gives meaning to his dual role as a critic of the Jewish bourgeoisie and a member of that class.

A 1910 portrait of Schnitzler and his family by Madame d'Ora conveys a sense of carefully constructed sartorial identity along class and gendered lines (Figure 6.13). Posing behind Olga and the children, Heinrich and Lili, who sit on a sofa upholstered in striped fabric, Schnitzler and his family have cultivated an image of carefree bons vivants decked out in sartorial splendor. The clothing choices are somewhat exaggerated, with an obvious preference for volume, as can be seen in the wide skirt of Olga's taffeta dress (at a time when the silhouettes of female fashions had begun to narrow), the wide-brimmed hats of both parents and young Heinrich, the puffed sleeves of Lili's white dress, and Heinrich's velvet suit with large lace collar and sleeve cuffs. The family's chosen styles clearly reference popular middle-class fashions of the period, and yet the

Figure 6.14 Fashion plates from the menswear brochure *Wiener Herrenmode: Frühjahr und Sommer 1918* (Vienna: Verlag der Internationalen Moden-Zeichnung, 1918). Inv. Nr. 520.710 A. Courtesy of Österreichische Nationalbibliothek, Vienna

Figure 6.15 Fashion plates from the menswear brochure *Wiener Herrenmode: Frühjahr und Sommer 1918* (Vienna: Verlag der Internationalen Moden-Zeichnung, 1918). Inv. Nr. 520.710 A. Courtesy of Österreichische Nationalbibliothek, Vienna

sense of exaggeration allows Schnitzler to present himself and his family as standing somewhat beyond the strict confines of Vienna's *Bildungsbürgertum*. Consider, for example, his own dress. Overall, the light (possibly woven straw) hat and dark suit he dons are similar to mainstream fashions, such as those fashion plates included in the supplement of contemporary tailoring journal *Wiener Herrenmode* (Figures 6.14 and 6.15). However, it is the details of his dressed appearance—the hat worn at a jaunty angle and the wide, somewhat low collar—and Schnitzler's defiant stance, clenched fist held against his chest, that dramatize his visual appearance and underscore his role as a social critic, both embedded in and removed from the society he scrutinizes in his writing.

Stefan Zweig: Cosmopolitan European

Youthful photographs of Stefan Zweig depict an elegant, neatly groomed young man whose bearing suggests a sense of pride in his external presentation. Zweig was raised in a wealthy bourgeois family and his early poetry was published in 1897 while he was still a student at the Gymnasium Wasagasse in Vienna's ninth district. After completing his secondary education, Zweig enrolled at the University of Vienna where he completed a doctoral thesis on the philosophy of the French positivist critic Hippolyte Taine in

1904. Zweig would go on to forge an illustrious career as an author, writing in various genres—including poetry, plays, feuilletons, biographies of historical figures, novellas, and short stories—and fraternizing with literary and cultural luminaries across Europe and further afield. At the time of his untimely death by suicide in Brazil in February 1942, Zweig was one of the most widely translated authors in Europe. However, more than his identity as a renowned writer, Zweig's sartorial appearance reveals much about his self-identification as a Jewish "European" and his bourgeois Viennese milieu.

The younger son of a Moravian textile manufacturer father and Italian-born Austrian mother, Zweig has at times been referred to as an aesthete for his fastidious mode of dress and attention to material and visual culture, in both his writing and his private life.[52] In his short stories, novellas, and sole novel, he gave careful attention to the dress of his characters and their material surroundings.[53] The carefully selected accessories and trinkets that he wore, such as neckties in unobtrusive patterns, adorned almost always with a pearl tiepin, cufflinks, and a discreet ring on the little finger of his left hand, and the signature purple ink in which he wrote his letters and manuscripts (including using a purple typewriter ribbon), reinforce his aesthetic fastidiousness.[54]

A photograph (*c.* 1898) taken at the Kunst Salon Pietzner in Vienna's Innere Stadt depicts a seventeen-year-old Zweig standing next to his nineteen-year-old brother Alfred, who is seated, patrician-like on a sturdy chair with elaborately carved back and armrests (Figure 6.16). In contrast to his older brother, who looks confidently at the camera with

Figure 6.16 Alfred and Stefan Zweig photographed by Kunst Salon Pietzner, Vienna, 1898. Courtesy of Alfred Zweig Collection, Daniel A. Reed Library Archives & Special Collections, State University of New York at Fredonia, NY.

175

his curled, waxed moustache and hair trimmed in a vaguely militaristic manner, the young Stefan standing demurely behind Alfred with his hands hidden behind his back, in his tightly buttoned frock coat, carefully pomaded hair, faint smudge of moustache, and delicate pince-nez perched precariously on the bridge of his long nose looks very much the gentle, romantic aesthete as he gazes thoughtfully into the camera's lens.

Presenting the sharp contrasts between the two brothers, the photograph serves, in a sense, as an indication of the separate paths their lives would take and their roles in the family. Alfred was destined as the elder son to take over the family's textile business in Bohemia, while Stefan, the baby of the family, already having shown an aptitude for writing as a *Gymnasiast*, would become a much celebrated author both in the German-language realm and in the world at large.[55] These contrasts also point to two of Vienna's Jewish "types": the Germanic and somewhat militaristic precision and bearing of Alfred's outer appearance, alluding to his position as a member of the Jewish bourgeoisie with its dedication to *Bildung und Besitz* (self-cultivation and capital), and Stefan's softer, delicate stance marking him as one concerned foremost with intellectual pursuits, and his almost naïve dedication to the belief in internationalism and the brotherhood of all people.[56]

The styling of this photograph reveals traces of the Zweig family's middle-class milieu, albeit most probably taken at the Pietzner studio and not the family home. As Tanya Sheehan highlights in her study of nineteenth- and early twentieth-century studio photography practices among minorities in the United States, photographers employed the material trappings of the middle classes, as well as posing conventions in the styling of portraits to enable their sitters to feel as though they were participating in the context of white bourgeois respectability:

> These included books, prints and paintings of the "finest" quality, historic ephemera, stained glass draped with "splendid curtains," classically styled vases and marble busts, and even brightly colored singing birds. Taken together, these fine things—literature, art, furnishings and music—were closely tied to "pleasing expressions" under the skylight precisely because they were highly valued in the bourgeois cultural imagination.[57]

The sturdy, expensive-looking furniture, plush drapery, household plant, and painting hanging on the papered wall behind the Zweig brothers lend the studio an appearance of domesticity that not only expresses the sitters' class values but was a common tool used by portrait photographers in putting their sitters in a "genial, elevated tone of sentiment and emotion."[58]

Zweig's appearance, in both the Pietzner portrait and others is quite typical of contemporary male dress and styling. He does not appear bohemian in any sense but is, rather, very much the privileged son of the Viennese bourgeoisie, having been reared on its notions of sartorial and behavioral respectability (*Sittlichkeit*). Such preferences were common among other Jewish men of a similar background. The Zweig brothers were raised in a culturally assimilated household. Although a strict of observance of

Figure 6.17 Portrait of Stefan Zweig's great-great-grandfather Moses Josef Zweig (1832) published in Julius Röder, ed., *Die Nachkommen von Moses (Josef) Zweig und Elka (Katti) Chaja Sarah Spitzer: eine Nachfahrenliste* (Olmütz: 1932). Courtesy of Alfred Zweig Collection, Daniel A. Reed Library Archives & Special Collections, State University of New York at Fredonia, NY.

Judaism had long been abandoned—a portrait of their great-great-grandfather Moses Josef Zweig depicts a stereotypical *Ostjude* with a beard, sidelocks, and large *yarmulke* (Figure 6.17)—the family had not adopted Christianity—either out of genuine religious conviction or for professional and social advancement. Moriz and Ida Zweig, the parents of Alfred and Stefan, "remained Jews in more than a nominal sense," maintaining membership in communal organizations, fasting on *Yom Kippur*, and commemorating the *B'nei Mitzvah* of their sons.[59] Furthermore, the brothers Zweig matured during Karl Lueger's rise to prominence and the advent of Theodor Herzl's political Zionism, the latter exerting an influence on Stefan. During the early years of the new century, Stefan Zweig was involved with *Jung Jüdisch* (Young Jewish), a literary group founded by Nathan Birnbaum and Martin Buber, among others, that was active in Vienna and Berlin, with its central meeting point in Vienna at the Café Louvre on the Wipplingerstrasse.[60]

However, this affair with Zionism and Jewish nationalism was short-lived. Zweig would take pains to describe himself as a "European" writer and strove to write stories and feuilletons with universal themes appealing to a wider audience.[61] Even those works of fiction with "Jewish" (or rather biblical) themes conveyed a universal, humanistic message. His short story *Im Schnee* (*In the Snow*), first published in 1901 in the Zionist newspaper *Die Welt: Zentralorgan der Zionistischen Bewegung*, tells the story of Jewish refugees fleeing a pogrom during the Middle Ages who find themselves trapped in a snowstorm.[62] The novella evokes the pity of the reader for the persecuted Jews—not as Jews but rather for fellow human beings, Zweig insisted an absence of Jewish national feeling within.[63]

In a letter to Martin Buber dated May 8, 1916, Zweig formally expressed his reservations about identifying with Zionism or any kind of Jewish nationalism—indeed, national pride of any kind:

I am not proud [about being a Jew], because I reject pride or any achievement that is not my own, just as I am not proud of Vienna, despite being born there, or Goethe, because he was of my language, or the victories of "our" armies in which my blood did not flow. Everything that is prided in Jewishness, as I so often read, appears as a gaping insecurity, an inverted fear, and a twisted inferiority complex. What we are missing is <u>certainty</u>, <u>calmness</u>—I feel it in me as a Jew more and more.[64]

For many acculturated Viennese Jews, their Jewishness was a complicated matter: both a matter of fact and in some cases a burden. Stefan Zweig neither denied nor made a point of emphasizing his Jewish identification. He maintained relations with members of the Jewish *Bürgertum* in which he was raised; however, as an artist and a public persona, he was able to foster friendships with others outside this segment of society—something not always available to many of his coreligionists due to Vienna's antisemitic climate. Unlike Schnitzler, whose literary works often included overtly Jewish characters and themes as a comment on the antisemitic nature of Viennese society, Zweig's literary canon presents Jewish characters and the notion of Jewishness in line with his cosmopolitan, supranational worldview.[65]

Zweig, like many of his fellow middle-class Jews, conducted himself in a manner that appeared to correspond with the maxim coined by the Russian *Maskil* Judah Leib Gordon (1831–92): "Be a man in the street and a Jew at home." His sartorial habits, modern and following the accepted male fashions of the era, confirm this approach. Both brothers' dress choices in the 1898 Pietzner portrait would transform over time, reflecting both their maturation and the wider change in men's fashions. Although Alfred would go on after completing his secondary education at one of Vienna's *Realgymnasien* (technical secondary schools) to work for Moriz Zweig's textile company, and was described by his one-time sister-in-law Friderike Zweig as maintaining a "purely commercial standpoint of a prominent industrialist,"[66] surviving photographs lead to the conclusion that he did not inherit his father's ascetic dress habits or tastes.[67] In contrast to his more severe sartorial appearance in the Pietzner portrait, other photographs depict the young Alfred dressed in no less fastidious a manner, but in styles more akin to those favored by what Adolf Loos referred to as the *Gigerl*: hats worn at rakish angles, at times sporting a cane, high collars, and sharply tailored suits (Figure 6.18).

As he grew older, Alfred's choice of clothing became somewhat less "foppish" but no less carefully considered. One image depicts a middle-aged Alfred Zweig sitting on a cushioned bench at a polished wooden table by a white stucco wall (Figure 6.19). It is possible that this undated photograph was taken at a summer cottage or *Heuriger*. Alfred, in the midst of entering information into what might be a business ledger, pauses to stare sternly into the photographer's lens. His graying, receding hair is neatly combed and he sports the same style of moustache as his famous brother. His well-cut three-piece suit is of a tweed-like woolen fabric, and attention has been paid to smaller sartorial details such as the striped shirt and vari-toned, diagonally striped tie. He also wears cufflinks and rings on both hands. His sharply tailored attire puts him in stark contrast to his rustic surroundings. The photograph comes from a private family album, presenting a more "honest" glimpse into Alfred Zweig's attire in intimate settings. However, another photograph taken some years earlier at the atelier of the celebrated society photographer Franz Xaver Setzer broadcasts Alfred's deliberate self-fashioning: a confident industrialist

Figure 6.18 Photograph of Alfred Zweig as a young man, undated. Courtesy of Alfred Zweig Collection, Daniel A. Reed Library Archives & Special Collections, State University of New York at Fredonia, NY.

Figure 6.19 Photograph of Alfred Zweig, *c*. 1930s. Courtesy of Alfred Zweig Collection, Daniel A. Reed Library Archives & Special Collections, State University of New York at Fredonia, NY.

Figure 6.20 Alfred Zweig photographed by Franz Xaver Setzer, Vienna, 1920. Courtesy of Alfred Zweig Collection, Daniel A. Reed Library Archives & Special Collections, State University of New York at Fredonia, NY.

in a pinstripe suit, bow tie and horizontally striped shirt, Alfred Zweig stands at an angle to the camera, his arms crossed, and a slight smile visible beneath his trimmed moustache (Figure 6.20).

Such careful attention to dress was typical for Alfred Zweig. Numerous photographs of Alfred and his wife Stefanie (née Duschak) on holidays in the snow-covered Swiss Alps during the 1930s show him very much at odds with the environment. Dressed in outerwear—either belted trench coats or heavy overcoats with fur collars—breeches, tie and collar, and carrying a cane, Alfred Zweig does not appear in the guise of a man suited for skiing or hiking through the mountains (Figure 6.21). Nor do his adopted sartorial styles correspond to the more rustic styles advertised in contemporary Viennese men's fashion magazines and pattern books of the period, such as *Herren-Mode-Welt*, *The Gentleman*, and *Der Herr und seine Welt*.

To complete this image of the urban, sartorially conscious cosmopolitan—and in the context of the rise in nationalist and antisemitic sentiments during the late nineteenth and early twentieth centuries—such an image of the fashionable tourist had connotations of Jewish difference and evoked the irreconcilable divide between the *völkisch*, rural German and the urban, rootless Jew.[68] One image from a holiday spent in Arosa in 1934 features Alfred sitting on a wooden bench outside a rustic chalet or ski-hut with one of his beloved dachshunds (Figure 6.22). In stark contrast to the simple, raw setting, Alfred leans back comfortably against the bench. At first glance, he appears suitably attired for the snow

Figure 6.21 Stefanie and Alfred Zweig on holiday in Switzerland, 1930s. Courtesy of Alfred Zweig Collection, Daniel A. Reed Library Archives & Special Collections, State University of New York at Fredonia, NY

Figure 6.22 Alfred Zweig in Arosa, Switzerland, 1934. Courtesy of Alfred Zweig Collection, Daniel A. Reed Library Archives & Special Collections, State University of New York at Fredonia, NY.

in a coat, knitted hat, long scarf, and sunglasses to protect his eyes from the snow's glare. A closer observation reveals the coat's rather thin fabric and his white collared shirt and necktie. A ring is on the little finger of his left hand and the handle of his cane can be seen poking up between the wooden slats of the bench. Even his beloved dachshund has been dressed in a knitted rug and studded harness, which Alfred grips with his right hand.

In contrast to Alfred, Stefan's dressed appearance blends more easily into provincial environs. Images from Salzburg depict Stefan Zweig in far more casual attire, often without a tie, with an open-collared shirt, and at times wearing short trousers. In photographs from this period of his life, Zweig adopted a more leisured attire: light summer suits with short trousers, tweeds, and traditional leather shorts (*Lederhosen*) with long socks (Figure 6.23). Oliver Matuschek explains that Zweig's adoption of the local *Tracht*, or at least a variation of it, differed from that common among many Austrian and German Jews of the same period who aggressively asserted their loyalty to German culture. Rather, Zweig's casual, provincial attire was adopted as such styles were considered the height of fashion in Salzburg.[69] In her memoir of Zweig, Friderike Zweig (Zweig's first wife) recalled the designer and purveyor of fashion Sepp Lanz in particular, whose *Trachtenmoden* became so popular with both local and international visitors to the annual *Salzburger Festspiele* that he was later able to establish a business in Hawaii.[70] However, with this adoption of local styles for the purposes of visual conformity with the local population, there is still a sense of the individual asserting her or his loyalty to or identification with the hegemonic culture. Thus, whether Zweig adopted the local *Tracht* out of a sense of deliberate identification with the dominant *Volk* or simply for the purposes of visual conformity, a sense of the former is still present. Nor was his adopted provincial sartorial identity warmly accepted by everyone; as Matuschek asserts, Zweig's attire "attracted the unflattering sobriquet of *Salontiroler*, in some quarters—roughly, 'Alpine Tourist.'"[71]

These and other photographic examples correspond to written accounts of Stefan Zweig and his familial milieu. Like his relaxed and "*völkisch*" Salzburger attire, the clothes he wore during other periods of his life matched his dedication to universal (read "European") culture. As a proud "European" he made a point of not standing out. Unlike his contemporaries Peter Altenberg and Arthur Schnitzler, his clothing preferences were not unusual but carefully followed the maxims of correct male dressing. This is not to say that Zweig's dress patterns were mediocre. The German writer Irmgard Keun (1905–82) once described Zweig on a visit to Ostend during the 1930s as looking "very decorative—exactly like a cinema-goer's notion of a famous writer. Cosmopolitan, elegant, dapper, with a gentle melancholy in his dark gaze."[72] Surviving photographic evidence confirms that he took great care in the selection of his clothing and accessories. Photographs of Zweig taken during the 1920s and 1930s reveal his conservative but considered attire. His sartorial preferences evidently adapted to the changing fashions of the times—wearing suits that varied in cut, color, texture, and weight of fabric, his shirts were either plain or patterned, as was his choice of neckwear (Figures 6.24 and 6.25).

While the unremarkable nature of his choices of attire might seem insignificant in relation to his national or ethnic feeling, they are intrinsically dependent on his self-fashioning and performance of male Jewish-European identification. As a Jew coming of age during a

Figure 6.23 Friderike and Stefan Zweig in Salzburg, photographed by Ludwig Boedecker, published in *Die Dame* 17, 1922. Courtesy of Getty Images

Figure 6.24 Stefan Zweig photographed by Franz Xaver Setzer, Vienna, 1920. Archiv Setzer-Tschiedel. Courtesy of GettyImages

period of increasing antisemitism, Zweig found that his answer to the Jewish Question rested on a dedication to universal human values. A Jew, he declared through his public silence on the matter, was unremarkable and had no need to stand out from the crowd by emphasizing his difference through political activity or by adopting extraordinary sartorial practices. At the same time, his cosmopolitan nature and belief in lack of territorial bonds placed the Jew in a position specially situated to deal with the question of nationality. Zweig believed strongly in the Jew's role as a mediator among the people of the world, and

Figure 6.25 Photograph of Stefan Zweig, 1930s. Courtesy of Alfred Zweig Collection, Daniel A. Reed Library Archives & Special Collections, State University of New York at Fredonia, NY.

therefore regarded the establishment of a Jewish national state as a negation of the Jewish destiny.[73] Although unexpressed, Zweig's sartorially conservative appearance was evident not simply of Jewish assimilation and acculturation (albeit a product of this milieu) but representative of his views regarding the Jew's role in Western civilization.

Peter Altenberg: Bohemian Assimilationist

Peter Altenberg stands out for the peculiarity of his dress among the Viennese bourgeoisie and its bohemian offspring. Several surviving photographs, such as one from 1912 (Figure 6.26), mark Altenberg's choices of attire as eccentric. In this photograph, he wears a wide overcoat of a light-colored fabric (presumably wool) with a faint check pattern. The sleeves are wide (with a tab at the cuff on the seam-side of the sleeve), as is the coat's collar. A flat, tartan tam o' shanter-like bonnet perched on his head and his large drooping "walrus" moustache give him the appearance of a stereotypical Scot (sans kilt) and not the son of a Jewish merchant. With his left hand, he clasps his (leather or suede) gloves and cane, while his right hand is buried in his coat pocket as he stares stoically ahead. Although there is a sense of seriousness common in photographic portraits of the late nineteenth and early twentieth centuries, Altenberg consciously turns his gaze away from the camera, as if to reject the social conventions of portraiture.[74]

Figure 6.26 Photograph of Peter Altenberg addressed to Lotte Franzos, 1912. Handschriftensammlung, Inv. No. H.I.N. 115816. Courtesy of Wienbibliothek im Rathaus, Vienna.

There is nothing in Altenberg's physiognomy or bearing that can be coded as particularly "Jewish," neither in the stereotypical characteristics attributed to poorer *Ostjuden* newly arrived in Vienna from the empire's easternmost provinces (or those former *Ostjuden* who had already transformed themselves into so-called parvenus), nor in any of the sartorial habits or visual codes that were prevalent among Vienna's Jewish bourgeoisie. Altenberg's rejection of conventional aesthetic and sartorial styles does not translate into an elimination of style; rather, as Susan Sontag notes, "antipathy to 'style' is always antipathy to a given style," in favor of another.[75] Thus, at a time when "the Jew came to represent the counter-ideal of beauty in the popular German imagination,"[76] Altenberg's atypical style of dressing can be understood as a deliberate attempt to distance himself from Vienna's middle-class Jewry.

Peter Altenberg was born Richard Engländer to middle-class Jewish parents—Moriz Engländer, a migrant from Pest, and Viennese-born Pauline Schweinburg—in the "Jewish" environment of the Leopoldstadt where he spent his early childhood.[77] During his childhood, the family moved to an apartment in the Innere Stadt in the vicinity of Vienna's main synagogue in the Seitenstettengasse. Despite exposure to Jewish society at a young age, in both the first and second districts, Altenberg and his siblings were raised in a secular household dedicated to the ideals of *Bildung*, with their father more interested in French culture and literature than imparting his children with a strong Jewish identity. Altenberg recalled of his father:

> My father is a merchant. He has one peculiarity: he only reads French books. For forty years. A wonderful portrait of his idol hangs above his bed: Victor Hugo. In the evenings he sits in a dark red armchair and reads the "Revue des deux Mondes" while wearing a blue gown with wide velvet collar à la Victor Hugo.[78]

Like many sons of middle-class Jewish families, Altenberg enrolled in a law degree at the University of Vienna in 1877 after completing his secondary schooling, only to change two years later to a medicine degree. Like his contemporary Arthur Schnitzler, Altenberg came to the realization that he was unsuited for a career in medicine. Withdrawing from his studies again in what Harold B. Segel refers to as "an emerging pattern of instability," Altenberg relocated to Stuttgart in order to undertake an apprenticeship at Julius Weise's *Hofbuchhandlung* in 1880.[79] After further failed attempts at study and work, Altenberg was declared unfit for work by a psychiatrist and drifted further into a bohemian lifestyle, living at first with his brother Georg and then in numerous hotels.[80] It was during this period that Altenberg began to spend much of his time in coffeehouses, particularly the cafés Löwenbräu, Grienstiedl, and Central.

It was, in fact, in Café Central that Altenberg was first "discovered" as a writer. According to his own recollection, Altenberg was writing a sketch based on a report of a local girl who disappeared en route to a piano lesson when Arthur Schnitzler and his literary colleagues Hugo von Hofmannsthal, Felix Salten, Richard Beer-Hofmann, and Hermann Bahr entered the café and noticed him writing. Schnitzler read his piece and passed it on to his colleagues, and Beer-Hofmann arranged a literary evening at which the sketch was read aloud. After this debut, members of Vienna's literary milieu began to take an interest in Altenberg's writing, which was subsequently sent to the renowned Berlin publisher Samuel Fischer who published the work and, in Altenberg's own words, "so wurde ich!"[81] Altenberg joked that had he not been writing a sketch but rather a bill for all the unpaid coffees had had consumed over the past months, he might never have been discovered as a writer, and thus he came to be a *Schnorrer* (sponger or freeloader).[82]

Altenberg was indeed known as a *Schnorrer*, living off the benevolence of his friends and acquaintances between paychecks. Although as an author he wrote multiple sketches and short poems—cultivating the *Kleinkunst* (short prose) style[83]—he was more famous for his appearance. Andrew Barker asserts that Altenberg was a widely recognized character in Vienna at the *fin de siècle* and was often caricatured in the works of other writers.[84] His visual appearance was carefully constructed to reflect his becoming not only the writer but also the individual he wished to be.

Like many of their contemporaries, Altenberg and two of his four siblings officially resigned from the IKG and converted to Catholicism.[85] Indeed, after his resignation from the Jewish community in 1900, he became increasingly hostile to Viennese Jewry, using common antisemitic tropes that quite clearly placed acculturated middle-class Jews in the same racial and cultural categories as their poorer, traditional coreligionists. He also made a point of underlining his supposedly non-Jewish appearance and manners, and his ability to pass as a Gentile[86]—likely influenced by the rising antisemitism in Vienna. Altenberg fixated upon the notion of not looking Jewish. After a visit to Gmunden in the Salzkammergut, he wrote of his ability to pass as a Gentile, in both appearance and behavior—employing language that evokes a supposed Jewish deviousness.[87]

His rejection of conventional middle-class male dress expressed a conscious decision to reject his Jewish upbringing. It was not simply that Altenberg often appeared in oversized or loose-fitting clothing. In a photograph from 1915 addressed to his friend Béla von Gomperz, Altenberg stands in what appears to be a rural environment, leaning on a cane while holding a vase of flowers in his other hand (Figure 6.27). He wears a short, double-breasted peacoat with a high closure, metal buttons, wide trousers, a soft turndown collar, and satin bow. A light-colored *Tiroler*-style hat perches on his head at a slight angle, with what appears to be a feather poking out of its braided band. Although this somewhat casual attire gave him a *völkisch* appearance and was thus not too peculiar for a provincial setting—albeit different to the *Trachtenmode* adopted by other Viennese tourists—he appears to have retained elements of this dressed appearance in studio portraits and other photographs from Vienna as well. Writing of *Volkstracht* during the following decade, the Swiss journalist Rudolf von Tavel (1866–1934) argued that its importance lay in signifying the wearer's belonging to a certain *Volksstamm* (ethnicity) or class.[88] By adopting a *völkisch*-style hat as part of his everyday appearance rather than a form of holiday fashion, Altenberg may have been signaling his desire to appear less "Jewish" and a member of the German *Volk*. This attire appears in multiple portraits. In a photograph from 1916, he wears the same jacket, albeit with a slightly different hat—a porkpie hat rather than the *Tirolerhut* (Figure 6.28). His attire is completely at odds with

Figure 6.27 Photograph of Peter Altenberg addressed to Béla von Gomperz, undated. Hanschriftensammlung, Inv. No. H.I.N. 206693. Courtesy of Wienbibliothek im Rathaus, Vienna.

Figure 6.28 Photograph of Peter Altenberg, 1916. Handschriftensammlung, Inv. No. H.I.N. 2044180. Courtesy of Wienbibliothek im Rathaus, Vienna.

Figure 6.29 Photograph of Peter Altenberg addressed to his brother Georg Engländer, May 1913. Handschriftensammlung, H.I.N. 243307. Courtesy of Wienbibliothek im Rathaus, Vienna.

his middle-class background. Beneath his jacket he wears a soft shirt with a turndown collar, and its loud striped fabric clashes with the stripes of his bow tie.

The surviving images exist in black and white or sepia tone, which obscures the actual colors of Altenberg's clothing. Without other evidence, it is impossible to know if the colors were as eccentric as the garments themselves. A 1913 sepia tone photograph addressed to his brother Georg Engländer suggests one possibility. Colored over with what is most likely pencil, Altenberg's checkered overcoat is green, the tweed jacket in a shade of brown, his patterned bowtie is orange, the checkered shirt red and the *Tiroler*-style hat cream or white with a green braided band (Figure 6.29). The fact that the garments were depicted in these colors does not mean that they were accurate. However, given the eccentricity of Altenberg's garment choices, it is probable that the choice of colors matched the reality, following the practice of coloring photographs by hand throughout the nineteenth and early decades of the twentieth centuries.[89] Alternatively, Altenberg may have been expressing artistic license in imagining a flamboyant appearance. In any case, his "suit"—both its supposed colors and the individual garments—subverts notions of accepted male sartorial sobriety.

A photograph taken several years later, in 1918, by his friend Emil Franzos, presents the writer standing in Vienna's *Rathauspark* during summer (Figure 6.30).[90] Altenberg stands smugly, eyebrow cocked, right hand on his hip, and a book clasped in his left. His clothing looks particularly out of place for both the time and location of this photograph. He wears a long, mid-calf-length, dark overcoat, and a pinstriped jacket of some sort

Figure 6.30 Peter Altenberg in the Rathauspark photographed by Emil Franzos, Vienna, 1918. Handschriftensammlung, H.I.N. 116224. Courtesy of Wienbibliothek im Rathaus, Vienna.

with a belt around his waist (so that this style resembles a military tunic; relevant considering this photograph was taken a few months short of the end of the First World War) and at a jaunty angle. From this belt hangs his pince-nez. His shirt collar is low and soft, as opposed to the high, white starched style prevalent at the time, and he wears an untidily knotted tie around his neck. His trousers are in a checkered fabric. The clash of patterns—the jacket's stripe and the check of the trousers—definitely disregards all manner of correct male dressing as espoused by his close friend Adolf Loos and men's fashion and lifestyle magazines such as *Die Herrenwelt*, published during the years of the First World War.[91]

Most striking about this ensemble is Altenberg's choice of sandals. These are likely the same "*Holz-Sandalen*" (wooden sandals) he referred to in a letter to the Franzoses, which he was known to wear.[92] The sandals appear to be out of place not only with the rest of his attire but also with regard to the location of this photograph: the *Rathauspark*, an inner-city park in front of Vienna's Neo-Gothic town hall. Posing for Emil Franzos's camera, Altenberg looks more suited for a day at the seaside than a stroll through cosmopolitan Vienna. The Ringstrasse, onto which the *Rathaus* faces was, during the late nineteenth and early twentieth centuries, the kind of public space that served the individual as a stage upon which one could parade before society.[93] Altenberg's strange collection of garments garnished with his sandals showcasing his bare toes would have been a particularly peculiar sight among the upwardly mobile upper-middle-class men and women dressed in their Sunday best.

The Viennese bourgeoisie during this period maintained a fascination with the English, particularly with the culture of the English gentry.[94] Male dress and lifestyle magazines from the early decades of the twentieth century contained numerous references to English male fashions and the notion of dandyism, particularly in reference to Beau Brummell.[95] Altenberg's overall soft dressing and bold choice of footwear point to another possible English connection. During this period in Great Britain, the English socialist poet and homosexual rights activist Edward Carpenter campaigned for the radical reform of male dress. Among Carpenter's ideas of male dressing was the adoption of softer, less restrictive garments, as opposed to the man in the suit, of whom he wrote in 1886, "might almost as well be in one's own coffin as in the stiff layers upon layers of buckram-like clothing commonly worn nowadays."[96] One particular element of this campaign was the call to adopt sandals as a rational form of male footwear.[97] This was relevant not only in the adoption by both men of a specific type of footwear but also in that both were concerned with the restyling of masculine self and a rejection of the strict conventions of contemporary men's dress. Altenberg, for example, has been described as attempting to develop a markedly "feminine" style, both in his softer sartorial preferences and in his cultivation of a typically "feminine" style of handwriting.[98] Like Carpenter's male dress reform, Altenberg's clothing choices reveal his conscious decision to challenge the perceived norms of masculinity in *fin-de-siècle* Vienna.

Karl Kraus: A Renegade Jew

One of the most striking characteristics of portraits of Karl Kraus (1874–1936) is the rigidity of his dress practices. His stark dressing suggests a lack of interest in fashion beyond the desire to be correctly dressed. Such patterns of dress—sharp, un-extravagant, and unwavering in their consistency—correspond to his general attitude toward the written word and its bastardization by others. Kraus was a steadfast proponent of the "purity" of the German language and culture. Accusations levelled against him as a "self-hating Jew" were often made in reference to his acerbic criticism of fellow Viennese Jews who distorted the sacred language for what he considered to be their own gain—they were likely to be the ones most interested in style, taste, and fashion.

Kraus was born in Gitschin (Jičin), Bohemia, the eighth child of a wealthy paper manufacturer Jakob Kraus and his wife Ernestine (née Kantor), who relocated to the Austrian capital three years after his birth. After leaving university without a degree, a short-lived and unsuccessful career as an actor, and turning on his fellow members of *Jung Wien*, Kraus was employed as Viennese correspondent for the *Breslauer Zeitung* in 1897.[99] During this period, Theodor Herzl published his pamphlet calling for the establishment of a Jewish State (1896). In his dreams of a grand Jewish national reawakening, Herzl strongly utilized the ideals of *Bildung*, *Sittlichkeit*, and *Deutschtum*. What was presented as an ideology of Jewish self-ennoblement and self-determination was more a project in German cultural colonization. Jews, as a colonized people, would act as agents of German colonialism in bringing the ideals of *Bildung* and German culture to an "uncivilized" Palestine (or wherever else the Jewish State might be founded), as well as to the "uncivilized" *Ostjuden*.[100] For Kraus, the self-appointed defender of the German language against its misuse (particularly by other Jews), it was not enough to simply laugh at Herzl's grand plans, as many of Vienna's Jewish *Bildungsbürgertum* did. Rather, such dreams needed to be shattered—in both an ideological and a linguistic sense.[101]

Kraus's attack on Herzl's Zionist ideology and his boss, the editor of the *Neue Freie Presse* (NFP), Moriz Benedikt (who had unsuccessfully attempted to purchase Kraus's allegiance by offering him a position on his editorial staff)[102] stemmed not only from his devotion to the German language but also from the added dimension of his strained relationship with Jewishness. A keen supporter of Jewish assimilation, Kraus converted to Catholicism in 1899, later renouncing that denomination, too, for Protestantism.[103] The most frequent victims of Kraus's vitriolic attacks in his self-published journal *Die Fackel* (*The Torch*) (1899–1936) were members of Vienna's Jewish bourgeoisie, in his eyes the worst offenders of the bastardization of the German language. Harold B. Segel notes that Kraus "never lost an opportunity to expose the Jew behind an assumed non-Jewish name or to knock the putative Jewish features, mannerisms, or style of speech of his adversaries."[104]

Referred to at times as a self-hating Jew, Kraus did not so much hate other Jews as believe, according to his own explanation, that they had gone astray from the true path of righteousness because of what he saw as their debauched aping of the Gentile élite.[105] This was most apparent in his abhorrence of the feuilleton genre, particularly that of the NFP with Herzl as its feuilleton editor. He viewed the feuilleton as a representation of the "mixing of literary modes, which undermined the moral and artistic integrity of the writer"[106] in its pastiche-like path to prominence, unsympathetic to proper literary forms, and morals. He may even have been jealous of other Jewish men in Vienna who so uncaringly went about their daily lives as a way of hoisting themselves into the role of a new cultural élite, a path that had previously been closed to them. This is also suggested in his attack of the converted Jew Heinrich Heine (1797–1856), who can be seen as the progenitor of Jewish artists who converted for professional advancement.[107]

Robert S. Wistrich argues that despite Kraus's repeated attacks on Jewish individuals in Vienna's cultural and literary milieu during the late nineteenth and early twentieth centuries, the moniker of self-hating Jew does not fit, as Kraus's attacks of the reactionary aristocracy and the Gentile bourgeoisie were no less virulent. Rather than attacking Jews as Jews, Kraus devoted himself to condemning bastardization of language and morality at the hands of these individuals,[108] a bastardization that he juxtaposed with the metaphor of the Israelites forsaking God in favor of false idols.[109] Although reserving his anger for a people "gone astray" from the path of righteousness, the poor company Kraus kept in figures like the racial theorist Jörg Lanz von Liebenfels (1874–1954) and the British-born philosopher Houston Stewart Chamberlain (1855–1927)—both proponents of antisemitic racial theories—may have distorted post-Shoah judgments of Kraus. While he himself was no peddler in racial antisemitism, his associations, perceived friendships, and professional collaboration with figures who were racists, bring into question the validity of his critique of Viennese Jewry.

Despite Kraus's antipathy to Herzl ("der König von Zion"), both men shared a similar view of the middle-class Jewish milieu from which they sprang. Herzl's 1902 utopian novel *Altneuland* depicts Vienna's Jewish *Bildungsbürgertum* in a similarly unsavory light. The hypocritical, self-loathing, materially and morally debauched behavior and lifestyles of the milieu—particularly evident in the sarcastic, self-deprecating characters of Grün and Blau at the dinner party hosted at the home of the wealthy clothing manufacturer Moriz Löffler—is contrasted with the autonomous Jewish federation in Ottoman Palestine.[110] Both men highlighted the elements of their milieu that appalled them; what differed was the manner in which they sought to address the "problem." Herzl advocated for Jewry's transformation through self-ennoblement and national rejuvenation. In contrast, Kraus supported assimilation and linguistic purity as the remedies for all that was wrong with contemporary Jewry.[111]

But how did Kraus's aversion to what he saw as the hypocrisy of Vienna's Jewish bourgeoisie manifest itself in sartorial terms? In truth, he appears to have dressed in the same manner as those he lampooned in the pages of *Die Fackel*. Unlike his friend Peter Altenberg, to whom he often played the role of patron, his rejection of the Jewish milieu of his childhood did not take on a deliberate subversion of conventional male dress practices. His sartorial patterns were plain, perhaps even a little conservative. In contrast to his close friend, the self-styled expert on modern aesthetics Adolf Loos,[112] who by the 1920s appears to have adopted soft, turndown shirt collars in keeping with fashion, contemporaneous photographs of Kraus well into the 1920s (and leading into the 1930s) indicate his persistent use of the stiff, wingtip variety. Indeed, in the tight-buttoned, stiff conservatism of Kraus's sartorial habits there is a sense of formality—not pomposity and ceremony, as was the case with "der König von Zion" but a sense of seriousness that can be observed in his overall appearance.

In an 1888 portrait by Nickolaus Stockmann, Kraus as a fourteen-year-old looked mature beyond his years (Figure 6.31). Despite his youthful face and swept hairstyle in a similar manner to the young Schnitzler, he poses confidently, his arms crossed against his chest, leaning in a semi-casual manner against a table or plinth covered with a damask cloth, a chair with plush upholstery off to the side. He wears a dark jacket and waistcoat, light trousers with a faint check pattern, a white shirt, and a simple black bow tie. Unlike the stiff wing collar of later portraits, his collar is turndown—perhaps symbolic of his youthful career prospects before his abandonment of formal study and failure to succeed at a career in the theater.[113] It was during the decade following this portrait that Kraus refused Moriz Benedikt's job offer at the NFP and instead founded his own journal in 1899.

Photographs of Kraus taken in the decade after his founding of *Die Fackel* present him in a changed light. Gone is the hopeful-looking boy and in his place is a severe individual with jutting cheekbones and a pained expression stretched across his face. His hairstyle, too, evokes a sense of unpretentious severity, such as the closely cropped messy fringe he commonly wore, including in a series of portraits by Madame d'Ora (1908) (Figure 6.32). The almost careless styling of his hair is at odds with his attire. In

Figure 6.31 Karl Kraus photographed by Nickolaus Stockmann, Vienna, 1888. Courtesy of GettyImages.

both instances he wears a typical dark lounge suit with a high-cut jacket and his iconic wingtip collar. Whereas in the d'Ora portraits he wears a simple black bow tie, in the later portrait he wears a severe, plain necktie. His posture adds to the sense of frustration and severity, particularly in the second image, where his hands are crossed awkwardly in front of him.

It is not that Kraus was unable to pose comfortably in front of the camera. There are numerous images—both formal studio portraits and informal photographs—in which he appears very much at ease. In his study of photography and its social meanings, Pierre Bourdieu avers that individuals sitting (or standing) before the camera do not pose themselves in a natural manner, but rather in a way that commands respect.[114] By adopting a certain pose or stance, the individual being photographed "presents oneself to be looked at as one seeks to be looked at . . . presents one's own image."[115] In this light,

Figure 6.32 Karl Kraus photographed by Madame d'Ora, Vienna, 1908. 203.430 D. Courtesy of Wiener Bildarchiv/Österreichische Nationalbibliothek, Vienna.

Kraus's staged appearance in earlier images can be understood as an expression of his desire to fashion himself as a young literary crusader; his conventional middle-class attire is a sign of his desire to behave in a "correct" fashion while his untidy hairstyle jumps out from his otherwise understated appearance as a comment on his rejection and criticism of "decadent" bourgeois norms. In contrast, the apparent comfort he exudes in later portraits—particularly those by Trude Fleischmann and Charlotte Joël-Heinzelmann—suggest the sense of self-confidence of a more established writer.

Film evidence from the year 1934 in which Kraus reads excerpts from his writings is revealing of his character.[116] In these recorded recited excerpts from *Die Fackel* and his play *Die letzten Tage der Menschheit*, Kraus demonstrates the mastery of his public persona as a prophet of doom, speaking in a clear, evocative voice. He begins his recitations softly and calmly, increasing the momentum of dramatic recital as the pieces progress. But it is not only his vocal style that is remarkable. In his self-appointed role as defender of language sent to arraign bourgeois Jews, there is almost a sense of the seriousness of the Talmudic scholar, particularly in the visual manner of his readings. Kraus's erratic gesticulations and the manner in which he absorbs himself entirely in his texts recalls Orthodox rabbinical students passionately arguing over Talmud tractates.[117] The drama of Kraus's manner contrasts with the plainness of his physiognomic and sartorial appearance. A slight, hunched man with shortly cropped hair and delicate spectacles that draw attention to his weak vision, Kraus wears a simple dark jacket, dark bow tie, and white shirt, complete with the ubiquitous stiff, wing collar. His clothing is neither ceremonial nor casual but serious and somewhat businesslike, the clothes of a man who has set himself a serious task.[118]

Kraus's clothing remained unremarkable throughout surviving photographs taken over the course of his adult life, changing only slightly with the general course of male fashion (apart from his collar styles, it seems, which tended to remain static, unlike his favored styles of tailoring). Unlike Arthur Schnitzler, Kraus avoided any sartorial extravagance that would mark him as a bohemian writer and, unlike Stefan Zweig, he appeared not to indulge in the fine details of men's accessories. All in all, his dress patterns seemed to correspond to the sober style of the "Great Masculine Renunciation." An exception appears to be a certain plaid smoking jacket with a satin shawl lapel that he wore in a series of photographs from 1928 by the Viennese Jewish photographer Trude Fleischmann (Figure 6.33). The photographs are not colored, so the colors of the fabrics

Figure 6.33 Karl Kraus photographed by Trude Fleischmann, Vienna, 1928. Courtesy of GettyImages.

used for this jacket are unknown, but the plaid pattern and the shiny texture of the satin lapels provide a contrast to the sober conservatism of the plain suits he wore in other photographs.

Despite his stark sartorial appearance in photographs and film recordings, Kraus was not immune to the influences of fashion. Surviving receipts indicate that he was a customer of the renowned tailors Goldman & Salatsch, both purchasing his clothing from the atelier and having them serviced there. A surviving receipt from Goldman & Salatsch issued in November 1917 lists his purchases and services rendered over the previous year: a sports jacket ("*Saccoanzug*") on November 7, 1916, a jacket and waistcoat in silk ("*Jaquet und Gilet mit Seide*") on March 28, 1917, and for having a suit laundered a ironed on April 10, 1917.[119] Likewise, receipts have survived from the tailor Franz Woska—located at Wohllebengasse 19 in Wieden (district IV)—from the years 1908 and 1915 (the latter of which lists purchases from December 1914 to March 1915). Unfortunately, although these receipts list Kraus's purchases, the garment descriptions are limited to garment types, such as "*Saco Anzug*" (sports jacket), "*Winterrock*" (winter jacket), "*Überzieher*" (overcoat), "*Reithose*" (riding breeches), and "*Mantel*" (coat). As a result, the appearance of the garments—their fabrics, colors, and cuts—can only be speculated based on contemporary male fashions and photographs of Kraus. However, the occasional detail, such as "*Perl[-]Knöpfe*" (pearl buttons) does shed some light on Kraus's clothing preferences and that he showed an interest in matters of sartorial taste.[120]

* * *

The photographic and other evidence of Freud, Schnitzler, Zweig, and Kraus, like that of other men of their time, reveals a multiplicity of similar sartorial patterns adopted by these individuals, rather than an identical, uniform dress. With the exception of Altenberg, who Elana Shapira asserts represents the age-old figure of the wandering Jew,[121] the similarity in the dress habits of these men can be found instead in their overall conformity to accepted male attire of the period. The dark suits, white collars, and neckwear they favored placed them firmly in the sphere of contemporary male clothing consumption, not only in a European context—as outlined by classic studies of male dress by Christopher Breward—but in a wider Western cultural sphere that included men from as far as North America and Australia.[122] Although clothing was not a central element of their literary concerns, it both surfaced as a theme of literary device in their writings and played an important role in the construction of the visual and ideological identification of these five men. Their sartorial patterns, practices, and preferences reveal that each of these men took pains to fashion his appearance in a manner that best expressed his position in Viennese society. Examining the dressed appearance of these men betrays little about their status as Jews. After all, as this chapter has explained, these men were from a similar middle-class milieu that, in its dedication to the values and ideals of *Bildung*, *Sittlichkeit*, and *Deutschtum*, preferred visual and cultural conformity with the corresponding Gentile socioeconomic classes. It is through, what Shapira refers to as their "tailored authorship"[123]—a combination of their attire, gaze, and presence within photography—that helped establish them as distinct icons of Viennese modernism. Moreover, it is in the details of male clothing—particularly the suit—in the face of its perceived opacity and uniformity that diversity of style is sharply highlighted. The individual styles they chose did not overtly broadcast their ethnic or religious identification. It is only in understanding the complex and varied relationship these men maintained to Jewishness and their Jewish identities that certain patterns of dress begin to emerge. This explains, for example, why Sigmund Freud, a "godless Jew" and intellectual hoping to be taken seriously in Vienna's conservative and antisemitic medical community, embraced the conventional English tailoring and fabrics, or why Peter Altenberg completely eschewed the sartorial norms and "good taste" of bourgeois respectability.

CONCLUSION

Acculturated middle-class Jews made up only part of a diverse and strong segment of Viennese society. Despite the prevalence of antisemitism, Jewish writers and critics, politicians and industrialists, scientists and artists, continued to contribute to the flowering of Viennese modernism. Men, both renowned and unknown, followed sartorial fashions and attired themselves in modes that they felt best expressed their social and political identification. In addition to its use as a form of self-fashioning, clothing and its relationship to the body were important in dealing with hostility, whether through adoption of conventional fashions, or eccentric or radical styles that might express allegiance to specific cultural or political ideologies. In the introduction to her edited volume about Jewish life in Vienna's Leopoldstadt, Ruth Beckermann presents a photo of a "typical" Jewish family. The older generation appear in the guise of typical Orthodox Jews, the patriarch with a large beard and dressed in ubiquitous dark clothing and a black felt hat, and the matriarch wearing a wig, in the typical manner of married Orthodox women. The younger generation, however, are dressed in the prevalent styles of the wider society, an indication of the intergenerational acculturation process. Beckermann asserts that it was expressly through their dress that this family's acculturation as well as the various ways Viennese Jews dealt with their intersecting identification could be measured.[1] For the two younger men, in particular, their dress patterns suggest conflicting notions of Jewish identity, conflicting both with each other and with their parents' generation. The man who wears a suit and tie, which Beckermann remarks was common among men of various class backgrounds, may have been expressing a bourgeois identity. His brother also wears a suit; however, the tie is absent and his collar is worn open over his jacket lapels, a sign, Beckermann suggests, of his Zionist or Socialist convictions and his desire to distance himself from bourgeois society.[2]

What Beckermann describes is not novel. As this book has argued, men's dress and the way in which it was worn could be both opaque and transparent. Sartorial patterns, practices, and preferences meant more than a uniform of modern masculinity; for acculturating and acculturated Jewish men, dressed appearances went beyond attempts at visual assimilation. Like the family depicted in Beckermann's introduction, clothing might express political ideologies, cultural affiliations, and even social and professional identification—as the examples of clerical garments and "private" attire of Viennese rabbis have shown.

As Elana Shapira has demonstrated with regard to Jewish patrons of architecture, the dress and fashion industries similarly afforded Jewish men the opportunity to participate in the city's realm of fashion by conforming to accepted modes of dress ("opt in") as well as actively negating conventions of bourgeois respectability and sobriety ("opt out"), and they did this as both consumers and purveyors of fashion.³ Although Vienna took many of its fashion cues from London and Paris, during the interwar period it was recognized as one of Europe's fashion capitals in its own right, with a reputation for quality. The high proportion of Jews working in the fashion and apparel industries meant not only that Jewish practitioners created and distributed fashions consumed by most of the population but also that Viennese fashion came to be regarded as somehow "Jewish," even if it was not overtly expressed. Similarly, the acclaim won by the many writers, artists, critics, and thinkers of Jewish origin as representatives of Viennese culture meant that, wittingly or not, Jewish men became visual examples of the diverse Viennese male sartorial modes in a wider European arena. Men like Sigmund Freud and Theodor Herzl in their conventional tailored suits could be regarded as Viennese dandies attesting to the quality and respectability of the city's male fashions, while Peter Altenberg and Arthur Schnitzler with their playful attire represented the more eccentric modes of fashionable Viennese male consumption.

The period between 1867 and 1938 has often been portrayed as a golden era of Viennese Jewry. Within this span of seven decades, Viennese Jewry and Austrian Jewry as a whole not only enjoyed unprecedented legal and civic equality but also involved themselves in all areas of Viennese society—political, scientific, economic, and artistic. In his oft-quoted memoir, the German-Jewish writer Jakob Wassermann expressed his bewilderment at the confidence and visibility of Viennese Jewry as he encountered it upon relocating to the Austrian capital from Bavaria:

> I recognized fairly soon that the entire public was dominated by Jews. The banks, the press, the theater, literature, society events—everything was in the hands of Jews. One did not have to look very far for an explanation. The nobility was completely indifferent. With the exception of a few non-conformists and outcasts, a few who were aloof and enlightened, they not only maintained an uneasy distance from the intellectual and artistic life, but they also feared and scorned it. . . . The court, the petit bourgeoisie, and the Jews gave the city its character. That the Jews were the most versatile group that kept all others in incessant motion is not particularly astonishing. Nonetheless, I was amazed at the quantity of Jewish physicians, lawyers, club members, snobs, dandies, workers, actors, newspersons, and poets.⁴

The Jewish contribution to the development of Viennese culture might be understood as a way of "giving back" to the city and state that had offered them equality, as well as a way of asserting their enduring and dynamic presence in the city and its culture.

As this book has shown, Viennese Jews grappled with their Jewish identities and the concept of Jewishness on many different levels. In a multiethnic society in which they unofficially constituted one *Volksstamm* among many, their Jewish identities were often a fact of life, regardless of whether they engaged with it or not. Even those Jews who converted to Christian denominations and/or married Gentile partners were aware of the social perception of their Jewish "difference." The dissolution of the multiethnic and multilinguistic Habsburg Empire and the subsequent creation of successor states like

Czechoslovakia, Poland, and Yugoslavia meant that most non-German and non-Magyar Austro-Hungarians fulfilled the desires of national determination that had plagued the Austro-Hungarian political arena for much of the nineteenth century. Of the various "peoples" of the former empire, Austrian Jews were among those who found themselves an ethnic minority among a largely homogenous German nation.

During the interwar period, Vienna suffered from political and civic turmoil, including civil war, political coups, the assassination of the chancellor Engelbert Dollfuss (1892–1934), and political pressure from the neighboring National Socialist regime. While antisemitism flared up in the political and social discourse, and Jewish university students faced abuse from fellow students aligned with the National Socialists,[5] the political movement later to be declared illegal under the Dollfuss-Schuschnigg regime, most Jews continued their lives as they had under the Habsburgs. As Lisa Silverman has asserted in reference to the tripartite model of Austro-Jewish self-identification first highlighted by Marsha L. Rozenblit,[6] Viennese Jews felt comfortable in their adopted home city. Despite the prevalence of antisemitism, they felt themselves very much a part of Viennese and Austrian society: politically Austrian, ethnically and/or religiously Jewish, and culturally Viennese.[7] Richard Thieberger, for example, recalled answering "Austrian," "Viennese," and "Jewish" when asked for his national, residential, and religious details while filling in an official form upon his matriculation.[8]

The Anschluss of March 1938 put a definitive end to both Vienna's Jewish "Golden Autumn"[9] and its status as a fashion capital. Commencing with the German Wehrmacht crossing the Austro-German frontier on March 12, the Anschluss culminated with Adolf Hitler driving through the streets of Vienna on March 15, met by cheering crowds who had eagerly awaited his arrival. On the Heldenplatz in front of the former Imperial Palace (*Hofburg*), Hitler addressed a glowing crowd of 200,000. The National Socialists set to work at once dismantling the Austrian state and enacting anti-Jewish measures. It has been said that Austrian Jewry experienced from one moment to the next what their German counterparts had suffered over the course of five years. While in Germany, anti-Jewish measures had slowly been introduced since Hitler's induction as chancellor, Austrian Jews were met with a barrage of state-sponsored discrimination as well as virulent local antisemitism. Iconic images from the period show Viennese Jews being forced on hands and knees to scrub graffiti from the pavement while crowds of jeering onlookers surrounded them.[10]

For many, the deluge of state-sponsored antisemitism came as a shock and prompted them into emigration, with the encouragement of the new Nazi government which opened the *Zentralstelle für jüdische Auswanderung in Wien* (Central Agency for Jewish Emigration in Vienna), headed by Adolf Eichmann and operating out of the former Palais Albert Rothschild on Prinz-Eugen Strasse 20–22 in Wieden (district IV). Notwithstanding the difficulties associated with acquiring entry visas to other countries as well as exit visas from the Reich, a great number of Viennese Jews managed to flee Austria. Of the approximate 170,000 Jews living in Vienna in 1938, close to 129,000 were able to leave the country, the majority to the Americas, the United Kingdom, and Shanghai—the latter being one of the few places in the world that still readily accepted

Jewish refugees without an entry visa.[11] It is ironic that Viennese Jews, once castigated as "rootless cosmopolitans" whose roots were everywhere and nowhere at once, would be forced out into the world, and often not welcomed enthusiastically.

Among the five writers whose sartorial habits were analyzed in Chapter 6, only Sigmund Freud and Stefan Zweig were still alive in 1938. Having left Austria in 1934, Zweig was already living in London at the time of the Anschluss. His brother Alfred and widowed mother Ida, however, were still in Vienna. By the end of March, Alfred and his wife Stefanie, as Czechoslovak citizens, traveled unhindered to Switzerland and eventually settled in the United States. Ida, however, a woman well into her eighties, was too frail to make the journey and died alone in Vienna in August that same year.[12] Freud, as a world-renowned scientist, received a permit for the United Kingdom, obtained on his behalf by his Welsh colleague and biographer Ernest Jones, and relocated to London in early June 1938, where he succumbed to cancer the following year.[13]

Most of the Jews who remained in Vienna were deported to concentration camps and ghettos in Nazi-occupied Poland and other parts of Eastern Europe, notably Łódź, Minsk, Riga, and Theresienstadt (Terezín), where many died of malnutrition, disease, exhaustion, and violence at the hands of the Nazis and their local collaborators. Deportations began immediately after the Anschluss, with many Jewish men—particularly political and other prominent figures—being arrested and interned at Dachau concentration camp near Munich.[14] A small number of Viennese Jews, however, survived the war in the city, either in hiding, protected by Gentile spouses or friends, or by working for the Nazis.[15]

In addition to destroying the once vibrant and large Jewish community, the Nazis also destroyed the city's fashion and apparel industries. Among the thousands of businesses forcibly "Aryanized" were those in the dress and luxury sectors. Only a number of the many famous, Jewish-owned luxury stores still exist, albeit under new ownership: the men's tailoring shops Kniže (Graben) and Jungmann & Neffe (Albertinaplatz), and the department store Gerngross (Mariahilferstrasse). The myriad other Jewish-owned clothing establishments catering to all levels of Viennese society no longer exist. Some buildings remain, serving as reminders to the once burgeoning Viennese fashion industry, albeit used today for different purposes. The shop on the Graben once housing the textile company E. Braun & Co. now houses a branch of the Swedish fast-fashion retailer H&M,[16] and the famous Looshaus on the Michaelerplatz that Adolf Loos designed for Michael Goldman, owner of the Goldman & Salatsch tailoring company, is now home to a branch of the Austrian Raiffeisen Bankengruppe.

The appropriation of Vienna's Jewish-owned dress and luxury companies had a drastic effect on Vienna's fashion industry. Just as Hugo Bettauer prophesized in his 1922 dystopian novel, Die Stadt ohne Juden, the expulsion of Vienna's Jewish population resulted in the city's loss of status as a fashion capital. Although the result was not exactly what Bettauer portrayed—Vienna did not become a large provincial town whose inhabitants went around in Trachtenmoden—factors such as the destruction of a large segment of the city's fashion industry, and Nazi notions of beauty and family purity certainly influenced the city's external character.

The involvement of Jews in Vienna's *fin-de-siècle* world of fashion went beyond the roles of consumer, creator, and purveyor. Jewish men used fashionable clothing as a way of creating and expressing specific identities—both to themselves and to others. Despite having sartorial patterns, practices, and preferences that were maintained by the wider society, their choices continued to play a central role in the persistence of external notions of Jewishness. The adoption of modern clothing, particularly the suit, by Jewish men corresponded with the broad period of their emancipation over the course of the nineteenth century. Former signs of sartorial Jewishness were made redundant and, barring xenophobic notions of Jewish physiognomic appearance and behavioral patterns, the Jewish man became invisible among other "modern" men who donned the same garments. This does not mean that a change of clothing always signaled an attempt to become "invisible," or that when it did the outcome was successful. On the contrary, certain forms of behavior and habits—social, political, educational, residential, and professional—continued to be used by antisemites to distinguish a Jew from the Gentile body politic. However, to an individual in the street, a man walking toward him in "identical" attire was no longer instantly recognizable as a Jew based on his dressed appearance alone. Sometimes it infuriated antisemites, who leveled accusations against the suit's wearers for trying to mask their Jewishness. As Alain Finkielkraut asserts, "Anti-Semitism turned racist only on the fateful day when, as a consequence of Emancipation, you could no longer pick Jews out of the crowd at first glance. . . . Racial hatred and its blind rage were essentially the Jew's punishment for no longer placing their difference on display."[17] The piles of clothing, including suits, stripped from incoming prisoners at concentration and extermination camps during the Shoah are testimony, in moving and multifaceted ways, of the failure of the suit and indeed modern clothing in general to be any protection for Jewish men at all. Engaging with the latest material culture was in the end no protection against antisemitism and the modern machine of Nazism.

NOTES

Introduction

1 Anne Hollander, *Sex and Suits* (New York: Alfred A. Knopf, 1994); David Kuchta, *The Three-Piece Suit and Modern Masculinity: England, 1550–1850* (Berkeley, CA: University of California Press, 2002).

2 Throughout his 1879 pamphlet, *Der Sieg des Judenthums über das Germanenthum*, Marr refers to "semitism," but it was not until later that he would employ the term "antisemitism" in his writing. See Wilhelm Marr, *Der Sieg des Judenthums über das Germanenthum: Vom nicht confessionellen Standpunkt aus betrachtet* (Bern: Rudolph Costenoble, 1879).

3 See Y. Michal Bodemann, "Coldly Admiring the Jews: Werner Sombart and Classical German Sociology on Nationalism and Race," in *Antisemitism and the Constitution of Sociology*, ed. Marcel Stoetzler (Lincoln, NE: Nebraska University Press, 2014), 110–34.

4 See Heinz-Georg Marten, "Racism, Social-Darwinism, Anti-Semitism and Aryan Supremacy," *The International journal of the History of Sport* 16, no. 2 (1991): 23–41.

5 Panizza's choice of name for the novella's antihero is a clear reference to the Jewish villain Veitel Itzig in Gustav Freytag's novel *Soll und Haben* (1855). It was also the pseudonym of Heinrich Holzschuher (1798–1847) who wrote antisemitic sketches in mock-Yiddish. See Annika Reichwald, *Das Phantasma der Assimilation* (Göttingen: Vandenhoeck & Rupprecht, 2017), 310–11.

6 Adolf Hitler, *Mein Kampf*, trans. James Murphy (New York: Fredonia Classics, 2003 [1925]), 117–18.

7 Oskar Panizza, "The Operated Jew," in *The Operated Jew: Two Tales of Anti-Semitism*, ed. and trans. Jack Zipes (New York: Routledge, 1991), 51.

8 Ibid., 66–7.

9 The change of name from Itzig Faitel Stern to Siegfried Freudenstern is itself a joke, with the title character's new name being equally recognizable as "Jewish," and alluding to the popularity of typical German names, such as Siegfried, Sigismund, and Moriz among assimilating and acculturating Jews during the nineteenth century. Even the adoption of the surname "Freudenstern" with its use of the Jewish-sounding suffix "-stern" (like "-mann," "-berg," and "-stein") makes light of the manner in which the Jew Stern unsuccessfully attempts to mask his origins.

10 There is, however, the presence of one particular, important sartorial tool in Stern/Freudenstern's metamorphosis, and this is the barbed belt which forces the wearer to stand erect on pains of bodily damage—ironic as the belt itself causes bodily damage by placing strain on Stern/Freudenstern's natural physique.

11 Ellen Moers, *The Dandy: Brummell to Beerbohm* (New York: The Viking Press, 1960), 17–38.

12 *Kikeriki* 37, no. 3 (January 10, 1897): 1.

13 Panizza, "The Operated Jew," 57–8.

14 Morris B. Kaplan, "Refiguring the Jewish Question: Arendt, Proust, and the Politics of Sexuality," in *Feminist Interpretations of Hannah Arendt*, ed. Bonnie Honig (University Park, PA: The Pennsylvania State University Press, 1995), 116.

15 Panizza, "The Operated Jew," 64.

16 Ibid., 74.

17 Hermann Bahr quoted in Elana Shapira, *Style and Seduction: Jewish Patrons, Architecture, and Design in Fin de Siècle Vienna* (Waltham, MA: Brandeis University Press, 2016), 74.

18 Although distinct, the figures of the "Jew" and "Jewess" are connected, with the (male) "Jew" perceived as being feminine in *fin-de-siècle* antisemitic discourse. See, for example, Sander L. Gilman, "Salome, Syphilis, Sarah Bernhardt and the 'Modern Jewess'," *The German Quarterly* 66, no. 2 (1993): 195–211.

19 Sander Gilman, *The Jew's Body* (New York: Routledge, 1991), 5.

20 Ibid., 3.

21 Sigmund Freud quoted in Jacques Le Rider, *Modernity and Crisis of Identity: Culture and Society in Fin-de-Siècle Vienna*, trans. Rosemary Morris (Cambridge: Polity Press, 1993), 168.

22 Gilman, *The Jew's Body*, 18.

23 Zygmunt Bauman, *Modernity and Ambivalence* (Cambridge: Polity Press, 1991), 89. Although the concept of Jewishness relates to Gentile notions of expressions of Jewish character, this concept is also tied to internal expressions of Jewish identification and being Jewish, as related to the notion of *Yiddishkeit*.

24 See Richard Weikart, "The Impact of Social Darwinism on Anti-Semitic Ideology in Germany and Austria, 1860–1945," in *Jewish Tradition and the Challenge of Darwinism*, ed. Geoffrey Cantor and Marc Swetlitz (Chicago, IL: University of Chicago Press, 2006), 93–115.

25 Ibid., 95.

26 See Alain F. Corcos, *The Myth of the Jewish Race: A Biologist's Point of View* (Bethlehem, PA: Lehigh University Press, 2005), 42–53; Mitchell B. Hart, ed., *Jews & Race: Writings on Identity & Difference, 1880–1940* (Waltham, MA: Brandeis University Press, 2011).

27 Elana Shapira discusses the importance of Jewish self-identification in a modernizing society in her study of Jewish art patrons in *fin-de-siecle* Vienna. See Shapira, *Style and Section*.

28 Ian Reifowitz, *Imagining an Austrian Nation: Joseph Samuel Bloch and the Search for a Multiethnic Austrian Society, 1846–1919* (Boulder, CO: East European Monographs, 2003), 25–6.

29 Deborah Hertz, *How Jews Became Germans: The History of Conversion and Assimilation in Berlin* (New Haven, CT: Yale University Press, 2007), 141–3.

30 See, for example, Gabriel M. Goldstein and Elizabeth E. Greenberg, eds., *A Perfect Fit: The Garment Industry and American Jewry, 1860–1960* (Lubbock, TX: Texas University Press, 2012); Roberta S. Kremer, ed., *Broken Threads: The Destruction of the Jewish Fashion Industry in Germany and Austria* (Oxford: Berg, 2007); Adam D. Mendelsohn, *The Rag Race: How Jews Sewed Their War to Success in America and the British Empire* (New York: New York University Press, 2015); Edna Nahshon, ed., *Jews and Shoes* (Oxford: Berg, 2008); Alfred Rubens, *A History of Jewish Dress* (London: Weidenfeld and Nicolson, 1973); Eric Silverman, *A Cultural History of Jewish Dress* (London: Bloomsbury, 2013).

31   Eduard Fuchs, "'Bourgeois Dress' (1902)," in *The Rise of Fashion: A Reader*, ed. Daniel Leonard Purdy (Minneapolis, MN: University of Minnesota Press, 2004), 318.

32   Hollander, *Sex and Suits*, 91.

33   Christopher Breward, *The Suit: Form, Function and Style* (London: Reaktion Books, 2016), 13.

34   Hollander, *Sex and Suits*, 97.

35   Kuchta, *The Three-Piece Suit and Modern Masculinity*.

36   Ibid., 2.

37   Michael Zakim, *Ready-Made Democracy: A History of Men's Dress in the American Republic, 1760–1860* (Chicago, IL: University of Chicago Press, 2003), 126.

38   Breward, *The Suit*, 52.

39   Ibid., 76.

40   Christopher Breward, *The Hidden Consumer: Masculinities, Fashion and City Life, 1860–1914* (Manchester: Manchester University Press, 1999).

41   John C. Flügel, *The Psychology of Clothes* (London: The Hogarth Press, 1966[1930]), 110ff.

42   Michael C. Carter, "Formality and Informality in (Mainly) Men's Dress," in *Being Prepared: Aspects of Dress and Dressing* (Sydney: Puncher & Wattmann, 2017), 127–72.

Chapter 1

1   Franz Friedrich Masaidek, *Wien und die Wiener aus der Spottvogelperspektive: Wien's Sehens-, Merk- und Nichtswürdigkeiten* (Vienna: R. von Waldheim, 1873), 5.

2   Michael John and Albert Lichtblau, *Schmelztiegel Wien—Einst und Jetzt: Zur Geschichte und Gegenwart von Zuwanderung und Minderheiten* (Vienna: Böhlau Verlag, 1990).

3   Masaidek, *Wien und die Wiener*, 5.

4   Peter Gay, *Freud, Jews and Other Germans: Masters and Victims in Modernist Culture* (Oxford: Oxford University Press, 1978), 10–11.

5   See Ernst Bruckmüller, *The Austrian Nation: Cultural Consciousness and Socio-Political Processes*, trans. Lowell A. Bangerter (Riverside, CA: Ariadne Press, 2003).

6   Robert A. Kann, *A History of the Habsburg Empire, 1526–1918* (Berkeley, CA: The University of California Press, 1974), 433–5; Julie Thorpe, *Pan-Germanism and the Austrofascist State, 1933–1938* (Manchester: Manchester University Press, 2011), 19–21.

7   See John Deak, *Forging a Multinational State: State Making in Imperial Austria from the Enlightenment to the First World War* (Stanford, CA: Stanford University Press, 2015); R. J. W. Evans, *Austria, Hungary, and the Habsburgs: Essays on Central Europe, c. 1683–1867* (Oxford: Oxford University Press, 2006); Kann, *A History of the Habsburg Empire*.

8   See Evans, *Austria, Hungary, and the Habsburgs*, in particular Chapter 10 "The Habsburgs and the Hungarian Problem, 1790–1848," 173–92.

9   Kann, *A History of the Habsburg Empire*, 349–50.

10   Ibid., 439–41.

11   Edward Timms, *Karl Kraus: Apocalyptic Satirist, Vol. 1: Culture and Catastrophe in Habsburg Vienna* (New Haven, CT: Yale University Press, 1986), 16.

12   See Peter Thaler, "National History—National Imagery: The Role of History in Postwar Austrian Nation Building," *Central European History* 32, no. 3 (1999): 277–309 (in particular 284–97).

13   Article 19 of the Austrian Constitution stated, "All ethnic groups (*Volksstämme*) in the state have equal rights and every ethnic group has the inviolable right to preserve and cultivate its nationality and language." Quoted in Kann, *A History of the Habsburg Empire*, 339.

14   Steven Beller, *Vienna and the Jews, 1867–1938: A Cultural History* (Cambridge: Cambridge University Press, 1989), 44.

15   Marsha L. Rozenblit, *Reconstructing a National Identity: The Jews of Habsburg Austria During World War I* (New York: Oxford University Press, 2001), 23–4.

16   On Czechs and the Czech language in Austria and Vienna in particular, see Jakub S. Beneš, *Workers & Nationalism: Czech and German Social Democracy in Habsburg Austria, 1890–1918* (Oxford: Oxford University Press, 2017); Pavel Kladiwa, "The Czech Community and Czech as a 'Language of Daily Use,' in Vienna, 1880–1910," *Prager wirtschafts- und sozialhistorische Mitteilungen—Prague Economic and Social History Papers* 20, no. 2 (2014): 26–47.

17   Lisa Silverman, *Becoming Austrians: Jews and Culture Between the World Wars* (New York: Oxford University Press, 2012), 14.

18   Michael John, "Migration in Austria: An Overview of the 1920s to 2000s," in *Understanding Multiculturalism: The Habsburg Central European Experience*, ed. Johannes Feichtinger and Gary B. Cohen (New York: Berghahn, 2014), 123.

19   Marsha L. Rozenblit, *The Jews of Vienna, 1867–1914: Assimilation and Identity* (Albany, NY: State University of New York, 1983), 17. Rozenblit notes, "The 1857 census counted only the *einheimisch* residents, i.e., those who had Viennese *Heimatsrecht*. This number [6,217] represents only those who had legal domiciliary rights in Vienna." The census did not include those Jews who lived illegally in Vienna while being registered as living in other towns and villages. Michael John and Albert Lichtblau put the total Jewish population for the year 1857 at 15,116 (3.2 percent). See John and Lichtblau, *Schmelztiegel Wien*, 36.

20   See William O. McCagg Jr., *A History of Habsburg Jews, 1670–1918* (Bloomington, IN: Indiana University Press, 1989).

21   After the failed 1848–9 revolution, Franz Joseph I would make it easier for Habsburg Jews to settle in Vienna; however, the final restrictions on Jewish purchase of real estate were not removed until 1860, and Jews were not granted equality with other Austrians until 1867.

22   See Michael Laurence Miller, *Rabbis and Revolution: The Jews of Moravia in the Age of Emancipation* (Stanford, CA: Stanford University Press, 2011).

23   Rozenblit, *The Jews of Vienna*, 27–8; Marsha L. Rozenblit, "The Struggle over Religious Reform in Nineteenth-Century Vienna," *AJS Review* 14, no. 2 (Autumn 1989): 213–17.

24   Rozenblit, *The Jews of Vienna*, 13–45.

25   David Biale, David Assaf, Benjamin Brown, Uriel Gellman, Samuel C. Heilman, Moshe Rosman, Gadi Sagiv and Marcin Wodziński, *Hasidism: A New History* (Princeton, NJ: Princeton University Press, 2018), 583.

26   Klaus Hödl, *Als Bettler in die Leopoldstadt: Galizische Juden auf dem Weg nach Wien*, 2nd ed. (Vienna: Böhlau Verlag, 1994), 140–1.

27   Harriet Pass Freidenreich, *Jewish Politics in Vienna, 1918–1938* (Bloomington, IN: Indiana University Press, 1991), 22–3. See also Robert S. Wistrich, *The Jews of Vienna in the Age of Franz Joseph* (Oxford: The Littman Library of Jewish Civilization, 1989), in particular,

Chapter 4, "Three Viennese Preachers," 98–130, and Chapter 5, "Liberalism, *Deutschtum,* and Assimilation," 131–63.

28 Ibid., 148.

29 See Freidenreich, *Jewish Politics in Vienna,* 213.

30 Wistrich, *The Jews of Vienna in the Age of Franz Joseph,* 41.

31 Ibid., 6–7.

32 On the history of Jews in Vienna, see Max Grunwald, *Vienna* (Philadelphia, PA: The Jewish Publication Society of America, 1936); Sigmund Mayer, *Die Wiener Juden: Kommerz, Kultur, Politik, 1700–1900* (Vienna: R. Löwit Verlag, 1917; Hans Tietze, *Die Juden Wiens: Geschichte—Wirtschaft—Kultur* (Leipzig: E. P. Tal, 1935).

33 John and Lichtblau, *Schmelztiegel Wien,* 145.

34 Rozenblit, *The Jews of Vienna,* 75–6.

35 Ibid., 78; and Magistrats-Abteiling XXI für Statistik, ed., *Statistisches Jahrbuch der Stadt Wien für das Jahr 1901* (Vienna: Verlag des Wiener Magistrates, 1903), 50–1.

36 Ruth Beckermann, ed., *Die Mazzesinsel: Juden in der Wiener Leopoldstadt, 1918–1938* (Vienna: Löcker Verlag, 1984). Despite its pejorative origins, the term developed a sense of nostalgia and is used today in an endearing manner by Jews and Gentiles alike.

37 Mayer, *Die Wiener Juden,* 463. The *Schalothstube* Mayer describes was a typical feature of traditional Jewish Sabbath throughout Central and Eastern Europe, where Jews could leave their Schaloth (also known as "cholent" or "chulent") in the ovens of local bakers to cook overnight for Sabbath lunch.

38 Kurt Tauber, "To Greta: The Biography of Kurt Tauber," unpublished memoir, Leo Baeck Institute [LBI], (1995), ME 1234. MM II 43, 1–2.

39 Kurt H. Schaffir, "My Personal History, 1923–1940," unpublished memoir, LBI (1989), ME 1980. MM II 22, 13.

40 See Peter McNeil, "Despots of Elegance: Men's Fashion, 1715–1915," in *Reigning Men: Fashion in Menswear, 1715–2015,* ed. Sharon Sadako Takeda, Kaye Durland Spilker, and Clarissa M. Esquerra (Munich: Los Angeles County Museum of Art, and DelMonica Books, 2016), 235–47.

41 Wistrich, *The Jews of Vienna in the Age of Franz Joseph,* 58.

42 Auguste Glauber, "Who We Are and Why we Are Here," unpublished memoir, LBI (1985), ME 1137. MM II 33, 2a.

43 Ibid.

44 Todd M. Endelman, "Gender and Conversion Revisited," in *Gender and Jewish History,* ed. Marion A. Kaplan and Deborah Dash Moore (Bloomington, IN: Indiana University Press, 2011), 177.

45 Moriz Gallia, a Moravian-born Jewish industrialist who converted to Catholicism with his wife Hermine in 1910 (some years after having their children baptized) left money in his will to the Jewish communities in Vienna and his hometown Bisenz (Bzenec), as well as other Jewish charities. No money was left, however, to any Catholic organizations. See Tim Bonyhady, *Good Living Street: The Fortunes of My Viennese Family* (Crows Nest, NSW: Allen & Unwin, 2014), 204.

46 Raymond H. C. Teske Jr. and Bardin H. Nelson, "Acculturation and Assimilation: A Clarification," *American Ethnologist* 1, no. 2 (1974): 358–65.

47   Ibid., 359.

48   Milton M. Gordon, *Assimilation in American Life: The Role of Race, Religion, and National Origins* (New York: Oxford University Press, 1964).

49   Leo Spitzer, *Lives in Between: Assimilation and Marginality in Austria, Brazil, and West Africa, 1780–1945* (Cambridge: Cambridge University Press, 1989), 28.

50   Rozenblit, *The Jews of Vienna*, 148–53.

51   Spitzer, *Lives in Between*, 90–1.

52   Hödl, *Als Bettler in die Leopoldstadt*, 240–2.

53   See Wistrich, *The Jews of Vienna in the Age of Franz Joseph*, in particular Chapter 4, "Three Viennese Preachers," 98–130, and Chapter 5, "Liberalism, *Deutschtum*, and Assimilation," 131–63.

54   Bauman, *Modernity and Ambivalence*, 72.

55   Ibid., 107–8.

56   Georg Simmel, "The Stranger," in *The Sociology of Georg Simmel*, trans. and ed. Kurt H. Wolff (New York: The Free Press, 1950), 402.

57   As a child, Simmel's Jewish parents had him baptized as a Protestant.

58   Simmel, "The Stranger," 403.

59   Bauman, *Modernity and Ambivalence*, 71.

60   See Ivar Oxaal, Michael Pollak, and Gerhard Botz, eds., *Jews, Antisemitism and Culture in Vienna* (London: Routledge and Kegan Paul, 1987).

61   Rozenblit, *Reconstructing a National Identity*, 18.

62   Emil Brix, "Assimilation in the Late Habsburg Monarchy," in *Österreich-Konzeptionen und jüdisches Selbstverständnis: Identitäts-Transfiguationen im 19. Und 20. Jahrhundert*, ed. Hanni Mittelmann and Armin A. Wallas (Tübingen: Max Niemeyer Verlag, 2001), 37; Albert Lichtbalu, "'Galitsianer' and the Mobility of Stereotypes," *Jewish Culture and History* 11, no. 1&2 (2009): 93.

63   Recognized nationalities included German, Magyar, Czech, Slovak, Pole, Ruthenian, Romanian, Slovene, Serbo-Croat, and Italian. In addition to Judaism, other recognized religions included Roman Catholicism, Greek Catholicism, Armenian Catholicism, Greek Orthodoxy, Armenian Orthodoxy, Evangelism, Anglicanism, Apostolic Christianity, Baptism, Methodism, and Islam. See Magistrats-Abteilung XXI für Statistik, *Statistisches Jahrbuch der Stadt Wien für das Jahr 1901*, 430.

64   Rozenblit, *Reconstructing a National Identity*, 19.

65   Ibid., 24.

66   Joseph Samuel Bloch, "Nichts gelernt und nichts vergessen," *Dr. Bloch's Oesterreichische Wochenschrift: Centralorgan für die gesammten Interessen des Judenthums* 34, no. 24 (June 22, 1917): 390.

67   Franz Theodor Csokor, *3. November 1918: Drei Akte* (Vienna: Wiener Bibliophilien-Gesellschaft, 1968[1936]), 51. For an excellent analysis of the play's address of Jewish patriotism, see Lisa Silverman, "'Nicht jüdeln': Jews and Habsburg Loyalty in Franz Theodor Csokor's *Dritter November 1918*," *Religions* 8, no. 60 (2017): 1–11, doi.10.3390/rel8040060.

68   Rozenblit, *Reconstructing a National Identity*, 4.

69   Silverman, *Becoming Austrians*, 16.

70 Smaller communities did indeed exist in other Austrian towns and villages, memorialized in the manner of *Yizkor* books after the Second World War in Hugo Gold, *Geschichte der Juden in Österreich: Ein Gedenkbuch* (Tel Aviv: Olamenu, 1971). See also Verena Wagner, *Jüdisches Leben in Linz, 1849–1943*, 2 vols (Linz: Wagner Verlag, 2008).

71 Robert Musil quoted in Bruckmüller, *The Austrian Nation*, 120.

72 Janek Wasserman, *Black Vienna: The Radical Right in the Red City, 1918–1938* (Ithaca, NY: Cornell University Press, 2014), 18.

73 Freidenreich, *Jewish Politics in Vienna*, 212.

74 Rozenblit, *The Jews of Vienna*, 132–6.

75 In 1900 more than a quarter of all Jewish apostates (including those declaring *Konfessionslosigkeit*) converted to Protestant denominations. See Stefan Sedlaczek, Wilhelm Löwy, and Wilhelm Becke, eds., *Statistisches Jahrbuch der Stadt Wien für das Jahr 1900* (Vienna: Verlag des Wiener Magistrates, 1902), 376.

76 Rozenblit, *The Jews of Vienna*, 134.

77 Ibid., 128–9; Endelman, "Gender and Conversion Revisited," 177–8.

78 See Hannah Arendt, *The Origins of Totalitarianism* (New York: Harcourt Brace Jovanovich, 1973), 56–68.

79 See, for example, Bonyhady, *Good Living Street*.

80 For marriage patterns among Vienna's wealthiest Jewish families, see Georg Gaugusch, *Wer Einmal War: Das jüdische Großbürgertum Wiens, 1800–1938*, 2 vols. (Vienna: Amalthea Signum Verlag, 2011–16).

81 George L. Mosse, "Jewish Emancipation: Between *Bildung* and Respectability," in *The Jewish Response to German Culture: From the Enlightenment to the Second World War*, ed. Jehuda Reinharz and Walter Schatzberg (Hanover, NH: University Press of New England, 1985), 1–16.

82 See, for example, Beller, *Vienna and the Jews*; Shapira, *Style and Seduction*.

83 Designed by the French architect Gabriel-Hippolyte Destailleur and built between 1876 and 1884, the French Renaissance-style palace later acquired a sinister connotation after it was seized by the Gestapo in 1938 and used as its headquarters, as well as Adolf Eichmann's Central Agency for Jewish Emigration in Vienna. Roman Sandgruber, *Traumzeit für Millionäre: Die 929 reichsten Wienerinnen und Wiener im Jahr 1910* (Vienna: Sytria Premium, 2013), 239.

84 Bonyhady, *Good Living Street*, 130–8.

85 Roman Sandgruber notes that some of the élite families, such as the Rothschilds and the Ephrussis, rejected modern art and decorated their homes only with old masters and antique furniture. See Sandgruber, *Traumzeit für Millionäre*, 30, 33.

86 See Shapira, *Style and Seduction*, 115–66.

87 Masaidek, *Wien und die Wiener*, 30.

88 Well-known writers were representative of this segment of the Jewish population. Stefan Zweig, for example, kept an apartment in the eighth district (Kochgasse 8) prior to relocating to Salzburg after the First World War, Karl Kraus in the fourth (Lothringerstrasse 6), while Richard Beer-Hofmann commissioned the architect Josef Hoffmann to design his villa in the eighteenth (Hasenauerstrasse 59).

89 *Buchgasse* translates as "book lane."

90 Oliver Matuschek, *Three Lives: A Biography of Stefan Zweig*, trans. Allan Blunden (London: Pushkin Press, 2011), 37.

91 Ibid., 30.

92 Postcard from Rosalie Landstone to Hedy (Hetty) Landstone, National Library of Israel, ARC*1905/3.

93 Friedrich Torberg, *Die Tante Jolesch: oder, Der Untergang des Abendlandes in Anekdoten* (Munich: Deutscher Taschenbuch Verlag, 2013).

94 Harry Rich in discussion with author, April 19, 2016.

95 Lisl Ziegler in discussion with author, August 19, 2015.

96 Susan Warhaftig (née Tillemann) in discussion with author, July 3, 2022.

97 Freidenreich, *Jewish Politics in Vienna*, 119.

98 Rozenblit, "The Struggle Over Religious Reform in Nineteenth-Century Vienna." Rozenblit describes the communal politics with regards to the desire for some within the Viennese community to reform their style of worship along the lines of German Reform Judaism and those who preferred a traditional style of worship.

99 Walter K. Weitzman, "The Politics of the Viennese Jewish Community 1890–1914," in *Jews, Antisemitism and Culture in Vienna*, ed. Ivar Oxaal, Michael Pollak, and Gerhard Botz (London and New York: Routledge and Kegan Paul, 1987), 123.

100 See David Sorkin, *The Transformation of German Jewry, 1780–1840* (Detroit, MI: Wayne State University Press, 1999).

101 See, for example, John W. Boyer, *Political Radicalism in Late Imperial Vienna: Origins of the Christian Social Movements, 1848–1897* (Chicago, IL: The University of Chicago Press, 1981); Wasserman, *Black Vienna*; Robert S. Wistrich, "Social Democracy and Judeophobia in Imperial Vienna," in *From Ambivalence to Betrayal: The Left, the Jews, and Israel* (Lincoln, NE: The University of Nebraska Press, 2012), 250–71.

Chapter 2

1 Bauman, *Modernity and Ambivalence*, 71.

2 Beller, *Vienna and the Jews*.

3 Gay, *Freud, Jews and Other Germans*, 19.

4 Ibid., 98.

5 Jacob Golomb, "Stefan Zweig's Tragedy as a Nietzschean *Grenzjude*," in *Jüdische Aspekte Jung-Wiens im Kulturkontext des »Fin de Siècle«*, ed. Sarah Fraiman-Morris (Tübingen: Max Niemayer Verlag, 2005), 79.

6 Sander L. Gilman, "Race and Madness in I. J. Singer's *The Family Carnovsky*," in *Difference and Pathology: Stereotypes of Sexuality, Race, and Madness* (Ithaca, NY: Cornell University Press, 1985), 163–74.

7 The philosopher and psychiatrist Frantz Fanon described a similar accusation leveled against acculturating Afro-Caribbeans and Africans who adopted French language and culture. Much of what Fanon describes regarding the acculturation aspirations of France's colonial subjects bears a resemblance to the experience of European Jews during the broad

period of emancipation and acculturation. See Frantz Fanon, *Black Skin, White Masks*, trans. Charles Lam Markmann (London: Pluto Press, 1986).

8   Franz Friedrich Masaidek, *Lose Gedanken* (Vienna: Ostdeustchen Rundschau, 1891), 8.

9   Efrat Tseëlon, *The Masque of Femininity: The Presentation of Women in Everyday Life* (London: Sage Publications, 1995), 34–7.

10   Karl Kraus, "The Eroticism of Clothes [1906]," in *The Rise of Fashion: A Reader*, ed. Daniel Leonard Purdy (Minneapolis, MN: University of Minnesota Press, 2004), 241.

11   *Kikeriki* 35, no. 99 (December 12, 1895): 1.

12   The motif of the *Judensau* commonly featured a group of Jewish men surrounding a large sow, sucking at its teats and licking its excrement. On antisemitic iconography within historical European Christianity, see Jan Dienstbier, "The Metamorphosis of the *Judensau*," in *Visual Antisemitism in Central Europe: Imagery of Hatred*, ed. Jakub Hauser and Eva Janáčová (Berlin: Walter de Gruyter, 2021), 1–34.

13   Hödl, *Als Bettler in die Leopoldstadt*, 242. See also Jeanette R. Malkin and Freddie Rokem, eds., *Jews and the Making of Modern German Theater* (Iowa City, IA: University of Iowa Press, 2010) on the central role Jews played in German and Austrian theater during the *fin-de-siècle* and interwar periods.

14   See Neil R. Davison, "'The Jew' as Homme/Femme-Fatale: Jewish (Art)ifice, *Trilby*, and Dreyfus," *Jewish Social Studies* 8, no. 2–3 (2002): 75–111.

15   See Andrew Barker, "Race, Sex and Character in Schnitzler's *Fräulein Else*," *German Life and Letters* 54, no. 1 (January 2001): 1–9.

16   Arthur Schnitzler, *Fräulein Else*, trans. G. H. Lyon (London: Pushkin Press, 2001), 14.

17   Tamás Farkas, "Jewish Name Magyarization in Hungary," *AHEA: E-Journal of the American Hungarian Educators Association* 5, no. 1 (2012): 1–16, https://ahea.net/e-journal/volume-5-2012; Kalman Weiser, "'Kopl Not Filaret, Sore Not Salomea': Debates About Jewish Naming Practices in Pre-WWII Poland," *East European Jewish Affairs* 50, no. 1–2 (2020): 134–56, doi: 10.1080/13501674.2020.1774274.

18   Schnitzler, Fräulein Else, 24.

19   Ibid., 21.

20   Ibid., 97–100.

21   Ibid., 100.

22   See Chapter 5.

23   JMW Archive, Inv. Nr. 11828.

24   JMW Archive, Inv. Nr. 11779.

25   Shapira, *Style and Seduction*.

26   Michael B. Miller, *The Bon Marché: Bourgeois Culture and the Department Store, 1869–1920* (Princeton, NJ: Princeton University Press, 1981), 29–30.

27   Paul Lerner, *Consuming Temple: Jews, Department Stores, and the Consumer Revolution in Germany, 1880–1914* (Ithaca, NY: Cornell University Press, 2015), 37.

28   Ibid., 92.

29   Miller, *The Bon Marché*, 25, 34–5.

30   Zakim, *Ready-Made Democracy*, 70.

31   Ibid.

32   Ibid.

33   Breward, *The Hidden Consumer*, 28.

34   Fritzi Ritterman, in discussion with the author, August 5, 2015.

35   See Lerner, *Consuming Temple*; Kremer, *Broken*; Astrid Peterle, ed., *Kauft bei Juden! Geschichte einer Wiener Geschäftskultur—Buy from Jews! Story of a Viennese Store Culture* (Vienna: Amalthea and Jüdisches Museum Wien, 2017).

36   Gerda Buxbaum, *Mode aus Wien, 1815–1938* (Salzburg and Vienna: Residenz Verlag, 1986), 25; Peter McNeil, "The Beauty of the Everyday," in *Dressing Sydney: The Jewish Fashion Story*, ed. Sydney Jewish Museum (Darlinghurst, NSW: Sydney Jewish Museum, 2012), 139.

37   Ibid., 146.

38   Lore Krempel, *Die deutsche Modezeitschrift: Ihre Geschichte und Entwicklung nebst einer Bibliographie der deutschen, englischen und französischen Modezeitschriften* (Coburg: Tageblatt-Haus, 1935), 101–2. See also Sandgruber, *Traumzeit für Millionäre*, 72–3, 309; Frauke Severit, *Ea von Allesch: Wenn aus Frauen Menschen werden: Eine Biographie* (Wiesbaden: Deutscher Universitäts-Verlag, 1999), 133–4.

39   The Austro-Silesian August Herzmansky was not Jewish himself, but the Jewish Delfiner family purchased the company in 1933. See Astrid Peterle, "Wien im Kaufrausch! Die Blüte der Wiener Kaufhäuser und k.u.k. Hoflieferanten—Vienna Goes Shopping! The Heyday of the Viennese Retail Stores and Court-Appointed Suppliers," in *Kauft bei Juden! Geschichte einer Wiener Geschäftskultur—Buy from Jews! Story of a Viennese Store Culture*, ed. Astrid Peterle (Vienna: Amalthea and Jüdisches Museum Wien, 2017), 80–1.

40   Uri M. Kupferschmidt, *European Department Stores and Middle Eastern Consumers: The Orosdi-Back Saga* (Istanbul: Ottoman Bank Archive and Research Centre, 2007), 16.

41   Georg Glockemeier, *Zur Wiener Judenfrage* (Leipzig: Johannes Günther Verlag, 1936), 108.

42   Ibid., 71–82. For the same period, Michael John and Albert Lichtblau offer alternate figures: 67.6 percent of furriers, 39.8 percent of jewelers, 73.3 percent of those involved in the textile trade, and 53 percent of shoe merchants. See John and Lichtblau, *Schmelztiegel Wien*, 34.

43   Stefan Zweig, *The World of Yesterday*, trans. Anthea Bell (London: Pushkin Press, 2011[1942]), 32–3.

44   Sandgruber, *Traumzeit für Millionäre*, 120–1.

45   Elana Shapira, "Modernism and Jewish Identity in Early Twentieth-Century Vienna: Fritz Waerndorfer and His House for an Art Lover," *Studies in the Decorative Arts* 13, no. 2 (Spring-Summer 2006): 85–6.

46   Shapira, *Style and Seduction*.

47   Moriz Gallia and his family's involvement in the Wiener Werkstätte and the Vienna Secession is recounted in a memoir by his great-grandson. See Bonyhady, *Good Living Street*.

48   Angela Völker, *Textiles of the Wiener Werkstätte, 1910–1932* (London: Thames and Hudson, 1994), 8; Werner J. Schweiger, *Wiener Werkstätte: Design in Vienna, 1903–1932* (London: Thames and Hudson, 1984), 97, 114–16; Mirjam Zadoff, *Next Year in Marienbad: The Lost Worlds of Jewish Spa Culture*, trans. William Templer (Philadelphia, PA: University of Pennsylvania Press, 2012), 231.

49 See Julie M. Johnson, *The Memory Factory: The Forgotten Women Artists of Vienna, 1900* (West Lafayette, IN: Purdue University Press, 2012).

50 Kremer, *Broken Threads*.

51 Georg Gaugusch, "Wilhelm Jungmann & Neffe: 150 Jahre einer Wiener Firma—Wilhelm Jungmann & Neffe: 150 Years of a Viennese Company," in *Kauft bei Juden! Geschichte einer Wiener Geschäftskultur—Buy from Jews! Story of a Viennese Store Culture*, ed. Astrid Peterle (Vienna: Amalthea and Jüdisches Museum Wien, 2017), 95–6.

52 Ibid., 99.

53 Catharina Christ, "Jüdische k. und k. Hoflieferanten in der Textilbranche mit Niederlassung in Wien in der Zeit von 1870 bis 1938" (MA diss., University of Vienna, 2006), 65–6.

54 Gaugusch, "Wilhelm Jungmann & Neffe," 96, 104–5.

55 Wilhelm Jungmann & Neffe customer register, private collection of Georg Gaugusch, Vienna.

56 Christ, "Jüdische k. und k. Hoflieferanten."

57 Peterle, ed., *Kauft bei Juden!*

58 Paul Lerner, "Circulation and Representation: Jews, Department Stores and Cosmopolitan Consumption in Germany, c. 1880s–1930s," *European Review of History* 17, no. 3 (June 2010): 395–414.

59 Dora Heinz, "Viennese Men's Fashions," in *The Imperial Style: Fashions of the Habsburg Era: Based on the Exhibition Fashions of the Habsburg Era: Austria-Hungary at the Metropolitan Museum of Art, December 1979–August 1980*, ed. Polly Cone (New York: The Metropolitan Museum of Art, 1980), 102.

60 Reingard Witzmann, "The Beautiful Viennese: Fashions from the Times of Maria Theresa to the End of the Congress of Vienna," in *The Imperial Style: Fashions of the Habsburg Era: Based on the Exhibition Fashions of the Habsburg Era: Austria-Hungary at the Metropolitan Museum of Art, December 1979–August 1980*, ed. Polly Cone (New York: The Metropolitan Museum of Art, 1980), 37.

61 Helga Kessler, "Viennese Biedermeier Fashion," in *The Imperial Style: Fashions of the Habsburg Era: Based on the Exhibition Fashions of the Habsburg Era: Austria-Hungary at the Metropolitan Museum of Art, December 1979–August 1980*, ed. Polly Cone (New York: The Metropolitan Museum of Art, 1980), 43.

62 Monica Kunzel-Runtscheiner, "The Magic of the Uniform: Dress Codes, Fashion Dictates and the Spread of Civilian Uniforms through the Congress of Vienna," in *Fashion Drive: Extreme Clothing in the Visual Arts*, ed. Catherine Hug and Christoph Becker (Bielefeld: Kunsthaus Zürich and Kerber Culture, 2018), 155.

63 Comte A. de La Garde-Chambonas, *Anecdotal Recollections of the Congress of Vienna*, trans. Albert D. Vandam (London: Chapman & Hall, 1902).

64 Kessler, "Viennese Biedermeier Fashion," 43.

65 French, and to a lesser extent English, language and culture played similar roles in the modernization and secularization of Jews across Europe, North Africa, and the Near East, particularly in their utilization by the schools of the Alliance Israélite Universelle, a French-Jewish organization founded in Paris in 1860. See, for example, Julia Phillips Cohen and Sarah Abrevaya Stein, eds., *Sephardi Lives: A Documentary History, 1700–1950* (Stanford, CA: Stanford University Press, 2014); Peter Drucker, "'Disengaging from the Muslim Spirit': The Alliance Israélite Universelle and Moroccan Jews,"

Journal of Middle East Women's Studies 11, no. 1 (2015): 3–23, doi:0.1215/15525864-2832322; Jonathan Sciarcon, "Expanding the Mission: The Alliance Israélite Universelle, the Anglo-Jewish Association and the Jewish Boys' School in Basra, 1890–1903," *International Journal of Contemporary Iraqi Studies* 9, no. 3 (2015): 191–207, doi:10.1386/ijcis.9.3.191_1.

66   Buxbaum, *Mode aus Wien*, 89.

67   Matuschek, *Three Lives*, 32.

68   Altenberg cited in Heinz Lunzer, "Kindheit, Jugend in einer wohlhabenden Kaufmannsfamilie," in *Peter Altenberg, Extracte des Lebens: einem Schriftsteller auf der Spur*, ed. Heinz Lunzer and Victoria Lunzer-Talos (Salzburg: Residenz Verlag, 2003), 18.

69   Buxbaum, *Mode aus Wien*, 201.

70   Ibid., 89.

71   Ibid., 203.

72   Sandgruber, *Traumzeit für Millionäre*, 59.

73   Beyond Vienna, periodicals focusing on women's fashionable dress often contained references to Paris in the titles, such as *Oglasnik Parižke Mode* (Zagreb), *Nové pařížské mody* (Prague), *Dziennik Mód Paryskich* (Lwów), *Mody Paryzkie* (Warsaw).

74   See Rebecca Gates-Coon, "Anglophile Households and British Travellers in Late Eighteenth-Century Vienna: 'A Very Numerous and Pleasant English Colony'," *Britain and the World* 12, no. 2 (2019): 130–50, doi:10.3366/brw.2019.0323. Although not the central focus of her scholarship, Elana Shapira often refers to the Viennese bourgeois affinity for English culture in her study of modern design and Jewish patronage in the Austrian capital. See, for example, Elana Shapira, "Adolf Loos and the Fashioning of 'the Other': Memory, Fashion, and Interiors," *Interiors* 2, no. 2 (2011): 213–37.

75   Kuchta, *The Three-Piece Suit and Modern Masculinity*, 112.

76   On German bourgeois Anglophilia, see Andrew Francis Bell, "Anglophilia: The Hamburg Bourgeoisie and the Importation of English Middle Class Culture in the Wilhelmine Era" (PhD diss., Brown University, 2001). The Viennese *Deutsch-Englischer-Reise-Curier/English-German-Tourists-Courier* (1904–1914), a bilingual tourists' periodical that contained articles, reviews of hotels throughout Europe, and advertisements for clothing boutiques, restaurants and other businesses is also informative.

77   Adolf Loos, *Spoken into the Void: Collected Essays, 1897–1900*, trans. Jane O. Newman and John H. Smith (Cambridge, MA: The MIT Press, 1982). See also Janet Stewart, *Fashioning Vienna: Adolf Loos's Cultural Criticism* (London: Routledge, 2000).

78   In a sense, Loos was drawing on an earlier tradition of using "foreign" material culture for the purposes of improving the local.

79   See, for example, Otto Weininger, *Sex and Character: An Investigation of Fundamental Principles*, trans. Ladislaus Löb, Daniel Steuer, and Laura Marcus, eds. (Bloomington, IN: Indiana University Press, 2005[1903]).

80   Such as the Viennese *Die Wiener Elegante* (1842–72), *Wiener Moden-Zeitung* (1862–63), and *Internationale Moden-Zeitung: Central Organ europäischer Herren-Moden mit Wiener und Pariser Original-Moden-Bildern* (1871–1934).

81   Such as *Die Herrenwelt* (1916–17), *Der Herr und seine Welt* (1927–40), *Der Herr von heute* (1928–34), *Der gut angezogene Herr* (1936–38).

82   Zakim, *Ready-Made Democracy*, 77.

83   Anja Meyerrose, *Herren im Anzug: Eine transatlantische Geschichte von Klassengesellschaften im langen 19. Jahrhundert* (Cologne: Böhlau Verlag, 2016).

84   As in Vienna, men in other cities of the Dual Monarchy, such as Budapest, Zagreb, and Prague, adhered to the model of English sartorial respectability. In Zagreb, M. Arnstein's Englezki Magazin (English Shop), located at Ilica 41, advertised the city's largest repository of English clothing and articles for men and boys. It is interesting to note that although referring to male customers and male articles of clothing, the advertisement included illustrations of women's attire. See, for example, an advertisement for Englezki Magazin in *Agramer Zeitung*, April 4, 1895, 8.

85   "Umwälzung der Herrenmode," *Wiener Presse*, June 20, 1887, 3; "Herrenmode," *Wiener Presse*, February 25, 1889, 3; "Neue Herrenmode," *Welt Blatt*, March 17, 1901, 14.

86   See, for example, "Rothe Ballkravaten," *Innsbrucker Nachrichten*, February 16, 1885, 6; "Englische Moden," *Bukowiner Rundschau*, May 24, 1892, 3; "Gehrock und Hose," *Mährisches Tagblatt*, March 8, 1905, 5; L. "Herrenmode," *Agramer Zeitung*, March 28, 1911, 2–3; "Das Abendkleid des Jägers," *Die Herrenwelt* 1, no. 4 (1916): 12; "Der grüne Hut," *Die Herrenwelt* 1, no. 4 (1916): 9–11. Similar articles also appeared in publications including *Pilsner Tagblatt*, *Czernowitzer Allgemeine Zeitung*, and *Neues Wiener Journal*.

87   "Die Weste des Prinzen von Wales: Die neuesten Schöpfungen," *Neues Wiener Tagblatt*, June 19, 1898, 3.

88   Alternatively, the slower pace of men's fashion—as remarked by the author of the article in question—may have contributed to attitudes that periodicals catering specifically to men's dress were unnecessary, in contrast to those dedicated to ever-changing women's fashion.

89   Ibid.

90   Ibid.

91   Eberle also advertised music-related prints, including sheet music for synagogues, in the Jewish weekly, *Die Wahrheit* (1885–1938).

92   *Fashions for Gentlemen* 4 (April 1912).

93   In addition to German and English, the journal was also printed with French and Hungarian text.

94   "Vornehme Herren. Zur Erziehung der Erwachsenen," *Die Herrenwelt* 1, no. 1 (January 1916): 3–4.

95   Ibid.

96   Ibid.

97   Mary Gluck describes the similar role of etiquette magazines aimed at the aspiring middle class in Budapest during the latter decades of the nineteenth century. See Mary Gluck, *Invisible Jewish Budapest: Metropolitan Culture at the Fin de Siècle* (Madison, WI: The University of Wisconsin Press, 2016), 181–5.

98   Gesa C. Teichert, *Mode. Macht. Männer: Kulturwissenschaftliche Überlegungen zur bügerlichen Herrenmode des 19. Jahrhunderts* (Berlin: Lit Verlag, 2013), 112.

99   "Vornehme Herren," 4.

100   See "Briefkasten," *Die Herrenwelt* 2, no. 1 (February 1917): 23.

101   See, for example, Martin Freud, *Glory Reflected: Sigmund Freud—Man and Father* (London: Angus and Robertson, 1957), 125.

102 Ulrich R. Furst, "Windows to My Youth," unpublished memoir, LBI (1993), ME 902. MM II 14, 47–50. Furst's uncle was the renowned Prague-born Jewish writer Leo Perutz (1882–1957).

103 Although it often included content on men's fashion, *Die Bühne* was dedicated to theater and other aspects of Viennese popular culture, and not men's fashion as such. Many magazines published in Vienna were also consumed in Germany and Switzerland, and often contained advertisements for men's outfitters and other apparel companies in those countries in addition to those in Austria.

104 "Neue Stoffe, neue Farben, neue Muster für Sie—meine Herren!" *Der gut angezogene Herr* (Autumn/Winter 1936): 11.

105 Hilde Helmers, "Also sprach Adolphe Menjou: Der bekannte Bonvivant des Films und anerkannte Arbeiter Elegantiarum verteidigt die Ansicht, daß gutangezogene Männer im Leben Erfolg haben," *Der Herr von heute: ein Monatsblatt für die Herrenwelt* (April 1931): 8.

106 Jindřich Toman, "Conversational Modernism: Talking Czech Men into Being Gentlemen by Way of *The Gentleman*, 1924–30," *Central Europe* 13, no. 1–2 (2015): 19–35, doi:10.1080 /14790963.2025.1107321.

107 Although the author does not indicate how *Tracht* appears in this instance, the terms "*Tracht*" and "*Volkstracht*" refer to the traditional folk costumes worn by rural populations for special ceremonies and events, and the readers would be familiar with the styles the editor was referring to. *Trachten* and their popularized form of *Trachtenmoden* will be explored in more detail in Chapter 4.

108 "Die Hochzeitskleidung des Herrn," *Der gut angezogene Herr* (autumn–winter 1936): 9.

109 Furst, "Windows to My Youth," 40–1.

110 "Wählen Sie meine Herren!" *Der gut angezogene Herr* (autumn–winter 1936/1937): 6.

111 Edgar Liss, "Der schlecht angezogene Herr," *Der Herr von heute* (March 1931): 10.

112 See Stewart, *Fashioning Vienna*.

113 See Adolf Loos, *Spoken into the Void*.

114 Named for (in order of each name) his father, all four grandparents (both grandfathers were named Franz, while his grandmothers were both named Franziska), two uncles, and his mother.

115 For a comprehensive study of Loos's life and work, see Burkhardt Rukschcio and Roland Schachel, *Adolf Loos: Leben und Werk* (Salzburg: Residenz Verlag, 1982).

116 Frederic Bedoire, *The Jewish Contribution to Modern Architecture, 1830–1930*, trans. Roger Tanner (Jersey City, NJ: KTAV Publishing House, 2004), 338.

117 Stewart, *Fashioning Vienna*, 67.

118 Shapira, "Adolf Loos and the Fashioning of 'the Other.'"

119 Ibid.

120 See Chapter 6.

121 Elana Shapira, "Jewish Identity, Mass Consumption, and Modern Design," in *Longing, Belonging, and the Making of Jewish Consumer Culture*, ed. Gideon Reuveni and Nils Roemer (Leiden: Brill 2010), 63.

122 Adolf Loos, "Die Emanzipation des Judenthums," quoted in Bedoire, *The Jewish Contribution to Modern Architecture*, 334–5. There is also a sense of orientalism in

comparing supposedly "traditional" Jewish garb—the clothing of east European Jews with its allegedly Turkish origins—with the styles of the Secession that drew heavily on "oriental" vernaculars.

123 See Shapira, "Adolf Loos and the Fashioning of 'the Other,'" 216–17.

124 See Shapira, "Jewish Identity, Mass Consumption, and Modern Design."

125 George Clare remembered that growing up in the 1920s, his grandmother's flat remained as a museum piece from the 1880s: "Not a chair, not one of the heavy plush burgundy curtains, not one antimacassar had been replaced. Everything remained exactly as it had been on the day when Dr Ludwig Klaar and his young wife Julie moved into the house at Josefstädterstrasse so many years before." George Clare, *Last Waltz in Vienna* (London: Pan Books, 2007), 38.

126 Elana Shapira, "Tailored Authorship: Adolf Loos and the Ethos of Men's Fashion," in *Leben mit Loos*, ed. Inge Podbrecky and Rainald Franz (Vienna: Böhlau Verlag, 2008), 54.

127 Loos would also design Kniže stores in Berlin (1924) and Paris (1927). See Rukschcio and Roland Schachel, *Adolf Loos*, 49.

128 See Archiv der IKG Wien, *Geburtsbuch der Israelitischen Kultusgemeinde Wien, L, 1887–1888*, entry no. 1265, https://www.familysearch.org/ark:/61903/3:1:33S7-8B24-722?i =92&cc=2028320&personaUrl=%2Fark%3A%2F61903%2F1%3A1%3A81KG-L1T2.

129 Deutsch-Dryden is better remembered for and credited with creating the so-called "new woman" in German advertising while serving as the creative director of the Berlin fashion magazine *Die Dame*. In fact, in Vienna, Deutsch-Dryden also designed for Wolff's wife Helene (née Krása), whose women's boutique Hello was also located on the Graben. See Mila Geneva, *Women in Weimar Fashion: Discourses and Displays in German Culture, 1918–1933* (Rochester, NY: Camden House, 2008), 66; Anthony Lipmann, *Divinely Elegant: The World of Ernst Dryden* (London: Pavilion Books, 1989).

130 Ibid., 62.

131 Ibid., 66.

132 Stewart, *Fashioning Vienna*, 110. In this case, the kaftan (also spelled "caftan") refers to a variety of long robes or coats worn by Hasidic men in Eastern Europe. These garments were known in Yiddish by specific names such as "bekeshe" or "kapote."

133 Loos [1898] quoted in Ibid., 54.

134 Klaus Hödl, "Viennese Newspapers and Jewish Reading Habits around 1900," *Jewish Culture and History* 17, no. 3 (2016): 194, http://dx.doi.org/10.1080/1462169X.2016 /1221034.

135 Adolf Loos, "Men's Fashion," in *Spoken into the Void: Collected Essays, 1897–1900*, trans. Jane O. Newman and John H. Smith (Cambridge, MA: The MIT Press, 1982), 11. The piece first appeared in the *Neue Freie Presse*, May 22, 1898, under the title "Die Herrenmode."

136 See Jules Lubbock, "Adolf Loos and the English Dandy," *Architectural Review* 174, no. 1038 (1983): 43–5; Charles Baudelaire, *The Painter of Modern Life and Other Essays*, trans. Jonathan Mayne (London: Phaidon Press, 1995); Rhonda K. Garelick, *Rising Star: Dandyism, Gender, and Performance in the Fin de Siècle* (Princeton, NJ: Princeton University Press).

137 See Ibid.

138 Brummell famously remarked that the greatest triumph was when someone described him as well dressed but could not pinpoint why. See Teichert, *Mode. Macht. Männer*, 154.

139 Panayotis Tournikiotis, *Adolf Loos* (New York: Princeton Architectural Press, 1994), 56.

140 See Adolf Loos, "The Principle of Cladding," in *Spoken into the Void: Collected Essays, 1897–1900*, trans. Jane O. Newman and John H. Smith (Cambridge, MA: The MIT Press, 1982), 66–9.

141 See, for example, Lubbock, "Adolf Loos and the English Dandy," 46.

142 Stewart, *Fashioning Vienna*, 189.

143 Loos, "Men's Fashion," 12.

144 Adolf Loos, "Praise for the Present," in *Adolf Loos: Why a Man Should be Well-Dressed*, trans. Michael Edward Troy (Vienna: Metroverlag, 2001), 16.

145 Stewart, *Fashioning Vienna*, 49.

146 Ibid., 59.

147 Loos, "Men's Fashion," 11.

148 Zakim, *Ready-Made Democracy*, 96.

149 Stewart, *Fashioning Vienna*, 66.

150 Shapira, "Adolf Loos and the Fashioning of the 'Other'," 226.

151 Ibid.

Chapter 3

1 Stephen Greenblatt, *Renaissance Self-Fashioning: From More to Shakespeare* (Chicago, IL: The University of Chicago Press, 1980), 2.

2 John Styles, "Fashion and Innovation in Early Modern Europe," in *Fashioning the Early Modern: Dress, Textiles, and Innovation in Europe, 1500–1800*, ed. Evelyn Welch (Oxford: Oxford University Press, 2017), 34.

3 Beller, *Vienna and the Jews*, 152.

4 Ibid., 153.

5 See McCagg Jr., *A History of Habsburg Jews*.

6 See Barbara Staudinger, "Unerwünschte Fremde. Galizische Juden in Wien: Zwischen Integration, Wohlfahr und Antisemitismus," in *"Ostjuden": Geschichte und Mythos*, ed. Philipp Metauer and Barbara Staudinger (Innsbruck: Studien Verlag, 2015), 29–48.

7 Kladiwa, "The Czech Community and Czech as a 'Language of Daily Use' in Vienna, 1880–1910," 27.

8 See Israel Bartal, *The Jews of Eastern Europe, 1772–1881*, trans. Chaya Naor (Philadelphia, PA: The University of Pennsylvania Press, 2005); Gershon David Hundert, *Jews in Poland-Lithuania in the Eighteenth Century: A Genealogy of Modernity* (Berkeley, CA: University of California Press, 2004), 95–8.

9 Vanita Reddy, *Fashioning Diaspora: Beauty, Femininity, and South Asian American Culture* (Philadelphia, PA: Temple University Press, 2016), 5.

10 Marion A. Kaplan, "Gender and Jewish History in Imperial Germany," in *Assimilation and Community: The Jews in Nineteenth-Century Europe*, ed. Jonathan Frankel and Steven J. Zipperstein (Cambridge: Cambridge University Press, 1992), 199–224.

11 Marsha L. Rozenblit, "Jewish Assimilation in Habsburg Vienna," in *Assimilation and Community: The Jews in Nineteenth-Century Europe*, ed. Jonathan Frankel and Steven J. Zipperstein (Cambridge: Cambridge University Press, 1992), 225–45.

12 Archiv der IKG Wien, *Geburtsbuch der Israelitischen Kultusgemeinde Wien, 1904 Jan–June*, entry no. 178. *FamilySearch*, https://www.familysearch.org/ark:/61903/3:1:333S7-LB29 -5BS?i=30&wc=MQB682S%3A344266801%2C344266802%2C344501801&cc=2028320, accessed June 6, 2018.

13 This information was provided partly by Stern's daughter, Eva Engel, in conversation with author, November 14, 2017.

14 Index of the Jewish Records of Vienna and Lower Austria, entry no. 280456. *GenTeam: Die genealogische Datenbank*, https://genteam.at/index.php?option=com_db53&id=280456 &limitstart=10&n=czopp&v=&view=detail&lang=en, accessed July 31, 2021.

15 See Benyamin Lukin, "Berdychiv," *YIVO Encyclopedia of Jews in Eastern Europe*, accessed July 24, 2021, https://yivoencyclopedia.org/article.aspx/Berdychiv.

16 Edmund De Waal, *The Hare with Amber Eyes: A Hidden Inheritance* (London: Vintage, 2011), 180. See also James McAuley, *The House of Fragile Things: Jewish Art Collectors and the Fall of France* (New Haven, CT: Yale University Press, 2021), which explores the experiences of members of the Paris branch within the larger network of French-Jewish art collectors.

17 Berta Zuckerkandl-Szeps's sister Sophie (1862–1937) was the wife of Paul Clemenceau, who was the brother of the later French president Georges Clemenceau (1841–1929). As the daughter of a successful newspaper magnate, Moriz Szeps (1835–1902), and a highly regarded critic in her own right, Zuckerkandl-Szeps was hostess to a popular literary salon that brought together many members of Vienna's artistic and scholastic milieu as well as visiting cultural luminaries. See Berta Zuckerkandl, *Österreich* intim: *Erinnerungen, 1882–1942*, ed. Reinhard Federmann (Vienna: Amalthea, 2013). See Chapter 6 of this book, which includes a discussion of Zweig's family background in relation to his clothing.

18 Sandgruber, *Traumzeit für Millionäre*, 15.

19 Ibid., 32–3. Sandgruber asserts that Ephrussi was not cut out for his profession in banking (Ibid., 33), therefore supporting Stefan Zweig's assertion that education and culture (*Bildung*) were of paramount importance to Vienna's Jewish bourgeoisie above their dedication to commerce and amassing wealth. See Zweig, *The World of Yesterday*, 32–4.

20 Raphael Mahler quoted in Jonathan Frankel, "Assimilation and the Jews in Nineteenth-Century Europe: Towards a New Historiography?" in *Assimilation and Community: The Jews in Nineteenth-Century Europe*, ed. Jonathan Frankel and Steven J. Zipperstein (Cambridge: Cambridge University Press, 1992), 8.

21 See Wistrich, *The Jews of Vienna in the Age of Franz Joseph*, in particular, "Three Viennese Preachers," 98–130 and "Liberalism, *Deutschtum*, and Assimilation," 131–63.

22 Miller, *Rabbis and Revolution*, 44.

23 The former hailing from Derslawitz (Drslavice), Moravia and the latter from Dukla, Galicia.

24 Rozenblit, *The Jews of Vienna*, 148.

25 Rozenblit, "The Struggle Over Religious Reform," 182.

26 Wistrich, *The Jews of Vienna in the Age of Franz Joseph*, 98.

27 Ibid., 99.

28   Ibid., 100. See also the debate on the use of Hebrew in German Reform congregations that took place at the Reform Rabbinical Conference at Frankfurt on July 16, 1845, reprinted as "Hebrew as the Language of Jewish Prayer," in *The Jew in the Modern World: A Documentary History*, ed. Paul R. Mendes-Flohr and Jehuda Reinharz (New York: Oxford University Press, 1980), 158–62; Michael A. Meyer, "Women in the Thought and Practice of the European Jewish Reform Movement," in *Gender and Jewish History*, ed. Marion A. Kaplan and Deborah Dash Moore (Bloomington, IN: Indiana University Press, 2011), 139–57.

29   Rozenblit, "The Struggle Over Religious Reform," 180–1.

30   The *metzitzah* custom involved the *mohel* (ritual circumcizor) drawing blood away from the wound by placing his mouth on the infant's circumcision and sucking blood away from the incision. Horowitz and Mannheimer abolished the practice for hygienic reasons, mandating the use of a sponge instead of oral suction. See Julie Lieber, "Infidelity and Intimacy in Nineteenth-Century Vienna: Gender and Orthodoxy as Reflected in the Response of Rabbi Eleazar Horowitz," *Nashim: A Journal of Jewish Women's Studies & Gender Issues* 21 (2011): 27. For a brief overview of Horowitz's life and tenure as rabbi in Vienna, see Grunwald, *Vienna*, 375–8.

31   See Howard Lupovitch, "Between Orthodox Judaism and Neology: The Origins of the Status Quo Movement," *Jewish Social Studies* 9, no. 2 (2003): 123–53; and Assaf Yedidya, "Orthodox Reactions to 'Wissenschaft des Judentums,'" *Modern Judaism: A Journal of Jewish Ideas & Experience* 30, no. 1 (February 2010): 69–94, doi:10.1093/mj/kjp021.

32   Meyer, "Women in the Thought and Practice of the European Jewish Reform Movement," 140–1.

33   Rozenblit demonstrates that the organ remained a pressing issue for Viennese congregations throughout the nineteenth century, with Mannheimer abandoning his desire to introduce an organ into the synagogue, which "would only provide a Christian intrusion into Judaism." Rozenblit, "The Struggle Over Religious Reform," 190. Nevertheless, some Viennese synagogues would introduce the organ to the synagogue service over the course of the nineteenth and early twentieth centuries. See Robert Kanfer, "The Family Memories of Robert Kanfer: Vienna—London—Cheltenham—Vienna," unpublished memoir, LBI (2005), ME 1518. MM III 20, 8; Hans Stein, "Vienna Childhood Memories," unpublished memoir, LBI (1998), ME 1180. MM II 36, 24.

34   Rozenblit, ""The Struggle Over Religious Reform," 190–5.

35   Ibid., 182.

36   Miller, *Rabbis and Revolution*, 51–2, 140–3.

37   Rozenblit, ""The Struggle Over Religious Reform," 186.

38   See Wistrich, Chapter 4, "Three Viennese Preachers," in *The Jews of Vienna in the Age of Franz Joseph*, 98–129.

39   See, for example, Leonard J. Greenspoon, ed., *Fashioning Jews: Clothing, Culture, and Commerce* (West Lafayette, IN: Purdue University Press, 2013); Silverman, *A Cultural History of Jewish Dress*.

40   Tamar Somogyi, *Die Schejnen und die Prosten: Untersuchungen zum Schönheitsideal der Ostjuden in Bezug auf Körper und Kleidung unter besonderer Berücksichtigung des Chassidismus* (Berlin: Dietrich Reimer Verlag, 1983), 123–6. See also Adam Jasienski, "A Savage Magnificence: Ottomanizing Fashion and the Politics of Display in Early Modern East-Central Europe," *Muqarnas* 31, no. 1 (2014): 173–205.

41   Miller, *Rabbis and Revolution*, 63.

42   Asher Salah, "How Should a Rabbi Be Dressed? The Question of Rabbinical Attire in Italy from Renaissance to Emancipation (Sixteenth–Nineteenth Centuries)," in *Fashioning Jews: Clothing, Culture, and Commerce*, ed. Leonard J. Greenspoon (West Lafayette, IN: Purdue University Press, 2013), 55.

43   Ibid., 60–1.

44   Born in Hamburg to Rabbi Raphael and Gela (née Herz) Hirsch, Samson Raphael Hirsch was given a traditional Jewish as well as a secular, German education and would go on to become a leading figure in German Orthodoxy. Hirsch has been attributed as being the progenitor of the Modern Orthodox Movement. See, for example, Sorkin, "Religious Tradition," in *The Transformation of German Jewry*, 156–71.

45   It is significant that those rabbis living in a predominantly Catholic society, as in France, adopted clerical garb resembling that of their Christian (Catholic) counterparts, in contrast to their rabbinical colleagues residing in societies where Protestantism dominated.

46   Salah, "How Should a Rabbi Be Dressed?" 55.

47   Rozenblit, "The Struggle over Religious Reform."

48   See John Harvey, *Men in Black* (London: Reaktion Books, 1995), in particular Chapter 2, "Black in History," 41–69, and Chapter 3, "From Black in Spain to Black in Shakespeare," 71–113.

49   Franz Tesar, *Wiener Herrenkleidung* (Vienna: Selbstverlag der Genossenschaft der Kleidermacher Wiens, 1911).

50   The Philippi Collection of ritual headwear identifies the tall hat (of varying shapes) often worn by rabbis and cantors as a *mitznefet* (also written as *mitsnephet* or *misnafat*), the name derived from the turban of the same name worn by Jewish High Priests in biblical times. See "Modelle, Ausführungen, Varianten und Farben," The Philippi collection, accessed January 10, 2018, http://www.dieter-philippi.de/en/the-philippi-collection/head-coverings-1. However, in the 2009 printed catalogue of the Philippi Collection, the name "*Miznäfät*" (the German spelling of the aforementioned terms) is indicated specifically for a white version of this octagonal hat worn by some rabbis on the Jewish High Holy Days *Rosh Hashanah* and *Yom Kippur*, and a black low cylindrical hat worn by some Sephardic rabbis, such as those worn by Sephardic chief rabbis in present-day State of Israel. Other similar forms of rabbinical headwear in the collection are labelled as "*Migbaot*" and "*Kantorenhut*" (cantor's hat). See Dieter Philippi, *Sammlung Philippi: Kopfbedeckung in Glaube, Religion und Spiritualität* (Leipzig: Benno, 2009), 345–47, 350–3.

51   Wistrich, *The Jews of Vienna in the Age of Franz Joseph*, 123. In his diaries, Theodor Herzl recalled a visit of Güdemann to his apartment where the latter was displeased to find Herzl illuminating the Christmas tree for his children. See Theodor Herzl, *Theodor Herzls Tagebücher*, vol. 1 (Berlin: Jüdischer Verlag, 1922), 328.

52   Jack Wertheimer, "'The Unwanted Element': East European Jews in Imperial Germany," *Leo Baeck Institute Yearbook* 26 (1981): 23.

53   See Hödl, *Als Bettler in die Leopoldstadt*. Ruth Beckermann's edited volume also provides an insight into the attitudes of Viennese Jews—of both "western" and "eastern" origins—toward *Galitsianer* immigrants in the Leopoldstadt during the First World War and interwar period. See Beckermann, *Die Mazzesinsel*.

54   Otto Grossman, "The Wandering Jew Nearing Journey's End," unpublished memoir, LBI (undated), MS 304. MSF 22, PID: 761945, 3.

55   Stein, "Vienna Childhood Memories," 5.

56   Wistrich, *The Jews of Vienna in the Age of Franz Joseph*, 53.

57   See, for example, Oxaal, Pollak, and Botz, eds, *Jews, Antisemitism and Culture in Vienna*.

58   Franz Kafka, "Ein Bericht für eine Akademie," *Der Jude* 2, no. 8 (1917): 559–65. Shulamit Volkov explains that the figure of the *Ostjude* in Germany was used by antisemites to attack *Westjuden*. See Shulamit Volkov, "The Dynamics of Dissimilation: *Ostjuden* and German Jews," in *The Jewish Response to German Culture: From the Enlightenment to the Second World War*, ed. Jehuda Reinharz and Walter Schatzberg (Hanover, NH: University Press of New England, 1985), 203.

59   Schaffir, "My Personal History," 26.

60   Volkov, "The Dynamics of Dissimilation," 205.

61   See Freidenreich, *Jewish Politics in Vienna*.

62   See, for example, the range of clothing-based advertisements in *Jüdisches Volksblatt*, March 3, 1899.

63   Beller, *Vienna and the Jews*, 43–70; Gary B. Cohen, "Jews Among Vienna's Educated Middle Class Elements at the Turn of the Century: A Comment on Steven Beller," in *A Social and Economic History of Central European Jewry*, ed. Yehuda Don and Victor Karady (New Brunswick, NJ: Transaction Publications, 1990), 179–89; Rozenblit, *The Jews of Vienna*, 99–125.

64   Wistrich, *The Jews of Vienna in the Age of Franz Joseph*, 58.

65   Joseph Tenenbaum, *Galitsiye mayn alte heym* (Buenos Aires: Tsentral-Farband fun Poylishe Yidn in Argentinye, 1952), 84–5.

66   Joshua Shanes, *Diaspora Nationalism and Jewish Identity in Habsburg Galicia* (Cambridge: Cambridge University Press, 2012), 25–30; Volkov, "The Dynamics of Dissimilation," 203–4.

67   Eva Bostock in discussion with the author, September 2, 2015. See also Leah Apfelbaum, "This is My Life: Eva Bostock," unpublished memoir (Hunters Hill, NSW: The Montefiore Life History Program, 2010).

68   Ibid., 4.

69   Ibid., 3.

70   Bostock, discussion.

71   Apfelbaum, "This is My Life," 5.

72   Evelyn Adunka and Gabriele Anderl, *Jüdisches Leben in der Wiener Vorstadt Ottakring und Hernals* (Vienna: Mandelbaum, 2012).

73   Clare, *Last Waltz in Vienna*, 83.

74   With their training in chemistry, Kürschner and Walter would found Valkiere, a company specializing in household polishes. Both would go on to marry women of a similar Galician background. In 1932 Kürschner married Elsa Kleiner, the Viennese-born daughter of Galician Jewish parents. This information was provided by Nuchim and Elsa Kürschner's daughter Ruth. Author's personal communication with Ruth Kurschner, August 12, 2015.

75   Klaus Hödl demonstrates that the act of dressing in historicist fancy-dress afforded Jews the ability to associate with the myth of "*Alt-Wien*," a period in which Jews were (largely) absent from the city. See Klaus Hödl, "The Quest for Amusement: Jewish Leisure Activities in Vienna, circa 1900," *Jewish Culture and History* 14, no. 1 (2013): 1–17, doi:10.1080/1462 169X.2012.708504.

76 De Waal, *The Hare with Amber Eyes*, 154–64. See also Thorstein Veblen, *The Theory of the Leisure Class: An Economic Study of Institutions* (New York: Modern Library, 2011[1899]).

77 The portraits in question depict Serena Pulitzer Lederer (1899), Marie Henneberg (1901), Margaret Stonborough-Wittgenstein (1905), and Fritza Riedler (1906). In addition to the similarity of the gowns worn by these sitters, Klimt accentuated their dark "Semitic" features, that is, dark hair and eyes against their pale, sometimes olive-tinted skin.

78 Bonyhady, *Good Living Street*, 130–8.

79 Ibid., 32.

80 Wistrich, *The Jews of Vienna in the Age of Franz Joseph*, 138.

81 Zweig, *The World of Yesterday*, 32–3.

82 Knut Beck, Jeffery B. Berlin, and Natascha Weschenbach-Feggeler, eds., *Stefan Zweig: Briefe, 1897–1914* (Frankfurt am Main: Fischer, 1995), 62.

83 As a result of the Anschluss, Eva was unable to attend university, and instead trained for a short period as a nurse before fleeing to England. Bostock, discussion with author. On antisemitism in Austrian universities and other institutions during the interwar period, see Bruce F. Pauley, *From Prejudice to Persecution: A History of Austrian Anti-Semitism* (Chapel Hill, NC: The University of North Carolina Press, 1991), in particular Chapter 7, "Academic Anti-Semitism in the Early Postwar Years," 89–101, and Chapter 9 "Segregation and Renewed Violence," 117–30.

84 Apfelbaum, *This is My Life*, 6.

85 See, for example, Armin Eidherr, "Die jiddische Kultur in Wien der Zwischenkriegszeit und ihre Positionierungen in Bezug auf Akkulturation, Diasporanationalismus und Zionismus," *Wien und die jüdische Erfahrung, 1900–1938: Akkulturation—Antisemitismus—Zionismus*, ed. Frank Stern and Barbara Eichinger (Vienna: Böhlau Verlag, 2009), 175–95.

86 Dominic A. Pacyga, *American Warsaw: The Rise, Fall, and Rebirth of Polish Chicago* (Chicago, IL: The University of Chicago Press, 2019), 7.

87 Wilhelm Marr, *Der Weg zum Siege des Germanenthums über das Judenthum* (Berlin: Otto Hentze, 1880), 10.

88 Steven Beller, "Dis-Oriented Jews? Orientalism, Assimilation, and Modernism in Vienna, 1900," in *Design Dialogue: Jews, Culture and Viennese Modernism/Design Dialog: Juden, Kultur und Wiener Moderne*, ed. Elana Shapira (Vienna: Böhlau Verlag, 2018), 301.

89 Moritz Güdemann, quoted in Wistrich, *The Jews of Vienna in the Age of Franz Joseph*, 98.

90 See Wistrich, *The Jews of Vienna in the Age of Franz Joseph*, 305–7.

91 See Joseph S. Bloch, *Erinnerungen aus meinem Leben* (Vienna: R. Löwit, 1922).

92 During the trial, Rohling argued as an "expert" that ritual murder for the purpose of using Christian blood during Jewish rituals was widespread. Bloch denounced Rohling in a series of articles published in the *Wiener Allgemeine Zeitung*, after which the latter attempted to sue him for libel. The politician and prominent member of the Viennese Jewish community Sigmund Mayer described Bloch as "the only man in Europe who had the courage to force Rohling into a trial that destroyed the horrible man. I only mean to honor the truth when I say that through this courageous act he has done world Jewry a great service, for which I do not believe sufficient gratitude has been shown." Sigmund Mayer, *Ein jüdischer Kaufmann, 1831 bis 1911: Lebenserinnerungen* (Leipzig: Duncker & Humblot, 1911), 308.

93 Later published as *Dr. Bloch's oesterreichische Wochenschrift* and *Dr. Bloch's Wochenschrift*.

94 Bloch quoted in Wistrich, *The Jews of Vienna in the Age of Franz Joseph*, 289.

95 Reifowitz, *Imagining an Austrian Nation*, 96.

96 Kann, *A History of the Habsburg Empire*, 442; David Rechter, *Becoming Habsburg: The Jews of Austrian Bukovina, 1774–1918* (Oxford: Littman Library of Jewish Civilization, 2013), 116.

97 Rozenblit, *Reconstructing a National Identity*, 29–30; Larry Wolff, *The Idea of Galicia: History and Fantasy in Habsburg Political Culture* (Stanford, CA: Stanford University Press, 2010), 264.

98 Ibid., 319–26. Among other Jewish subcultures in Eastern Europe, Galician Jews were recognized for their dedication to the emperor and a supranational Austrian ideal. The celebrated Yiddish playwright S. An-ski (1863–1920)—pseudonym of the Russian-born Shloyme Rappaport—highlighted this sense of *Kaiser*-mania among his *Galitsianer* coreligionists and their superiority complex with regard to their coreligionists in Tsarist Russia. See Ibid., 353–54.

99 Joseph Samuel Bloch, *Der nationale Zwist und die Juden in Österreich* (Vienna: Gottlieb, 1886), 41. The original text reads: "Wenn eine spezifisch österreichische Nationalität construirt werden könnte, so würden die Juden ihren Grundstock bilden."

100 Grunwald, *Vienna*, 440. A native of Zabrze, Upper Silesia, Max Grunwald (1871–1953) studied in Breslau before serving as a rabbi at congregations in Hamburg and Vienna. Grunwald married Bloch's daughter Margarethe.

101 Ibid.

102 Reifowitz, *Imagining an Austrian Nation*, 6–7.

103 Wistrich, *The Jews of Vienna in the Age of Franz Joseph*, 295–7.

104 Two of the prominent cultural-political organizations that arose as alternatives to Zionism and other Jewish nationalisms were the General Jewish Labor Bund—a secular, anti-Zionist, Yiddish-centered, socialist movement in Poland, Lithuania, and Russia—and the Agudath Israel/Agudas Yisroel—a politically conservative, Orthodox, anti-Zionist organization concerned with the interests of Orthodox Jewry. See Zvi Gitelman, "A Century of Jewish Politics in Eastern Europe: The Legacy of the Bund and the Zionist Movement," *East European Politics and Societies* 11, no. 3 (1997): 543–59; and Ezra Mendelsohn, "The Politics of Agudas Yisroel in Inter-War Poland," *East European Jewish Affairs* 2, no. 2 (1972): 47–60.

105 Masaidek, *Lose Gedanken*, 3. The text translates as: "One Rabbi Bloch fosters more antisemitism than ten Schönerers."

106 See, for example, the caricature that appeared on the front cover of *Kikeriki* 30, no. 1 (January 2, 1890).

107 Grunwald, *Vienna*, 439.

108 Reifowitz, *Imagining an Austrian Nation*, 147–8.

109 See Theodor Herzl, "Selbstbiographie," in *Theodor Herzls Zionistische Schriften*, ed. Leon Kellner (Berlin: Jüdischer Verlag, 1920), 7–10; Herzl, *Theodor Herzls Tagebücher*. Although useful for understanding Herzl's familial influences, it should be noted that this ego-literature was written after his "conversion" to Zionism, and therefore a strong element of "refashioning" is present.

110 Georges Yitshak Weisz, *Theodor Herzl: A New Reading*, trans. Diana File and Len Schramm (Jerusalem: Gefen Publishing House, 2013), 44–56; Wistrich, *The Jews of Vienna in the Age of Franz Joseph*, particularly "Theodor Herzl: The Making of a Political Messiah," 421–57.

111 Werner Hanak, "Von Bärten und Propheten; Oder: Theodor Herzl, Hermann Bahr und die Folgen des 'antisemitic turns' der Wiener 1880er Jahre," in *Design Dialogue: Jews, Culture and Viennese Modernism/Design Dialog: Juden, Kulur und Wiener Moderne,* ed. Elana Shapira (Vienna: Böhlau Verlag, 2018), 315–16. See also Shlomo Avineri, *Herzl: Theodor Herzl and the Foundation of the Jewish State,* trans. Haim Watzman (London: Phoenix, 2014), 56–7.

112 Ibid., 58.

113 Weisz, however, attests that it was probable that the young Herzl had been influenced by his grandfather Simon Loeb Herzl (1797–1879), a close follower of the Sephardic, Sarajevo-born Rabbi Judah Alkalai (1798–1878), who wrote about a Jewish return to Zion. See Weisz, *Theodor Herzl,* 48–9.

114 Herzl, *Tagebücher,* vol. 1, 8. See also Avineri, *Herzl,* 100–1.

115 Michael Burri, "Theodor Herzl and Richard Schaukal: Self-Styled Nobility and the Sources of Bourgeois Belligerence in Prewar Vienna," in *Rethinking Vienna 1900,* ed. Steven Beller (New York: Berghahn Books, 2001), 105–31.

116 Steven Beller quoted in Ibid., 118.

117 The pageant took place in the year following the Herzl family's move to Vienna and it is probable that it made an impression on the young student Theodor.

118 Jacques Kornberg, preface to Theodor Herzl, *Old New Land,* trans. Lotta Levensohn (Princeton, NJ: Markus Wiener Publishers, 1997), xviii.

119 Theodor Herzl, *The Jewish State,* trans. Jacob M. Alkow (New York: Dover Publications, 1988[1896]). See also his vision for the transformation of the Palestinian Arab population in Herzl, *Old New Land.*

120 Herzl, *The Jewish State,* 115. This sentiment corresponds to Michael Zakim's notions about the suit's democratizing properties. See Zakim, *Ready-Made Democracy.*

121 Herzl quoted in Burri, "Theodor Herzl and Richard Schaukal," 124.

122 Hermann Bahr quoted in Hanak, "Von Bärten und Propheten," 318. It is significant that Bahr describes Herzl's youthful appearance as "Assyrian" when as a youth Herzl did not yet sport the full beard he would become known for. Bahr's later description is thus certainly influenced by later imagery of Herzl—especially Ephraim Moses Lilien's biblically themed Zionist artwork that depicts Herzl in the guise of biblical figures dressed in the style of ancient Assyria. Stefan Zweig similarly recalled his first meeting with Herzl, offering orientalist binaries of the latter's noble appearance as a "Bedouin desert sheikh," in contrast to his "black morning coat, well-cut in an obviously Parisian style." See Zweig, *The World of Yesterday,* 127–8.

123 Artur Kamczycki, "Orientalism: Herzl and His Beard," *Journal of Modern Jewish Studies* 12, no. 1 (2013): 90–116, doi:10.1080/14725886.2012.757475; Lynne M. Swarts, *Gender, Orientalism and the Jewish Nation: Women in the Work of Ephraim Moses Lilien at the German Fin de Siècle* (New York: Bloomsbury, 2020), 41.

124 Herzl died in 1904, four years prior to the creation of Lilien's illustrations.

125 Hildegard Frübis notes the strong resemblance between the lithographs and a photograph titled *Junger Mann mit weißem Kopftuch (Young Man with a White Keffieh)* taken during Lilien's 1906 visit to Palestine. See Hildegard Frübis, "Ephraim Moses Lilien: The Figure of the 'Beautiful Jewess,' the Orient, the Bible, and Zionism," trans. Andrew Boreham, in *Orientalism, Gender, and the Jews: Literary and Artistic Transformations of European National Discourses,* ed. Ulrike Brunotte, Anna-Dorothea Ludewig, and Axel Stähler (Berlin: De Gruyter, 2015), 88.

126 Todd Samuel Presner, "'Clear Heads, Solid Stomachs, and Hard Muscles': Max Nordau and the Aesthetics of Jewish Regeneration," *Modernism/Modernity* 10, no. 2 (April 2003): 269–96.

127 Erich Burin, "Das Kaffeehausjudentum," *Jüdische Turnzeitung* 11, no. 5/6 (May–June 1910): 74–5.

128 Richard I. Cohen, *Jewish Icons: Art and Society in Modern Europe* (Berkeley, CA: University of California Press, 1998), 242.

129 Ibid.

130 See Sandra M. Sufian, *Healing the Land and the Nation: Malaria and Zionist Project in Palestine, 1920–1947* (Chicago, IL: The University of Chicago Press, 2007).

131 Flügel, *The Psychology of Clothes*, 110ff.

132 On black clothing, respectability, and dandified self-fashioning, see Harvey, *Men in Black*, in particular 31–6.

133 Kamczycki, "Orientalism."

134 Ibid., 97–8.

135 Ibid., 91–3.

Chapter 4

1   "Die armen Antisemiten," *Kikeriki* 30, no. 58 (July 20, 1890): 2.

2   I am grateful to Professor Liliane Weissberg for bringing this connection to my attention.

3   Kurt Grunwald, "Europe's Railways and Jewish Enterprise: German Jews as Pioneers of Railway Promotion," *Leo Baeck Institute Year Book* 12, no. 1 (1967): 163–209; Dominik Kaim et al., "Railway Network of Galicia and Austrian Silesia (1847–1914)," *Journal of Maps* 16, no. 1 (2020): 132–7, doi:10.1080/17445647.2020.1762774.

4   Grunwald, "Europe's Railways," 205.

5   Masaidek, *Wien und die Wiener*, 4–5.

6   Rozenblit, *The Jews of Vienna*, 17.

7   Freidenrich, *Jewish Politics in Interwar Vienna*, 213.

8   Carl E. Schorske, *Fin-de-Siècle Vienna: Politics and Culture* (Cambridge: Cambridge University Press, 1979), 32–3; Péter Hanák, "Urbanization and Civilization: Vienna and Budapest in the Nineteenth Century," in *The Garden and the Workshop": Essays on the Cultural History of Vienna and Budapest* (Princeton, NJ: Princeton University Press, 1998), 9–12.

9   Adolf Loos, "Die Potemkin'sche Stadt," *Ver Sacrum* 1, no. 7 (July 1898): 19–21.

10 Timms, *Karl Kraus*, 1: 22.

11 Schorske, *Fin-de-Siècle Vienna*, 46–62; and Shapira, *Style and Seduction*, 21–56.

12 Elana Shapira, "Imagining the Jew: A Clash of Civilisations," in *Facing the Modern: The Portrait in Vienna, 1900*, ed. Gemma Blackshaw (London: National Gallery and Yale University Press, 2013), 155–71.

13 See, for example, Pieter M. Judson, "Do Multiple Languages Mean a Multicultural Society? Nationalist 'Frontiers' in Rural Austria, 1880–1918," in *Understanding Multiculturalism:*

The Habsburg Central European Experience, ed. Johannes Feichtinger and Gary B. Cohen (New York: Berghahn Books, 2014), 61–82.

14   On the complexities of Austrian "national" identification, see Bruckmüller, *The Austrian Nation*.

15   See Michael L. Miller and Scott Ury, eds., *Cosmopolitanism, Nationalism and the Jews of East Central Europe* (Abingdon: Routledge, 2015).

16   Arendt, *The Origins of Totalitarianism*, 239–40.

17   Margaret C. Jacob, "The Cosmopolitan as a Lived Category," *Dædalus* 37, no. 3 (Summer 2008): 18.

18   Bauman, *Modernity and Ambivalence*, 61.

19   For a thorough analysis of how Jews dealt with the Austrian identity during the late Habsburg and interwar periods, see Oxaal, Pollak, and Botz, eds., *Jews, Antisemitism and Culture in Vienna*; Rozenblit, *Reconstructing a National Identity*; Silverman, *Becoming Austrians*.

20   Michael L. Miller and Scott Ury, "Cosmopolitanism: The End of Jewishness?" *European Review of History* 17, no. 3 (June 2010): 340.

21   See Cathy S. Gelbin and Sander L. Gilman, "How Did We Get Here From There?" in *Cosmopolitanisms and the Jews* (Ann Arbor, MI: University of Michigan Press, 2017), 1–30 for an excellent review of literary debates surrounding Jews and Cosmopolitanism. In contrast, Jews have also been castigated for being too insular and "a failure to be cosmopolitan at all." See Robert D. Fine, "Cosmopolitanism and the Critique of Antisemitism: Two Faces of Universality," *European Review of History: Revue européenne d'histoire* 23, no. 5–6 (2016): 770, doi:10.1080/13507486.2016.1203877.

22   Cathy S. Gelbin, "Nomadic Cosmopolitanism: Jewish Prototypes of the Cosmopolitan in the Writings of Stefan Zweig, Joseph Roth and Lion Feuchtwanger, 1918–1933," *Jewish Culture and History* 16, no. 2 (2015): 157–77, doi:10.1080/1462169X.2015.1084147; Harry Zohn, "Stefan Zweig, the European and the Jew," *Leo Baeck Institute Yearbook* 27, no. 1 (1982): 323–36.

23   Mark H. Gelber, *Stefan Zweig, Judentum und Zionismus* (Innsbruck: Studien Verlag, 2014).

24   This is ironic when considering the dress of Hasidic Jews and their characterization as insular and non-cosmopolitan. Hasidic styles of dress are thought to be derived from those of the sixteenth-century Polish *szlachta*, in turn influenced by Ottoman styles. See Somogyi, *Die Schejnen und die Prosten*, 117–18.

25   Fuchs, "Bourgeois Dress (1902)," 318.

26   Ibid., 319.

27   Ibid., 320.

28   See Todd M. Endelman, *The Jews of Britain, 1656–2000* (Berkeley, CA: University of California Press, 2000), in particular Chapter 4, "Native Jews and Foreign Jews (1870–1914)," 127–80.

29   See, for example, Jürgen Habermas, *The Structural Transformation of the Public Sphere: An Inquiry into a Category of Bourgeois Society*, trans. Thomas Burger (Cambridge: Polity Press, 1989); Alistair O'Neill, *London After a Fashion* (London: Reaktion Books, 2007); Richard Sennett, *Flesh and Stone: The City and the Body in Western Civilization* (New York: W. W. Norton and Company, 1996).

30   Tag Gronberg, "The Inner Man: Interior and Masculinity in Early Twentieth-Century Vienna," *Oxford Art Journal* 24, no. 1 (2001): 71.

31   Ibid. See also the discussion on the domestic sphere and bourgeois performativity in *fin-de-siècle* Budapest in Hanák, "Urbanization and Civilization," 24–32.

32   See, for example, Charlotte Ashby, Tag Gronberg, and Simon Shaw-Miller, eds., *The Viennese Café and Fin-de-Siècle Culture* (New York: Berghahn Books, 2015); Bedoire, *The Jewish Contribution to Modern Architecture*; Mona Domosh, "Those 'Gorgeous Incongruities': Politics and Public Space on the Streets of Nineteenth-Century New York City," *Annals of Association of American Geographers* 88, no. 2 (1998): 209–26; Schorske, *Fin-de-Siècle Vienna*; Sennett, *Flesh and Stone*.

33   Anne Hollander, "The Clothed Image: Picture and Performance," *New Literary History* 2, no. 3 (Spring 1971): 487.

34   Denis Diderot, "Regrets on Parting with My Old Dressing Gown: Or, A Warning to Those Who Have More Taste than Money," in *The Eighteenth Century*, ed. Peter McNeil, vol. 2, *Fashion: Critical and Primary Sources* (Oxford: Berg, 2009), 22–5.

35   See Mary Costello, "Adolf Loos's Kärntner Bar: Reception, Reinvention, Reproduction," in *The Viennese Café and Fin-de-Siècle Culture*, ed. Charlotte Ashby, Tag Gronberg, and Simon Shaw-Miller (New York: Berghahn Books, 2015), 138–57.

36   Steven Beller, "'The Jew Belongs in the Coffeehouse': Jews, Central Europe and Modernity," in *The Viennese Café and Fin-de-Siècle Culture*, ed. Charlotte Ashby, Tag Gronberg, and Simon Shaw-Miller (New York: Berghahn Books, 2015), 54–5.

37   Christoph Grafe, "The Architecture of Cafés, Coffee Houses and Public Bars," in *Cafés and Bars: The Architecture of Public Display*, ed. Christoph Grafe and Franziska Bollery (New York: Routledge, 2007), 7.

38   See Shapira, *Style and Seduction*; Mark Wigley, *White Walls, Designer Dresses: The Fashioning of Modern Architecture* (Cambridge, MA: The MIT Press, 2001).

39   Shapira, *Style and Seduction*, 182.

40   Tournikiotis, *Adolf Loos*, 51.

41   Shachar Pinsker, "Between 'The House of Study' and the Coffeehouse: The Central European Café as a Site for Hebrew and Yiddish Modernism," in *The Viennese Café and Fin-de-Siècle Culture*, ed. Charlotte Ashby, Tag Gronberg, and Simon Shaw-Miller (New York: Berghahn Books, 2015), 87.

42   The "founding myth" of Viennese coffeehouses concerns a highly dramatized episode in which Jerzy Franciszek Kulczycki (known in German as "Georg Franz Kolschitzky"), a noble from the Polish-Lithuanian Commonwealth, helped end the Ottoman siege of Vienna in 1683 by dressing as a Turk and penetrating enemy lines. For his service, Kulczycki was purported to have been awarded several sacks of coffee beans abandoned by the Ottoman army, and permission to open Vienna's first coffeehouse. The orientalist and exoticized characterization of the tale is further influenced by the ambiguity of Kulczycki's national origins: in different versions of the story, he is characterized as a Pole, Ukrainian, Serbo-Croat, or simply Viennese. The first Viennese coffeehouse, however, has been traced to Armenian proprietors. The association of Jews and the Viennese coffeehouse is intricately connected to widespread perceptions of Jews as an eastern, oriental people. See Tag Gronberg, "Coffeehouse Orientalism," in *The Viennese Café and Fin-de-Siècle Culture*, ed. Charlotte Ashby, Tag Gronberg, and Simon Shaw-Miller (New York: Berghahn Books, 2015), 59–77.

43   Shapira, *Style and Seduction*, 182.

44 Ibid., 180–1.

45 In her study of Loos's bar and its replica at Trinity College at the University of Dublin, Mary Costello notes that the choice and use of materials in the American Bar's interior architecture and furnishings have been characterized as "masculine." This is not only due to their selection, such as "hard, polished surfaces, dark colours, and materials such as leather and mahogany," as well as English textiles, but also in the way in which they were used to create a space that required its inhabitants to move and sit in ways that were considered masculine. See Costello, "Adolf Loos's Kärntner Bar," 139–40; Otakar Máčel, "American Bar (Kärntner Bar)," in *Cafés and Bars: The Architecture of Public Display*, ed. Christoph Grafe and Franziska Bollery (New York: Routledge, 2007), 140–4.

46 *Neue Freie Presse*, January 21, 1909, 13.

47 Costello, "Adolf Loos's Kärntner Bar," 140. In her memoir, Claire Loos (1904–42), the architect's third wife, explains that women found the gender ban intolerable and resorted to protest. See Claire Beck Loos, *Adolf Loos: A Private Portrait*, ed. Carrie Patterson (Los Angeles, CA: DoppelHouse Press, 2011), 144.

48 Reprinted as Peter Altenberg, "Adolf Loos' 'American Bar'," in *Das Wiener Kaffeehaus*, ed. Kurt-Jürgen Heering (Berlin: Insel Verlag, 2013), 98–100.

49 Costello, "Adolf Loos's Kärntner Bar," 152.

50 See, for example, Ashby, Gronberg, and Shaw-Miller, eds., *The Viennese Café*; Robert Liberles, *Jews Welcome Coffee: Tradition and Innovation in Early Modern Germany* (Waltham, MA: Brandeis University Press, 2012); Shachar M. Pinsker, *A Rich Brew: How Cafés Created Modern Jewish Culture* (New York: New York University Press, 2018).

51 Friedrich Uhl, "Wiener Kaffeehäuser," *Wiener Zeitung*, May 31, 1900, 3–5.

52 Between 1869 and 1880, Vienna's Jewish population grew from 40,230 to 73,222, or 82 percent. See Rozenblit, *The Jews of Vienna*, 17–18.

53 Although Jürgen Habermas explained that the coffeehouse was instrumental to the development of cultural life and the dissemination of critical discourse in seventeenth- and eighteenth-century England, he claims that the public discourse of the late nineteenth and early twentieth centuries became overshadowed by mass press consumption. Charlotte Ashby, however, asserts that this thesis cannot be applied to the *Wiener Kaffeehaus* due to the political situation in Austria prior to 1848. Charlotte Ashby, "The Cafés of Vienna: Space and Sociability," in *The Viennese Café and Fin-de-Siècle Culture*, ed. Charlotte Ashby, Tag Gronberg, and Simon Shaw-Miller (New York: Berghahn Books, 2015), 10–11. See also Habermas, *The Structural Transformation of the Public Sphere*.

54 Beller, "The Jew Belongs in the Coffeehouse."

55 Ibid., 54. *Burschenschaften* did not always exclude Jewish members. Prior to the renewed wave of antisemitism during the 1870s, Jewish students at German-language universities had often participated in *Burschenschaften*, even those of the more right-wing, pan-German variety—such as Theodor Herzl's involvement in the *Akademische Burschenschaft Albia*. For a comparative study of Jewish students at German universities during the nineteenth century and their involvement in the social and cultural life, see Keith H. Pickus, *Constructing Modern Identities: Jewish University Students in Germany, 1815–1914* (Detroit, MI: Wayne State University Press, 1999).

56 Gluck, *Invisible Jewish Budapest*, 189.

57 Gronberg, "Coffeehouse Orientalism." See also Chapter 3, "Vienna: The 'Matzo Island' and the Functioning Myths of the Viennese Café," 98–141, in Pinsker, *A Rich Brew*.

58 Ibid.

59 Beller, "'The Jew Belongs in the Coffeehouse'," 52. The *Heuriger*—"new wine," literally "this year," in Austrian dialect—was a particular Viennese institution: a kind of wine garden set amidst the vineyards on the outskirts of Vienna. Traditionally, the proprietor of the *Heuriger* served wine to his customers who were required to bring their own food. The modern *Heuriger* serves both the year's yield and traditional Austrian cuisine. Beller argues that during the late nineteenth and early twentieth centuries, the *Heuriger* and the *Kaffeehaus* came to be coded, as a result of their regular patrons, as "German" and "Jewish," respectively. See Beller, *Vienna and the Jews*, 183.

60 See Ashby, "The Cafés of Vienna."

61 Uhl, "Wiener Kaffeehäuser," 3.

62 Breward, *The Suit*, 52.

63 The series of watercolors was presented to the chairman of the IKG, Heinrich Klinger, on the occasion of his seventieth birthday in 1902.

64 Rudolf Klein, *The Great Synagogue of Budapest* (Budapest: TERC, 2008), 23.

65 Vienna's IKG followed Orthodox traditions, and therefore men and women sat separately in its many synagogues. In contrast to Orthodoxy, women play an active and equal role in other streams of Judaism, including Reform and Conservative.

66 Silverman, *A Cultural History of Jewish Dress*, xvii–xviii.

67 Karen Anijar, "Jewish Genes, Jewish Jeans: A Fashionable Body," in *Religion, Dress and the Body*, ed. Linda B. Arthur (London: Berg, 1999), 184.

68 Pinsker, *A Rich Brew*, 105.

69 See, for example, the establishments advertised in Jewish periodicals, such as *Die Wahrheit*.

70 Beller, "'The Jew Belongs in the Coffeehouse'."

71 See Beller, *Vienna and the Jews*, 188–206.

72 Boyer, *Political Antisemitism in Late Imperial Vienna*.

73 Fritz Wittels, "Der heilige Lueger," *Die Bühne* 2, no. 17 (March 5, 1925): 30.

74 Ibid., 31.

75 Gilman, Chapter 1, "The Jewish Voice: Chicken Soup or the Penalties of Sounding Too Jewish," in *The Jew's Body*, 10–37.

76 Wittels, "Der heilige Lueger," 32. The original German reads: "Uije, bis um zehne hab' ich schon drei Juden g'fressen!"

77 Ibid., 33. The original German reads: "Ja könnt's denn ös G'scherten kan Jud'n von unserem hochverehrten Bürgermeister unterscheiden?"

78 Mayer, *Ein jüdischer Kaufmann*, 296.

79 Bloch, *Erinnerungen aus meinem Leben*, 250.

80 John M. Efron, "The 'Kaftanjude' and the 'Kaffeehausjude': Two Models of Jewish Insanity: A Discussion of Causes and Cures among German Jewish Psychiatrists," *Leo Baeck Institute Yearbook* 37, no. 1 (1992): 169–88; Sander L. Gilman, "Jews and Mental Illness: Medical Metaphors, Anti-Semitism, and the Jewish Response," *Journal of the History of Behavioral Sciences* 20, no. 2 (April 1984): 150–9.

81 Martin Engländer, *Die auffallend häufigen Krankheitserscheinungen der jüdischen Rasse* (Vienna: J. L. Pollak, 1902).

82 Gilman, *The Jew's Body*, 49.

83 Silverman, *Becoming Austrians*, 44.

84 Glockemeier, *Zur Wiener Judenfrage*, 68.

85 Vienna's 1923 Jewish population of 201,513 can be compared with Budapest's 215,560 in 1920, and Prague's 31,751 in 1921. For a more detailed comparison of the Jewish populations of these three cities during the interwar period, see William O. McCagg, "The Jewish Population in Interwar Central Europe: A Structural Study of Jewry at Vienna, Budapest, and Prague," in *A Social and Economic History of Central European Jewry*, ed. Yehuda Don and Victor Karady (New Brunswick, NJ: Transaction Publishers, 1990), 47–81.

86 Silverman, *Becoming Austrians*, 22.

87 Rozenblit, *Reconstructing a National Identity*, 24. See also Hanni Mittelmann and Armin A. Wallas, "Österreich-Konzeption und jüdisches Selbstverständnis: Identitäts-Transfiguration im 19. Und 20. Jahrhundert," in *Österreich-Konzeption und jüdisches Selbstverständnis: Identitäts-Transfiguration im 19. Und 20. Jahrhundert*, ed. Hanni Mittelmann and Armin A. Wallas (Tübingen: Max Niemeyer Verlag, 2001), 1–10.

88 Glockemeier, *Zur Wiener Judenfrage*.

89 Ibid., 5. The original German reads: "Eine *gerechte* und *rechtzeitige* Lösung der Wiener Judenfrage," italics in the original.

90 Kunschak quoted in Ibid. The original German reads: "Entweder man löst die Judenfrage rechtzeitig, Eingebungen der Vernunft und Menschlichkeit folgend, oder sie wird gelöst werden, wie das unvernünftige Tier seinen Feind angeht, im Toben wildgewordenen Instinktes."

91 Julie Thorpe, *Pan-Germanism and the Austro-Fascist State, 1922–38* (Manchester: Manchester University Press, 2011), 157.

92 Glockemeier, *Zur Wiener Judenfrage*, 88. Presenting statistics (raw numbers and percentages) of Jews in various professional fields and industries, Glockemeier contends, "Die vorstehenden Darlegungen lassen keine Zweifel daran, daß die Juden Wien gleichsam erobert haben. Sie haben wirtschaftlich und damit auch politisch eine Machtstellung erlangt, die außer Verhältnis zu ihrer Zahl steht." (The above explanations leave no doubt that the Jews have, so to speak, conquered Vienna. They have achieved an economic and political position of power that is disproportionate to their numbers.)

93 Ibid., 94.

94 See, for example, Hilary Hope Herzog, *"Vienna is Different": Jewish Writers in Austria from the Fin de Siècle to the Present* (New York: Berghahn Books, 2011), 142–7; Silverman, *Becoming Austrians*, 51–60.

95 Hugo Bettauer, *Die Stadt ohne Juden: Ein Roman von übermorgen* (Berlin: Omnium Verlag, 2013[1922]), 9–11.

96 Ibid., 11.

97 Bettauer, *Die Stadt ohne Juden*, 119.

98 Ibid., 48.

99 Ibid., 72. The rustic styles described by Bettauer correspond to actual men's fashions for *Sommerfrischen* and hiking expeditions as depicted in the 1930s Viennese pattern books *Herren-Mode-Welt* and *The Gentleman: English Fashion* (both published by the Jewish-owned publishing house, Bachwitz).

100 Bettauer, *Die Stadt ohne Juden*, 73.

101 Scott Spector, *Modernism Without Jews? German-Jewish Subjects and Histories* (Bloomington, IN: Indiana University Press, 2017), 22–3.

102 In 1923, out of a total Austrian Jewish population of 220,208, 91.5 percent lived in Vienna. Pauley, *From Prejudice to Persecution*, 209. See also Michael John, "Jews as Consumers and Providers in provincial Towns: The Example of Linz and Salzburg, 1900–1938," in *Longing, Belonging, and the Making of Jewish Consumer Culture*, ed. Gideon Reuveni and Nils Roemer (Leiden: Brill, 2010), 139–62.

103 A longer version of this subchapter appears as "*Lederhosen, Dirndl* and a Sense of Belonging: Jews and *Trachten* in Pre-1938 Austria," *TEXTILE: Cloth and Culture* (2022), do i:10.1080/14759756.2022.2141037.

104 Hans Haas, "Der Traum vom Dazugehören—Juden auf Sommerfrische," in *Der Geschmack der Vergänglichkeit: Jüdische Sommerfrische in Salzburg*, ed. Robert Kriechbaumer (Vienna: Böhlau Verlag, 2002), 41–57.

105 Deborah R. Coen, *Vienna in the Age of Uncertainty: Science, Liberalism, and Private Life* (Chicago, IL: The University of Chicago Press, 2007), 17.

106 Torberg, *Die Tante Jolesch*, 92.

107 See Chapter 6 of this book.

108 See Robert Kriechbaumer, ed., *Der Geschmack der Vergänglichkeit: Jüdische Sommerfrische in Salzburg* (Vienna: Böhlau Verlag, 2002). Viennese Jews did not exclusively holiday in the Salzkammergut but also visited the Mediterranean, South Tyrol, and Bohemian spa towns—such as Karlsbad (Karlovy Vary), Franzensbad (Františkovy Lázně), and Marienbad (Márianské Lázně)—the latter, albeit for medicinal purposes. See Zadoff, *Next Year in Marienbad*.

109 Such pamphlets were commonly published in various Salzkammergut locales as well as Bohemian spa towns.

110 Jakob von Falke, *Die deutsche Trachten- und Modenwelt: Ein Beitrag zur deutschen Culturgeschichte*, vol. 1 (Leipzig: Gustav Mayer, 1858), vi.

111 Buxbaum, *Mode aus Wien*, 332.

112 Rebecca Houze, *Textiles, Fashion, and Design Reform in Austria-Hungary Before the First World War: Principles of Dress* (Farnham: Ashgate, 2015), 250.

113 Benedict Anderson, *Imagined Communities: Reflections on the Origin and Spread of Nationalism* (London: Verso, 2006[1983]); Rogers Brubaker, *Citizenship and Nationhood in France and Germany* (Cambridge, MA: Harvard University Press, 1992); Bruckmüller, *The Austrian Nation*.

114 Alexander Maxwell, *Patriots Against Fashion: Clothing and Nationalism in Europe's Age of Revolutions* (Basingstoke: Palgrave Macmillan, 2014), 3.

115 Houze, *Textiles*, 250.

116 "Was ist die Mode?" *Neuigkeits Welt-Blatt*, October 8, 1881.

117 Anton Schlossar, "Die Volkstrachten in Steiermark," *Neue illustrirte Zeitung*, October 21, 1883, 54.

118 Lerner, *The Consuming Temple*, 23ff.

119 Zakim, *Ready-Made Democracy*.

120 Lillian M. Bader, "One Life Is Not Enough: Autobiographical Vignettes," unpublished memoir, LBI (1956), ME 784. MM II 4, 38.

121 Freud, *Glory Reflected*, 93.

122 Ibid., 13–14.

123 Jacqueline Vansant, *Reclaiming Heimat: Trauma and Mourning in Memoirs by Jewish Austrian Reémigrés* (Detroit, MI: Wayne State University Press, 2001), 14–15.

124 Raphael Samuel, *Theatres of Memory: Past and Present in Contemporary Culture* (London: Verso, 2012), 330–3.

125 Eva Engel in discussion with author, November 14, 2017.

126 See Bruckmüller, *The Austrian Nation*.

127 Rozenblit, *Reconstructing a National Identity*, 4–5; Silverman, *Becoming Austrian*, 16.

128 Herzog, *"Vienna is Different,"* 102.

129 Engel, discussion. Eva recalled an incident, when living in Auckland, New Zealand, during the 1940s after fleeing the Anschluss, in which her mother caught her secretly lighting Hanukkah candles in her bedroom—influenced by her teacher at the local *kheyder*—and ridiculed her for it.

130 Ulrike Kammerhofer-Aggermann, "Dirndl, Lederhose und Sommerfrischenidylle," in *Der Geschmack der Vergänglichkeit: Jüdische Sommerfrische in Salzburg*, ed. Robert Kriechbaumer (Vienna: Böhlau Verlag, 2002), 329.

131 Engel, discussion.

132 Haas, "Der Traum von Dazugehören," 56.

133 SJM Object No. M2019/012:001.

134 Konrad Kwiet, "The Second Time Around: The Re-Acculturation of German-Jewish Refugees in Australia," *The Journal of Holocaust Education* 10, no. 1 (2001): 34–9. The use of *Trachten* as a form of fancy dress rather than explicit sartorial indicators of national identity is significant in the context of Jewish refugees in 1940s Australia and New Zealand—as in other parts of the Anglophone world—both at war with Nazi Germany. To don *Trachten* in the same manner they had in Austria or Germany during a time when their linguistic, cultural, and "national" origins already made them suspect in the eyes of the predominantly Anglo-Saxon host societies would have likely endangered the welfare of the refugees during a period of wartime hysteria and xenophobia. See Konrad Kwiet, "'Be Patient and Reasonable!': The Internment of German-Jewish Refugees in Australia," trans. Jane Sydenham-Kwiet, *Australian Journal of Politics and History* 31, no. 1 (1985): 61–77.

135 Kammerhofer-Aggermann, "Dirndl, Lederhose und Sommerfrischenidylle," 319.

136 However, acculturated and secular Viennese Jews were not the only ones to visit *Sommerfrischen*, nor did all Jewish visitors don *Trachten* or *Trachtenmoden*. Vienna's Orthodox Jews also visited Austria's rural resort towns, some of which catered to their religious needs with kosher restaurants and hotels. Advertisements for such establishments regularly appeared in Jewish periodicals. For example, the June 28, 1935, issue of the Orthodox-leaning *Jüdische Presse* advertised a number of kosher hotels and pensions in various Austrian, Czechoslovak, Hungarian, and Yugoslav resort towns, including Kurhotel Bristol (Bad Gastein), Villenpension Kreuzberg (Breitenstein am Semmering), Ferienheim der Agudas-Jisroel-Mädchengruppe Wien (Forchtenau), Hotel Metropole in Bad Sliač (Kežmarok), Termalbad Vyhne (Vyhne), Pension Schreiber (Tatranská Lomnica), Pension Landau (Balatonszárszó), Rogaška Slatina (Rohitsch [Rogatec]), and Pension Weiss (Abbazia [Opatija]). See *Jüdische Presse*, June 28, 1935, 6.

Chapter 5

1   Eduard Fuchs, *Die Juden in der Karikatur: Ein Beitrag zur Kulturgeschichte* (Munich: Albert Langen Verlag, 1921), 3.

2   Ibid., 4.

3   Thomas Milton Kemnitz, "The Caricature as a Historical Source," *The Journal of Interdisciplinary History* 4, no. 1 (1973): 92–3.

4   Ibid., 86.

5   John Richard Moores, *Representations of France in English Satirical Prints, 1740–1832* (Basingstoke: Palgrave Macmillan, 2015), 1.

6   Ibid., 1–2.

7   Mark Bills, *The Art of Satire: London in Caricature* (London: Philip Wilson Publishers and the Museum of London, 2006), 18.

8   Ibid.

9   Lawrence H. Streicher, "On a Theory of Political Cartoons," *Cosmopolitan Studies in Society and History* 9, no. 4 (1967): 431. Streicher goes so far as to argue that caricature is to visual art what satire is to literature.

10 Bills, *The Art of Satire*, 13; Diana Donald, *Followers of Fashion: Graphic Satires from the Georgian Period* (London: Hayward Gallery Publishing and the British Museum, 2007), 7; Moores, *Representations of France in English Satirical Prints*, 8.

11 Donald, *Followers of Fashion*, 7.

12 Ann Taylor Allen, *Satire and Society in Wilhelmine Germany: Kladderadatsch & Simplicissimus, 1890–1914* (Lexington, KY: University of Kentucky Press, 1984), 4.

13 Peter McNeil, "Ideology, Fashion and the Darlys' 'Macaroni' Prints," in *Dress and Ideology: Fashioning Identity from Antiquity to the Present*, ed. Shoshana-Rose Marzel and Guy D. Stiebel (London: Bloomsbury, 2015), 119.

14 Donald, *Followers of Fashion*, 9.

15 Pamela C. Berger, "The Roots of Anti-Semitism in Medieval Imagery: An Overview," *Religion and the Arts* 4, no. 1 (March 2000): 4–42; Steven F. Kruger, "Becoming Christian, Becoming Male?" in *Becoming Male in the Middle Ages*, ed. Jeffrey Jerome Cohen and Bonnie Wheeler (New York: Garland Publishing, 2000), 21–41.

16 Berger, "The Roots of Anti-Semitism in Medieval Visual Imagery," 35–7.

17 Fuchs, *Die Juden in der Karikatur*, 97.

18 William Collins Donahue, *The End of Modernism: Elias Canetti's Auto-da-Fé* (Chapel Hill, NC: University of North Carolina Press, 2001), 117.

19 See Salo Aizenberg, *Hatemail: Anti-Semitism on Picture Postcards* (Lincoln, NE: University of Nebraska Press, 2013), 190–9. *Der kleine Cohn* is just one example of a fictional Jewish individual used as a reference for Jewry in its entirety. Other popular *fin-de-siècle* Jewish caricatures included Wilhelm Busch's *Schmulchen Schievelbeiner* (German), *Itzig Spitzig* and *Salomon Seiffensteiner* (the latter two appearing in Adolf Ágai's satirical Budapest magazine *Borsszem Jankó*). See Mary Gluck, "The Budapest Flâneur: Urban Modernity, Popular Culture, and the 'Jewish Question' in Fin-de-Siècle Hungary," *Jewish Social Studies* 10, no. 3 (Spring/Summer 2004): 1–22.

20 Matthew Baigell, *The Implacable Urge to Defame: Cartoon Jews in the American Press, 1877–1935* (Syracuse, NY: Syracuse University Press, 2017), 3.

21 McCagg, *A History of Habsburg Jews*, 156–7.

22 See Werner Bergmann and Ulrich Wyrwa. "The Making of Antisemitism as a Political Movement: Political History as Cultural History (1878–1914): An Introduction," *Quest: Issues in Contemporary Jewish History*, no. 3 (July 2012): 1–15, doi: 10.48248/issn.2037-741X/16.

23 At the *fin de siècle*, Jews in Bohemia and Moravia, for example, were largely German-speaking and adherents of German culture, with only a minority identifying with Czech culture and language. For this reason, Jews were commonly seen as agents of German imperialism and thus enemies of the Czech national cause—in much the same way they served in the minds of non-Magyars as agents of Magyar imperialism in Transleithania. See, for example, Kateřina Čapková, *Czechs, Germans, Jews? National Identity and the Jews of Bohemia*, trans. Derek and Marzia Paton (New York: Berghahn Books, 2012).

24 Wistrich, *The Jews of Vienna in the Age of Franz Joseph*, 211–14.

25 Allen, *Satire and Society in Wilhelmine Germany*, 2–3.

26 See Julia Secklehner, "Simple Entertainment? *Die Muskete* and 'Weak' Antisemitism in Interwar Vienna," in *Visual Antisemitism in Central Europe: Imagery of Hatred*, ed. Jakub Hauser and Eva Janáčová (Berlin: De Gruyter, 2021), 123–43.

27 Edward Timms describes Austrian Liberalism as "the radiant new creed" to which Viennese and other Austrian Jews devoted themselves. The "growing discrepancy" between Liberalism and the rest of Austrian society ultimately isolated liberal-minded Jews from the wider society in which Liberalism had lost influence. Timms, *Karl Kraus*, 1:20–21.

28 See, for example, *Der Floh*, February 16, 1890, 3.

29 Jeffery W. Beglaw, "The German National Attack on the Czech Minority in Vienna, 1897–1914, as Reflected in the Satirical Journal *Kikeriki*, and its Role as a Centrifugal Force in the Dissolution of Austria-Hungary" (MA diss., Simon Fraser University, 2004).

30 See series of postcards by U. Baasch (Plauen, Germany) in JMW Archive, Inv. Nr. 11660; 11661; 11662; 11664; 11665; 11667.

31 David Low, *Ye Madde Designer* (London: The Studio, 1935), 18. Citing Low's "tabs of identity," Lawrence H. Streicher notes that these tabs became masks that obscured the individual's true identity and became "more 'real' than the subject's actual face with all its changeability and variations." See Streicher, "On a Theory of Political Caricature," 436.

32 While text is important in conveying the intricacies of such images, Matthew Baigell notes that "it was not always necessary to read the captions" of cartoons to identify a Jewish subject, who was easily recognizable by stereotyped physiognomy. See Baigell, *The Implacable Urge to Defame*, 11.

33 Julia Secklehner, "Bolshevik Jews, Aryan Vienna? Popular Antisemitism in 'Der Kikeriki', 1918–1933," *Leo Baeck Institute Yearbook* 63, no. 1 (2018): 157, https://doi.org/10.1093/leobaeck/yby011.

34 Pseudonym of Ottokar Franz Ebersberg.

35 See W. A. Coupe, "*Kikeriki* und die Minderheiten der Donaumonarchie," in *Satire–Parodie Pamphlet–Caricature: en Autriche à l'époque de François-Joseph (1848–1914)*, ed. Gilbert Ravy and Jeanne Benay (Rouen: Université de Rouen, 1999), 61–88.

36 For example, in the February 18, 1906, issue of *Kikeriki*, only two of the issue's eight caricatures did not include Jewish stereotypes—not including the literary satires that explicitly mentioned or implied Jewishness.

37 Juliette Adam quoted in W. E. Yates, *Theatre in Vienna: A Critical History, 1776–1995* (Cambridge: Cambridge University Press, 1996), 175.

38 *Kikeriki* 30, no. 14 (February 16, 1890): 4.

39 *Wiener Luft*, no. 1 (January 4, 1890): 5.

40 *Kikeriki* 40, no. 6 (January 21, 1900): 2.

41 Alma Mahler-Werfel, *Diaries, 1898–1902*, trans. Anthony Beaumont, ed. Anthony Beaumont and Susanne Rode-Breymann (London: Faber & Faber, 1998), 399.

42 *Der Floh* 29, no. 23 (June 6, 1897): 5.

43 *Kikeriki* 30, no. 2 (January 5, 1890): 1.

44 *Kikeriki* 30, no. 34 (April 27, 1890): 3.

45 *Wiener Luft*, no. 5 (February 1, 1890): 1.

   The Yiddishized German caption roughly translates as: "You terrible spendthrift! Weren't we already soaked to the skin in the rain the day before yesterday?"

46 See Efron, "The 'Kaftanjude' and the 'Kaffeehausjude'"; Gilman, *The Jew's Body*, 96–100.

47 Steven E. Aschheim, *Brothers and Strangers: The East European Jew in German and German Jewish Consciousness, 1800–1923* (Madison, WI: The University of Wisconsin Press, 1982).

48 See cartoon in *Kikeriki* 65, no. 11 (March 15, 1925): 4.

49 While most Jewish caricatures in the Viennese satirical press are depicted as speaking a Yiddishized German, there are some examples of caricatures in which Jews are depicted speaking High German.

50 Additionally, the topic of their conversation ridicules the Jewish dedication toward high culture, accusing *Bildung*-obsessed Jews of ignorance of the culture they so strongly admire.

51 Arendt, *The Origins of Totalitarianism*, in particular 56–68.

52 Allen, *Satire and Society in Wilhelmine Germany*, 190. Although Allen's study focuses on the Berlin and Munich journals *Kladderadatsch* (1848–1955) and *Simplicissimus* (1896–1967), the same can be said of other European *Witzblätter*, such as the Viennese journals addressed in this chapter, and the Budapest *Borsszem Jankó* founded and edited by the Jewish satirist Adolf Ágai (né Rosenzweig, 1836–1916).

53 Ibid., 191.

54 JMW Archive Inv. Nr. 11817.

55 Joanne Entwistle, *The Fashioned Body: Fashion, Dress and Modern Social Theory*, 2nd ed. (Cambridge: Polity Press, 2015), 35.

56 See David Brenner, "Out of the Ghetto and into the Tiergarten: Redefining the Jewish Parvenu and His Origins in *Ost und West*," *The German Quarterly* 66, no. 2 (1993): 176–94.

57 Theodor Herzl, *Altneuland* (Leipzig: Hermann Seemann Nachfolger, [1902]).

58 Arendt, *The Origins of Totalitarianism*, 56–68.

59 See, for example, *Invisible Jewish Budapest*, in particular 35–7 and 104–38, in which the Hungarian Jewish humorist Adolf Ágai's satirical utopian writings and satirical magazine *Borsszem Jankó* are examined as an example of Jewish self-reflection in the Hungarian capital.

60 Herzl's efforts to transform European Jewry from pariahs and parvenus expose his attitudes toward the Jewish bourgeoisie. For example, after attending a dinner party in Berlin, he

wrote to his parents, "Yesterday there was a *Grande soiree* at Treitel's. Thirty or forty ugly little Jews and Jewesses. Not a consoling sight." It is unsurprising that a man with such attitudes would strive to change Jewry's image. Quoted in Kamczycki, "Orientalism." 92.

61 Endelman, "Gender and Conversion Revisited," 177–8.

62 Rozenblit, *The Jews of Vienna*, 127–46.

63 Ibid., 129. In offering the rates of Jewish intermarriage in Vienna for the years 1895 and 1910 (an average of 3.8 percent and 8.1 percent, respectively—an increase of over 4 percent in fifteen years), Rozenblit cites the *Statistisches Jahrbuch der Stadt Wien*. However, these statistics are unreliable, as Rozenblit asserts they include only Jews married to *konfessionslos* individuals (the only legal interdenominational marriage at the time) and therefore do not take into account those Jews who had declared themselves *konfessionslos* or converted to Christianity. Likewise, such statistics do not take into account those Jews who married *konfessionslos* partners of Jewish origin, or converted Jews marrying each other—both of which were also common. Thus, the rate of ethnic-intermarriage (couples of corresponding Jewish and non-Jewish "ethnic" origin) is impossible to determine without examining the family backgrounds of the individuals involved, and not simply their legal religious status.

64 *Der Floh* 30, no. 40 (October 2, 1898): 4. I am grateful to Dr. Elana Shapira for bringing this particular image to my attention.

65 Gilman, *The Jew's Body*, 102.

66 See, for example, *Der Floh* 22, no. 13 (March 30, 1890): 8; *Kikeriki* 59, no. 26 (June 29, 1919): 3–4; *Kikeriki* 62, no. 4 (January 22, 1922): 4.

67 See Liliane Weissberg, "Literary Culture and Jewish Space around 1800: The Berlin Salons Revisited," in *Modern Jewish Literatures: Intersections and Boundaries*, ed. Sheila E. Jelen, Michael P. Kramer, and L. Scott Lerner (Philadelphia, PA: University of Pennsylvania Press, 2011), 24–43.

68 Sandgruber, *Traumzeit für Millionäre*, 170.

69 In contrast, Marsha L. Rozenblit asserts that most female converts from Judaism were workers and artisans who converted in order to marry Gentile men from the same professional classes. See Rozenblit, *The Jews of Vienna*, 139.

70 See Aizenberg, *Hatemail*; Zadoff, *Next Year in Marienbad*, 100–3. Zadoff notes that antisemitic postcards were also distributed by Jewish vendors.

71 This trope was peddled even by Viennese Jews themselves. In his memoir, Stefan Zweig asserted that Jews dominated Vienna's artistic and cultural milieu, claiming, "Anyone who wished to introduce a novelty to Vienna, anyone from outside seeking understanding and an audience there, had to rely on the Jewish bourgeoisie." Zweig, *The World of Yesterday*, 43.

72 *Wiener Luft*, no. 3 (January 18, 1890): 4.

73 *Wiener Luft*, no. 14 (April 5, 1890): 4.

74 See Glockemeier, *Zur Wiener Judenfrage*, 71–87.

75 Werner Sombart, *The Jews and Modern Capitalism*, trans. M. Epstein (Kitchener, ON: Batoche Books, 2001[1911]). However, Sombart differentiated between "eastern" and "western" Jews, and at a 1912 symposium encouraged the latter to distance themselves from the former. See Aschheim, *Brothers and Strangers*, 48. Sombart was not the first to call attention to the supposed link between Jews and capitalism—a concept popularized by Karl Marx in the 1840s. See Karl Marx, "On the Jewish Question [1843]," in *Marx on Religion*, ed. John Raines (Philadelphia, PA: Temple University Press, 2002), 65–9.

76 Rozenblit, *The Jews of Vienna*, 148.

77 *Kikeriki* 46, no. 53 (July 5, 1906): 3.

78 "Papa, Papa, there is a man on the esplanade who can imitate a Christian!"

79 The trope of Jews ridiculing or insulting Christians draws from a long history of accusations against Jewish defilement of Christian traditions and symbols. See, for example, Magda Teter, *Sinners on Trial: Jews and Sacrilege After the Reformation* (Cambridge, MA: Harvard University Press, 2011).

80 There is an additional joke in this image that concerns the futility and stupidity of judgment and stereotyping. In his surprise at a Jewish man imitating a Christian— surrounded by laughing onlookers—the child also recognizes what his parents refuse to discuss: the comical aping of a Gentile majority that the cartoonist accuses all Jewish individuals present of committing.

81 There were exceptions to this German hegemony. In Carniola, for example, Slovenes were granted a degree of linguistic autonomy during the Taafe era (1879–1893), with the Slovene language used increasingly in schools and the administration, and bureaucrats living in Slovene-speaking areas were expected to have proficiency in the Slovene language. In Galicia, Poles were given almost complete autonomy, with Polish being the primary language of business in the Diet of Galicia and Lodomeria. See, for example, Alfred Fischel, ed., *Das österreichische Sprachenrecht* (Brünn: Friedrich Irrgang, 1910), 224; Jonathan Kwan, *Liberalism and the Habsburg Monarchy, 1861–1895* (Basingstoke: Palgrave Macmillan, 2013), 181–3; Wolff, *The Idea of Galicia*.

82 Beglaw, "The German National Attack on the Czech Minority in Vienna."

83 Masaidek, *Wien und die Wiener aus der Spottvogelperspektive*, 68, 70.

84 *Kikeriki* 46, no. 14 (February 18, 1906): 2.

85 Even his bald head appears like a *yarmulke* amidst a crown of unruly, dark "Jewish" hair.

86 *Wiener Luft*, no. 9 (March 1, 1890): 2.

87 "Können Sie mir vielleicht sagen, wo die nicht ist?"

88 See Gilman, "The Jewish Voice: Chicken Soup or the Penalties of Sounding too Jewish," in *The Jew's Body*, 10–37.

89 See, for example, *Kikeriki* 59, no. 15 (April 13, 1919): 7.

90 See, for example, *Kikeriki* 59, no. 26 (June 29, 1919): 7. This trope was not new. Years before the large-scale arrival of Galician refugees during the war years, *Kikeriki* periodically ran cartoons of *Ostjuden* swamping Vienna's *Nordbahnhof*—see *Kikeriki* 37, no. 8 (January 28, 1897): 2; *Kikeriki* 51, no. 17 (February 26, 1911): 3.

91 See, for example, *Kikeriki* 59, no. 27 (July 6, 1919): 3.

92 *Kikeriki* 65 no. 23 (June 7, 1925): 7.

93 The original German reads: "Man sieht jetzt nur mehr Kohns und Schloime, beschnitten sind sogar die Bäume!"

94 For example, going through every 1900 issue of *Kikeriki*, I found at least thirty-two cartoons in which well-known and generic Jewish characters appeared as either central or background figures. In contrast, in January 1897 alone (nine issues) I counted twenty-three images of this type—not including the illustrated heading for the classified section which appeared in every Sunday issue and included antisemitic caricatures. During the First World War, however, the frequency of antisemitic cartoons and non-visual pieces seemed to decrease, with *Kikeriki* tending to focus more on Europe's political situation, with an increase in antisemitic content in 1919.

95 Beglaw, "The German National Attack on the Czech Minority in Vienna," 73.

96 Like the antisemitic archetypes discussed earlier in this chapter, there was a common crossover between these two kinds of caricatures.

97 *Der Floh* 29, no. 12 (March 21, 1897): 1.

98 The Salzgries was a street in Vienna's first district in the vicinity of the Danube canal and Vienna's main synagogue and IKG headquarters on the Seitenstettengasse. Many Jews lived and worked in this area.

99 *Kikeriki* 40, no. 15 (February 22, 1900): 4. It is relevant to note that of the two crying Jews in the left of the image, one appears to be stealing a bunch of garlic from his friend's pocket. This is a clear reference to supposed Jewish deviousness, where one Jew will have no scruples cheating his fellow. Additionally, garlic had strong Jewish connotations in antisemitic texts and was connected to the *foeter judaicus*—the Jewish smell. Caricatures depicted Jewish figures eating garlic, which was suggested as contributing to their foul odor. See Maria Diemling, "'As the Jews Like to Eat Garlick': Garlic in the Christian-Jewish Polemical Discourse in Early Modern Germany," in *Food and Judaism: Studies in Jewish Civilization 15*, ed. Leonard J. Greenspoon, Ronald A. Simkins, and Gerald Shapiro (Omaha, NE: Creighton University Press, 2004), 215–34.

100 Wistrich, *The Jews of Vienna in the Age of Franz Joseph*, 234.

101 Ibid. See also Boyer, *Culture and Political Crisis in Vienna*, 500. In an essay addressing Stefan Zweig's rose-tinted memoir about *fin-de-siècle* Vienna, Hannah Arendt lambasts his apologetic dismissal of Lueger's antisemitism, particularly given that Zweig, as a celebrity and therefore given greater access to circles usually closed to Jews, did not endure it. See Hannah Arendt, "Stefan Zweig: Jews in the World of Yesterday," in *The Jewish Writings*, ed. Jerome Kohn and Ron H. Feldman (New York: Schocken Books 2007), 321.

102 Mayer, *Die Juden Wiens*, 475.

103 Arthur Schnitzler quoted in Herzog, *"Vienna is Different,"* 19. Original in Arthur Schnitzler, *Jugend in Wien: Eine Autobiographie*, ed. Therese Nickl and Heinrich Schnitzler (Frankfurt am Main: Fischer Taschenbuch Verlag, 2011), 322.

104 *Kikeriki* 40, no. 14 (February 18, 1900): 2.

105 *Kikeriki* 46, no. 14 (February 18, 1906): 7.

106 The original German reads: "Eintritt nur für Offiziere, hohe Würdenträger, Diplomaten, etc." *Kikeriki* 40, no. 6 (January 21, 1900): 3.

Chapter 6

1 Parts of this chapter, in particular sections on Freud, Zweig, and Altenberg, appear in Jonathan C. Kaplan, "Looking and Behaving: Sartorial Politics and Jewish Men in *Fin-de-Siècle* Vienna," *Critical Studies in Men's Fashion* 5, no. 1 & 2 (2018): 5–23, doi:10.1386/csmf.5.1-2.5_1; Jonathan C. Kaplan, "The Man in the Suit: Jewish Men and Fashion in *Fin-de-Siècle* Vienna," *Fashion Theory* 25, no. 3 (2021): 339–66, doi:10.1080/136270 4X.2020.1746115.

2 Wistrich, *The Jews of Vienna in the Age of Franz Joseph*, 497.

3 Simmel, "The Stranger."

4 Georg Simmel, "Fashion," *The American Journal of Sociology* 62, no. 2 (May 1957[1904]): 546.

5   Michael Carter, *Being Prepared: Aspects of Dress and Dressing* (Glebe, NSW: Puncher & Wattmann, 2017), 136–7.

6   See Peter Gay, *Freud: A Life for Our Time* (London: Papermac, 1989), 4–5; Liliane Weissberg, "Ariadne's Thread," *MLN* 125, no. 3 (2010): 661–81, doi:10.1353/mln.0.0267.

7   See Janine Burke, *The Gods of Freud: Sigmund Freud's Art Collection* (Milsons Point, NSW: Random House Australia, 2006); Gay, "Sigmund Freud: A German and His Discontents," in *Freud, Jews and Other Germans*, 29–92; Ernest Jones, *Sigmund Freud: Life and Work*, 3 vols. (London: Hogarth Press, 1972–74); Adam Philips, *Becoming Freud: The Making of a Psychoanalyst* (New Haven, CT: Yale University Press, 2014).

8   Weissberg, "Ariadne's Thread," 681.

9   Freud, *Glory Reflected*, 25.

10   Flügel, *The Psychology of Clothes*, 113.

11   Shapira, "Adolf Loos and the Fashioning of 'The Other,'" 221.

12   Sitting bent over a book, there is something reminiscent of the east European Talmud scholars, perhaps found among Freud's own ancestors. In this manner there is a sense of Freud as the secular heir to this long tradition of Jewish scholarship.

13   Christopher Breward discusses the role of clothing in the construction of public personas and its centrality to middle-class ideals of professionalism. Breward writes, "Professional standing was presented as a position to be striven for and earned. The onus on duty and respectability that it entailed ensured a greater concentration on the correctness of its physical manifestations." Breward, *The Hidden Consumer*, 77.

14   I am grateful to Dr. Elana Shapira for this information.

15   Freud quoted in Gay, *Freud, Jews and Other Germans*, 90.

16   Sigmund Freud, *Three Contributions to the Sexual Theory*, trans. A. A. Brill (New York: The Journal of Nervous and Mental Disease Publishing Company, 1910). See also Jordan Osserman, *Circumcision on the Couch: The Cultural, Psychological, and Gendered Dimensions of the World's Oldest Surgery* (London: Bloomsbury, 2022).

17   Gay, *Freud, Jews and Other Germans*, 76–7.

18   McNeil, "Despots of Elegance," 236.

19   Teichert, *Mode. Macht. Männer*, 155.

20   Ibid., 158.

21   Zweig, *The World of Yesterday*, 56–7.

22   Teichert, *Mode. Macht. Männer*, 175.

23   Freud, *Glory Reflected*, 24.

24   George Latimer Apperson, *The Social History of Smoking* (London: Martin Secker, 1914), 159; Penelope Byrde, *The Male Image: Men's Fashion in England, 1300–1970* (London: B. T. Batsford, 1979), 153.

25   See Chapter 4 of this book.

26   Freud, *Glory Reflected*, 125.

27   Loos, "Men's Fashion."

28   The date of the dinner party is not provided; however, it would have had to have taken place some years prior to the 1894 letter as Johann Schnitzler died in 1893.

29   Zuckerkandl, *Österreich intim*, 31.

30   Ibid., 32.

31   Moriz Szeps (1835–1902) and Julius Szeps (1867–1924), respectively.

32   Shira Brisman, "Biographies," in *Jewish Women and Their Salon: The Power of Conversation*, ed. Emily D. Bilski and Emily Braun (New York: The Jewish Museum/New Haven, CT: Yale University Press, 2005), 211–13; Lisa Silverman, "Jewish Intellectual Women and the Public Sphere in Inter-War Vienna," in *Women in Europe between the Wars: Politics, Culture and Society*, ed. Angela Kershaw and Angela Kimyongür (Aldershot: Ashgate, 2007), 158–9.

33   Martin Swales, *Arthur Schnitzler: A Critical Study* (London: Oxford University Press, 1971), 28.

34   The IKG birth records record Schnitzler's Jewish name as "Mendel." Archiv der IKG Wien, *Geburtsbuch der Israelitischen Kultusgemeinde Wien, C, 1858–1964*, entry no. 2948. *FamilySearch*, https://www.familysearch.org/ark:/61903/3:1:33S7-9BKB-DRX?i=181 &wc=MQB6438%3A344266801%2C344266802%2C344410201%3Fcc%3D2028320&cc =2028320.

35   Schnitzler, *Jugend in Wien*, 11–17. Palais Schey von Koromla was commissioned by Friedrich Schey Freiherr von Koromla (1815–81), son of Amalia Markbreieter's brother József Schey. See Bedoire, *The Jewish Contribution to Modern Architecture*, 318.

36   Ritchie Robertson, introduction to *Arthur Schnitzler: Round Dance and Other Plays*, trans, J. M. Q. Davies (Oxford University Press, 2004), viii.

37   Ibid.

38   Ibid., x.

39   See Beller, *Vienna and the Jews*, 12–13, 22.

40   Archiv der IKG Wien, *Index zu den Trauungsbüchern der Israelitischen Kultusgemeinde Wien, 1902–1903*, date August 26, 1903. Accessed May 18, 2018, via *Family Search*, https://www.familysearch.org/ark:/61903/3:1:33S7-9B23-VNQ?i=130&wc=4692-DXK %3A344266801%2C344266302%2C344573301&cc=2028320.

41   For Lili Schnitzler's birth records, see Archiv der IKG Wien, *Geburtsbuch der Israelitischen Kultusgemeinde Wien, 1909*, entry no. 1648. Accessed May 18, 2018, via *FamilySearch*, https://www.familysearch.org/ark:/61903/3:1:33S7-9B2Q-XLG?i=210&wc=4692-DX6 %3A344266801%2C344266802%2C344528901&cc=2028320. Details of Heinrich Schnitzler's birth (August 9, 1902) are listed in the Index of the Jewish Records of Vienna and Lower Austria. Accessed May 18, 2018, via *GenTeam: die genealogische Datenbank*, https://www.genteam.at/index/php?option=com_db53&id=145940&limitstart=40&n =schnitzler&v=&view=detail&lang=en.

42   Schnitzler quoted in Harry Zohn, "The Jewish World of Arthur Schnitzler (1862–1931)," *The Jewish Quarterly* 10 (1963): 29. By referring to "genuine German writers," there is still an implication that the German-Jewish writer is not as genuine as his or her Gentile counterpart.

43   Rozenblit, *Reconstructing a National Identity*, 4.

44   See Clare Rose, *Making, Selling and Wearing Boys' Clothes in Late-Victorian England* (Farnham: Ashgate, 2010), in particular, Chapter 1, "Raggedness and Respectability," 23–54, which deals with these twin notions in society and the role of clothing in generating a boy's image.

45   On masculinity, facial hair and its maintenance during the second half of the nineteenth century, see Sharon Twickler, "Combing Masculine Identity in the Age of the Moustache,

1860–1900," in *New Perspectives on the History of Facial Hair: Framing the Face*, ed. Jennifer Evans and Alun Withey (Cham: Palgrave Macmillan, 2018), 149–68.

46   Graham Clarke, *The Photograph* (Oxford: Oxford University Press, 1997), 15.

47   Geoffrey Batchen, "Vernacular Photographies," in *Each Wild Idea: Writing, Photography, History* (Cambridge, MA: The MIT Press, 2001), 62.

48   Teichert, *Mode. Macht. Männer*, 137.

49   Zuckerkandl, *Österreich* intim, 32. What Zuckerkandl-Szpes related to her sister in Paris concerned Johann Schnitzler's dismay towards his son's desire to embark on a literary career, rather than following him into the medical field (in which the younger Schnitzler had also been trained). In his treatise of *fin-de-siècle* Vienna, Carl E. Schorske argues that young writers' embrace of the arts and development of new forms was a firm rejection of the world of their fathers. See Schorske, *Fin-de-Siècle Vienna*.

50   Arthur Schnitzler, *The Road into the Open (Der Weg ins Freie)*, trans. Roger Byers (Berkeley, CA: University of California Press, 1992[1908]).

51   See Breward, *The Hidden Consumer*.

52   Lionel Bradley Steiman, "Stefan Zweig: The Education of an Aesthete and His Response to War and Politics" (PhD diss., University of Pennsylvania, 1970).

53   See, for example, Stefan Zweig, *Beware of Pity*, trans. Phyllis Blewitt and Trevor Blewitt (London: Cassell, 1953[1939]).

54   Ink seems to have been a coded message among late nineteenth-century writers, green ink being associated with the circles of aesthetes and Oscar Wilde. Peter McNeil observes that the color green was equally "associated with the 'diabolism and artificiality' that came to characterize *fin de siècle* art and literature," and the goddess Venus, thus conveying erotic connotations. See Peter McNeil, "'Everything Degenerates': The Queer Buttonhole," in *Floriographie: Die Sprache der Blumen*, ed. Isabel Kranz, Alexander Schwan, and Eike Wittrock (Berlin: Wilhelm Fink, 2016), 401–3.

55   Prior to the Second World War, Stefan Zweig enjoyed huge literary success and was one of the most widely translated European authors of the period. His work was translated into multiple European and non-European languages, including Arabic and Turkish. Friedhelm Hoffmann, "Zur arabischen Stefan-Zweig-Rezeption," *Zweigheft* 17 (July 2017): 27–34.

56   See Zweig's pacifist writings that first appeared in Austrian and German newspapers and as lectures during the early twentieth century, in Stefan Zweig, *Messages from a Lost World: Europe on the Brink*, trans. Will Stone (London: Pushkin Press, 2016).

57   Tanya Sheehan, "Looking Pleasant, Feeling White: The Social Politics of the Photographic Smile," in *Feeling Photography*, ed. Elspeth H. Brown and Thy Phu (Durham, NC: Duke University Press, 2014), 130.

58   Ibid.

59   Spitzer, *Lives in Between*, 98.

60   Mark Gelber, "Interfaces between Young Vienna and the Young Jewish Poetic Movement: Richard Beer Hofmann and Stefan Zweig," in *Jüdische Aspeckte Junge-Wiens in Kulturkontext des "Fin de Siècle,"* ed. Sarah Fraiman-Morris (Tübingen: Max Niemayer Verlag, 2005), 63. Gelber describes the literary group as "an integral part of German cultural Zionism."

61   This is evident in the widespread popularity of his writing before the Second World War, at which time Zweig was one of the most widely read and widely translated author in Europe, with his work being translated into most European languages.

62   Stefan Zweig, "Im Schnee," *Die Welt* 5, no. 31 (1901): 10–13.

63   Mark H. Gelber, *Melancholy Pride: Nation, Race, and Gender in the German Literature of Cultural Zionism* (Tübingen: Max Niemayer Verlag, 2000), 67. Gelber argues that despite Zweig's insistence that this work lacked any Jewish national feeling, Martin Buber, editor of *Die Welt*, felt differently and republished it in the *Jüdischer Almanach* in 1904.

64   NLI, M. Buber Archive, 933-13. Translation my own.

65   Herzog, *"Vienna is Different,"* 127.

66   Friderike Zweig, *Stefan Zweig*, trans. Erna McArthur (London: W. H. Allen, 1946), 219.

67   For an analysis of Moriz Zweig's sartorial habits, see Jonathan C. Kaplan, "Refashioning the Jewish Body: An Examination of the Sartorial Habits of the Family of Viennese Writer Stefan Zweig (1881–1942)," *The Journal of Dress History* 5, no. 1 (2021): 56–87.

68   Silverman, *Becoming Austrians*, 22–3.

69   Matuschek, *Three Lives*, 250.

70   Zweig, *Stefan Zweig*, 202. In America, Lanz went into business with the brothers Werner and Kurt Scharff, German refugees who arrived in New York in 1937. See "German Brothers Began Shops in West," *Desert Sun*, April 11, 1978, 8; Rose Mary Pederson Budge, "Practical, Pretty Lanz Celebrating 50 Years," *Desert News*, December 23, 1988, https://www.desertnews.com/article/28001/PRACTICAL-PRETTY-LANZ-CELEBRATING-50-YEARS.html, accessed December 13, 2017; Dennis Hevesi, "Werner Scharff, 90, Designer of Classic Warm Nightgown Dies," *The New York Times*, August 31, 2006, http://www.nytimes.com/2006/08/31/business/31scharff.html, accessed December 13, 2017.

71   Matuschek, *Three Lives*, 250.

72   Irmgard Keun quoted in Matuschek, *Three Lives*, 312–13.

73   Letter from Stefan Zweig to Martin Buber, January/February 1918. NLI, M. Buber Archive, 933-21.

74   Clarke, *The Photograph*, 105.

75   Susan Sontag, "On Style [1965]," in *Against Interpretation and Other Essays* (New York: Picador, 1996), 18.

76   Sharon Gillerman, "Samson in Vienna: The Theatrics of Jewish Masculinity," *Jewish Social Studies* 9, no. 2 (2003): 79.

77   Richard Engländer adopted the nom de plume after a childhood (unrequited) romance with a young girl nicknamed "Peter" and "Altenberg" after a town on the Danube. See Shapira, *Style and Seduction*, 175.

78   Altenberg quoted in Lunzer, "Kindheit, Jugend in einer wohlhabenden Kaufmannsfamilie," 18.

79   Harold B. Segel, *The Vienna Coffeehouse Wits, 1890–1938* (West Lafayette, IN: Purdue University Press, 1993), 110.

80   Ibid., 111.

81   "And so I came to be!" Peter Altenberg, "So wurde ich," in *Das Wiener Kaffeehaus*, ed. Kurt-Jürgen Heering (Berlin: Insel Verlag, 2013), 123.

82   Ibid., 125.

83   Segel, "Peter Altenberg," 120.

84   Andrew Barker, "Peter Altenberg: Das Werk und das literarische Umfeld," in *Peter Altenberg, Extracte des Lebens: Einem Schriftsteller auf der Spur*, ed. Heinz Lunzer and Victoria Luzner-Talos (Salzburg: Residenz Verlag, 2003), 10.

85 See Gaugusch, *Wer Einmal War*, 1:566–7.

86 Victoria Lunzer-Talos, "Judentum—Antisemitismus," in *Peter Altenberg, Extracte des Lebens: Einem Schriftsteller auf der Spur*, ed. Heinz Lunzer and Victoria Luzner-Talos (Salzburg: Residenz Verlag, 2003), 53–7.

87 Ibid., 54.

88 Rudolf von Tavel, "Was ist uns die Volkstracht?" *Heimatschutz: Zeitschrift der Schweizerischen Vereinigung für Heimatschutz* 22, no. 6 (1927): 82.

89 See Mike Crawford, "Hand Colouring and Hand Toning," in *Encyclopedia of Twentieth-Century Photography: Volume 1: A–F*, ed. Lynne Warren (New York: Routledge, 2006), 669–70.

90 An inscription by Lotte Franzos, the photographer's wife, on the back of the photograph reads "Peter mit ‚Vita Ipsa' [book by Altenberg published the same year] im Rathauspark, August 1918, aufgenommen von meinem Mann." Wienbibliothek im Rathaus, Handschriftensammlung: I.N.116.224.

91 Loos, "Men's Fashion."

92 Letter from Peter Altenberg to Emil and Lotte Franzos, July 6, 1916. Wienbibliothek im Rathaus, Handschriftensammlung: I.N.115.814.

93 See De Waal, *The Hare with Amber Eyes*, 116–25; Gronberg, "The Inner Man," 71. The Ringstrasse was an appropriate location for the act of parading oneself before society. For Loos, who referred to the Austrian capital as "Die Potemkin'sche Stadt" for its abundance of conflicting ornamentation and architectural styles, the Ringstrasse and parvenu slaves to fashion went hand in hand. See Loos, "Die Potemkin'sche Stadt."

94 See Chapter 2. "Fashioning the Self, Dressing Society: Dress and Identity in Europe's Third Jewish Capital."

95 The continued reference to English male fashion articles, particularly in reference to garment types, in the publication *Die Herrenwelt*, published in the midst of the First World War, continued a long conversation between continental Europe and Great Britain that was already well established by the mid-eighteenth century, the period of Anglomania. At a time when Austria was at war with Great Britain, the English names of garments (i.e., Chesterfield, Ulster, cutaway, smoking, etc.) remained unchanged, whereas other English-language words common in Vienna were censored and substituted for a German equivalent, sometimes with awkward results. In fact, in its July 1916 issue, the journal's editor ran an article that was highly critical of the debates taking place in the Berlin Chamber of Commerce regarding the Germanization of foreign terms used in the menswear trade. The author of the article rejected any attempts by government bodies to Germanize non-German words that were in common use, arguing that such matters would disrupt business and create confusion among consumers. See "Das Fremdwort in der Herrenmode," *Die Herrenmode* no. 6 (July 1916): 13. It indicates how tenacious English expressions were in men's fashion practice, just as French terms were very common in women's (such a comparison would require further study).

96 Carpenter quoted in Breward, *The Suit*, 39.

97 Michael Bronski, "The Male Body in the Western Mind," *Harvard Gay & Lesbian Review* 54 (1998): 28–31.

98 Shapira, *Style and Seduction*, 175–6.

99 Herzog, "*Vienna is Different*," 57; Wilma Abeles Iggers, *Karl Kraus: A Viennese Critic of the Twentieth Century* (The Hague: Martinus Nijhoff, 1967), 1

100 Herzl, *The Jewish State*.

101 Tietze, *Die Juden*, 269–70.

102 Paul Reitter, *The Anti-Journalist: Karl Kraus and Jewish Self-Fashioning in Fin-de-Siècle Europe* (Chicago, IL: The University of Chicago Press, 2008), 82–3. Moriz Benedikt (1849–1920), the Moravian-born longtime editor-in-chief of the *Neue Freie Presse* was a strong supporter of Austrian Liberalism, an opponent of his feuilleton editor Herzl's Zionist project, and one of Kraus's main targets in his attack of the Jewish bourgeoisie. See Österreichische Nationalbibliothek, ed., *Handbuch österreichischer Autorinnen und Autoren jüdischer Herkunft 18. Bis 20. Jahrhundert*, vol. 1, A–1, 1-4541 (Munich: K. G. Saur, 2002), 95. For more on Benedikt's reaction to Herzl's Zionism while the latter was employed at the *Neue Freie Presse*, see Wistrich, *The Jews of Vienna in the Age of Franz Joseph*, 446–9.

103 Ibid., 514.

104 Segel, ed., *The Vienna Coffeehouse Wits*, 60.

105 Edward Timms, *Karl Kraus: Apocalyptic Satirist, Vol. 2: The Post-War Crisis and the Rise of the Swastika* (New Haven, CT: Yale University Press, 2005), 210.

106 Wistrich, *The Jews of Vienna in the Age of Franz Joseph*, 501.

107 Heinrich Heine's conversion to Christianity is said to have been purely a means of rising to social and professional prominence. In the poet's own words, he wrote a letter to the Berliner banker Moses Moser (1796–1838) that he would not have undergone conversion "if the law permitted stealing silver spoons." Quoted in Endelman, "Gender and Conversion Revisited," 175.

108 Wistrich, *The Jews of Vienna in the Age of Franz Joseph*, 505.

109 In a 1913 issue of *Die Fackel*, Kraus wrote, "I believe I can say this about myself, that I go along with the development of Judaism up to the Exodus, but that I don't participate in the dance around the Golden Calf—and from that point on share only in those characteristics which were also found in the defenders of God and the avengers of a people gone astray." Kraus quoted in Ibid., 497–8. See original in Karl Kraus, "Er ist doch ä Jud," *Die Fackel* 15, no. 386 (October 29, 1913): 3.

110 Herzl, *Altneuland*.

111 In addition to his resentment of the Jewish bourgeoisie, Kraus both pitied and reviled *Ostjuden* and the Yiddish language, which he characterized as "oriental enclaves in European civilization." Wistrich, *The Jews of Vienna in the Age of Franz Joseph*, 513–14; see also Günter Schütt, *Karl Kraus und sein Verhältnis zum (Ost-)Judentum* (Vienna: Mandelbaum Verlag, 2017).

112 When Kraus was baptized as a Catholic in 1911—twelve years after formally resigning from the IKG and declaring himself *konfessionslos*—Loos served as his baptismal godfather. See Andreas Stuhlmann, *"Die Literatur—das sind wir und unsere Feinde": Literarische Polemik bei Heinrich Heine und Karl Kraus* (Würzburg: Königshausen & Neumann, 2010), 186.

113 Wistrich, *The Jews of Vienna in the Age of Franz Joseph*, 499–500.

114 Pierre Bourdieu, "The Social Definition of Photography," in *Photography: A Middle-Brow Art*, trans. Shaun Whiteside (Cambridge: Polity Press 1990), 80.

115 Ibid., 83.

116 "Karl Kraus aus eigenen Schriften (Tonfilm, 1934)," YouTube video, 18:04, from a recording of Karl Kraus reading excerpts from his writing, recorded by Albrecht Viktor Blum in

Prague, 1934. Posted by "cbartolf," March 9, 2014, https://www.youtube.com/watch?v=rg
-uGpBhs2g.

117 The German-Jewish theater critic Alfred Kerr, né Kempner (1867–1948), described the
tone of Kraus's writings as "Talmudic." See Reitter, *The Anti-Journalist*, 92.

118 Breward, *The Hidden Consumer*, 77–9.

119 Wienbibliothek im Rathaus, I.N.241.143.

120 Wienbibliothek im Rathaus, I.N.241.145 and I.N.241.146.

121 Elana Shapira, "Imaging the Jew," 163.

122 See, for example, Hissako Anjo and Antonia Finnane, "Tailoring in China and Japan:
Cultural Transfer and Cutting Techniques in the Early Twentieth Century," in *Dressing
Global Bodies: The Political Power of Dress in World History*, ed. Beverly Lemire and
Giorgio Riello (London: Routledge, 2019), 263–88; Melissa Bellanta, "Business Fashion:
Masculinity, Class and Dress in 1870s Australia," *Australian Historical Studies* 28, no.
2 (2017): 189–212; Mina Roces, "'These Guys Came Out Looking Like Movie Actors':
Filipino Dress and Consumer Practices in the United States, 1920s–1930s," *Pacific
Historical Review* 85, no. 4 (2016): 532–76.

123 Shapira, "Tailored Authorship."

Conclusion

1 Beckerman, *Die Mazzesinsel*, 9.

2 Ibid.

3 Shapira, *Style and Seduction*, 204.

4 Jakob Wassermann, *Mein Weg als Deutscher und Jude* (Berlin: S. Fischer Verlag, 1922),
102–3.

5 Pauley, *From Prejudice to Persecution*, 96–9.

6 Rozenblit, *Reconstructing a National Identity*, 4.

7 Silverman, *Becoming Austrians*, 16.

8 Richard Thieberger, "Assimilated Jewish Youth and Viennese Cultural Life Around 1930," in
Jews, Antisemitism and Culture in Vienna, ed. Ivar Oxaal, Michael Pollak, and Gerhard Botz
(London: Routledge and Kegan Paul, 1987), 180.

9 See Spiel, *Vienna's Golden Autumn*.

10 On the experience of Viennese Jews after the Anschluss, see, for example, Leonard H.
Ehrlich and Edith Ehrlich, *Choices Under Duress of the Holocaust: Benjamin Murmelstein
and the Fate of Viennese Jewry, Vol. 1: Vienna*, ed. Carl S. Ehrlich (Lubbock, TX: Texas Tech
University Press, 2018); Ilana Fritz Offenberger, *The Jews of Nazi Vienna, 1938–1945: Rescue
and Destruction* (Cham: Palgrave Macmillan, 2017); Doron Rabinovici, *Eichmann's Jews:
The Jewish Administration of Holocaust Vienna, 1938–1945*, trans. Nick Somers (Cambridge:
Polity Press, 2011).

11 See Irene Eber, *Wartime Shanghai and the Jewish Refugees from Central Europe: Survival, Co-
Existence, and Identity in a Multi-Ethnic City* (Berlin: Walter de Gruyter, 2013).

12 On the fate of Stefan Zweig's mother and brother, see Matuschek, *Three Lives*, 314–15.
Alfred Zweig's certificate of naturalization as a citizen of the United States lists his former

nationality as "Czechoslovakian." See Naturalization Certificate in Alfred Zweig Collection: Alfred Zweig Documents, Daniel A. Reed Library Archives & Special Collections.

13 At Freud's funeral at the Golders Green Crematorium, eulogies were given by both Stefan Zweig and Ernest Jones. Jones, *Sigmund Freud*, 3:263.

14 See Ehrlich and Ehrlich, *Choices under Duress*, 41–4. In the "early days," when the German government still encouraged Jewish emigration before the Second World War, Jewish men interned at Dachau were often released if they were able to obtain entry to another country and promised to leave immediately.

15 See Rabinovici, *Eichmann's Jews*, in particular Chapter 11 "The Kultusgemeinde: Authorities without Power," 143–93.

16 The Braun family were able to emigrate to the United States where they opened a linen shop in Manhattan under the same name. During the war the original E. Braun & Co. was managed by a former employee, Franziska Färber, who continued to work for the company when the family of Myer-Braun returned to Vienna after the war. Astrid Peterle, "Kauft (nicht) bei Juden! Zerstörung einer Wiener Geschäftskultur, 1938–1945—(Don't) Buy from Jews! Destruction of a Viennese Store Culture, 1938–1945," in *Kauft bei Juden! Geschichte einer Wiener Geschäftskultur—Buy from Jews! Story of a Viennese Store Culture*, ed. Astrid Peterle (Vienna: Amalthea Verlag and Jüdisches Museum Wien, 2017), 164–79.

17 Alain Finkielkraut, *The Imaginary Jew*, trans. Kevin O'Neill and David Suchoff (Lincoln, NE: University of Nebraska Press, 1994), 83.

BIBLIOGRAPHY

Primary Sources (Pre-1938)

(a) Archives

Archiv der Israelitische Kultusgemeinde Wien (IKG)
Daniel A. Reed Library Archives & Special Collections, State University of New York
Jüdisches Museum Wien Archiv, Vienna (JMW)
Leo Baeck Institute, New York (LBI)
National Library of Israel, Jerusalem (NLI)
Sydney Jewish Museum, Sydney (SJM)
Wienbibliothek im Rathaus

(b) Correspondence

Rosalie Landstone. Correspondence. Arthur Schnitzler Collection, National Library of Israel, Jerusalem.
Martin Buber and Stefan Zweig. Correspondence. M. Buber Collection, National Library of Israel, Jerusalem.

(c) Newspapers and Magazines

Agramer Zeitung
Bukowiner Rundschau
Czernowitzer Allgemeine Zeitung
Der Floh
Der gut angezogene Herr
Der Herr und seine Welt
Der Herr von heute
Deutsch-Englischer-Reise-Curier/English-German-Tourists-Courier
Die Bühne
Die Herrenwelt
Die Wahrheit
Die Welt
Dr. Bloch's oesterreichische Wochenschrift
Fashions for Gentlemen
Herren-Mode-Welt
Innsbrucker Nachrichten
Internationale Moden-Zeitung
Ischler Cur-Liste
Jüdische Presse
Jüdisches Volksblatt

Kikeriki: Humoristisches Volksblatt
Mährisches Tagblatt
Neue Freie Presse
Neue Illustrirte Zeitung
Neues Wiener Journal
Neues Wiener Tagblatt
Pilsner Tagblatt
Neuigkeits Welt-Blatt
Wiener Herrenmode
Wiener Luft
Wiener Moden-Zeitung
Wiener Presse
Wiener Zeitung

(d) Books and Articles

Altenberg, Peter. "Adolf Loos' 'American Bar.'" In *Das Wiener Kaffeehaus*, edited by Kurt-Jürgen Heering, 98–100. Berlin: Insel Verlag, 2013.
Altenberg, Peter. "So wurde ich." In *Das Wiener Kaffeehaus*, edited by Kurt-Jürgen Heering, 123–5. Berlin: Insel Verlag, 2013.
Apperson, George Latimer. *The Social History of Smoking*. London: Martin Secker, 1914.
Bettauer, Hugo. *Die Stadt ohne Juden: Ein Roman von übermorgen*. Berlin: Omnium Verlag, 2013 [1922].
Bloch, Joseph Samuel. *Der nationale Zwist und die Juden in Österreich*. Vienna: Gottlieb, 1886.
Bloch, Joseph Samuel. *Erinnerungen aus meinem Leben*. Vienna: R. Löwit, 1922.
Burin, Erich. "Das Kaffeehausjudentum." *Jüdische Turnzeitung* 11, no. 5/6 (May–June 1910): 74–5.
Csokor, Franz Theodor. *3. November 1918: Drei Akte*. Vienna: Wiener Bibliophilen-Gesellschaft, 1968 [1936].
Engländer, Martin. *Die auffallend häufigen Krankheitserscheinungen der jüdischen Rasse*. Vienna: J. L. Pollak, 1902.
Falke, Jakob von. *Die deutsche Trachten- und Modenwelt: Ein Beitrag zur deutschen Culturgeschichte*. Vol. 1. Leipzig: Gustav Mayer, 1858.
Fischel, Alfred, ed. *Das österreichische Sprachenrecht*. Brünn: Friedrich Irrgang, 1910.
Flügel, John C. *The Psychology of Clothes*. London: The Hogarth Press, 1966 [1930].
Freud, Sigmund. *Three Contributions to the Sexual Theory*. Translated by A. A. Brill. New York: The Journal of Nervous and Mental Disease Publishing Company, 1910.
Fuchs, Eduard. *Die Juden in der Karikatur: Ein Beitrag zur Kulturgeschichte*. Munich: Albert Langen Verlag, 1921.
Fuchs, Eduard. "'Bourgeois Dress' (1902)." In *The Rise of Fashion: A Reader*, edited by Daniel Leonard Purdy, 317–27. Minneapolis, MN: University of Minnesota Press, 2004.
Glockemeier, Georg. *Zur Wiener Judenfrage*. Leipzig: Johannes Günther Verlag, 1936.
Grunwald, Max. *Vienna*. Philadelphia, PA: The Jewish Publication Society of America, 1936.
Herzl, Theodor. *Altneuland*. Leipzig: Hermann Seemann Nachfolger, 1902.
Herzl, Theodor. "Selbstbiographie." In *Theodor Herzls Zionistische Schriften*, edited by Leon Kellner, 7–10. Berlin: Jüdischer Verlag, 1920.
Herzl, Theodor. *Theodor Herzls Tagebücher*. Vol. 1. Berlin: Jüdischer Verlag, 1922.
Herzl, Theodor. *The Jewish State*. Translated by Jacob M. Alkow. New York: Dover Publications, 1988 [1896].

Bibliography

Herzl, Theodor. *Old New Land*. Translated by Lotta Levensohn. Princeton, NJ: Markus Wiener Publishers, 1997.

Hitler, Adolf. *Mein Kampf*. Translated by James Murphy. New York: Fredonia Classics, 2003 [1925].

Kafka, Franz. "Ein Bericht für eine Akademie." *Der Jude* 2, no. 8 (1917): 559–65.

Kraus, Karl. "Er ist doch ä Jud." *Die Fackel* 15, no. 386 (October 29, 1913): 3.

Kraus, Karl. "The Eroticism of Clothes [1906]." In *The Rise of Fashion: A Reader*, edited by Daniel Leonard Purdy, 239–44. Minneapolis, MN: University of Minnesota Press, 2004.

Krempel, Lore. *Die deutsche Modezeitschrift: Ihre Geschichte und Entwicklung nebst einer Bibliographie der deutschen, englischen und französischen Modezeitschriften*. Coburg: Tageblatt-Haus, 1935.

La Garde-Chambonas, Comte A. de. *Anecdotal Recollections of the Congress of Vienna*. Translated by Albert D. Vandam. London: Chapman & Hall, 1902.

Loos, Adolf. "Die Herrenmode." *Neue Freie Presse*, May 22, 1898.

Loos, Adolf. "Die Potemkin'sche Stadt." *Ver Sacrum* 1, no. 7 (July 1898): 19–21.

Loos, Adolf. "Men's Fashion." In *Spoken into the Void: Collected Essays 1897–1900*, translated by Jane O. Newman and John H. Smith, 10–14. Cambridge, MA: The MIT Press, 1982.

Loos, Adolf. "The Principle of Cladding." In *Spoken into the Void: Collected Essays 1897–1900*, translated by Jane O. Newman and John H. Smith, 66–9. Cambridge, MA: The MIT Press, 1982.

Loos, Adolf. *Spoken into the Void: Collected Essays, 1897–1900*. Translated by Jane O. Newman and John H. Smith. Cambridge, MA: The MIT Press, 1982.

Loos, Adolf. "Praise for the Present." In *Adolf Loos: Why a Man Should be Well-Dressed*, translated by Michael Edward Troy, 13–17. Vienna: Metroverlag, 2001.

Low, David. *Ye Madde Designer*. London: The Studio, 1935.

Magistrats-Abteiling XXI für Statistik, ed. *Statistisches Jahrbuch der Stadt Wien für das Jahr 1901*. Vienna: Verlag des Wiener Magistrates, 1903.

Mahler-Werfel, Alma. *Diaries, 1898–1902*. Translated by Anthony Beaumont, edited by Anthony Beaumont and Susanne Rode-Breymann. London: Faber & Faber, 1998.

Marr, Wilhelm. *Der Weg zum Siege des Germanenthums über das Judenthum*. Berlin: Otto Hentze, 1880.

Marr, Wilhelm. *Der Sieg des Judenthums über das Germanenthum: Vom nicht confessionellen Standpunkt aus betrachtet*. Bern: Rudolph Costenoble, 1879.

Marx, Karl. "On the Jewish Question [1843]." In *Marx on Religion*, edited by John Raines, 65–9. Philadelphia, PA: Temple University Press, 2002.

Masaidek, Franz Friedrich. *Wien und die Wiener aus der Spottvogelperspektive: Wien's Sehens-, Merk- und Nichtswürdigkeiten*. Vienna: R. von Waldheim, 1873.

Masaidek, Franz Friedrich. *Lose Gedanken*. Vienna: Ostdeustchen Rundschau, 1891.

Mayer, Sigmund. *Ein jüdischer Kaufmann, 1831 bis 1911: Lebenserinnerungen*. Leipzig: Duncker & Humblot, 1911.

Mayer, Sigmund. *Die Wiener Juden: Kommerz, Kultur, Politik, 1700–1900*. Vienna: R. Löwit Verlag, 1917.

Panizza, Oskar. "The Operated Jew." In *The Operated Jew, Two Tales of Anti-Semitism*, edited and translated by Jack Zipes, 42–74. New York: Routledge, 1991.

Schlossar, Anton. "Die Volkstrachten in Steiermark." *Neue illustrirte Zeitung*, October 21, 1883, 54.

Schnitzler, Arthur. *The Road into the Open (Der Weg ins Freie)*. Translated by Roger Byer. Berkeley, CA: University of California Press, 1992 [1908].

Schnitzler, Arthur. *Fräulein Else*. Translated by G. H. Lyon. London: Pushkin Press, 2001 [1924].

Schnitzler, Arthur. *Jugend in Wien: Eine Autobiographie*. Edited by Therese Nickl and Heinrich Schnitzler. Frankfurt am Main: Fischer Taschenbuch Verlag, 2011.

Sedlaczek, Stefan, Wilhelm Löwy and Wilhelm Becke, eds. *Statistisches Jahrbuch der Stadt Wien für das Jahr 1900*. Vienna: Verlag des Wiener Magistrates, 1902.

Simmel, Georg. "The Stranger." In *The Sociology of Georg Simmel*, translated and edited by Kurt H. Wolff, 402–8. New York: The Free Press, 1950.

Simmel, Georg. "Fashion." *The American Journal of Sociology* 62, no. 2 (May 1957 [1904]): 541–8.

Sombart, Werner. *The Jews and Modern Capitalism*. Translated by M. Epstein. Kitchener, ON: Batoche Books, 2001 [1911].

Tavel, Rudolf von. "Was ist uns die Volkstracht?" *Heimatschutz: Zeitschrift der Schweizerischen Vereinigung für Heimatschutz* 22, no. 6 (1927): 81–91.

Tesar, Franz. *Wiener Herrenkleidung*. Vienna: Selbstverlag der Genossenschaft der Kleidermacher Wiens, 1911.

Tietze, Hans. *Die Juden Wiens: Geschichte—Wirtschaft—Kultur*. Leipzig: E.P. Tal, 1935.

Uhl, Friedrich. "Wiener Kaffeehäuser." *Wiener Zeitung*, May 31, 1900, 3–5.

Veblen, Thorstein. *The Theory of the Leisure Class: An Economic Study of Institutions*. New York: Modern Library, 2011 [1899].

Wassermann, Jakob. *Mein Weg als Deutscher und Jude*. Berlin: S. Fischer Verlag, 1922.

Weininger, Otto. *Sex and Character: An Investigation of Fundamental Principles*. Translated by Ladislaus Löb, edited by Daniel Steuer and Laura Marcus. Bloomington, IN: Indiana University Press, 2005 [1903].

Wittels, Fritz. "Der heilige Lueger." *Die Bühne* 2, no. 17 (March 5, 1925): 30–3.

Zuckerkandl, Berta. *Österreich intim: Erinnerungen, 1882–1942*. Edited by Reinhard Federmann. Vienna: Amalthea, 2013.

Zweig, Stefan. *Beware of Pity*. Translated by Phyllis Blewitt and Trevor Blewitt. London: Cassell, 1953 [1939].

Zweig, Stefan. "Im Schnee." *Die Welt* 5, no. 31 (1901): 10–13.

Zweig, Stefan. *The World of Yesterday*. Translated by Anthea Bell. London: Pushkin Press, 2011 [1942].

Zweig, Stefan. *Messages from a Lost World: Europe on the Brink*. Translated by Will Stone. London: Pushkin Press, 2016.

(e) Unpublished Memoirs and Manuscripts

Apfelbaum, Leah. "This Is My Life: Eva Bostock." Unpublished memoir. Hunters Hill, NSW: The Montefiore Life History Program, 2010.

Bader, Lillian M. "One Life Is not Enough: Autobiographical Vignettes." Unpublished memoir. Leo Baeck Institute (1956), ME 784. MM II 4.

Furst, Ulrich R. "Windows to my Youth." Unpublished memoir. Leo Baeck Institute (1993), ME 902. MM II 14.

Glauber, Auguste. "Who We Are and Why We Are Here." Unpublished memoir. Leo Baeck Institute, ME 1137. MM II 33.

Grossman, Otto. "The Wandering Jew Nearing Journey's End." Unpublished memoir. Leo Baeck Institute (undated), MS 304. MSF 22, PID: 761945.

Kanfer, Robert. "The Family Memories of Robert Kanfer: Vienna—London—Cheltenham—Vienna." Unpublished memoir, Leo Baeck Institute, ME 1518. MM III 20.

Schaffir, Kurt H. "My Personal History, 1923–1940." Unpublished memoir, Leo Baeck Institute (1989), ME 1980. MM II 22.

Stein, Hans. "Vienna Childhood Memories." Unpublished memoir. Leo Baeck Institute (1998), ME 1180. MM II 36.

Tauber, Kurt. "To Greta: The Biography of Kurt Tauber." Unpublished memoir, Leo Baeck Institute [LBI], ME 1234. MM II 43.

Bibliography

(f) Sources Consulted Online

Archiv der IKG Wien. *Geburtsbuch der Israelitischen Kultusgemeinde Wien, C, 1858–1864*, entry no. 2948. Accessed via *FamilySearch*, https://www.familysearch.org/ark:/61903/3:1 :33S7-9BKB-DRX?i=181&wc=MQB6438%3A344266801%2C344266802%2C344410201 %3Fcc%3D2028320&cc=2028320.

Archiv der IKG Wien. *Geburtsbuch der Israelitischen Kultusgemeinde Wien, L, 1887–1888*, entry no. 1265. Accessed via https://www.familysearch.org/ark:/61903/3:1:33S7-8B24-722?i=92&cc =2028320&personaUrl=%2Fark%3A%2F61903%2F1%3A1%3A81KG-L1T2.

Archiv der IKG Wien. *Geburtsbuch der Israelitischen Kultusgemeinde Wien, 1904 Jan–June*, entry no. 178. Accessed via *FamilySearch*, https://www.familysearch.org/ark:/61903/3:1 :333S7-LB29-5BS?i=30&wc=MQB682S%3A344266801%2C344266802%2C344501801&cc =2028320, accessed June 6, 2018.

Archiv der IKG Wien. *Geburtsbuch der Israelitischen Kultusgemeinde Wien, 1909*, entry no. 1648. Accessed via *FamilySearch*, https://www.familysearch.org/ark:/61903/3:1:33S7-9B2Q-XLG?i =210&wc=4692-DX6%3A344266801%2C344266802%2C344528901&cc=2028320

Archiv der IKG Wien. *Index zu den Trauungsbüchern der Israelitischen Kultusgemeinde Wien, 1902–1903*, date August 26, 1903. Accessed via *Family Search*, https://www.familysearch.org /ark:/61903/3:1:33S7-9B23-VNQ?i=130&wc=4692-DXK%3A344266801%2C344266302 %2C344573301&cc=2028320.

Index of the Jewish Records of Vienna and Lower Austria. Accessed May 18, 2018, via *GenTeam: die genealogische Datenbank*, https://www.genteam.at/index/php?option=com_db53&id =145940&limitstart=40&n=schnitzler&v=&view=detail&lang=en

Index of the Jewish Records of Vienna and Lower Austria, entry no. 280456. Accessed May 18, 2018, via *GenTeam: Die genealogische Datenbank*, https://genteam.at/index.php?option=com_ db53&id=280456&limitstart=10&n=czopp&v=&view=detail&lang=en, accessed July 31, 2021.

"Karl Kraus aus eigenen Schriften (Tonfilm, 1934)." YouTube video, 18:04, from a recording of Karl Kraus reading excerpts from his writing, recorded by Albrecht Viktor Blum in Prague, 1934. Posted by "cbartolf," March 9, 2014, https://www.youtube.com/watch?v=rg -uGpBhs2g.

(g) Oral History Interviews and Personal Correspondence

Eva Bostock in discussion with author, September 2, 2015.

Eva Engel in discussion with author, November 14, 2017.

Ruth Kurschner, email to author, August 12, 2015.

Harry Rich in discussion with author, April 19, 2016.

Fritzi Ritterman, in discussion with author, August 5, 2015.

Susan Warhaftig, in discussion with author, July 3, 2022.

Lisl Ziegler in discussion with author, August 19, 2015.

Secondary Sources

(a) Books and Chapters in Edited Books

Anderson, Benedict. *Imagined Communities: Reflections on the Origin and Spread of Nationalism*. London: Verso, 2006.

Adunka, Evelyn, and Gabriele Anderl. *Jüdisches Leben in der Wiener Vorstadt Ottakring und Hernals*. Vienna: Mandelbaum, 2012.

Aizenberg, Salo. *Hatemail: Anti-Semitism on Picture Postcards*. Lincoln, NE: University of Nebraska Press, 2013.

Allen, Ann Taylor. *Satire and Society in Wilhelmine Germany: Kladderadatsch & Simplicissimus, 1890–1914*. Lexington, KY: University of Kentucky Press, 1984.

Anijar, Karen. "Jewish Genes, Jewish Jeans: A Fashionable Body." In *Religion Dress and the Body*, edited by Linda B. Arthur, 181–200. London: Berg, 1999.

Anjo, Hissako, and Antonia Finnane. "Tailoring in China and Japan: Cultural Transfer and Cutting Techniques in the Early Twentieth Century." In *Dressing Global Bodies: The Political Power of Dress in World History*, edited by Beverly Lemire and Giorgio Riello, 263–88. London: Routledge, 2019.

Arendt, Hannah. *The Origins of Totalitarianism*. New York: Harcourt Brace Jovanovich, 1973.

Arendt, Hannah. "Stefan Zweig: Jews in the World of Yesterday." In *The Jewish Writings*, edited by Jerome Kohn and Ron H. Feldman, 317–28. New York: Schocken Books 2007.

Aschheim, Steven E. *Brothers and Strangers: The East European Jew in German and German Jewish Consciousness, 1800–1923*. Madison, WI: The University of Wisconsin Press, 1982.

Ashby, Charlotte. "The Cafés of Vienna: Space and Sociability." In *The Viennese Café and Fin-de-Siècle Culture*, edited by Charlotte Ashby, Tag Gronberg and Simon Shaw-Miller, 9–31. New York: Berghahn Books, 2015.

Ashby, Charlotte, Tag Gronberg and Simon Shaw-Miller, eds. *The Viennese Café and Fin-de-Siècle Culture*. New York: Berghahn Books, 2015.

Avineri, Shlomo. *Herzl: Theodor Herzl and the Foundation of the Jewish State*. Translated by Haim Watzman. London: Phoenix, 2014.

Baigell, Matthew. *The Implacable Urge to Defame: Cartoon Jews in the American Press, 1877–1935*. Syracuse, NY: Syracuse University Press, 2017.

Barker, Andrew. "Peter Altenberg: Das Werk und das literarische Umfeld." In *Peter Altenberg, Extracte des Lebens: Einem Schriftsteller auf der Spur*, edited by Heinz Lunzer and Victoria Luzner-Talos, 9–16. Salzburg: Residenz Verlag, 2003.

Bartal, Israel. *The Jews of Eastern Europe, 1772–1881*. Translated by Chaya Naor. Philadelphia, PA: The University of Pennsylvania Press, 2005.

Batchen, Geoffrey. "Vernacular Photographies." In *Each Wild Idea: Writing, Photography, History*, 56–80. Cambridge, MA: The MIT Press, 2001.

Baudelaire, Charles. *The Painter of Modern Life and Other Essays*. Translated by Jonathan Mayne. London: Phaidon Press, 1995.

Bauman, Zygmunt. *Modernity and Ambivalence*. Cambridge: Polity Press, 1991.

Beck, Knut, Jeffery B. Berlin and Natascha Weschenbach-Feggeler, eds. *Stefan Zweig: Briefe, 1897–1914*. Frankfurt am Main: Fischer, 1995.

Beckermann, Ruth, ed. *Die Mazzesinsel: Juden in der Wiener Leopoldstadt, 1918–1938*. Vienna: Löcker Verlag, 1984.

Bedoire, Frederic. *The Jewish Contribution to Modern Architecture, 1830–1930*. Translated by Roger Tanner. Jersey City, NJ: KTAV Publishing House, 2004.

Beller, Steven. *Vienna and the Jews, 1867–1938: A Cultural History*. Cambridge: Cambridge University Press, 1989.

Beller, Steven. "'The Jew Belongs in the Coffeehouse': Jews, Central Europe and Modernity." In *The Viennese Café and Fin-de-Siècle Culture*, edited by Charlotte Ashby, Tag Gronberg and Simon Shaw-Miller, 50–8. New York: Berghahn Books, 2015.

Beller, Steven. "Dis-Oriented Jews? Orientalism, Assimilation, and Modernism in Vienna 1900." In *Design Dialogue: Jews, Culture and Viennese Modernism/Design Dialog: Juden, Kultur und Wiener Moderne*, edited by Elana Shapira, 299–311. Vienna: Böhlau Verlag, 2018.

Beneš, Jakub S. *Workers & Nationalism: Czech and German Social Democracy in Habsburg Austria, 1890–1918*. Oxford: Oxford University Press, 2017.

Bibliography

Biale, David, David Assaf, Benjamin Brown, Uriel Gellman, Samuel C. Heilman, Moshe Rosman, Gadi Sagiv and Marcin Wodziński. *Hasidism: A New History*. Princeton, NJ: Princeton University Press, 2018.

Bills, Mark. *The Art of Satire: London in Caricature*. London: Philip Wilson Publishers and the Museum of London, 2006.

Bodemann, Y. Michal. "Coldly Admiring the Jews: Werner Sombart and Classical German Sociology on Nationalism and Race." In *Antisemitism and the Constitution of Sociology*, edited by Marcel Stoetzler, 110–34. Lincoln, NE: Nebraska University Press, 2014.

Bonyhady, Tim. *Good Living Street: The Fortunes of My Viennese Family*. Crows Nest, NSW: Allen & Unwin, 2014.

Bourdieu, Pierre. "The Social Definition of Photography." In *Photography: A Middle-Brow Art*. Translated by Shaun Whiteside, 73–93. Cambridge, MA: Polity Press 1990.

Boyer, John W. *Political Radicalism in Late Imperial Vienna: Origins of the Christian Social Movements, 1848–1897*. Chicago, IL: The University of Chicago Press, 1981.

Breward, Christopher. *The Hidden Consumer: Masculinities, Fashion and City Life, 1860–1914*. Manchester: Manchester University Press, 1999.

Breward, Christopher. *The Suit: Form, Function and Style*. London: Reaktion Books, 2016.

Brisman, Shira. "Biographies." In *Jewish Women and Their Salon: The Power of Conversation*, edited by Emily D. Bilski and Emily Braun, 195–213. New York: The Jewish Museum/New Haven, CT: Yale University Press, 2005.

Brix, Emil. "Assimilation in the Late Habsburg Monarchy." In *Österreich-Konzeptionen und jüdisches Selbstverständnis: Identitäts-Transfigurationen im 19. Und 20. Jahrhundert*, edited by Hanni Mittelmann and Armin A. Wallas, 29–41. Tübingen: Max Niemeyer Verlag, 2001.

Brubaker, Rogers. *Citizenship and Nationhood in France and Germany*. Cambridge, MA: Harvard University Press, 1992.

Bruckmüller, Ernst. *The Austrian Nation: Cultural Consciousness and Socio-Political Processes*. Translated by Lowell A. Bangerter. Riverside, CA: Ariadne Press, 2003.

Burke, Janine. *The Gods of Freud: Sigmund Freud's Art Collection*. Milsons Point, NSW: Random House Australia, 2006.

Burri, Michael. "Theodor Herzl and Richard Schaukal: Self-Styled Nobility and the Sources of Bourgeois Belligerence in Prewar Vienna." In *Rethinking Vienna 1900*, edited by Steven Beller, 105–31. New York: Berghahn Books, 2001.

Buxbaum, Gerda. *Mode aus Wien, 1815–1938*. Salzburg: Residenz Verlag, 1986.

Byrde, Penelope. *The Male Image: Men's Fashion in England, 1300–1970*. London: B. T. Batsford, 1979.

Čapková, Kateřina. *Czechs, Germans, Jews? National Identity and the Jews of Bohemia*. Translated by Derek and Marzia Paton. New York: Berghahn Books, 2012.

Carter, Michael. *Being Prepared: Aspects of Dress and Dressing*. Sydney: Puncher & Wattmann, 2017.

Clare, George. *Last Waltz in Vienna*. London: Pan Books, 2007.

Clarke, Graham. *The Photograph*. Oxford: Oxford University Press, 1997.

Coen, Deborah R. *Vienna in the Age of Uncertainty: Science, Liberalism, and Private Life*. Chicago, IL: The University of Chicago Press, 2007.

Cohen, Gary B. "Jews Among Vienna's Educated Middle Class Elements at the Turn of the Century: A Comment on Steven Beller." In *A Social and Economic History of Central European Jewry*, edited by Yehuda Don and Victor Karady, 179–89. New Brunswick, NJ: Transaction Publications, 1990.

Cohen, Julia Phillips, and Sarah Abrevaya Stein, eds. *Sephardi Lives: A Documentary History, 1700–1950*. Stanford, CA: Stanford University Press, 2014.

Cohen, Richard I. *Jewish Icons: Art and Society in Modern Europe*. Berkley, CA: University of California Press, 1998.

Corcos, Alain F. *The Myth of the Jewish Race: A Biologist's Point of View*. Bethlehem, PA: Lehigh University Press, 2005.

Costello, Mary. "Adolf Loos's Kärntner Bar: Reception, Reinvention, Reproduction." In *The Viennese Café and Fin-de-Siècle Culture*, edited by Charlotte Ashby, Tag Gronberg and Simon Shaw-Miller, 138–57. New York: Berghahn Books, 2015.

Coupe, W. A. "*Kikeriki* und die Minderheiten der Donaumonarchie." In *Satire–Parodie Pamphlet–Caricature: en Autriche à l'époque de François-Joseph (1848–1914)*, edited by Gilbert Ravy and Jeanne Benay, 61–88. Rouen: Université de Rouen, 1999.

Crawford, Mike. "Hand Colouring and Hand Toning." In *Encyclopedia of Twentieth-Century Photography: Volume 1: A–F*, edited by Lynne Warren, 669–70. New York: Routledge, 2006.

Deak, John. *Forging a Multinational State: State Making in Imperial Austria from the Enlightenment to the First World War*. Stanford, CA: Stanford University Press, 2015.

De Waal, Edmund. *The Hare with Amber Eyes: A Hidden Inheritance*. London: Vintage, 2011.

Diderot, Denis. "Regrets on Parting with My Old Dressing Gown: Or, A Warning to Those Who Have More Taste than Money." In *The Eighteenth Century*, edited by Peter McNeil, 22–5. Vol. 2. *Fashion: Critical and Primary Sources*. Oxford: Berg, 2009.

Dienstbier, Jan. "The Metamorphosis of the *Judensau*." In *Visual Antisemitism in Central Europe: Imagery of Hatred*, edited by Jakub Hauser and Eva Janáčová, 1–34. Berlin: Walter de Gruyter, 2021.

Diemling, Maria. "'As the Jews Like to Eat Garlick': Garlic in the Christian-Jewish Polemical Discourse in Early Modern Germany." In *Food and Judaism: Studies in Jewish Civilization 15*, edited by Leonard J. Greenspoon, Ronald A. Simkins and Gerald Shapiro, 215–34. Omaha, NE: Creighton University Press, 2004.

Donahue, William Collins. *The End of Modernism: Elias Canetti's Auto-da-Fé*. Chapel Hill, NC: University of North Carolina Press, 2001.

Donald, Diana. *Followers of Fashion: Graphic Satires from the Georgian Period*. London: Hayward Gallery Publishing and the British Museum, 2007.

Ehrlich, Leonard H. and Edith Ehrlich. *Choices under Duress of the Holocaust: Benjamin Murmelstein and the Fate of Viennese Jewry. Vol. 1. Vienna*, edited by Carl S. Ehrlich. Lubbock, TX: Texas Tech University Press, 2018.

Eidherr, Armin. "Die jiddische Kultur in Wien der Zwischenkriegszeit und ihre Positionierungen in Bezug auf Akkulturation, Diasporanationalismus und Zionismus." *Wien und die jüdische Erfahrung, 1900–1938: Akkulturation—Antisemitismus—Zionismus*, edited by Frank Stern and Barbara Eichinger, 175–95. Vienna: Böhlau Verlag, 2009.

Endelman, Todd M. *The Jews of Britain, 1656–2000*. Berkeley, CA: University of California Press, 2000.

Endelman, Todd M. "Gender and Conversion Revisited." In *Gender and Jewish History*, edited by Marion A. Kaplan and Deborah Dash Moore, 170–86. Bloomington, IN: Indiana University Press, 2011.

Entwistle, Joanne. *The Fashioned Body: Fashion, Dress and Modern Social Theory*. 2nd ed. Cambridge, MA: Polity Press, 2015.

Eber, Irene. *Wartime Shanghai and the Jewish Refugees from Central Europe: Survival, Co-Existence, and Identity in a Multi-Ethnic City*. Berlin: Walter de Gruyter, 2013.

Evans, R. J. W. *Austria, Hungary, and the Habsburgs: Essays on Central Europe, c. 1683–1867*. Oxford: Oxford University Press, 2006.

Fanon, Frantz. *Black Skin, White Masks*. Translated by Charles Lam Markmann. London: Pluto Press, 1986.

Bibliography

Finkielkraut, Alain. *The Imaginary Jew*. Translated by Kevin O'Neill and David Suchoff. Lincoln, NE: University of Nebraska Press, 1994.

Frankel, Jonathan. "Assimilation and the Jews in Nineteenth-Century Europe: Towards a New Historiography?" In *Assimilation and Community: The Jews in Nineteenth-Century Europe*, edited by Jonathan Frankel and Steven J. Zipperstein, 1–37. Cambridge: Cambridge University Press, 1992.

Freidenreich, Harriet Pass. *Jewish Politics in Vienna, 1918–1938*. Bloomington, IN: Indiana University Press, 1991.

Freud, Martin. *Glory Reflected: Sigmund Freud—Man and Father*. London: Angus and Robertson, 1957.

Frübis, Hildegard. "Ephraim Moses Lilien: The Figure of the 'Beautiful Jewess,' the Orient, the Bible, and Zionism." Translated by Andrew Boreham. In *Orientalism, Gender, and the Jews: Literary and Artistic Transformations of European National Discourses*, edited by Ulrike Brunotte, Anna-Dorothea Ludewig and Axel Stähler, 82–97. Berlin: De Gruyter, 2015.

Garelick, Rhonda K. *Rising Star: Dandyism, Gender, and Performance in the Fin de Siècle*. Princeton, NJ: Princeton University Press.

Ganeva, Mila. *Women in Weimar Fashion: Discourses and Displays in German Culture, 1918–1933*. Rochester, NY: Camden House, 2008.

Gaugusch, Georg. *Wer Einmal War: Das jüdische Großbürgertum Wiens, 1800–1938*. 2 Vols. Vienna: Amalthea Signum Verlag, 2011–16.

Gaugusch, Georg. "Wilhelm Jungmann & Neffe: 150 Jahre einer Wiener Firma—Wilhelm Jungmann & Neffe: 150 Years of a Viennese Company." In *Kauft bei Juden! Geschichte einer Wiener Geschäftskultur—Buy from Jews! Story of a Viennese Store Culture*, edited by Astrid Peterle, 94–113. Vienna: Amalthea and Jüdisches Museum Wien, 2017.

Gay, Peter. *Freud, Jews and Other Germans: Masters and Victims in Modernist Culture*. Oxford: Oxford University Press, 1978.

Gay, Peter. *Freud: A Life for Our Time*. London: Papermac, 1989.

Gelber, Mark H. *Melancholy Pride: Nation, Race, and Gender in the German Literature of Cultural Zionism*. Tübingen: Max Niemayer Verlag, 2000.

Gelber, Mark H. "Interfaces between Young Vienna and the Young Jewish Poetic Movement: Richard Beer Hofmann and Stefan Zweig." In *Jüdische Aspekte Junge-Wiens in Kulturkontext des »Fin de Siècle«*, edited by Sarah Fraiman-Morris, 75–93. Tübingen: Max Niemayer Verlag, 2005.

Gelber, Mark H. *Stefan Zweig, Judentum und Zionismus*. Innsbruck: Studien Verlag, 2014.

Gelbin, Cathy S. and Sander L. Gilman. *Cosmopolitanisms and the Jews*. Ann Arbor, MI: University of Michigan Press, 2017.

Gilman, Sander L. "Race and Madness in I. J. Singer's *The Family Carnovsky*." In *Difference and Pathology: Stereotypes of Sexuality, Race, and Madness*, 163–74. Ithaca, NY: Cornell University Press, 1985.

Gilman, Sander. *The Jew's Body*. New York: Routledge, 1991.

Gluck, Mary. *Invisible Jewish Budapest: Metropolitan Culture at the Fin de Siècle*. Madison, WI: The University of Wisconsin Press, 2016.

Gold, Hugo. *Geschichte der Juden in Österreich: Ein Gedenkbuch*. Tel Aviv: Olamenu, 1971.

Goldstein, Gabriel M., and Elizabeth E. Greenberg, eds. *A Perfect Fit: The Garment Industry and American Jewry, 1860–1960*. Lubbock, TX: Texas University Press, 2012.

Golomb, Jacob. "Stefan Zweig's Tragedy as a Nietzschean *Grenzjude*." In *Jüdische Aspekte Jung-Wiens im Kulturkontext des »Fin de Siècle«*, edited by Sarah Fraiman-Morris, 75–93. Tübingen: Max Niemayer Verlag, 2005.

Gordon, Milton M. *Assimilation in American Life: The Role of Race, Religion, and National Origins*. New York: Oxford University Press, 1964.

Grafe, Christoph. "The Architecture of Cafés, Coffee Houses and Public Bars." In *Cafés and Bars: The Architecture of Public Display*, edited by Christoph Grafe and Franziska Bollery, 4–41. New York: Routledge, 2007.

Greenblatt, Stephen. *Renaissance Self-Fashioning: From More to Shakespeare*. Chicago, IL: The University of Chicago Press, 1980.

Greenspoon, Leonard J., ed. *Fashioning Jews: Clothing, Culture, and Commerce*. West Lafayette, IN: Purdue University Press, 2013.

Gronberg, Tag. "Coffeehouse Orientalism." In *The Viennese Café and Fin-de-Siècle Culture*, edited by Charlotte Ashby, Tag Gronberg and Simon Shaw-Miller, 59–77. New York: Berghahn Books, 2015.

Haas, Hans. "Der Traum vom Dazugehören—Juden auf Sommerfrische." In *Der Geschmack der Vergänglichkeit: Jüdische Sommerfrische in Salzburg*, edited by Robert Kriechbaumer, 41–57. Vienna: Böhlau Verlag, 2002.

Habermas, Jürgen. *The Structural Transformation of the Public Sphere: An Inquiry into a Category of Bourgeois Society*. Translated by Thomas Burger. Cambridge: Polity Press, 1989.

Hanák, Péter. "Urbanization and Civilization: Vienna and Budapest in the Nineteenth Century." In *The Garden and the Workshop" Essays on the Cultural History of Vienna and Budapest*, 3–43. Princeton, NJ: Princeton University Press, 1998.

Hanak, Werner. "Von Bärten und Propheten; Oder: Theodor Herzl, Hermann Bahr und die Folgen des 'antisemitic turns' der Wiener 1880er Jahre." In *Design Dialogue: Jews, Culture and Viennese Modernism/Design Dialog: Juden, Kulur und Wiener Moderne*, edited by Elana Shapira, 313–28. Vienna: Böhlau Verlag, 2018.

Hart, Mitchell B., ed. *Jews & Race: Writings on Identity & Difference, 1880–1940*. Waltham, MA: Brandeis University Press, 2011.

Harvey, John. *Men in Black*. London: Reaktion Books, 1995.

Heinz, Dora. "Viennese Men's Fashions." In *The Imperial Style: Fashions of the Habsburg Era: Based on the Exhibition Fashions of the Habsburg Era: Austria-Hungary at the Metropolitan Museum of Art, December 1979–August 1980*, edited by Polly Cone, 101–8. New York: The Metropolitan Museum of Art, 1980.

Hertz, Deborah. *How Jews Became Germans: The History of Conversation and Assimilation in Berlin*. New Haven, CT: Yale University Press, 2007.

Herzog, Hilary Hope. *"Vienna Is Different": Jewish Writers in Austria from the Fin de Siècle to the Present*. New York: Berghahn Books, 2011.

Hödl, Klaus. *Als Bettler in die Leopoldstadt: Galizische Juden auf dem Weg nach Wien*, 2nd ed. Vienna: Böhlau Verlag, 1994.

Hollander, Anne. *Sex and Suits*. New York: Alfred A. Knopf, 1994.

Houze, Rebecca. *Textiles, Fashion, and Design Reform in Austria-Hungary Before the First World War: Principles of Dress*. Farnham: Ashgate, 2015.

Hundert, Gershon David. *Jews in Poland-Lithuania in the Eighteenth Century: A Genealogy of Modernity*. Berkeley, CA: University of California Press, 2004.

Iggers, Wilma Abeles. *Karl Kraus: A Viennese Critic of the Twentieth Century*. The Hague: Martinus Nijhoff, 1967.

John, Michael. "Jews as Consumers and Providers in provincial Towns: The Example of Linz and Salzburg, 1900–1938." In *Longing, Belonging, and the Making of Jewish Consumer Culture*, edited by Gideon Reuveni and Nils Roemer, 139–62. Leiden: Brill, 2010.

John, Michael. "Migration in Austria: An Overview of the 1920s to 2000s." In *Understanding Multiculturalism: The Habsburg Central European Experience*, edited by Johannes Feichtinger and Gary B. Cohen, 122–57. New York: Berghahn, 2014.

John, Michael, and Albert Lichtblau. *Schmelztiegel Wien—Einst und Jetzt: Zur Geschichte und Gegenwart von Zuwanderung und Minderheiten*. Vienna: Böhlau Verlag, 1990.

Bibliography

Johnson, Julie M. *The Memory Factory: The Forgotten Women Artists of Vienna 1900*. West Lafayette, IN: Purdue University Press, 2012.

Jones, Ernest. *Sigmund Freud: Life and Work*, 3 vols. London: Hogarth Press, 1972–74.

Judson, Pieter M. "Do Multiple Languages Mean a Multicultural Society? Nationalist 'Frontiers' in Rural Austria, 1880–1918." In *Understanding Multiculturalism: The Habsburg Central European Experience*, edited by Johannes Feichtinger and Gary B. Cohen, 61–82. New York: Berghahn Books, 2014.

Kammerhofer-Aggermann, Ulrike. "Dirndl, Lederhose und Sommerfrischenidylle." In *Der Geschmack der Vergänglichkeit: Jüdische Sommerfrische in Salzburg*, edited by Robert Kriechbaumer, 317–34. Vienna: Böhlau Verlag, 2002.

Kann, Robert A. *A History of the Habsburg Empire, 1526–1918*. Berkeley, CA: The University of California Press, 1974.

Kaplan, Marion A. "Gender and Jewish History in Imperial Germany." In *Assimilation and Community: The Jews in Nineteenth-Century Europe*, edited by Jonathan Frankel and Steven J. Zipperstein, 199–224. Cambridge: Cambridge University Press, 1992.

Kaplan, Morris B. "Refiguring the Jewish Question: Arendt, Proust, and the Politics of Sexuality." In *Feminist Interpretations of Hannah Arendt*, edited by Bonnie Honig, 105–33. University Park, PA: The Pennsylvania State University Press, 1995.

Kessler, Helga. "Viennese Biedermeier Fashion." In *The Imperial Style: Fashions of the Habsburg Era: Based on the Exhibition Fashions of the Habsburg Era: Austria-Hungary at the Metropolitan Museum of Art, December 1979–August 1980*, edited by Polly Cone, 43–63. New York: The Metropolitan Museum of Art, 1980.

Klein, Rudolf. *The Great Synagogue of Budapest*. Budapest: TERC, 2008.

Kremer, Roberta S., ed. *Broken Threads: The Destruction of the Jewish Fashion Industry in Germany and Austria*. Oxford: Berg, 2007.

Kriechbaumer, Robert, ed. *Der Geschmack der Vergänglichkeit: Jüdische Sommerfrische in Salzburg*. Vienna: Böhlau Verlag, 2002.

Kruger, Steven F. "Becoming Christian, Becoming Male?" In *Becoming Male in the Middle Ages*, edited by Jeffrey Jerome Cohen and Bonnie Wheeler, 21–41. New York: Garland Publishing, 2000.

Kuchta, David. *The Three-Piece Suit and Modern Masculinity: England, 1550–1850*. Berkeley, CA: University of California Press, 2002.

Kunzel-Runtscheiner, Monica. "The Magic of the Uniform: Dress Codes, Fashion Dictates and the Spread of Civilian Uniforms Through the Congress of Vienna." In *Fashion Drive: Extreme Clothing in the Visual Arts*, edited by Catherine Hug and Christoph Becker, 150–7. Bielefeld: Kunsthaus Zürich and Kerber Culture, 2018.

Kupferschmidt, Uri M. *European Department Stores and Middle Eastern Consumers: The Orosdi-Back Saga*. Istanbul: Ottoman Bank Archive and Research Centre, 2007.

Kwan, Jonathan. *Liberalism and the Habsburg Monarchy, 1861–1895*. Basingstoke: Palgrave Macmillan, 2013.

Le Rider, Jacques. *Modernity and Crisis of Identity: Culture and Society in Fin-de-Siècle Vienna*. Translated by Rosemary Morris. Cambridge: Polity Press, 1993.

Lerner, Paul. *Consuming Temple: Jews, Department Stores, and the Consumer Revolution in Germany, 1880–1914*. Ithaca, NY: Cornell University Press, 2015.

Liberles, Robert. *Jews Welcome Coffee: Tradition and Innovation in Early Modern Germany*. Waltham, MA: Brandeis University Press, 2012.

Lipmann, Anthony. *Divinely Elegant: The World of Ernst Dryden*. London: Pavilion Books, 1989.

Loos, Claire Beck. *Adolf Loos: A Private Portrait*. Edited by Carrie Patterson. Los Angeles: DoppelHouse Press, 2011.

Lunzer, Heinz. "Kindheit, Jugend in einer wohlhabenden Kaufmannsfamilie." In *Peter Altenberg, Extracte des Lebens: einem Schriftsteller auf der Spur*, edited by Heinz Lunzer and Victoria Lunzer-Talos, 18–23. Salzburg: Residenz Verlag, 2003.

Lunzer-Talos, Victoria. "Judentum—Antisemitismus." In *Peter Altenberg, Extracte des Lebens: Einem Schriftsteller auf der Spur*, edited by Heinz Lunzer and Victoria Luzner-Talos, 53–7. Salzburg: Residenz Verlag, 2003.

Máčel, Otakar. "American Bar (Kärntner Bar)." In *Cafés and Bars: The Architecture of Public Display*, edited by Christoph Grafe and Franziska Bollery, 140–4. New York: Routledge, 2007.

Malkin, Jeanette R., and Freddie Rokem, eds. *Jews and the Making of Modern German Theater*. Iowa City, IA: University of Iowa Press, 2010.

Matuschek, Oliver. *Three Lives: A Biography of Stefan Zweig*. Translated by Allan Blunden. London: Pushkin Press, 2011.

Maxwell, Alexander. *Patriots Against Fashion: Clothing and Nationalism in Europe's Age of Revolutions*. Basingstoke: Palgrave Macmillan, 2014.

McAuley, James. *The House of Fragile Things: Jewish Art Collectors and the Fall of France*. New Haven, CT: Yale University Press, 2021.

McCagg Jr., William O. *A History of Habsburg Jews, 1670–1918*. Bloomington, IN: Indiana University Press, 1989.

McCagg, William O. "The Jewish Population in Interwar Central Europe: A Structural Study of Jewry at Vienna, Budapest, and Prague." In *A Social and Economic History of Central European Jewry*, edited by Yehuda Don and Victor Karady, 47–81. New Brunswick, NJ: Transaction Publishers, 1990.

McNeil, Peter. "The Beauty of the Everyday." In *Dressing Sydney: The Jewish Fashion Story*, edited by Sydney Jewish Museum, 91–47. Darlinghurst, NSW: Sydney Jewish Museum, 2012.

McNeil, Peter. "Ideology, Fashion and the Darlys' 'Macaroni' Prints." In *Dress and Ideology: Fashioning Identity from Antiquity to the Present*, edited by Shoshana-Rose Marzel and Guy D. Stiebel, 111–36. London: Bloomsbury, 2015.

McNeil, Peter. "Despots of Elegance: Men's Fashion, 1715–1915." In *Reigning Men: Fashion in Menswear, 1715–2015*, edited by Sharon Sadako Takeda, Kaye Durland Spilker and Clarissa M. Esquerra, 235–47. Munich: Los Angeles County Museum of Art, and DelMonica Books, 2016.

McNeil, Peter. "'Everything Degenerates': The Queer Buttonhole." In *Floriographie: Die Sprache der Blumen*, edited by Isabel Kranz, Alexander Schwan and Eike Wittrock, 389–408. Berlin: Wilhelm Fink, 2016.

Mendelsohn, Adam D. *The Rag Race: How Jews Sewed Their War to Success in America and the British Empire*. New York: New York University Press, 2015.

Mendes-Flohr, Paul R., and Jehuda Reinharz, eds. *The Jew in the Modern World: A Documentary History*. New York: Oxford University Press, 1980.

Meyer, Michael A. "Women in the Thought and Practice of the European Jewish Reform Movement." In *Gender and Jewish History*, edited by Marion A. Kaplan and Deborah Dash Moore, 139–57. Bloomington, IN: Indiana University Press, 2011.

Meyerrose, Anja. *Herren im Anzug: Eine transatlantische Geschichte von Klassengesellschaften im langen 19. Jahrhundert*. Cologne: Böhlau Verlag, 2016.

Miller, Michael B. *The Bon Marché: Bourgeois Culture and the Department Store, 1869–1920*. Princeton, NJ: Princeton University Press, 1981.

Miller, Michael Laurence. *Rabbis and Revolution: The Jews of Moravia in the Age of Emancipation*. Stanford, CA: Stanford University Press, 2011.

Miller, Michael L., and Scott Ury, eds. *Cosmopolitanism, Nationalism and the Jews of East Central Europe*. Abingdon: Routledge, 2015.

Mittelmann, Hanni, and Armin A. Wallas. "Österreich-Konzeption und jüdisches Selbstverständnis: Identitäts-Transfigurationen im 19. Und 20. Jahrhundert." In *Österreich-Konzeption und jüdisches Selbstverständnis: Identitäts-Transfigurationen im 19. Und 20.*

Jahrhundert, edited by Hanni Mittelmann and Armin A. Wallas, 1–10. Tübingen: Max Niemeyer Verlag, 2001.

Moers, Ellen. *The Dandy: Brummell to Beerbohm.* New York: The Viking Press, 1960.

Moores, John Richard. *Representations of France in English Satirical Prints, 1740–1832.* Basingstoke: Palgrave Macmillan, 2015.

Mosse, George L. "Jewish Emancipation: Between *Bildung* and Respectability." In *The Jewish Response to German Culture: From the Enlightenment to the Second World War*, edited by Jehuda Reinharz and Walter Schatzberg, 1–16. Hanover, NH: University Press of New England, 1985.

Nahshon, Edna, ed. *Jews and Shoes.* Oxford: Berg, 2008.

Offenberger, Ilana Fritz. *The Jews of Nazi Vienna, 1938–1945: Rescue and Destruction.* Cham: Palgrave Macmillan, 2017.

O'Neill, Alistair. *London After a Fashion.* London: Reaktion Books, 2007.

Osserman, Jordan. *Circumcision on the Couch: The Cultural, Psychological, and Gendered Dimensions of the World's Oldest Surgery.* London: Bloomsbury, 2022.

Österreichische Nationalbibliothek, ed. *Handbuch österreichischer Autorinnen und Autoren jüdischer Herkunft 18. Bis 20. Jahrhundert.* Vol. 1. A–1, 1-4541. Munich: K.G. Saur, 2002.

Oxaal, Ivar, Michael Pollak and Gerhard Botz, eds. *Jews, Antisemitism and Culture in Vienna.* London: Routledge and Kegan Paul, 1987.

Pacyga, Dominic A. *American Warsaw: The Rise, Fall, and Rebirth of Polish Chicago.* Chicago, IL: The University of Chicago Press, 2019.

Pauley, Bruce F. *From Prejudice to Persecution: A History of Austrian Anti-Semitism.* Chapel Hill, NC: The University of North Carolina Press, 1991.

Peterle, Astrid, ed. *Kauft bei Juden! Geschichte einer Wiener Geschäftskultur—Buy from Jews! Story of a Viennese Store Culture.* Vienna: Amalthea and Jüdisches Museum Wien, 2017.

Peterle, Astrid. "Kauft (nicht) bei Juden! Zerstörung einer Wiener Geschäftskultur, 1938–1945—(Don't) Buy from Jews! Destruction of a Viennese Store Culture, 1938–1945." In *Kauft bei Juden! Geschichte einer Wiener Geschäftskultur—Buy from Jews! Story of a Viennese Store Culture*, edited by Astrid Peterle, 164–79. Vienna: Amalthea Verlag and Jüdisches Museum Wien, 2017.

Peterle, Astrid. "Wien im Kaufrausch! Die Blüte der Wiener Kaufhäuser und k.u.k. Hoflieferanten—Vienna Goes Sopping! The Heyday of the Viennese Retail Stores and Court-Appointed Suppliers." In *Kauft bei Juden! Geschichte einer Wiener Geschäftskultur—Buy from Jews! Story of a Viennese Store Culture*, edited by Astrid Peterle, 66–93. Vienna: Amalthea and Jüdisches Museum Wien, 2017.

Philippi, Dieter. *Sammlung Philippi: Kopfbedeckung in Glaube, Religion und Spiritualität.* Leipzig: Benno, 2009.

Philips, Adam. *Becoming Freud: The Making of a Psychoanalyst.* New Haven, CT: Yale University Press, 2014.

Pickus, Keith H. *Constructing Modern Identities: Jewish University Students in Germany, 1815–1914.* Detroit, MI: Wayne State University Press, 1999.

Pinsker, Shachar M. "Between 'The House of Study' and the Coffeehouse: The Central European Café as a Site for Hebrew and Yiddish Modernism." In *The Viennese Café and Fin-de-Siècle Culture*, edited by Charlotte Ashby, Tag Gronberg and Simon Shaw-Miller, 78–97. New York: Berghahn Books, 2015.

Pinsker, Shachar M. *A Rich Brew: How Cafés Created Modern Jewish Culture.* New York: New York University Press, 2018.

Rabinovici, Doron. *Eichmann's Jews: The Jewish Administration of Holocaust Vienna, 1938–1945.* Translated by Nick Somers. Cambridge, MA: Polity Press, 2011.

Rechter, David. *Becoming Habsburg: The Jews of Austrian Bukovina, 1774–1918.* Oxford: Littman Library of Jewish Civilization, 2013.

Reddy, Vanita. *Fashioning Diaspora: Beauty, Femininity, and South Asian American Culture.* Philadelphia, PA: Temple University Press, 2016.

Reichwald, Annika. *Das Phantasma der Assimilation: Interpretationen des »Jüdischen« in der deutschen Phantastik 1890–1930.* Göttingen: Vandenhoeck & Rupprecht, 2017.

Reifowitz, Ian. *Imagining an Austrian Nation: Joseph Samuel Bloch and the Search for a Multiethnic Austrian Society, 1846–1919.* Boulder, CO: East European Monographs, 2003.

Reitter, Paul. *The Anti-Journalist: Karl Kraus and Jewish Self-Fashioning in Fin-de-Siècle Europe.* Chicago, IL: The University of Chicago Press, 2008.

Robertson, Ritchie. "Introduction." In Arthur Schnitzler, *Round Dance and Other Plays.* Translated by J. M. Q. Davies, vii–xxiii. Oxford: Oxford University Press, 2004.

Rose, Clare. *Making, Selling and Wearing Boys' Clothes in Late-Victorian England.* Farnham: Ashgate, 2010.

Rozenblit, Marsha L. *The Jews of Vienna, 1867–1914: Assimilation and Identity.* Albany, NY: State University of New York, 1983.

Rozenblit, Marsha L. "Jewish Assimilation in Habsburg Vienna." In *Assimilation and Community: The Jews in Nineteenth-Century Europe,* edited by Jonathan Frankel and Steven J. Zipperstein, 225–45. Cambridge: Cambridge University Press, 1992.

Rozenblit, Marsha L. *Reconstructing a National Identity: The Jews of Habsburg Austria during World War I.* New York: Oxford University Press, 2001.

Rubens, Alfred. *A History of Jewish Dress.* London: Weidenfeld and Nicolson, 1973.

Rukschcio, Burkhardt, and Roland Schachel. *Adolf Loos: Leben und Werk.* Salzburg: Residenz Verlag, 1982.

Salah, Asher. "How should a Rabbi Be Dressed? The Question of Rabbinical Attire in Italy from Renaissance to Emancipation (Sixteenth–Nineteenth Centuries)." In *Fashioning Jews: Clothing, Culture, and Commerce,* edited by Leonard J. Greenspoon, 49–66. West Lafayette, IN: Purdue University Press, 2013.

Samuel, Raphael. *Theatres of Memory: Past and Present in Contemporary Culture.* London: Verso, 2012.

Sandgruber, Roman. *Traumzeit für Millionäre: Die 929 reichsten Wienerinnen und Wiener im Jahr 1910.* Vienna: Sytria Premium, 2013.

Schorske, Carl E. *Fin-de-Siècle Vienna: Politics and Culture.* Cambridge: Cambridge University Press, 1979.

Schütt, Günter. *Karl Kraus und sein Verhältnis zum (Ost-)Judentum.* Vienna: Mandelbaum Verlag, 2017.

Schweiger, Werner J. *Wiener Werkstätte: Design in Vienna, 1903–1932.* London: Thames and Hudson, 1984.

Secklehner, Julia. "Simple Entertainment? *Die Muskete* and 'Weak' Antisemitism in Interwar Vienna." In *Visual Antisemitism in Central Europe: Imagery of Hatred,* edited by Jakub Hauser and Eva Janáčová, 123–43. Berlin: De Gruyter, 2021.

Segel, Harold B. *The Vienna Coffeehouse Wits, 1890–1938.* West Lafayette, IN: Purdue University Press, 1993.

Sennett, Richard. *Flesh and Stone: The City and the Body in Western Civilization.* New York: W. W. Norton and Company, 1996.

Severit, Frauke. *Ea von Allesch: Wenn aus Frauen Menschen werden: Eine Biographie.* Wiesbaden: Deutscher Universitäts-Verlag, 1999.

Shanes, Joshua. *Diaspora Nationalism and Jewish Identity in Habsburg Galicia.* Cambridge: Cambridge University Press, 2012.

Shapira, Elana. "Tailored Authorship: Adolf Loos and the Ethos of Men's Fashion." In *Leben mit Loos,* edited by Inge Podbrecky and Rainald Franz, 53–72. Vienna: Böhlau Verlag, 2008.

Bibliography

Shapira, Elana. "Jewish Identity, Mass Consumption, and Modern Design." In *Longing, Belonging, and the Making of Jewish Consumer Culture*, edited by Gideon Reuveni and Nils Roemer, 61–90. Leiden: Brill, 2010.

Shapira, Elana. "Imagining the Jew: A Clash of Civilisations." In *Facing the Modern: The Portrait in Vienna 1900*, edited by Gemma Blackshaw, 155–71. London: National Gallery and Yale University Press, 2013.

Shapira, Elana. *Style and Seduction: Jewish Patrons, Architecture, and Design in Fin de Siècle Vienna*. Waltham, MA: Brandeis University Press, 2016.

Sheehan, Tanya. "Looking Pleasant, Feeling White: The Social Politics of the Photographic Smile." In *Feeling Photography*, edited by Elspeth H. Brown and Thy Phu, 127–57. Durham, NC: Duke University Press, 2014.

Silverman, Eric. *A Cultural History of Jewish Dress*. London: Bloomsbury, 2013.

Silverman, Lisa. "Jewish Intellectual Women and the Public Sphere in Inter-War Vienna." In *Women in Europe between the Wars: Politics, Culture and Society*, edited by Angela Kershaw and Angela Kimyongür, 155–69. Aldershot: Ashgate, 2007.

Silverman, Lisa. *Becoming Austrians: Jews and Culture Between the World Wars*. New York: Oxford University Press, 2012.

Somogyi, Tamar. *Die Schejnen und die Prosten: Untersuchungen zum Schönheitsideal der Ostjuden in Bezug auf Körper und Kleidung unter besonderer Berücksichtigung des Chassidismus*. Berlin: Dietrich Reimer Verlag, 1983.

Sontag, Susan. "On Style [1965]." In *Against Interpretation and Other Essays*, 15–36. New York: Picador, 1996.

Sorkin, David. *The Transformation of German Jewry, 1780–1840*. Detroit, MI: Wayne State University Press, 1999.

Spector, Scott. *Modernism Without Jews? German-Jewish Subjects and Histories*. Bloomington, IN: Indiana University Press, 2017.

Spitzer, Leo. *Lives in Between: Assimilation and Marginality in Austria, Brazil, and West Africa, 1780–1945*. Cambridge: Cambridge University Press, 1989.

Staudinger, Barbara. "Unerwünschte Fremde. Galizische Juden in Wien: Zwischen Integration, Wohlfahr und Antisemitismus." In *"Ostjuden": Geschichte und Mythos*, edited by Philipp Metauer and Barbara Staudinger, 29–48. Innsbruck: Studien Verlag, 2015.

Stewart, Janet. *Fashioning Vienna: Adolf Loos's Cultural Criticism*. London: Routledge, 2000.

Stuhlmann, Andreas. *"Die Literatur—das sind wir und unsere Feinde": Literarische Polemik bei Heinrich Heine und Karl Kraus*. Würzburg: Königshausen & Neumann, 2010.

Styles, John. "Fashion and Innovation in Early Modern Europe." In *Fashioning the Early Modern: Dress, Textiles, and Innovation in Europe, 1500–1800*, edited by Evelyn Welch, 33–55. Oxford: Oxford University Press, 2017.

Sufian, Sandra M. *Healing the Land and the Nation: Malaria and Zionist Project in Palestine, 1920–1947*. Chicago, IL: The University of Chicago Press, 2007.

Swales, Martin. *Arthur Schnitzler: A Critical Study*. London: Oxford University Press, 1971.

Swarts, Lynne M. *Gender, Orientalism and the Jewish Nation: Women in the Work of Ephraim Moses Lilien at the German Fin de Siècle*. New York: Bloomsbury, 2020.

Teichert, Gesa C. *Mode. Macht. Männer: Kulturwissenschaftliche Überlegungen zur bügerlichen Herrenmode des 19. Jahrhunderts*. Berlin: Lit Verlag, 2013.

Tenenbaum, Joseph. *Galitsiye mayn alte heym*. Buenos Aires: Tsentral-Farband fun Poylishe Yidn in Argentinye, 1952.

Thieberger, Richard. "Assimilated Jewish Youth and Viennese Cultural Life Around 1930." In *Jews Antisemitism and Culture in Vienna*, edited by Ivar Oxaal, Michael Pollak and Gerhard Botz, 174–84. London: Routledge and Kegan Paul, 1987.

Twickler, Sharon. "Combing Masculine Identity in the Age of the Moustache, 1860–1900." In *New Perspectives on the History of Facial Hair: Framing the Face*, edited by Jennifer Evans and Alun Withey, 149–68. Cham: Palgrave Macmillan, 2018.

Timms, Edward. *Karl Kraus: Apocalyptic Satirist. Vol. 1. Culture and Catastrophe in Habsburg Vienna*. New Haven, CT: Yale University Press, 1986.

Timms, Edward. *Karl Kraus: Apocalyptic Satirist. Vol. 2. The Post-War Crisis and the Rise of the Swastika*. New Haven, CT: Yale University Press, 2005.

Thorpe, Julie. *Pan-Germanism and the Austrofascist State, 1933–1938*. Manchester: Manchester University Press, 2011.

Torberg, Friedrich. *Die Tante Jolesch: oder, Der Untergang des Abendlandes in Anekdoten*. Munich: Deutscher Taschenbuch Verlag, 2013.

Tournikiotis, Panayotis. *Adolf Loos*. New York: Princeton Architectural Press, 1994.

Tseëlon, Efrat. *The Masque of Femininity: The Presentation of Women in Everyday Life*. London: Sage Publications, 1995.

Vansant, Jacqueline. *Reclaiming Heimat: Trauma and Mourning in Memoirs by Jewish Austrian Reémigrés*. Detroit, MI: Wayne State University Press, 2001.

Völker, Angela. *Textiles of the Wiener Werkstätte, 1910–1932*. London: Thames and Hudson, 1994.

Volkov, Shulamit. "The Dynamics of Dissimilation: *Ostjuden* and German Jews." In *The Jewish Response to German Culture: From the Enlightenment to the Second World War*, edited by Jehuda Reinharz and Walter Schatzberg, 195–211. Hanover, NH: University Press of New England, 1985.

Wagner, Verena. *Jüdisches Leben in Linz, 1849–1943*. 2 Vols. Linz: Wagner Verlag, 2008.

Wasserman, Janek. *Black Vienna: The Radical Right in the Red City, 1918–1938*. Ithaca, NY: Cornell University Press, 2014.

Weikart, Richard. "The Impact of Social Darwinism on Anti-Semitic Ideology in Germany and Austria, 1860–1945." In *Jewish Tradition and the Challenge of Darwinism*, edited by Geoffrey Cantor and Marc Swetlitz, 93–115. Chicago, IL: University of Chicago Press, 2006.

Weissberg, Liliane. "Literary Culture and Jewish Space around 1800: The Berlin Salons Revisited." In *Modern Jewish Literatures: Intersections and Boundaries*, edited by Sheila E. Jelen, Michael P. Kramer, and L. Scott Lerner, 24–43. Philadelphia, PA: University of Pennsylvania Press, 2011.

Weisz, Georges Yitshak. *Theodor Herzl: A New Reading*. Translated by Diana File and Len Schramm. Jerusalem: Gefen Publishing House, 2013.

Weitzman, Walter K. "The Politics of the Viennese Jewish Community 1890–1914." In *Jews, Antisemitism and Culture in Vienna*, edited by Ivar Oxaal, Michael Pollak and Gerhard Botz, 121–51. London and New York: Routledge and Kegan Paul, 1987.

Wigley, Mark. *White Walls, Designer Dresses: The Fashioning of Modern Architecture*. Cambridge, MA: The MIT Press, 2001.

Wistrich, Robert S. *The Jews of Vienna in the Age of Franz Joseph*. Oxford: The Littman Library of Jewish Civilization, 1989.

Wistrich, Robert S. *From Ambivalence to Betrayal: The Left, the Jews, and Israel*. Lincoln, NE: The University of Nebraska Press, 2012.

Witzmann, Reingard. "The Beautiful Viennese: Fashions from the Times of Maria Theresa to the End of the Congress of Vienna." In *The Imperial Style: Fashions of the Habsburg Era: Based on the Exhibition Fashions of the Habsburg Era: Austria-Hungary at the Metropolitan Museum of Art, December 1979–August 1980*, edited by Polly Cone, 35–41. New York: The Metropolitan Museum of Art, 1980.

Wolff, Larry. *The Idea of Galicia: History and Fantasy in Habsburg Political Culture*. Stanford, CA: Stanford University Press, 2010.

Bibliography

Yates, W. E. *Theatre in Vienna: A Critical History, 1776–1995*. Cambridge: Cambridge University Press, 1996.

Zadoff, Mirjam. *Next Year in Marienbad: The Lost Worlds of Jewish Spa Culture*. Translated by William Templer. Philadelphia, PA: University of Pennsylvania Press, 2012.

Zakim, Michael. *Ready-Made Democracy: A History of Men's Dress in the American Republic, 1760–1860*. Chicago, IL: University of Chicago Press, 2003.

Zweig, Friderike. *Stefan Zweig*. Translated by Erna McArthur. London: W.H. Allen, 1946.

(b) Articles

Barker, Andrew. "Race, Sex and Character in Schnitzler's *Fräulein Else*." *German Life and Letters* 54, no. 1 (January 2001): 1–9.

Bellanta, Melissa. "Business Fashion: Masculinity, Class and Dress in 1870s Australia." *Australian Historical Studies* 28, no. 2 (2017): 189–212.

Berger, Pamela C. "The Roots of Anti-Semitism in Medieval Imagery: An Overview." *Religion and the Arts* 4, no. 1 (March 2000): 4–42.

Bergmann, Werner, and Ulrich Wyrwa. "The Making of Antisemitism as a Political Movement: Political History as Cultural History (1878–1914): An Introduction." *Quest: Issues in Contemporary Jewish History* no. 3 (July 2012): 1–15, doi:10.48248/issn.2037-741X/16.

Brenner, David. "Out of the Ghetto and into the Tiergarten: Redefining the Jewish Parvenu and His Origins in *Ost und West*." *The German Quarterly* 66, no. 2 (1993): 176–94.

Bronski, Michael. "The Male Body in the Western Mind." *Harvard Gay & Lesbian Review* 54 (1998): 28–31.

Davison, Neil R. "'The Jew' as Homme/Femme-Fatale: Jewish (Art)ifice, *Trilby*, and Dreyfus." *Jewish Social Studies* 8, no. 2–3 (2002): 75–111.

Domosh, Mona. "Those 'Gorgeous Incongruities': Politics and Public Space on the Streets of Nineteenth-Century New York City." *Annals of Association of American Geographers* 88, no. 2 (1998): 209–26.

Drucker, Peter. "'Disengaging from the Muslim Spirit': The Alliance Israélite Universelle and Moroccan Jews." *Journal of Middle East Women's Studies* 11, no. 1 (2015): 3–23, doi:0.1215/15525864-2832322.

Efron, John M. "The 'Kaftanjude' and the 'Kaffeehausjude': Two Models of Jewish Insanity: A Discussion of Causes and Cures among German Jewish Psychiatrists." *Leo Baeck Institute Yearbook* 37, no. 1 (1992): 169–88.

Farkas, Tamás. "Jewish Name Magyarization in Hungary." *AHEA: E-Journal of the American Hungarian Educators Association* 5, no. 1 (2012): 1–16, https://ahea.net/e-journal/volume-5 -2012.

Fine, Robert D. "Cosmopolitanism and the Critique of Antisemitism: Two Faces of Universality." *European Review of History: Revue européenne d'histoire* 23, no. 5–6 (2016): 769–83, doi:10.10 80/13507486.2016.1203877.

Gates-Coon, Rebecca. "Anglophile Households and British Travellers in Late Eighteenth-Century Vienna: 'A Very Numerous and Pleasant English Colony.'" *Britain and the World* 12, no. 2 (2019): 130–50.

Gelbin, Cathy S. "Nomadic Cosmopolitanism: Jewish Prototypes of the Cosmopolitan in the Writings of Stefan Zweig, Joseph Roth and Lion Feuchtwanger, 1918–1933." *Jewish Culture and History* 16, no. 2 (2015): 157–77, doi:10.1080/1462169X.2015.1084147.

Gillerman, Sharon. "Samson in Vienna: The Theatrics of Jewish Masculinity." *Jewish Social Studies* 9, no. 2 (2003): 65–98.

Gilman, Sander L. "Jews and Mental Illness: Medical Metaphors, Anti-Semitism, and the Jewish Response." *Journal of the History of Behavioral Sciences* 20, no. 2 (April 1984): 150–9.

Gilman, Sander L. "Salome, Syphilis, Sarah Bernhardt and the 'Modern Jewess'." *The German Quarterly* 66, no. 2 (1993): 195–211.

Gitelman, Zvi. "A Century of Jewish Politics in Eastern Europe: The Legacy of the Bund and the Zionist Movement." *East European Politics and Societies* 11, no. 3 (1997): 543–59.

Gluck, Mary. "The Budapest Flâneur: Urban Modernity, Popular Culture, and the 'Jewish Question' in Fin-de-Siècle Hungary." *Jewish Social Studies* 10, no. 3 (Spring/Summer 2004): 1–22.

Gronberg, Tag. "The Inner Man: Interior and Masculinity in Early Twentieth-Century Vienna." *Oxford Art Journal* 24, no. 1 (2001): 67–88.

Grunwald, Kurt. "Europe's Railways and Jewish Enterprise: German Jews as Pioneers of Railway Promotion." *Leo Baeck Institute Year Book* 12, no. 1 (1967): 163–209.

Hödl, Klaus. "The Quest for Amusement: Jewish Leisure Activities in Vienna circa 1900." *Jewish Culture and History* 14, no. 1 (2013): 1–17, doi:10.1080/1462169X.2012.708504.

Hödl, Klaus. "Viennese Newspapers and Jewish Reading Habits around 1900." *Jewish Culture and History* 17, no. 3 (2016): 189–202, doi:10.1080/1462169X.2016/1221034.

Hoffmann, Friedhelm. "Zur arabischen Stefan-Zweig-Rezeption." *Zweigheft* 17 (July 2017): 27–34.

Hollander, Anne. "The Clothed Image: Picture and Performance." *New Literary History* 2, no. 3 (Spring 1971): 477–93.

Jacob, Margaret C. "The Cosmopolitan as a Lived Category." *Dædalus* 37, no. 3 (Summer 2008): 18–25.

Jasienski, Adam. "A Savage Magnificence: Ottomanizing Fashion and the Politics of Display in Early Modern East-Central Europe." *Muqarnas* 31, no. 1 (2014): 173–205.

Kaim, Dominik, Jakub Taczanowski, Marcin Szwagrzyk and Krzysztof Ostafin. "Railway Network of Galicia and Austrian Silesia (1847–1914)." *Journal of Maps* 16, no. 1 (2020): 132–7, doi:10.1080/17445647.2020.1762774

Kamczycki, Artur. "Orientalism: Herzl and His Beard." *Journal of Modern Jewish Studies* 12, no. 1 (2013): 90–116, doi:10.1080/14725886.2012.757475.

Kaplan, Jonathan C. "*Lederhosen, Dirndl* and a Sense of Belonging: Jews and *Trachten* in Pre-1938 Austria." *TEXTILE: Cloth and Culture* (2022), doi:10.1080/14759756.2022.2141037.

Kaplan, Jonathan C. "Looking and Behaving: Sartorial Politics and Jewish Men in *Fin-de-Siècle* Vienna." *Critical Studies in Men's Fashion* 5, no. 1&2 (2018): 5–23, doi:10.1386/csmf.5.1-2.5_1.

Kaplan, Jonathan C. "The Man in the Suit: Jewish Men and Fashion in *Fin-de-Siècle* Vienna." *Fashion Theory* 25, no. 3 (2021): 339–66, doi:10.1080/1362704X.2020.1746115.

Kaplan, Jonathan C. "Refashioning the Jewish Body: An Examination of the Sartorial Habits of the Family of Viennese Writer, Stefan Zweig (1881–1942)." *The Journal of Dress History* 5, no. 1 (2021): 56–87.

Kemnitz, Thomas Milton. "The Caricature as a Historical Source." *The Journal of Interdisciplinary History* 4, no. 1 (1973): 81–93.

Kladiwa, Pavel. "The Czech Community and Czech as a 'Language of Daily Use', in Vienna 1880–1910." *Prager wirtschafts- und sozialhistorische Mitteilungen—Prague Economic and Social History Papers* 20, no. 2 (2014): 26–47.

Kwiet, Konrad. "'Be Patient and Reasonable!': The Internment of German-Jewish Refugees in Australia." Translated by Jane Sydenham-Kwiet. *Australian Journal of Politics and History* 31, no. 1 (1985): 61–77.

Kwiet, Konrad. "The Second Time Around: The Re-Acculturation of German-Jewish Refugees in Australia." *The Journal of Holocaust Education* 10, no. 1 (2001): 34–9.

Lerner, Paul. "Circulation and Representation: Jews, Department Stores and Cosmopolitan Consumption in Germany, c. 1880s–1930s." *European Review of History* 17, no. 3 (June 2010): 395–414.

Lichtbalu, Albert. "'Galitsianer' and the Mobility of Stereotypes." *Jewish Culture and History* 11, no. 1&2 (2009): 84–105.

Bibliography

Lieber, Julie. "Infidelity and Intimacy in Nineteenth-Century Vienna: Gender and Orthodoxy as Reflected in the Responsa of Rabbi Eleazar Horowitz." *Nashim: A Journal of Jewish Women's Studies & Gender Issues* 21 (2011): 24–45.

Lubbock, Jules. "Adolf Loos and the English Dandy." *Architectural Review* 174, no. 1038 (1983): 43–49.

Lupovitch, Howard. "Between Orthodox Judaism and Neology: The Origins of the Status Quo Movement." *Jewish Social Studies* 9, no. 2 (2003): 123–53.

Marten, Heinz-Georg. "Racism, Social-Darwinism, Anti-Semitism and Aryan Supremacy." *The International Journal of the History of Sport* 16, no. 2 (1991): 23–41.

Mendelsohn, Ezra. "The Politics of Agudas Yisroel in Inter-War Poland." *East European Jewish Affairs* 2, no. 2 (1972): 47–60.

Miller, Michael L., and Scott Ury. "Cosmopolitanism: The End of Jewishness?" *European Review of History* 17, no. 3 (June 2010): 337–60.

Presner, Todd Samuel. "'Clear Heads, Solid Stomachs, and Hard Muscles': Max Nordau and the Aesthetics of Jewish Regeneration." *Modernism/Modernity* 10, no. 2 (April 2003): 269–96.

Roces, Mina. "'These Guys Came Out Looking Like Movie Actors': Filipino Dress and Consumer Practices in the United States, 1920s–1930s." *Pacific Historical Review* 85, no. 4 (2016): 532–76.

Rozenblit, Marsha L. "The Struggle over Religious Reform in Nineteenth-Century Vienna." *AJS Review* 14, no. 2 (Autumn 1989): 179–221.

Sciarcon, Jonathan. "Expanding the Mission: The Alliance Israélite Universelle, the Anglo-Jewish Assoication and the Jewish Boys' School in Basra, 1890–1903." *International Journal of Contemporary Iraqi Studies* 9, no. 3 (2015): 191–207, doi:10.1386/ijcis.9.3.191_1.

Secklehner, Julia. "Bolshevik Jews, Aryan Vienna? Popular Antisemitism in 'Der Kikeriki', 1918–1933." *Leo Baeck Institute Yearbook* 63, no. 1 (2018): 157–78, doi:10.1093/leobaeck/yby011.

Shapira, Elana. "Modernism and Jewish Identity in Early Twentieth-Century Vienna: Fritz Waerndorfer and His House for an Art Lover." *Studies in the Decorative Arts* 13, no. 2 (Spring–Summer 2006): 52–92.

Shapira, Elana. "Adolf Loos and the Fashioning of 'The Other': Memory, Fashion, and Interiors." *Interiors* 2, no. 2 (2011): 213–37.

Silverman, Lisa. "'Nicht jüdeln': Jews and Habsburg Loyalty in Franz Theodor Csokor's *Dritter November 1918*." *Religions* 8, no. 60 (2017): 1–11, doi:10.3390/rel8040060.

Streicher, Lawrence H. "On a Theory of Political Cartoons." *Cosmopolitan Studies in Society and History* 9, no. 4 (1967): 427–45.

Teske Jr., Raymond H. C., and Bardin H. Nelson. "Acculturation and Assimilation: A Clarification." *American Ethnologist* 1, no. 2 (1974): 358–65.

Thaler, Peter. "National History—National Imagery: The Role of History in Postwar Austrian Nation Building." *Central European History* 32, no. 3. (1999): 277–309.

Toman, Jindřich. "Conversational Modernism: Talking Czech Men into Being Gentlemen by Way of *The Gentleman*, 1924–30." *Central Europe* 13, no. 1–2 (2015): 19–35, doi:10.1080/1479 0963.2025.1107321.

Weiser, Kalman. "'Kopl Not Filaret, Sore Not Salomea': Debates About Jewish Naming Practices in Pre-WWII Poland." *East European Jewish Affairs* 50, no. 1–2 (2020): 134–56, doi:10.1080/1 3501674.2020.1774274.

Weissberg, Liliane. "Ariadne's Thread." *MLN* 125, no. 3 (2010): 661–81, doi:10.1353/mln.0.0267.

Wertheimer, Jack. "'The Unwanted Element': East European Jews in Imperial Germany." *Leo Baeck Institute Yearbook* 26 (1981): 23–46.

Yedidya, Assaf. "Orthodox Reactions to 'Wissenschaft des Judentums'." *Modern Judaism: A Journal of Jewish Ideas & Experience* 30, no. 1 (February 2010): 69–94, doi:10.1093/mj/kjp021.

Zohn, Harry. "The Jewish World of Arthur Schnitzler (1862–1931)." *The Jewish Quarterly* 10 (1963): 25–9.

Zohn, Harry. "Stefan Zweig, the European and the Jew." *Leo Baeck Institute Yearbook* 27, no. 1 (1982): 323–36.

(c) Newspapers and Magazines (Post-1938)

Budge, Rose Mary Pederson. "Practical, Pretty Lanz Celebrating 50 Years." *Desert News*, December 23, 1988. https://www.desertnews.com/article/28001/PRACTICAL-PRETTY -LANZ-CELEBRATING-50-YEARS.html, accessed December 13, 2017.

"German Brothers Began Shops in West." *Desert Sun*, April 11, 1978, 8.

Hevesi, Dennis. "Werner Scharff, 90, Designer of Classic Warm Nightgown Dies." *The New York Times*, August 31, 2006. http://www.nytimes.com/2006/08/31/business/31scharff.html, accessed December 13, 2017.

(d) Dissertations

Beglaw, Jeffery W. "The German National Attack on the Czech Minority in Vienna, 1897–1914, as Reflected in the Satirical Journal *Kikeriki*, and Its Role as a Centrifugal Force in the Dissolution of Austria-Hungary." MA diss., Simon Fraser University, 2004.

Bell, Andrew Francis. "Anglophilia: The Hamburg Bourgeoisie and the Importation of English Middle Class Culture in the Wilhelmine Era." PhD diss., Brown University, 2001.

Christ, Catharina. "Jüdische k. und k. Hoflieferanten in der Textilbranche mit Niederlassung in Wien in der Zeit von 1870 bis 1938." MA diss., University of Vienna, 2006.

Steiman, Lionel Bradley. "Stefan Zweig: The Education of an Aesthete and His Response to War and Politics." PhD diss., University of Pennsylvania, 1970.

(e) Web sources

Lukin, Benyamin. "Berdychiv." *YIVO Encyclopedia of Jews in Eastern Europe*. accessed July 24, 2021. https://yivoencyclopedia.org/article.aspx/Berdychiv.

Philippi, Dieter. "Modelle, Ausführungen, Varianten und Farben." *The Philippi Collection*. Accessed January 10, 2018. http://www.dieter-philippi.de/en/the-philippi-collection/head -coverings-1.

INDEX

Note: Page numbers in *italics* refer to figures and followed by 'n' refer to notes

Index

Index

www.ingramcontent.com/pod-product-compliance
Lightning Source LLC
Chambersburg PA
CBHW071844270326
41929CB00013B/2099

* 9 7 8 1 3 5 0 2 4 4 2 1 4 *